OLD POTTERY AND PORCELAIN

FIG. 1.—VIEW OF WEDGWOOD & SONS' WORKS AT ETRURIA.
By permission of Messrs. Josiah Wedgwood & Sons, Ltd.

THE HOME CONNOISSEUR SERIES

OLD POTTERY AND PORCELAIN

BY

FRED. W. BURGESS

AUTHOR OF "ANTIQUE FURNITURE," "HOUSEHOLD CURIOS," "CHATS ON OLD COPPER
AND BRASS," ETC.

WITH 130 ILLUSTRATIONS

NEW YORK

G. P. PUTNAM'S SONS

1916

Printed in Great Britain.

PREFACE

In the first volume of " The Home Connoisseur Series " such old home appointments as could rightly be grouped under the general heading of *Antique Furniture* were referred to, and the successive periods into which old furniture is usually classed were passed in review. In this, the second volume of the series, pottery, which, although at first crudely modelled and merely sun-baked, has always been deemed essential in every home, is treated upon.

Ceramic wares would appear to have a claim to priority in curios, in that they must have existed long before furniture, as we understand it, or any other household requisite, was used. The graves of prehistoric races contain evidences of pottery and of its provision for the use of those who thousands of years ago not only used it themselves but provided their dead with vessels of clay. These early peoples' views of the spirit-world and its requirements were hazy, but their beliefs have been the means of supplying modern man with authentic relics of those far-off days.

In preparing this work, the scope of which is defined in the simple title *Old Pottery and Porcelain*, the aim has been to provide home connoisseurs with a handy book of reference embracing general features of interest in all the groups and periods into which ceramics are usually classified.

As in the first volume of the series, I have grouped the subjects under clearly-defined periods and types, and have distinguished as far as possible the products of the different potteries. The clearer knowledge of these should lead to increased artistic effect in the home by the greater display of treasured belongings.

Changes are now being made in households which have

v

7862

been undisturbed for years, in some instances for a century or more, and rare pieces of pottery and porcelain are changing hands. Yet amidst surrounding unrest many continue to pursue their hobbies, chief among them those who love their " bits " of china.

The crude pottery of early days appeals to some ; others take greater interest in the choicer handiwork of skilled artists and decorators of more recent times. To cater for all who possess, or desire to possess, old pottery and porcelain, a wide field of research has had to be traversed, and it has been desirable to consult those who have made special study of certain branches of ceramic art. I would tender my thanks to all who have rendered assistance in this work, and especially those who have so kindly furnished me with descriptions and photographs of many beautiful pieces, and given permission to make use of materials they have collected, and take extracts from their books. Some specialists have carried their researches into heights far beyond the ken of home connoisseurs ; if, therefore, this less ambitious effort kindles enthusiasm in any of my readers these specialistic volumes will greatly assist them in their higher flights in pursuit of knowledge of advanced ceramics.

The British Museum authorities have accorded permission to reproduce some of the illustrations in their catalogues. Dr Hoyle, the Director of the National Museum of Wales, has been good enough to procure photographs of several unique pieces of Swansea and Nantgarw porcelain, of which there are many examples in the Museum. The Curator of the Free Public Museums in Liverpool sends illustrations and descriptions of some of the fine products of the old potteries once flourishing in Liverpool. I am indebted to the courtesy of the Curator of the Art Gallery and Museum of Belfast, and to the Curator of the National Museum of Ireland, in Dublin, for illustrations of rare Irish pottery ; especially to Mr Dudley Westropp, of the National Museum of Ireland, for much of the information about old Irish wares and for some of the illustrations used.

The Director of the Public Museums of Brighton, where the collection of pottery and china of the late Mr Henry Willett is now housed, gives permission to refer to the descriptions given in the Museum catalogue. Some remarkable examples of Hispano-Moresque pots have been specially photographed by the proprietors of the Spanish Art Gallery, in Conduit Street, London, for illustration in this work.

It is well known that some of the oldest potteries in this country have been worked continuously since the days when the founders produced those choice pieces which are now reckoned among our greatest treasures. From the museums of the old factories, and from their archives, come illustrations and descriptions of great interest. To all those who have contributed in this way I gladly acknowledge my indebtedness. My special thanks are due to Messrs Josiah Wedgwood & Sons, Ltd, who have furnished much valuable information about the wares for which the founder of the firm—the great Josiah—was so justly famed. The information in their catalogue has been very helpful, and the work of Mr J. C. Wedgwood on *Staffordshire Pottery and its History* has thrown much light upon the early workers in clay in that county. Several of the illustrations in this volume represent pieces now in the Works' Museum at Etruria, and the picture frontispiece shows the works as they are now, much of the old buildings remaining.

I acknowledge the services of the Royal Worcester Porcelain Company, Ltd, who still make so much that is beautiful at the old works in Worcester, from whence came those rare old vases and other pieces of porcelain in the olden time. The description of the processes of manufacture supplied by them should be useful, as it is reliable and authentic. The name of Adams of Tunstall is well known to collectors and to buyers of modern wares. Some of the illustrations given here are taken from the private collections of the firm and members of the family and their friends, as well as from examples in local museums. The courteous owners of the Fulham Pottery have supplied interesting accounts of their old pottery and of their works. The ancient Wrotham ware is illustrated by the kindness of the Curator of the Maidstone Museum, where there are so many fine examples.

Many private collectors have loaned illustrations and gone to much trouble in obtaining special photographs of exceptional pieces. Mr Merrington Smith, of Lowestoft, an authority on china made at the works, about which so little was known until discoveries in which he took a prominent part revealed the old moulds and fragments of pottery, has placed his interesting collection at my disposal. He has also obtained from some of his friends photos of choice " bits " of the rarer types of " Lowestoft."

The illustrations of apothecaries' drug pots are taken from specimens in the possession of Mr J. E. Jewell, of Piccadilly—a most unique collection.

Mr A. E. Clark, of Cambridge, contributes some charming glimpses of his well-filled cabinets of Leeds and other wares. Mr Cecil B. Morgan, the owner of a remarkable collection of Staffordshire figures by Ralph Wood, courteously accords permission to illustrate some of the examples now on view in the Whitworth Institute in Manchester.

The illustrations of old Chinese porcelain and the descriptions of these works of art have been contributed by the executors of the late Edwin Gorer ; the Gorer Gallery in New Bond Street is known to all advanced collectors of Oriental porcelain. Mr Albert Amor, of St James's Street, kindly furnishes photos of some rare pieces which have passed through his hands. To Mr Phillips, of Hitchin, who has loaned illustrations of many fine pieces, Mr C. G. Taylor, of Lowestoft, and others, I am under an obligation.

Some of the illustrations are from special drawings by my daughter, taken from examples in my own collection and the collections of friends ; and it is hoped they will prove helpful.

In the preface to my work on *Antique Furniture,* the first volume of this series, I referred to the peculiar charm of old furniture, and the refinement which hangs about

the environment of the " home connoisseur." The
addition of old pottery and porcelain adds to that charm ;
and the owner of such wares can count on the enhanced
pleasure and delight about the home in which they are in
evidence.

FRED. W. BURGESS.

London, 1916.

PREFACE

CONTENTS

xi

CONTENTS

LIST OF ILLUSTRATIONS

* Figs. 59, 59a, 60, 61 form a set and are lettered " A.D."

ILLUSTRATIONS OF MARKS

OLD POTTERY AND PORCELAIN

OLD POTTERY AND PORCELAIN

CHAPTER I

THE POTTER'S ART

In olden time—Preparing the materials—Operating the clay—
Kilns, old and new.

THE potter's art is one of the most interesting studies
which can engage the attention of the connoisseur or the
collector, and the making of pottery is, probably, the most
ancient of all industries. It is conceivable that almost
before the dawn of civilisation the mud deposits of the
rivers, or the clays of still older formations, were made use
of to fashion vessels modelled from natural objects. There
have been many more or less romantic suggestions as to
the first awakening of cunning craftmanship, before competition and observation engendered skilled production.
It has been said by some that the shells upon the seashore
suggested to primitive tribes the forms of food vessels;
they had for a time served the purpose of porringers and
bowls. No doubt some natural object of unusual shape
indicated that convenient models in clay—the material
at hand, which readily hardened in the sun, the case-
hardening results of which would have been noticed
—could be made. In course of time some intelligent
native would experiment with exposure to greater heat,
produced by artificial means, finding in it a more effective

1   A

hardening process. It has been pointed out that dwellers in the forest would find in the broken cocoanut an admirable food vessel which might be copied in clay and hardened by drying or heat by tribes who could not obtain the " cups " which Nature had provided, but who were in possession of clay or some earthy substance which would serve the purpose of the primitive modellers.

There is a vast stride between the first vessels of clay and even those which collectors secure as specimens of prehistoric pottery. Doubtless, many ineffective attempts were made before any satisfactory results were achieved, and the dawn of the pottery trade is lost in the dim past. There are, however, many very early vessels which are known to have been made thousands of years ago ; such pottery is widely distributed, and different materials were employed, some of much purer consistency than others. The collector applies the term " pottery " to all the early vessels, and to most of the commoner wares made of clay, moulded into form in a plastic state and then baked.

Clay is a widely distributed substance or material abounding in different minerals, although consisting largely of hydrated silicate of alumina. The foreign substances found in natural clays, such as lime and oxides of iron, influence the colour of the material and also of the vessel when the modelled clay has been fired. The potter depends upon his knowledge of the chemical changes brought about under certain conditions for the pottery he makes and fires. In primitive or prehistoric pottery, as will be seen in another chapter, the burnt clay was often porous, and owing to the unsatisfactory conditions under which it was made, it differed materially from a well-baked piece which becomes a hard substance and extremely lasting. The processes of manufacture dealt with in chapter iii., in so far as their final stages in more modern times are concerned, were in early days very simple.

In Olden Time.

The potter's art in times gone by, when much of the early pottery collectors seek and excavators discover was being made, was the product of village industries, wrought out of local clays. Those were the days before foreign substances were introduced in the manufacture of pottery, and later still porcelain. We do not know when the necessary mixing, working, and beating of clay were first properly understood, but no doubt at an early time man was sufficiently familiar with local clays to understand that whatever processes he adopted it was essential that the clay should be rendered plastic by the admixture of sufficient water, and that the substance should be made as even as possible, and uniform in quality, as the potter would early discover that inequalities cause irregular expansion during the firing.

There are Biblical records of the kneading of clay by hands, and trampling it by the feet. It was by such methods that the initial processes of manufacture were then performed, although judged by modern standards irregularly and somewhat inefficiently. The human hand has at all times proved the best factor in production, although in more modern times labour-saving contrivances have been found desirable. In some trades until quite recent days hand labour has been almost entirely employed ; in the potting industry, however, a mechanical contrivance, simple it is true, was introduced at a very early date.

The potter's wheel by which the work of the human hands was rendered more effective and more regular is indeed ancient, for there is evidence of its use by the Egyptians as early as 4000 B.C. The wheel which was so long the only mechanical contrivance aiding the potting craft, we are told, in the form used by the Egyptians, as is illustrated upon some of the existing fragments of Egyptian pottery, is still employed by native potters in many parts of India. Surely a striking tribute to the completeness of that early mechanical contrivance which served so well in the past, and is still deemed sufficient for the needs of to-day !

The old wheel was improved somewhat in Egypt under the Ptolemies. The first contrivance consisted of a small round table on a revolving pivot, and was spun as the potter moulded his vessel, and so formed its circular shape. The improvement was to have another circular table somewhat larger in size fixed a little lower on the same axis. The early worker set this in motion with his feet, leaving his hands free for the manipulation of the clay. Those who have watched the potter spinning a vessel have been amazed at the rapidity with which it was fashioned, and have recognised in the plastic clay a natural material yielding with the greatest ease to the deft touches of the skilled operator.

PREPARING THE MATERIALS.

It is probable that of all the craftsmen the potter has changed the least in his methods, notwithstanding that he was the first to introduce a mechanical appliance. The principles which governed the first makers are those which to-day actuate the makers of the most beautiful of modern ceramics. This is apparent at once to those who visit one of the larger works. Many of the manufacturers most courteously allow visitors to inspect the different processes, and collectors learn much from seeing for themselves the way in which the clay is skilfully manipulated, then decorated, and afterwards fired.

In the course of such a visit the simplicity of the whole proceedings strikes the visitor as remarkable. The potter deftly throws the clay, then by a few rapid touches shapes it and perhaps adds decoration, afterwards glazing it for the firing.

The entire process can be seen at the Worcester Royal Porcelain Works, where every one is shown the different stages, and the connoisseur can imagine that in watching the making of modern wares he is seeing the manufacture of some of those now rare and costly antiques which the admirer of all things old prizes so highly. Indeed Worcester seems to be a connecting link between the new and the old.

The clay seems to spring into shape with marvellous rapidity under skilled hands. It is said that " clay so sensitive in the hands of the potter exhibits the most subtle impression of the actor's will, and presents to us the minds and characters of the peoples who may have left no other trace behind." The learned Brongniart says : " I know of no art which presents in the study of its practice, its theory, and its history, so many interesting and varied considerations as the ceramic art."

As we might naturally expect in a works like those at Worcester, modern science has been brought to bear ; and although the principles of the potters of old are untouched, the effective carrying out of those principles is enhanced by the application of present-day discoveries. Thus electricity is now employed as the motive power in the " mill " at Worcester—that is, of course, a recent introduction, but even as of yore, in the mill flint, felspar, Cornish stone, calcined bones and other substances are ground up, and in pans are reduced with liquids to the consistency of thick cream. Sometimes a few hours suffice, at others, according to the materials operated, days elapse before the liquid substance is ready for its final sieve, which is of silk lawn, with about ten thousand meshes to the square inch.

In the clay sheds are clays which Nature has pulverised ; they are placed in vats containing blungers, which make the cream or slip which is in them run into reservoirs. Then in the slip house are mixing pots into which the slip is pumped.

Various processes are adopted to extract foreign substances; for instance, in the mixing pot is a shaft from which radiate arms, having arranged on them rows of magnets, which work through the slip and catch every particle of iron that may have got into the vats or has been mixed with the material.

From the mixing vat the material is pumped into the clay press, a machine with a number of chambers lined with linen bags, where the mass assumes the consistency of paste. The paste is then kneaded or beaten to make it tough, in which condition it is ready for the workmen. The clay paste, or dough as it is called, is then manipulated by " throwing," " pressing," or " casting."

OPERATING THE CLAY.

It is obvious that when the clay has been rendered plastic and is ready for the potter to begin operations he must have in his mind an outline, or before him a model or design, of what he intends to make. There are many who in times gone by possessed a creative genius and modelled as their fancy led them; but most workmen have at all times worked according to some carefully mapped out plan, even if the decorator has had a free hand and thus given his work a distinctive individuality. When it was intended to mould vessels the mould of plaster had to be prepared beforehand, and thus the craftsman produced many copies, but when the clay was to be thrown there was more latitude in the operation.

When the method adopted is that of simple throwing, the *modus operandi* is indeed simple as judged by the onlooker, but it requires skill born of experience, as the amateur would soon find out. First of all the thrower takes a ball of prepared clay which he " throws " upon the head of the wheel and presses it, the rotary movement causing the clay to rise under pressure as the wheel revolves. To watch this operation is to realise some of the reasons why many of the simple vessels of old took their peculiar forms, for they assumed those shapes which were most readily fashioned.

Many of the figures of Derby, Staffordshire, and elsewhere were " cast," and wonderfully perfect models were turned out of the moulds, touched up by hand, and as triumphs of human skill placed, perhaps with feverish anxiety, into the kiln, where, alas! so many beautiful pieces perished in the final stages of manufacture. In the old days when the potters were experimenting with new materials, and using clays and admixtures of which they knew comparatively little, many beautiful objects were spoiled or destroyed almost at the last moment, when hours and often days of anxious toil had been expended upon their modelling, and upon their artistic decoration.

The decoration of pottery and porcelain is in modern factories a distinct branch of work. In olden time many of the master potters were skilled artists, and in not a few instances a workman who had gained fame as a designer or decorator, having accumulated some little means, began to manufacture the wares he afterwards decorated. Then again the workman who was a skilled modeller often owed much of his reputation to the attractive way in which he coloured his products, or perhaps to the peculiar glaze he discovered and used. There are many notable examples of decorators winning world-wide fame, and their ability did much for the potter who employed them—in those days the individuality of the workman was a greater factor in production than it is to-day. (For further reference to decoration and ornament, see chapter iii.)

We can well understand the anxiety of the workman or

the master potter when a difficult piece had been modelled and coloured and at last consigned to the not always tender mercies of the kiln. It has ever been a matter of much importance to see that the correct heat was maintained and just the required amount of firing given.

KILNS, OLD AND NEW.

The kilns which once sufficed would not be considered efficient now, but they served their purpose well, and although the improved conditions under which firing is accomplished in modern works prevents many of the mistakes of former days, some beautiful pieces were made in olden time. The kiln of antiquity as depicted on Egyptian wall paintings was a tall circular chamber of brick with a perforated floor near the bottom. Fuel was introduced under a brick floor, the pottery being placed in the middle of the chamber. There is an old tablet from Corinth which shows an early Greek kiln with a place for the fuel on one side, and a door in the side of the upper chamber through which pottery could be put in and withdrawn. The rapidity and comparative ease with which kilns were erected in different parts of the country a century or two ago point to the very simple kilns of brick then built, and suggest that the conditions under which some of our choice examples and treasured museum specimens were made were far from idealistic, and the only wonder is that so great a measure of success attended the early master potters.

There are some technical differences between ovens and kilns. In the oven, when full, the door is bricked up and fire-holes on the outside are furnished with fuel which burns slowly, so that the moisture may be driven out of the ware not too rapidly, otherwise the clay would crack. In the modern oven the flame from the fire-hole has free access to the interior ; in the muffle kilns, however, in which some of the final processes of completion take place, no flame enters the inside of the kiln. Needless to say, different temperatures are needed according to the objects being burned, and also to some extent the materials used in their manufacture.

Briefly, the old principles adhered to may be summed up as follows : Every precaution is taken to secure the correct firing of every part of the object. Having been prepared for the biscuit oven the object is placed with others in a fire-clay saggar, in which it is protected during the firing. When the sagger is carefully filled, it is placed over another similar receptacle in the oven ; then after having been burnt for forty-eight hours or so and cooled for a similar period, the pottery or porcelain becomes biscuit and is removed from the oven. When cleaned off the biscuit is ready for the dipping room ; then follow dipping in tubs of glazes, drying, and stoving. The vessel is then ready for decorating, after which it is again fired and some other processes resorted to in order to obtain the desired fixing of the colours, finishing of the pottery, and final preparation for the market.

The potter's art has from the earliest times been subject to the improvement and development going on in the town or country of manufacture. Thus in many places common earthenware and early types of pottery have served, whereas in some countries where even in mediæval days art had risen to a great height, the potters were encouraged to produce beautiful and even costly vessels such as those objects of virtu which are pointed out as among the rarities in museum collections.

The great Josiah Wedgwood in the introduction to his catalogue, which he published in 1787, makes a striking allusion to the purposes of the potter, and to those in-fluences which have ever caused the art to progress ; for the potter's craft, just the same as many other manufacturing industries, has always been governed by the law of supply and demand. Wedgwood wrote : " The progress of the arts, at all times and in every country, depends chiefly upon the encouragement they receive from those who by their rank and affluence are legislators in taste ; and who alone are capable of bestowing rewards upon the labours of industry, and the exertions of genius. It is their influence that forms the character of every age ; they can turn the current of human pursuits at their pleasure, and be surrounded either with beauty or deformity, with men or barbarians. Great improvements cannot be made without powerful patronage ; no art ever was or can be carried to great perfection with feeble efforts, or at a small expense ; and it depends upon those who are possessed of riches and power whether individuals shall be ruined or rewarded for their ingenuity."

Some rare pieces, the work of the great master potter and his partners, are shown in Figs. 2, 3, and 6. Fig. 2 is a curious pattern piece for a vase labelled in the Wedgwood Works' Museum, " One of the first day's productions at Etruria, in Staffordshire, by Wedgwood and Bentley, June 13th, 1769." Fig. 3 is also a pattern piece marked on the bottom, " A good pattern, 1791." Another pattern for a vase is illustrated in Fig. 6.

FIG. 2. — A curious pattern piece for a VASE, labelled "One of the first day's productions at Etruria, in Staffordshire, by Wedgwood & Bentley, June 13th, 1769." The subject on the opposite side is "Hercules in the Garden of Hesperides." Now in the Works' Museum at Etruria.

FIG. 2.

FIG. 3.

FIG. 3.—A pattern piece in the Wedgwood Museum, marked on the bottom, "A good pattern, 1791."

Both examples reproduced by permission of Josiah Wedgwood & Sons, Ltd.

[To face page 10.

FIG. 5.

A Choice Collection of LEEDS AND OTHER CHINA housed in a
Corner Cupboard (*see* pp. 18 and 141).

FIG. 4.

CHAPTER II

Soft pottery, stoneware, and porcelain defined—English and foreign
clays—Hard and soft pastes—Special bodies and pastes.

THERE are two methods by which the connoisseur of china
learns to distinguish his specimens ; sometimes independently, at others in conjunction. These are the
materials of which the pottery or porcelain was composed,
and the marks of identification impressed or painted on by
the potters. The materials or substances of which the
ware was composed are something quite apart from its
subsequent treatment, that is, its decorations, and the
glaze by which the raw material either before or after firing
was coated. The finished wares include the cruder
pottery, such, for instance, early British and Romano-
British pottery found in ancient barrows, and buried in the
earth, the soft pottery so easily fusible ; stoneware, very
hard and infusible ; and porcelain, for the most part
white, semi-transparent, and only fused at a high temperature. Then again, there are the numerous varieties
included in these different groups, especially in those which
are represented in seventeenth, eighteenth, and early
nineteenth century products.

SOFT POTTERY, STONEWARE, AND PORCELAIN DEFINED.

M. Brongniart in 1854 laid down a well-defined classification relating to soft pottery, stoneware, and porcelain,

11

and that classification has been largely adhered to by descriptive writers, and those who have aimed at putting before their readers technical expositions of the different substances of which pottery and porcelain are or have been composed. This classification, with some modification in order to simplify it, is as follows :

1. SOFT POTTERY :

    (*a*) *Biscuit.*—Simple baked clay, porous and without gloss. *Example*, a common modern flower-pot.

    (*b*) *Glossy.*—Fine clay covered with an almost imperceptible vitreous glaze. *Example*, most Greek vases.

    (*c*) *Glazed.*—Clay covered with a perceptible coating of glass. *Example*, common white earthenware plates.

    (*d*) *Enamelled.*—Clay covered with a vitreous coating made opaque by white oxide of tin. *Example*, Italian majolica.

2. STONEWARE :

    (*a*) Very silicious clay covered with a lead vitreous glaze. *Example*, old grey Flemish ware.

    (*b*) Silicious clay covered with a salt glaze. *Example*, a modern brown ginger-beer bottle.

3. PORCELAIN :

    (*a*) *Hard porcelain.*—Natural kaolinic clay covered with a felspar glaze. *Example*, porcelain of China and Japan.

    (*b*) *Soft porcelain.*—Artificial paste covered with a lead vitreous glaze. *Example*, early Sèvres porcelain.

    (*For explanation of technical terms, see Glossary.*)

As it has been suggested, earthenware is opaque. It may be thick or it may be thin ; it may be soft like those wares made of common clay, or hard like the opaque stone-ware. Its opaqueness, however, is the chief characteristic which distinguishes between pottery and porcelain. The porcelain, semi-transparent, which was imported into England from Oriental countries in the eighteenth century, appeals at once to householders, to the artist and to the admirer of beautiful substances; and consequently to copy the Oriental porcelain became the aim of eighteenth-century potters. The raw material, as we have seen, is clay, but clay is of varying quality, and although the common clays found in so many parts of England served in olden time, it soon became necessary to introduce other varieties in order to secure reliable results.

English and Foreign Clays.

The modern methods of obtaining clay are not the same as those which appertained when " old china " was first made in England. The clay excavated from the mines in Cornwall became an important industry, as the result of experimental tests by the early potters, who found there materials which accorded with the analysis of Oriental porcelain made by skilled chemists. At one time the annual value of clay produced in Cornwall amounted to £250,000; but it has long receded. According to some authorities, the honour of the discovery of the value of the properties of Cornish clay must be accorded to William Cookworthy, of Plymouth, who was probably the first maker of real porcelain in this country. At the time when the clay from the neighbourhood of St Austell was so much in demand, the raw material—disintegrated granite—was obtained by very simple methods. The ground where the Cornish clay was known to be was disturbed or broken up, then streams of water were laid on, the result being a milk-white liquid, afterwards conducted by

" launders " into a cistern or tank, in which the pure creamy substance was deposited. After passing through several minor processes and washings, the deposit was dried until the consistency was achieved ; it was then cut into blocks or cubes and placed in drying sheds. From the mines the clay, sometimes packed in large casks, at others loose in lumps, was carted to the coast, from whence it was shipped in small coasting vessels, destined for the Staffordshire Potteries and other places.

The Cornish china clay or kaolin was practically the same substance as the raw material, the secret of the preparation for which was so zealously guarded for centuries by the Chinese. From Cornwall, too, was obtained the growan or moor stone, which was regarded by the Chinese as a necessary accompaniment, for it was the *pe-tun-tse* (small white paste) that the Chinese used to give porcelain its peculiar hard surface and vitreous body.

The kaolin discovered in the eighteenth century to exist in Cornwall took its name from the Chinese word signifying " a lofty ridge " ; the Chinese kaolin was chiefly obtained from a hill near King-te-chin.

The Carclaze (grey rock) mine, near St Austell, is an immense open mine of nearly a mile and a half in circumference, and fully 150 feet deep. Although extensively mined for clay, the pit has yielded tin, having been worked as a tin mine for fully four hundred years, and in later days chiefly operated for clay. The Cornish clay, of which there are several varieties, withstands great heat, a property of considerable importance. In Dorsetshire the blue clay is remarkably plastic, although it lacks the purity of the Cornish clay.

Since the discovery of the value of flint in pottery-making that must be considered one of the more important constituents in porcelain, the flint of commerce being ordinary chalk flint, calcined. Felspar and Cornish stone are also valuable materials. The chief value of the latter is its properties as an insoluble fluxing material, rendering the wares dark, dense, and vitreous. Felspar is, of course, an important ingredient in the composition of hard paste glazes. Then again another material, apparently foreign in nature, and yet readily blending, is calcined bone, prepared from washed bones burned to a red heat.

HARD AND SOFT PASTES.

The connoisseur has to distinguish between hard and soft pastes when depending upon his knowledge of materials in defining the different substances of which pottery and porcelain have been made at different times. Pottery is opaque, porcelain semi-transparent. The glaze, however, as will be seen from the explanation given in chapter iii., if hard may materially affect the opinion formed of the substance of the paste or body.

The " old china," which constitutes by far the larger class of much-sought-after specimens, consists of both hard paste and soft paste wares, both of which are to some extent translucent when held up to the light. Hard paste is true porcelain, the materials of which it is composed being natural substances, whereas soft paste is composed of artificial substances and materials in combination. The glazes may be hard or soft ; for the most part hard glaze is used on hard paste porcelain, and soft glaze on soft body wares.

There is a difference between transparent or semi-transparent porcelain and translucent. Some of the old Worcester porcelain transmits a faint greenish colour, and there are many peculiarities in connection with Chinese porcelain. Some of these are referred to in particular in chapter xxxi.

Biscuit china is an unglazed ware, distinct from the

so-called " biscuit," the trade term of pottery or porcelain before being fired or decorated. Some of the most typical examples of pure biscuit porcelain are found in the biscuit figures and those lovely mirrors framed with exquisite wreaths of flowers and leaves in biscuit.

Parian marble may be regarded as a kind of biscuit china, especially the so-called Parian statuary figures and groups. The soft paste takes colours different to the hard ; in the former there is a delicacy and soft appearance which it is difficult to explain but easy to realise when comparing similar colour effects produced on hard and soft paste porcelain.

Once again it may be pointed out that most of the Oriental porcelain is hard paste, so hard that it cannot be cut with a file, differing, however, from the old soft paste Chinese. When describing old Chinese porcelain, however, it is seldom that any attempt is made to differentiate between pottery and porcelain.

Special Bodies and Pastes.

The bodies and pastes mentioned in the foregoing paragraphs are those most commonly met with, and represent such materials as were well understood by potters in the eighteenth century. Many, however, endeavoured to preserve trade secrets and to alter the composition they used so as to make some peculiarity in their wares.

As will be seen from a perusal of the following chapters, very many early potters sought to gain fame by introducing new substances, and especially by regulating the proportionate mixing of ingredients, in this latter lying the secret of their success in many instances. There was open competition resulting from the common knowledge possessed by eighteenth-century potters, and Josiah Wedgwood, the great master potter of the Staffordshire Potteries, was not over-anxious to retain in his own hands the secrets he had discovered ; he had many copyists, but as it is probable he discovered more varieties of paste and body than anyone else, some of the results of his investigations may be quoted as instances of the variations in the composition of old porcelain and pottery, for much of Wedgwood's work was wrought in opaque substances.

Josiah Wedgwood introduced his tortoiseshell agate, mottled cream ware, and other compositions, producing at least twenty new bodies for the manufacture of earthenware. Then again, he not only invented new bodies to suit the special objects he had in view, but he devised many other methods of utilising them, otherwise it would have been impossible for him to have produced such marvellous effects as those achieved in the black basalt and jasper wares, his beautiful new material jasper being a great achievement, allowing for every variety of colour and relief. It was the aim of the old potters to distinguish their own wares by some peculiarity of material or ornament, more frequently by the former—and it is of the different peculiarities of the several potteries in England, and of the varied and striking characteristics of pottery and porcelain made in Oriental countries and on the Continent of Europe, that the collector needs to be familiar with, otherwise the difficulties in his way are many, and he is robbed of half the delights of collecting by his ignorance of the location of his specimens, and the peculiarities which make them so different from others.

The home connoisseur begins at once to assemble his specimens, and long before he has had any thought of becoming a specialist he arranges with taste, if not with a great regard to classification, his specimens. During late years cabinet-makers have given some attention to the provision of a variety of " old china " cabinets, and none need now be without a fitting receptacle for china. The more decorative the better the effect of a miscellaneous collection, although the specialist prefers a good assortment of some one kind rather than a mixed group. Mr A. E. Clarke of Cambridge, whose fine collections of china and specialised groups are referred to in another chapter, favours us with a peep at his beautiful cabinet corner cupboards filled with choice specimens and many bits such as the home connoisseur is likely to have. Those reproduced in Figs. 4 and 5 are well filled with pottery and porcelain, including fine Leeds ware, inscribed and dated.

CHAPTER III

Skilled operators at work—The designer and his inspirations—The effect of glazing upon colour—Enamel finishes—The chief glazes met with.

THE connoisseur of ceramics has to depend very largely upon decorations, glazes, and marks for the identification of his specimens. The vessel after being fashioned out of the clay, and in some instances fired, passes through other processes before it comes into the hands of the user, and subsequently of the collector. The decoration in some instances almost obscures the paste or the natural colouring of the clay ; in others it is light and dainty and leaves a very large proportion of the surface undecorated, the whole being subsequently coated over with glaze and finally fired. As it has already been explained, in some instances the decoration is under the glaze, in others over the glaze. Of these two important processes of manufacture the decorations of the ware obviously come first. They vary, however, and the several treatments meted out to the different wares by various potters are referred to at some length in the chapters recording the productions of the different potteries, both in this country and abroad. In olden time the decorations imparted were almost in-variably scratched or incised into the clay ; then attempts were made to fill in the incisions with coloured matter, some remarkable pieces being executed, like the famous Greek pottery and terra-cotta ware.

19

Slip painting is said to be a method as old as primitive pottery itself, and yet it is one which has been revived in more recent times. The ornamenting of old stoneware with splashes of red, blue, or green has in some instances been remarkably effective, producing a species of raised ornament, contrasting with the ground colour. In modern times this process of decoration has been used in architectural tiles; curiously enough many of the so-called modern forms of ornament are but improved styles which were adopted ages ago. Many of the more remarkable departures in ceramic decoration came from Oriental countries, and even yet potters in the West receive some of their more important inspirations from the East. Slip decorations were applied equally on old Roman ware and on the coarse seventeenth-century pottery of Staffordshire and other parts of England.

Skilled Operators at Work.

The decoration chiefly adopted by English potters in the eighteenth century was some process of ornamentation under the glaze, blue being the favourite colour, in that it seems to have been very well adapted to produce good results. Such decorations were either painted or printed under glaze. By way of contrast, however, it may be remarked that Oriental china was nearly always painted. The soft paste of the English potters absorbed some portion of the colour, causing it to sink in or run, consequently the patterns of Worcester, Salopian, and Staffordshire blue were not as sharply defined as the paintings upon hard paste Oriental wares. The Oriental method was to dry the already formed vessel, and then to apply the cobalt colouring to the paste before firing, after glazing, both glazing and firing taking place after the finished decoration. As regards these early blues it may be pointed out that the Plymouth blue is a darker shade than the Worcester and Salopian blues, which gave such excellent effect to the " Willow " and other well-known patterns.

The simple paintings upon pottery, and those remarkable although crudely-drawn figures, arabesques, and other decorations on Saracenic pottery and some of the early Eastern wares, are entirely distinct from the artistic decorations and the beautiful paintings which were so well suited to the better modelled shapes of pottery and afterwards porcelain in the eighteenth century. At that time the decoration consisted largely of two groups : the one exquisite paintings closely imitating natural objects, such as scenic views, flowers, birds, insects, and sea-shells, which were painted upon English china by skilled artists and by Chinese workmen, copyists of English pictures ; the other group consisted of transfer prints, some of those prints being remarkably effective, for they were made from well-known pictures at that time engraved and stippled by clever copperplate engravers and some of the best known artists of the eighteenth century. The art of copperplate engraving was practised by artists of repute who engraved their own pictures, as well as by those who more mechanically copied the paintings of others. In the artistic decorations the painters on china, just as some of the modellers, were men who had won great fame ; they included Billingsley, Flaxman, Rose, Turner, and even the great potters themselves, some of whom were artists of no mean repute, being associated with the decorations of fine porcelain.

Needless to say, the preparation of the vessel to be painted required great care. It was burnt in the oven for some forty-eight hours and afterwards cooled for a similar period, passing through other processes until ready for decorating and gilding, the latter process being a very important one. Some idea of the methods employed by modern artists, who to a large extent follow the lines laid down by the older operators, may be seen when visiting one of the large modern potteries, where skilled operators are at work, although their names may not be made public, or their reputation spread about to the same extent as the fame of the older artists in days when lesser numbers of skilled workmen were employed.

The decorating process is admirably described in a booklet published by the Royal Worcester Porcelain Company, in which it is said : " Visitors generally look forward with pleasure to the decorating department, as they find it interesting to watch the painters engaged on landscapes, birds, flowers, and other subjects, and the gilders enriching the work with all kinds of ornament in gold.   After the first ' wash in ' of the colours (which are prepared from metallic oxides) has been burned, and the painter has worked upon it for a second fire, the forms and finish both in style and colour begin to appear.   The painters are trained from about fourteen years of age under special instructors ; thus they acquire not only a facility in drawing, but a general knowledge of the manipulation of the colours and of the action of the fire upon them. Elaborate and finely executed patterns in gold are traced by hand ; this requiring special training to ensure correct drawing and clean finish.   Pure gold is used, and it is obtained from the assayer in brown grains like coffee.   It is then mixed with quicksilver (which fires away in the kiln) to reduce it for grinding, this process occupying about thirty hours, after which it is ready for the workmen. Painted work and gold are fired in special kilns, which occupy about eighteen hours to heat and to cool."

After removal from the enamel kiln, the ware is touched up where necessary, and if perfect sent to the burnishing room, where the dull gold is burnished with a tool made from bloodstone or agate.   That, briefly, is an outline of the processes through which old china passed, and the process is still being repeated.

The Designer and his Inspirations.

As it has already been suggested, there have always been original designs used as decorations of pottery and porcelain, side by side with others which were copies either of designs used by other potters or taken from paintings, prints, and natural objects. Nature and still life as well as the art of the sculptor have joined hands with the painter in furnishing subjects for the decorator of ceramics. Some of the choicest examples of ancient pottery, of Eastern porcelain, and of some of the more recent works of art, like the Wedgwood copies of the celebrated Portland vase, were suggested by religion, mythology, and history. The religion and mythology of the ancients furnished them with their chief inspirations in art, architecture, and in applied designs. The Oriental porcelain of China is literally covered with reflections of Confucianism, Taoism, Buddhism, and the attributes inseparable from those different beliefs and myths. Gods, demons, men, and animals are mixed up in a wonderful systematic confusion, and the old porcelain of the Oriental world in its decorations presents to the student in picture form a history to be studied. The student of Greek vases, in common with the artist who studies the frieze of the Parthenon, Egyptian sculptures, the paintings on mummy cases, and other ancient relics, finds the subject matter which filled the minds of those old potters and their artists who so cleverly decorated their wares. The painted ornament on archaic vases, consisting of concentric circles, spirals, and other designs, was obviously suggested by textile fabrics, presenting another source of ornament. On some of the Phœnician and other vases there are

representations of seaweeds and marine animals, pointing
to knowledge of the sea and the creatures swimming therein.
Then again on other ancient pottery, like the Assyrian,
there are warlike subjects. The men represented in
chariots in Assyrian style would be familiar to those who
moulded and shaped the wares.

Scattered along the shores of the Mediterranean has
been found pottery, painted in dull ochre colour on biscuit
clay, representing animals on a ground sprinkled with
flowers. There are leopards, goats, and swans. There
are also sphinxes and, on many, designs which might be
called " history in ornament." With the remarkable
domestic scenes painted on Greek pottery the student of
that ware is familiar. The details, too, of such decoration,
although sometimes trifling, are wonderfully accurate, and
just as the forms of the vessels suggest their uses, so the
decoration indicates beliefs and daily happenings. There
are stories of the gods, scenes of the heroic age, and pictures
from real life, like the gathering of grapes and olives.
There are marriage feasts and hunting scenes, sacrifices,
and even theatrical subjects.

The colouring of the clay is in itself a form of decoration
which may be used in combination with embossing,
moulding, and relief ornament. Thus there is the remarkable Samian red pottery of Roman days resembling the
still earlier pottery of the Greek island of Samos. There
are the wonderful colour reliefs produced by Wedgwood on
his marvellous jasper wares. Even the sombre black of
Etruscan ware is rendered marvellously beautiful by
ornament in relief ; not relief applied in slip, but relief by
moulding in cleverly cut moulds, and in many instances by
touching up by hand the most delicate figure work. And
so the story of decoration might be lengthened, until the
gem-like pictures on Sèvres vases, and the cameos and
beautiful modelling in colour and relief seen in its greatest

height in the eighteenth century in the productions of Wedgwood and some of his contemporaries, were reached.

There is another form of decoration which calls for special note in that it is one of the characteristics which distinguish some classes of Continental and English pottery. That is found in the ornament fashioned in clay, and applied to the original vessel as an independent decoration, either in the natural colour or painted according to Nature. The encrustations of floral embellishments on Bristol china—those delightful frames of the Bristol mirrors in white biscuit—provide the collector with infinite variety in form and beauty of design and modelling, yet without colour. On the other hand, Dresden vases, the flowers upon which are patterns in relief coloured in blue, gold, and other tints, provide a special porcelain referred to in chapter xxviii. In English ceramics there are similar decorations on Chelsea, Bow, and Coalport china, wonderfully formed flowers, the very petals botanically correct, painted from natural blooms, the form and colouring providing an important scheme of decoration, something entirely distinct and apart from geometrical patterns and conventional ornament.

The mixing of colours and the preparation of the different pigments have been secrets jealously guarded throughout the ages, and the keeping of those secrets enabled people in olden time to produce distinctive wares, and to make use of special forms of decoration by applying suitable colours to the ornament often invented for those particular pigments.

THE EFFECT OF GLAZING UPON COLOUR.

No scheme of ornament is completed until finally fired, but the effects of colouring and the finish to the modelling have in most instances been supplemented by a process of glazing. It is said that many of the old glazes long defying attempts to copy are no longer secrets or relics of a lost art, for science has come to the aid of the potter, and enabled him to discover chemical results, and to produce similar effects to those obtained by the Orientals and other potters who by their glazes produced such extraordinary surfaces and iridescent lustrous effects. As an instance of the rediscovery of lost arts, it may be mentioned that in 1870 William de Morgan in England, and Cantigalli of Florence, rediscovered the manufacture of iridescent lustre from copper and silver fired on the glaze, a special kind of glaze and ornament used by the Moors, in Spain, and by Italian potters. Then again in more modern times Continental and English potters have been able to produce the brilliant turquoise blue of the Persians and Chinese. They have also analysed Chinese glazes, and secured exceedingly satisfactory results. The single or self-colour glazes of the Chinese are soft and brilliant, the colour glaze being often so thick as to hide the body paste. In such coloured glazes the celadon or sea-green is one of the oldest, reaching perfection about the year 1500. Following this came the yellow glaze, the imperial colour of the Tsing Dynasty.

Early in the eighteenth century the brown glazes of China became fashionable, but among the minor varieties are black, some of the black vases being extremely valuable. The crackle porcelain of China presents another variety of glaze. The small cracks were filled in with Indian ink, sometimes red, at others black, producing remarkable effects. There have been many modern attempts to copy the crackle glaze, so that collectors should be careful that they are really obtaining " old crackle." The blue and white porcelain of China, another important class, has a glaze and colouring of its own. These varieties, together with egg-shell porcelain and enamelled colours, are referred to in chapters xxx., xxxi., and xxxii.

ENAMEL FINISHES.

Enamel, so often a characteristic of the glaze or super-covering of the porcelain, is, of course, another substance consisting of opaque matter, and therefore entirely concealing the body paint. It is a term given to earthenware with what is called an enamelled surface, the earlier enamelled ware being represented by the Delft pottery made late in the sixteenth and early in the seventeenth centuries in Holland, and afterwards imitated at Bristol, Liverpool, Lambeth, and other places. The transparent glass or glaze is usually rendered opaque by the addition of oxide of tin. This enamel, although often spoken of as glaze, is entirely distinct from true glaze, in that the enamel is rather a coating of opaque matter, imparting a better finish to the body, whereas true glaze is transparent or semi-transparent and does not entirely conceal the body paste, or the painting or decoration which has been applied to it. Enamel is, therefore, like pottery, opaque, whereas glaze is transparent, even more so than the semi-transparent porcelain. Another feature of importance to bear in mind is that glaze may be either coloured or almost colourless. It may entirely change the appearance of the body paste or it may simply add to its lustre.

THE CHIEF GLAZES MET WITH.

The two chief glazes may be described as follows :

LEAD GLAZE.—The lead glaze, which was one of the earliest glazes employed in this country, was made by dusting the ware over with sulphide of lead. This older and injurious process was improved upon by the use of a liquid lead glaze.

SALT GLAZE.—The salt glaze was an eighteenth-century invention or discovery, by which it was found that when common salt was thrown into the kiln, upon its vaporising a fine glaze was spread over the different wares exposed therein.

The glazes usually met with on Egyptian pottery were alkaline silicates coloured when desired by metallic oxides, differing from enamel in that they were free from oxide of tin, which would have rendered them opaque. Some of the colourings of glazes were produced as follows : Blue and green by protoxide of copper or cobalt ; purple and violet by oxide of manganese ; yellow by iron ; red by sub-oxide of copper, and black by magnetic oxide of iron. Blues and greens are produced in many shades, including ultramarine, turquoise, and indigo ; all the varieties of blue shading to green. Some of the little mummy figures are covered with a silicious glaze, brilliantly coloured with copper oxide. Although many Assyrian vases are of plain biscuit clay, undecorated or stamped in relief, there are some glazed or enamelled. The enamelled pottery from the Grecian islands, especially that executed under Egyptian influence, finds its decoration in coloured enamels ; and many of the Greek vases were in part enamelled, showing up the paintings in relief. In some instances the enamel used was of considerable thickness, causing relief in the ornament. The Greek vases of the later period were ornamented by red figures on a black enamelled ground with a hard metallic glaze, differing from the softer ornament of the earlier period.

Glazed pottery was not common with the Romans, although some examples are found. Remarkable effects by the use of enamel and glaze are noticed in the Persian pottery, especially the lustre colours which required a special firing, for the beauty of the lustre depended upon the decomposition of a metallic salt, usually silver or copper. Lustre ware was much favoured in England late in the eighteenth century, and some beautiful examples were produced, the special treatment resulting in earthenware

Fig. 6.—A pattern for Vase in the Works' Museum at Etruria.

Illustrated by permission of Josiah Wedgwood & Sons, Ltd.

Fig. 6.

Fig. 7.   Fig. 8.

Fig. 7.—Metropolitan Slipware Cup, inscribed "Obeay the King."

Fig. 8.—Posset Cup of Staffordshire Slipware, inscribed "Ralph Turnor."

In the British Museum.

[To face page 28.

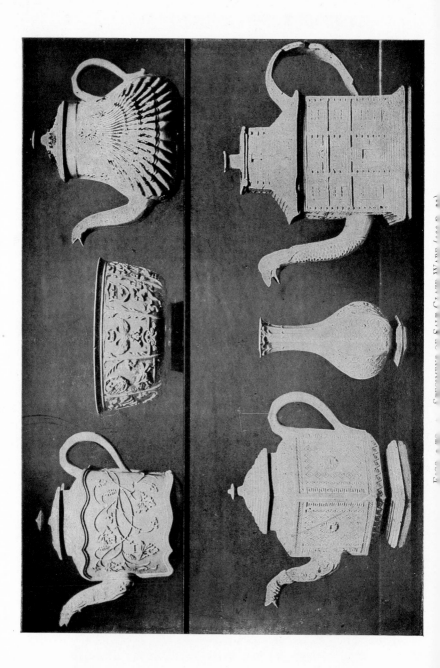

EXAMPLES OF SALT-GLAZE WARE (1720 & 1750).

To face page 29.]

which is so distinct as to provide the specialist with a kind of pottery of which he may secure many varieties from different countries (*see* chapter xxxviii.). The Persian pottery made under Chinese influence was glazed and decorated in quite a different style to the earlier Persian ware, the glaze being very thick. In the same way there is a distinct characteristic in the enamelled lustre ware produced in Sicily under Oriental influence.

The colouring of the Spanish potters, who imitated the technical methods of the Moors, and improved their own methods after a study of Persian pottery, included the application of a white enamel, a glaze rendered white and opaque, which when fired yielded a light cream colour, rich in lustre, produced by the addition of oxides of copper and silver. There was also a blue shade produced by cobalt oxides applied before the lustre glaze. Very rich indeed was the early Majolica pottery with deep ruby lustre.

In the sixteenth century the potters of France, especially Bernard Palissy, covered their remarkable wares, which were modelled in relief, with a tin enamel, sometimes using a lead glaze with a yellowish-cream tint. Lead glaze, too, was used in Germany, Flanders, and Holland from the fourteenth century onward, many of those wares being imported into England. Some of the cream ware was left unglazed, but a vitreous lead glaze, either colourless or tinted with oxide of cobalt, was usually employed. The glazes of the different wares made in England from the sixteenth century were varied. The cruder pottery of the seventeenth century was covered with a coarse lead glaze made from lead ore, sprinkled through a fine sieve on to the clay, producing a vitreous glaze. It was in that way that the old Staffordshire tygs, and the earthenware dishes made by Thomas Toft and others, were coated over.

Then came the salt glaze discovered about 1680, a simple method of glazing the wares in the kiln by throwing in handfuls of salt, the process, however, requiring a very high temperature. The glazes of more modern times, although varying in composition according to the recipes followed by different manufacturers, are for the most part transparent silicates of alumina, compounds of Cornish china stone, flint, and white lead. Borax and alkalis are added as a flux, in some instances reducing the quality of lead.

The application of the glaze varies, but the usual method is described by an authority as follows : " The materials for the glaze are finely ground with water and made into a thin white fluid. The biscuit pottery is rapidly dipped into vats of the milky mixture, and sufficient to form the glaze adheres to the absorbent clay in an even coating all over the surface. After being dried, the pottery is ready for the second firing of the glazing kiln, which is very similar in construction to the biscuit kiln, only as a rule rather smaller. It is packed in clay saddles as in the first firing, but a stronger heat is required to fuse the finer kinds of glaze than was necessary for the baking of the raw pottery."

The technical processes of manufacture are extremely interesting to the student and to those who desire to understand not only the composition of the substance, but the finish which produces different effects according to the treatment. There are many home connoisseurs, however, who are content to note the effects produced rather than the cause of the effect. Knowledge of ceramics to them comes from close inspection of specimens in representative collections. Fortunately collectors have access in London, and in other places, to very extensive collections where the work of different potters can be seen. The ceramic galleries of the Victoria and Albert Museum, at South Kensington, are full of rare pieces of Oriental and, indeed, of wares from all parts of the world ; the British Museum, too, contains a very fine collection.

The illustrations in this chapter are taken from the " British," and illustrate three distinct types of treatment. Figs. 7 and 8 indicate two varieties of slip decoration ; the first, Fig. 7, is an example of Metropolitan slip ware, a name given to that special type of ornament found in or about London, by the late Sir A. W. Franks. According to the British Museum catalogue the earliest dated example of this ware is of the year 1612 ; the one illustrated is inscribed, in the peculiar white slip, " OBEAY THE KING."

Another form of slip ware is given in Fig. 8, which is a posset cup of Staffordshire make, ornamented with combings, the inscription reading, " RALPH TURNOR."

The cream ware for the manufacture of which Wedgwood and others afterwards became famous is fully described in chapter xxii., where particulars of this ware and its decoration are given.

The salt glaze, the discovery of which was purely accidental, and yet of immense importance, became very generally used in Staffordshire in the eighteenth century ; few of the pieces are marked, they may therefore be collected and grouped according to their peculiar glaze rather than as being the products of any one maker. In chapter xxxviii. (Specialised Collections) further reference is made to salt glaze ware.

Figs. 9, 10, 11, 12, 13, and 14 are taken from examples in the British Museum ; their descriptions, briefly, are : Fig. 9, lovers' teapot ; Fig. 10, a bowl in high relief ornament ; Fig. 11, a shell-shaped teapot ; Fig. 12, a lozenge-shaped teapot; Fig. 13, a spill vase; and Fig. 14, a teapot of the cottage or house-like form, with a swan-necked spout —a very interesting group of salt glaze ware. As it is pointed out in the Museum catalogue, " the bulk of existing salt glaze consists of tea and coffee services and table ware." The manufacture of this ware ceased about 1780.

CHAPTER IV

PREHISTORIC POTTERY

Pottery from British barrows—Classification of finds—Summary of
forms of vessels—Egyptian prehistoric relics—Archaic pottery.

THE collection of prehistoric pottery belongs more particularly to the antiquarian than to the connoisseur of fine
art pottery and porcelain. In a representative ceramic
collection, however, it is interesting to possess at least a
few specimens of prehistoric pottery made by those peoples
who had scarcely begun to realise that in civilised com-
munities something more than the most primitive vessels
were necessary. The preservation of ancient pottery is
due, probably, to religious observances, superstitions, and
the common belief in a spirit world; for most of the objects
which have been discovered or turned up by the plough
have either been cinerary urns in which the ashes of the
departed dead were carefully preserved, or food vessels,
incense cups, and domestic pottery, buried with the dead
in the superstitious belief that in another world there might
be need of such pottery as served in the prehistoric world
of which we now know comparatively little. Of that
little, however, it is clear that those cave-dwellers of the
Paleolithic period and the prehistoric races of the Neolithic
Age made use of clay and burned it in order that the
vessels they had shaped might be more useful and lasting.

The sepulchral barrows of Scandinavia, France, and
other portions of Europe have yielded vast quantities of

ancient pottery, formed of coarse clay—brown, grey, or red. In some instances the clay has apparently been mixed with gravel, sand, and quartz crystals. Other ancient pottery, after being fashioned, was coated with a smooth slip. The examples found in British barrows are very similar to those discovered in Scandinavia and France. In referring then to the collectable objects, it will suffice to draw attention to those characteristics which are very noticeable in British specimens.

Many collectors possess a few examples of this ancient pottery, and others, while specialising chiefly on the more beautiful wares of comparatively recent times, may be induced by perusing these pages to think more kindly of the pottery made and used by those prehistoric races who once inhabited these islands and the continent of Europe, to which Britain was in the far past connected.

The burial places where the chieftains of prehistoric races found a last home have yielded the collector examples of the Neolithic and Bronze Ages, showing a remarkable similarity in the pottery found in almost every county in England. The materials of which these ancient vessels were formed vary somewhat, a natural condition to expect in that they were made locally and from the materials at hand. The forms and schemes of simple decorations are so curiously alike that we are forced to accept the theory which points to a common origin.

The cinerary urns, usually found full of burned bones, are of different sizes. There are not many less than twelve inches in height, whereas many are as large as eighteen inches. Some have handles, others are simply jars. The objects classed as food vessels vary in size and in shape, but always differ from the curious little vessels which for the want of a better name have been called incense cups. The ornament on these different vessels is exceedingly decorative, considering the crudeness of the

c

object, the primitive conditions under which this pottery was made, and the early days in which it was used. There are few, if any, sun-baked vessels found in British barrows, although some may have been hardened by the heat of the sun before firing. No doubt the burning of this ancient pottery was often done in a very careless way in an open fire ; indeed, some of the vessels show traces of having been blackened by the charcoal or fumes of the wood which supplied the heat.

In the consideration of some of the examples taken from barrows and ancient dwellings, it is well to point out the contents or finds of some well-known group of barrows, rather than take odd isolated examples which cannot be regarded as representative in any one district. The Staffordshire Potteries has become so essentially the centre of the twentieth-century potting industry in this country —although supplemented by Worcester, Derby, and other similarly well-known places—that to recall the chief features of prehistoric earthenware as found in that county will be of double interest. Indeed, it seems fitting to choose a locality like the county of Stafford, where not only does the potting industry at this time flourish, but where a century and a half ago Josiah Wedgwood and other great discoverers of ceramic secrets were struggling to gain the ascendency and to make their county the chief home of the trade.

At the time when Josiah Wedgwood was learning his art Staffordshire presented a very different appearance to what it does to-day ; even fifty or sixty years ago many parts of North Staffordshire were open heaths and moors over which the plough had not been drawn, and no building had then disturbed the ancient contour of the land. There were many barrows dotted over the landscape, and throughout the centuries which had elapsed since the prehistoric burials had taken place no one had dared to disturb the burying places of the dead. Yet within the last sixty years most of the remaining mounds have been broken up and explored, until it is difficult indeed to find an unopened barrow.

Mr Thomas Bateman, in conjunction with his son, Mr William Bateman, and some of his friends, spent nearly ten years in exploring the barrows in Staffordshire and some other counties, resulting in the acquirement of a vast number of interesting remains taken from them. Many prehistoric vessels thus discovered, after being classified, revealed much that had hitherto been unknown, and gave the present generation a much clearer insight into the purposes of the vessels made by ancient people, and showed their gradual attainment of some knowledge of art and manufacture. A large proportion of the famous Bateman collection was afterwards deposited in the Public Museum at Weston Park, Sheffield.

It has been suggested that very important groups of barrows (referred to at length in the *Victoria History of the Counties of England—Staffordshire*) in Staffordshire were connected with other burial places in Derbyshire.

Collectors class certain well-defined forms of prehistoric pottery under generic terms, such as food vessels, drinking cups, incense vessels, and cinerary urns, but those terms do not strictly indicate the original purposes or uses of the pottery ; indeed, doubtless in an age when vessels were few and their qualities and forms varied little, the same piece of pottery would be put to many different uses. It is curious to observe that although similar characteristics are met with in many districts, in certain places some vessels prevail more than others. In all, however, it has been found that clay vessels were purposely inserted in a tomb. In Staffordshire, it is said, drinking cups are the most conspicuous, occurring with unburnt burials ; and this type of vessel, probably the earliest form of decorated pottery, was made by man in the county of Stafford in the Bronze Age. The term "drinking cup" does not necessarily define its actual use, any more than the terms "incense cup" and "food vessel."

The drinking cup type of vessel found so extensively in Staffordshire has its counterpart in the drinking cups discovered in the barrows on Salisbury Plain and other parts of Wiltshire. Urns are of course found in districts where the bodies were cremated, and are often the most important finds in a large barrow. There are but few parts of Britain undisturbed by the plough or the builders' pickaxe now, but there are still a few places where excavations have been made within quite recent years, and accredited societies have placed on record discoveries of authentic specimens. One of the most important series of excavations has been that at Hengistbury Head, in Hampshire, where so many large urns have been found in the barrows. Those excavations were of some use to the antiquarian, too, for they revealed traces of a settlement where people evidently lived in huts made of wattle and daub. In the beaten clay floors of those ancient dwellings were sunk large earthenware jars which had apparently been used for the storage of corn.

In Doncaster Museum there are some excellent collections, the result of local excavations, including fine cinerary urns of a reddish terra-cotta colour; the commoner urns are usually of grey or yellow clay. It may be mentioned here that these so-called prehistoric burials in barrows continued until almost Romano-British days, and probably many of the vessels discovered on the sites where the people evidently lived together in huts and congregated in settlements were of a later or Romano-British period.

The ornament is a matter of some interest. In nearly all instances it consisted of horizontal lines running round the circumference of the vessel, these lines being frequently

connected with zig-zags or chevron-like markings. Such
ornamentations were impressed in the clay while it was
moist, and expert critical examination shows that the work
was done by some kind of instrument having a series of
tooth-like projections. Similar ornamentation has been
noticed on incense cups and food vessels found in Staffordshire, especially examples discovered in barrows at Castern,
Stanshope, and on urns found at Mouse Low and Top Low.
Some of the urns discovered in this latter district had
lozenge ornament. A very beautifully formed and somewhat curious incense cup was found at Throwley. On it
were both horizontal lines and chevrons; it had a well-
formed lip, and below the middle ridge of the body there
were two holes which had been pierced in the clay, thus
indicating its use as an incense cup. Such cups, it may be
mentioned, are generally associated with cremations.

Local museums are rich in fine pottery from ancient
barrows of local fame, and there are some noted collections,
which have been made by those who have devoted much
time and attention to the exploration of barrows, like the
Bateman Collection; but the finest and most complete
collection of ancient pottery is that which can be seen in the
British Museum. It is true there is a large store of early
pottery in the Guildhall Museum, but having been found in
London, which has been subjected to so many changes
and has been the dwelling-place of successive races, the
pottery found there has rarely been discovered in an undisturbed condition, and its real origin is uncertain.

In the British Museum, however, there are cases
containing examples from many finds, taken from undisturbed barrows in different places, so that the types can be
critically examined. There is pottery from Yorkshire and
Westmorland, where there was an elaborate system of
cremation, and many examples from the long barrows of
Worcestershire and Gloucestershire, where there were un-

burnt burials. Then again, there are relics the result of the
exploration of barrows of the later Bronze Age, where both
burnt and unburnt burials took place in barrows circular
and conical. Cremation appears to have been the common
usage in Cornwall, and very general, too, in some portions
of North Wales, whereas both systems were practised in
Northumberland and in Yorkshire.

Summarising the forms of the different vessels referred
to, the following descriptions are given in the British
Museum Guide: " (1) *Drinking cups*. The name is
based on Sir Richard Colt Hoare's assumption that the
tall cylindrical vessels of good thin ware, found almost
exclusively in unburnt interments, were intended to hold
liquid, either for refreshment during the journey to the
next world, or to propitiate the spirits of the dead in the
interests of the living. It is assumed that the drinking cup
fulfilled the same purpose as the food vessel. The earlier
kind, however, is practically confined to certain parts of
Britain. The ordinary form of the drinking cup has a
cylindrical neck which sometimes inclines to an inverted
cone, joined to a globular body, both portions being
covered with ornament, whereas the corresponding continental form, the *Schnur-becher*, has the body quite plain,
except for a fringe that served as a border to the ornamented neck. The sharp angle between the two com-
ponent parts was not constant ; and there are intermediate
forms between the angular and the bell or tulip pattern
that occurred in Germany and Holland. . . . The ornament is for the most part disposed in horizontal bands, but
in some cases the vertical treatment of the neck ornament
emphasises its distinction from the body. It is executed
by means of twisted thongs, impressed in the moist clay,
producing the characteristic cord pattern, and also by
pointed or shaped rods of bone or wood, forming herring-
bone or hatched patterns and stamped rings.

" (2) *Food vessels*.—These are found in considerable numbers in Ireland as well as in Britain, the majority having been deposited in unburnt bodies in round barrows. The ware is somewhat coarser than that of the class already described, and considerably thicker ; while the ornament, which is lavishly bestowed on the outside of the vessel, extends in some specimens outside the lip, and a cruciform design is by no means uncommon on the bottom. They are sometimes provided with covers, and with a number of lugs or ears round the contracted neck, which are either pierced for the insertion of a cord, or are merely ornamental survivals of such attachments. The mouldings round the neck and rim, and the delicate ornamentation on many specimens, render the food vessels on the whole the most attractive class of Bronze Age pottery in this country, and it is interesting to note that they are quite unrepresented outside the British Isles.

" (3) *Cinerary urns*.—As a class cinerary urns are undoubtedly later than the drinking cups and food vessels, and formed receptacles for the cremated remains of the dead. Their magnitude says something for the technical skill of the potter, who introduced grit, noticeable in the paste, which was necessary to prevent the clay from cracking during the process of firing. The usual type consists of two truncated forms placed base to base, the upper one forming a deep overlapping brim, to which the ornamentation is in many cases confined. Other shapes are, however, common, and specimens from one or two sites have the walls almost vertical, while the decoration was executed with a twisted thong, with a pointed tool, or with the finger point and finger-nail, the size of which suggests that the potters belonged to the female sex, as is generally the case among savages at the present day.

" (4) *Incense cups*.—These are intimately associated with the burning of the dead, but are not by any means as common as cinerary urns, inside which they are very frequently found. In shape and decoration they vary considerably, but are generally pierced in one or two places as if to assist combustion. Many have loops for suspension, while in some cases the bottom is ornamented with cruciform and other designs. They seem to have been placed in the grave after the body had been reduced to ashes."

The fine plate of twelve examples (*see* Fig. 15) is reproduced by special permission of the British Museum authorities and illustrates the types of prehistoric pottery described in the foregoing paragraphs. These and many other examples are to be seen in the cases round the galleries of the Museum.

EGYPTIAN.

The British Museum is rich in Egyptian antiquities, and many fine examples of the earliest domestic curios are to be seen in that extensive collection. In Egypt the use of marble and stone for even common objects came before pottery, the Museum collection containing some exceedingly fine stone and alabaster vases, among which are those of funeral type in granite, porphyry, jasper, and alabaster, many of which were found in the earlier grades of the Dynastic period. There are narrow vases in hard black stone, and large sepulchral limestone vessels, one remarkable exhibit being an alabaster table with a complete set of vessels made to hold oils and salves for the high priestly official Atena. The Pyramids were made of brick, and in those early days the Egyptians learned the use of fine coloured enamels ; rich in the clays deposited by the Nile, the Egyptians had ample opportunity of developing the potting industry as soon as they discovered how clay vessels could be shaped, modelled, and burned. In one of the wall

FIG. 15.—SEPULCHRAL POTTERY FROM BRITISH BARROWS.
In the British Museum.

[To face page 40.

FIG. 16.—Examples of EARLY GREEK POTTERY, including Lamp, Oil Bottles and Vases; some decorated in red and black.

In the Author's Collection.

FIG. 16.

FIG. 17.—BLACK GREEK VASES, including specimens from Pompei.

In the Author's Collection.

FIG. 17.

cases in the British Museum there is a representative collection of pottery dating from the Fourth Dynasty, B.C. 3700 to B.C. 1000. Among them are gracefully-shaped bottles, two-handled vases, and some ornamental pottery.

The term " Egyptian porcelain " has sometimes been given to the small mummy figures in blues and greens which were covered with a slip or glaze of an oxide of tin. It was, however, during the Ptolemaic period that so much graceful pottery was made in fine red and brown clays. Some pieces were decorative, others rather rudely coloured with shiny pigments. Of a later date, about the Twentieth Dynasty, examples are met with of the blue-glazed Egyptian porcelain, including vases, jars, bottles, and other vessels, many of them inscribed with the names of the reigning monarchs, some most decorative and beautifully ornamented. Among those in the British Museum are a blue-glazed porcelain jug with handle ornamented with the figure of a lady, in relief, making an offering at an altar ; a blue-glaze porcelain figure of the god Bes ; a porcelain dog-headed ape, a species found at the present day in Central Africa, celebrated for their intelligence and also for constant chattering from dawn until sunrise. For this reason the Egyptians believed that they were the spirits of the dawn which saluted the rising sun, and that when the sun had risen the spirits turned into apes. Among the relics of the Ptolemaic period are large glazed porcelain jugs, one in the Museum being ornamented with the figure of a princess making an offering at an altar, the handle being ornamented with bearded heads. There are numerous Egyptian jugs, bowls, and cups and saucers in terracotta, belonging to the Greco-Roman period. Such objects are still discovered in Egyptian tombs, but alas ! they have been much fabricated, and tourists in Egypt are often imposed upon, and extravagant prices charged for modern replicas purporting to be genuine antiques.

ARCHAIC POTTERY.

home connoisseur " can scarcely be expected to
ly into the mysteries of ancient pottery, far
removed from those discoveries which are made in this
country, although objects which have been brought over
in large quantities, like the prehistoric Greek vases and the
curios from ancient Egypt. The story of pottery and
porcelain, however, would be incomplete without a summarised reference to Phœnician and other archaic pottery,
and a brief reference to Assyrian, for recent discoveries
have brought to light many wonderful hoards of buried
pottery in Ancient Assyria, most of which finds its way into
museums and national collections. To take this latter
named class first, it may be pointed out that the ruined
palaces of Babylon and Nineveh have yielded much
pottery and bricks painted in various colours, some being
coated with vitrified enamels, others ornamented with
earth colours—ochres, and metallic oxides.

The vases and domestic vessels of Assyria have been
divided into four classes : (1) those made of biscuit clay
and undecorated ; (2) biscuit vessels afterwards painted ;
(3) vases enriched with stamp relief ; and (4) glazed and
enamelled-surfaced vessels. Many of these ancient jars
are most gracefully formed, and are not unlike some of
the Etruscan and early Greek pottery.

Recent discoveries in Southern Italy have brought to
light a vast quantity of Venetian pottery such as that
already referred to as having been sold in the London
auction rooms and brought over by visitors to Cyprus,
Rhodes, and other islands, and procured by tourists in
Egypt and other countries.

Summarising the forms and materials of archaic pottery,
it may be pointed out that these vessels so delicately
fashioned, often very thin in substance, have sometimes

very narrow necks and stems. They are thin, light, and well baked ; sometimes pale buff varying to straw colour and even whitish, those made of a darker clay being frequently coated with a white slip, which was composed of lime, silica, and alumina. The painted ornament on archaic vases may be divided into four classes : (1) concentric circles and hatchings, and various patterns obviously taken from textiles and metal work ; (2) crude ornamentation representing seaweed, marine animals, and sometimes birds ; (3) conventional designs, such as those in which the Egyptian lotus plant figures ; and lastly (4) the more ornamental vases which show some knowledge of art, and greater skill in painting animals and even men. This latter class, decorative and ornamental, represents the highest form of archaic art, and to some extent overlaps the artistic pottery of Greece, of which there are so many fine examples extant.

The British Museum is exceedingly rich in prehistoric pottery of every kind, not only in the ancient pottery found in this country in prehistoric barrows, and in course of excavating the sites of ancient settlements and towns, but in the pottery of prehistoric peoples all over the world. In the " Guide to the Department of Greek Antiquities in the British Museum " there is an interesting account of the art of the Etruscans, who made their appearance in Italy, probably entering from the north before the beginning of written history. Their territory was close to that of Rome, their struggle against the Romans ending in great battles fought B.C. 283. The original basis of Etruscan art is the primitive form of culture in which was a deep religious belief and elaborate ritual.

In the art of Etruria in its later days Greek influence is perceptible, and there was an interchange of wares between them, for many fine Greek vases have been found in Etruscan tombs. It is said the Etruscans never imitated

Greek wares with any success, but they adopted Greek
motives and utilised Greek mythology. In the British
Museum there is an early Etruscan pitcher in black ware,
the subject of its ornament being Theseus slaying the
Minotaur and Ariadne. There is also much Etruscan black
pottery on which patterns are made by incised lines and
partly moulded reliefs. Many of the vases exhibited have
been found during the course of excavations in Athens and
other parts of Greece, but mostly in islands and shores of
the Mediterranean which had been taken possession of by
Greek colonists in or before the sixth century B.C. The
early Greek vases have been for the most part found in
tombs, and their shapes vary according to the different
periods of art. Among the earlier examples may be
mentioned the *amphora*, a two-handled vase for storing
liquid ; the *hydria*, a pitcher for carrying water ; the
crater, a wide-mouthed vessel in which wine and water were
mixed for use ; the *lebes*, a bowl ; the *stamnos*, a rather
squat-shaped jar with two handles ; and the *psycter*, or
wine-cooler, all of which were of a somewhat large size.

Among the smaller objects which frequently come
under the notice of collectors are the *oinochoe*, a jug for
pouring out wine ; the *lekythos*, a narrow-necked jug for
pouring liquids slowly ; the *aryballos*, a small, round-bellied
jug for oil ; the *alabastrum*, a long, narrow vase with small
ears for ointment or perfume ; the *cantharos*, a drinking cup
with a tall stem and two handles ; the *kylix*, a wide and
shallow drinking cup, and a few other minor varieties.
Several examples of this archaic pottery are given in Figs.
16 and 17 ; most of the pieces came from islands in the
Græcean Archipelago, and others from Pompeii.

In the first Vase Room at the British Museum there is a
large collection of more advanced types of prehistoric
wares, chiefly from tombs in Paros and Antiparos. There
are numerous vases which have been found in Cyprus, the

later types showing a brown glaze, some with patterns incised, others with patterns painted on.

Some of the rarer examples of prehistoric pottery of the finer type are on the borderline between the prehistoric and that pottery made within the range of reliable history. One of these specimens now in the British Museum is known as the Burgon amphora, which is thought to have been one of the prize amphoræ which, filled with sacred olive oil, were given to the victors of the games held during the Panathenaic Festival. It was found at Athens filled with the ashes of its owner. On one side is the usual figure of Athene in black, the goddess' flesh being tinted white ; the inscription and some portions of her drapery are in crimson. On the reverse is the winner of the vase driving a biga.

Prehistoric pottery, and that pottery used when classic history was being written, is a prelude to the study and collection of the finer art treasures of later days. It forms an excellent basis on which to build ; for by the inclusion of a few pieces the story of the potter as seen in ceramic wares is rendered more complete. And although there is a gap between the pottery of those early races by whom this and other countries were at one time peopled and the pottery of days, the doings of which history has recorded, it is a necessary beginning, illustrating the story of primitive man and the things he made and used.

CHAPTER V

ROMAN AND ROMANO-BRITISH

Roman remains in Britain—A typical kiln—The early use of marks.

In the previous chapter reference has been made to the overlapping of the later Greek and the Roman pottery. No doubt when the Roman rule extended throughout the Peninsula, Greek pottery was used and reproduced by Roman potters. The Græco-Roman pottery found in Roman Colonies in Asia Minor was of a somewhat peculiar character, being glazed, often having more the appearance of glass than pottery, the thick vitreous glaze being very beautiful in appearance. The Roman pottery of the first century B.C. to the fifth century in the Christian era was very similar all throughout the Roman Empire. It was made in Italy, Spain, some parts of Germany, in France, and in Britain. That made in Britain, commonly known as Roman or Romano-British, may be treated separately in that the finds which have been made in this country are very extensive, furnishing fine examples in our museums, and also in private collections.

Many important discoveries of Roman ware have been made in all the countries enumerated, and the similarity of types in all these places shows that the Romans carried with them many of their domestic appliances, as well as reproducing similar patterns and designs in the countries where they settled. Numerous discoveries have been made in the neighbourhood of Cologne, from which it has been

46

thought likely that some of the red ware imported into Britain came from the Rhinish provinces, there being important kilns in the neighbourhood of Strassburg and Metz.

One of the principal varieties of old Roman pottery, the remains of which have been found in many countries, is a beautiful red glossy ware, designated Samian ware, the generic name being taken from the red pottery originally made in the Greek island of Samos. In colour it resembles red sealing-wax, and the moulded ornament and reliefs are very clearly cut, giving a most effective decoration, often covering the whole of the vessel. The clay consisted of silica, alumina, red oxide of iron, and lime. The enamel was also of a red vitreous character. The finest Samian ware is said to have been made in Italy and in Spain; some of it doubtless was made in Britain during the Roman occupation; other pottery, however, was probably imported, showing that it was valued even in those early times. Samian bowls have been discovered riveted with lead or bronze.

Another important type of unglazed ware consists of a soft and porous undecorated body, many of the objects being of simple forms not unlike Greek designs. Some of the amphoræ are quite large, so also are many urns and vessels for domestic use. These wares of biscuit pottery must of course be distinguished from the pottery covered with slip decoration in relief, some of the ornament being moulded and put on the body afterwards. There are fine examples in Colchester and other museums.

Black pottery of Roman make is another variety, the colour or tint being produced by direct contact with the smoke in the kiln. The most noted place in Britain where black pottery was made was at Castor in Northamptonshire, where there have been interesting discoveries of Roman kilns.

The Roman glazed pottery, which is scarce, was coated with a glass-like glaze.

The marks on Roman pottery are interesting, as they frequently indicate potters' names, which are impressed from oblong or circular incuse stamps. There are both Teutonic and Gaulish names, as well as those strictly Roman. The bricks and tiles used by the Roman generals who built houses for themselves in this country were made by the soldiers, and are frequently stamped with the name of the legion to which they belonged.

From the Roman potter we learn much, often seeing in the decoration on the red Samian ware, so exceedingly effective, in relief, something of the historical events in Roman history, of the legends and myths which were almost inseparable from the Roman thought, and even the actions of everyday life. In the early days of Roman supremacy, the art of Greece exercised a strong influence upon the work of the potters, many of the bowls and other vessels being highly decorated, covered over with well-modelled figures; gradually the Grecian mythological characters giving way to military figures, sports, and other occupations distinctly Roman. As it has been pointed out, Roman pottery was made in all the countries occupied by Roman troops. Doubtless the method of manufacture, the firing of the clay, and operating the kilns were similar in all countries, although the materials at hand in some instances were quite different and called for some special treatment.

ROMAN REMAINS IN ENGLAND.

The Roman pottery which has been found in this country, in many instances, includes those vessels brought over by Roman governors and others who settled here, the products of potteries in Italy and other parts of the

Continent, intermixed with the pottery undoubtedly made in England during Roman occupation.

Roman pottery discovered in England must of course be distinguished from collections of Roman pottery formed on the Continent of Europe, and especially in Italy. We cannot, however, accept all the fragments which have been found in England as of Romano-British make, for no doubt some of the choicer wares, like the Samian pottery, were brought over to this country in the days of Roman occupation. For four centuries there was an army of Roman soldiers in Britain, and during that long period many Roman villas were built, and a number of cities and important camps, where some of the nobles with their wives and families were settled. They imported choicer household goods, therefore, much that is beautiful and of exceptional merit artistically may have been brought over from Rome itself. England, however, possessed native clay, and Roman potters would improve upon the early British and Celtic wares, moulding and throwing the potters' clay, evolving similar shapes to those vessels they had been familiar with in other countries. One of the most noted Roman potteries in England was that at Castor, near Peterborough, where pots and pans and other vessels were made in large quantities. Upchurch, in Kent, was also a seat of the potting industry, as well as several places in the New Forest in Hampshire. Some of the most important finds of Roman pottery obviously made in this country come from Winchester and Colchester, and also from Bath, Chester, and other well-known Roman cities.

The Castor ware already referred to is distinctive, mostly grey or yellowish-brown, glazed with a reddish dull black.

One of the characteristics of the New Forest jars is the smooth porous body ; like Castor ware, it is grey or yellow-ish-buff, although often of a pale red or brown colour.

The reddish glaze is almost purple at times ; it is noted, too, for its banded or circular ornament.

Upchurch ware seems to have been made from a somewhat different clay which produced a slate colour or dark grey. The decoration on this pottery is quite distinct from other ornament used by Roman potters, being formed by the addition of raised spots and incised lines.

A Typical Kiln.

In London the Romans evidently used many large jars or vases, very fine amphoræ having been discovered. No doubt there was a great similarity in the Roman kilns. In a very interesting lecture delivered by Mr T. Arthur Acton, of Wrexham, to the members of the Chester and North Wales Archæological Society, some little time ago, the lecturer pointed out some of the characteristics of the Roman pot kilns at Holt. As the result of excavations it had been possible to uncover the kilns at Holt, which were said to be one of the finest series so far discovered. At the Roman settlement there was a legionary manufactury, in connection with the great fortress of Deva (Chester). It was there that the Romans made tiles, bricks, and every kind of pottery for their great fortress, and indeed for most of the camps in the west. The lecturer had traced the pottery made at Deva as having been transferred in ancient times to the Roman Wroxeter, and to many of the hill fortresses in Wales. It had been discovered how the main and cross flues were constructed and how they were fired. Describing a Roman kiln some years ago, one who inspected the remains then uncovered said there was a low arch for the insertion of the fuel, surmounted by a perforated floor made of clay slabs ; upon the floor rested the pots, and above the kiln had probably been a dome, long destroyed.

THE EARLY USE OF MARKS.

The marks on Roman pottery, often consisting of letters, and sometimes names in full, while exceedingly interesting, are not always means of identification in that the names of potters of that nation which had colonies in so many countries, and armies of occupation everywhere, have not been recorded in history. The master potter or the workman branded the vessels he was making with his initials or name, sometimes adding what may be called common marks ; thus on many pieces of Roman pottery there is a mark like a footprint, on the heel and sole of the foot being stamped initials. Many pieces and fragments of Roman pottery found in London bear the marks of early makers. London itself was an important station and the seat of pot works, andlocal clay appears to have been freely used. In many parts of the city, far down below the present roadways, are the remains of Roman roads, and among the rubbish heaps at that depth are found scraps of early English and Roman pottery. In the lower stratas, immediately above the solid beds of clay and gravel, pieces of the best pottery have been discovered.

From such marked examples as those referred to, we learn of the long-established practice of marking pottery. The features chiefly to remember in trying to decipher specimens is that such marks or names indicate the personality of the modeller, the potter, or possibly the owner of the kilns. Those who were fashioning Romano-British pottery were speaking in what is now a dead language, and they impressed their pottery with abbreviations which indicated to them, and to all who made use of the vessels they fashioned, the facts relating to their manufacture they wished to record. Curiously enough, some of their modes of expression and their abbreviations are equally as well known to-day to experts and connoisseurs, and to engravers and fabricators. There is the letter " F " for *fecit*, appropriately, after the name, indicating by whom it was made. Thus, from " Sabinvs, F," we learn that Sabinus *made it* ; a Samian vase marked " AMICI M," *Amici manu* (by the hand of Amicus), recorded by a well-known authority, shows by whom the actual work was performed. Yet another example may be given in the brand or mark " OF FILIC," *officina Felicis* (from the workshop of Felix) ; this mark evidently indicates the name of the owner of the kiln, and not that of the actual workman. These are but a few examples which might be multiplied almost indefinitely, for upwards of 1,100 separate Roman marks are known, showing the importance of the potting industry and of its wide distribution through the Roman Empire, represented in Britain perhaps as widely if not to a greater extent than in any other Roman colonies or possessions.

CHAPTER VI

EARLY ENGLISH

Few early examples preserved—The glazed wares of mediæval potteries—
Peasant pottery—Named and dated examples—Metropolitan and other
wares.

WHEN we leave the British pottery made by the craftsmen
of this country under Roman influence, the period which
follows is dark and obscure.   As in other commodities
when the influence of Roman control was withdrawn, the
people of Saxon England made little advance in the arts
and crafts.   In some instances they went backwards, in
others they merely practised those crafts they had learned,
without making any effort to advance them.   In some arts,
it is true, some little progress was made, but not in pottery.

It must be remembered that with the withdrawal of
the Roman army of occupation, the return of most of the
Roman nobles and their families to Italy, and the departure
of those who had for a time made England their home,
there was little intercourse with foreign countries.   At
that time the products of the British kilns seem to have
been very crude ; they were made for local use and the
roughest served.   This state of things continued throughout the earlier days of the Middle Ages, during which
pottery was poor, and apparently the work of unskilled
potters.   It is probable that the making of pottery was
not cultivated as a fine art by clay workers, most of whose
time was spent in making bricks and strictly utilitarian
pottery.

FEW EARLY EXAMPLES PRESERVED.

The decoration of earthenware at that time was crude,
like the forms and manufacture, and ornament was often
absent altogether.   Such was the condition of the pottery
trade in England for centuries.   It could scarcely be called
a trade ; the different objects were largely made for home
use, and for the use of the great landowners and barons
on whose lands the clay was found and the work performed.
The few remaining examples of Anglo-Saxon pottery tell
us little ; no doubt most pieces of special interest have
perished, largely on account of their inferior quality and the
ease with which they were broken and from time to time
renewed ; and also on account of the changes going on.
There were no cups or urns deposited with the bodies of
the dead such as those which had been buried with the
bodies of chieftains and others at an earlier time.   The
pagan faiths had given place to the Christian religion,
which carried with it none of those superstitions in which
pottery was deemed an essential provision for the needs of
the spirit world or the honoured dead in a future state.
In the Guildhall Museum in London there are a few terra-
cotta vases with embossed ornament of that period, but
they are not of sufficient importance to enable us to arrive
at any accurate idea of what the domestic pottery of that
time actually consisted, or its extent.   In this connection
it is well to remember that the use of pottery in household
matters was then, and for a long time afterwards, restricted.
In the early Middle Ages trenchers of bread served as
platters for the meat.   Then came wooden trenchers, for
wood was a handy material from which to cut serviceable
plates, and also bowls and other necessary culinary and
household utensils.

Progress was slow and centuries elapsed before the
pottery of the mediæval days, of which there are pieces

collectable, showed any marked improvement. The examples, limited to a few varieties, present great similarity of form, although doubtless made in very many different localities. They consisted of tygs, pilgrim bottles, jugs, and other objects; some of the quite early pieces were grotesque in form and decoration, foreshadowing the curious puzzle jugs which became so popular in Tudor times.

As it has already been suggested, the pottery made in England in mediæval days was the work of the peasant class; and those who were responsible for the work, possibly owners of the soil, were incapable of training workers or guiding them in their search for improvements in form or finish. Some exception must be made in the pottery produced in the neighbourhood of the great monastic establishments, where those who made tiles and decorative pottery for the embellishment of the beautiful abbeys and monasteries ornamented them with ecclesiastical emblems, their designs showing traces of much greater skill in draughtsmanship than the actual craftsmen were likely to have possessed. Pottery found in the neighbourhood of many well-known religious houses prove that it was possible even with the knowledge then acquired to produce tiles and other objects of superior colouring and finish.

The Glazed Wares of Mediæval Potters.

The use of greenish or yellow-glaze in English mediæval pottery is often regarded as a distinguishing mark, in that the objects so coated are quite different from anything made in Roman or Saxon times. At first the glaze seems to have been made and used very sparingly, and as it was chiefly applied to the inside of the vessel in the thirteenth and early part of the fourteenth centuries, it is reasonable to suppose that its original purport was utilitarian; and by applying it to the interior of the vessels it prevented the clay from absorbing the liquid contents, it was, there-fore, more cleanly in its use.

It was not long before potters began to ornament the exteriors by the use of glaze, chiefly by making irregular splashes, giving a quaint and not altogether unpleasing appearance to the fourteenth-century jugs and other pottery. The jugs, many of them about twelve inches in height, were furnished with strong, serviceable handles, and although rather tall in proportion to their width, they were very steady on the base.

The fifteenth century brought with it a change. The buff-coloured earthenware was then fired harder, the materials of which it was composed being more carefully selected and compounded. The greenish glaze on English pottery of that period was chiefly composed of powdered galena, thus imparting to it a lead glaze. The red oxide of lead was used at a later period, giving a red glaze, both glazes falling into disuse after the discovery of salt glaze.

The examples of fifteenth and sixteenth-century ware shown in Figs. 18 and 19 are selected from a large collection of Sussex pottery, most of the pieces made, probably, in the neighbourhood of Lewes, containing a very represen-tative group of domestic objects. Among the pieces illustrated are also jugs of late fourteenth-century forms (see Fig. 19); the body of these pieces is of a somewhat red-orange tint, whereas the fifteenth and sixteenth-century jugs are buff, tinged with yellow. The glaze of the fourteenth-century jugs is yellow-green, and slightly splashed with a deeper green. The jugs and beer mugs of the later period are irregularly glazed with greenish glazes varying in shade from yellow-green to artist's sap-green.

There is a fifteenth-century pilgrim bottle, shown in Fig. 18, and a fifteenth-century money-box, in the same group, the slit being just large enough to take the silver pennies and groats then in circulation. To open the box it

FIG. 18. — GROUP OF SUSSEX POTTERY, chiefly 15th and 16th century examples, made probably in the neighbourhood of Lewis. Besides Jars and Jugs are a Chafing Dish (top shelf, left-hand corner); two Money Boxes (middle row); and a Pilgrim Bottle (centre, bottom row).

In the Author's Collection.

FIG. 18.

FIG. 19.—On the top shelf are JUGS with vivid green glaze; middle shelf, two BELLARMINES, in the centre a CANDLESTICK; in the centre of the lower row is a fine 14TH CENTURY PIECE.

In the Author's Collection.

FIG. 19.

[To face page 56.

FIG. 20.

A DOUBLE-HANDLED VESSEL decorated in
yellow slip, with star-shaped
ornament and panels.

FIG. 21.

A FINE WROTHAM PIECE,
dated 1657.

FIG. 22.

MUG, dated 1656.

WROTHAM WARE JUGS.
In the Maidstone Museum.

To face page 57.]

was necessary to break either the side or the bottom, hence it is that nearly all museum specimens are found broken. The one in the collection referred to and illustrated here has been repaired ; another specimen in the same collection is broken on the side near the slit, a portion of which is intact. The candlesticks of that period varied in form, some being taller than others, some having handles. The one illustrated in Fig. 19 is quite small and without handle, although there is a useful sconce and a flange to catch the grease. One of the scarcer pieces in the collection is a chafing dish illustrated in Fig. 18. The upper part is irregular and somewhat chipped, the sides are perforated, and there is a triangular opening cut in the side to receive the heating material or substance. In the group are porringers and a bleeding-dish, as well as jugs showing minor differences in form in the rims and lips ; in some instances the handles are round, in others almost flat.

The English glazed wares which show superiority of finish are those made in the seventeenth century, when an artistic style of ornament, although crude in the light of modern potting, became noticeable. The slip ornament which gave such a distinct type to the wares of that period made in very many villages was very simple in character. It was applied to patterns and shapes in many instances not unlike those of earlier periods, but the improved ornament and more regular designs gave the wares an appearance indicating a marked advance.

At that time the potters of the Staffordshire Potteries, or rather the district which was afterwards to be known by that name, were not much more advanced in the art than the clay-workers in scores of villages widely scattered and separated from one another by almost tractless forests. It is clear that seventeenth-century wares were successfully made in Derbyshire, Cheshire, Kent, Yorkshire, Lancashire, and Hampshire in England, and in several parts of

Wales; similarity of use caused much similarity of form, and the limited knowledge of materials prevented great differences in ornament or glaze.

Another factor in production having an important bearing upon the great similarity in pottery made in places far apart is found in the so-called travelling potter, a man who journeyed from place to place and rested for a time when he found suitable material, an expectant people, and consequently a ready market for his wares. His apparatus was simple enough, and he soon set to work to throw, mould, decorate, and bake—following his accustomed style and fashioning replicas of what he had made elsewhere, continuing their manufacture until local demand was satisfied. He then packed his scanty store of materials and tools, and his kiln fell into disuse—for a time at least.

PEASANT POTTERY.

As it has been stated, most of the pottery in use in the seventeenth century was made by men without any advanced knowledge of the potters' art. It was essentially peasant pottery. Opportunities of manufacture as well as some thought for convenience of use no doubt influenced those early and often very ignorant workers. There were common forms. The qualities of the local clays, the difference in the chemical action of their constituents, used in conjunction with the metallic oxides of iron, manganese, and copper, caused some difference in colour and in the durability of the ware.

In the first part of the seventeenth century there were indications of improved conditions of living, and buyers and users would be a little more critical in the choice of the wares they purchased. The leather black-jacks, although not put away altogether, were supplemented by the more convenient and more cleanly pottery. Staffordshire tygs then became famous, and posset pots, beer jugs, and even large dishes were made for use in farm-houses as well as in the homes of the wealthy. It was about that time that certain localities became known as places where something better than mere peasant pottery could be bought.

NAMED AND DATED PIECES.

It gradually became an established custom to date and name vessels which must, obviously, have been made specially for their owners. This custom was much practised in Staffordshire, and many examples are known. To collect named and dated specimens is of great historic interest, as the often recorded names of local families carry us back to older associations; and such vessels are reminiscent of the Tudor oak and furniture with a collection of which these old dated wares accord so well. There are many examples of slip ware in private collections and in the older baronial halls and manor houses, where they have often been since the days when leathern black-jacks and wooden trenchers gave place to shining pewter and pottery. Most of the larger provincial museums have a few examples of dated slip wares, although perhaps the most representative pieces are in the London museums.

The following list, arranged alphabetically, will give some little idea of the period during which these dated wares were made and also of where some of them may be seen.

CHARLES BIRD, 1736, a two-handled cup. British Museum.

ANN BRIT, 1686, a posset cup. Norwich Museum.

ELIZABETH BORFATE, 1680, a tyg. British Museum.

WILLIAM CHATTERLEY, 1696, a posset cup. British Museum.

JOSEPH GLASS, 1703, a posset pot. British Museum.

FILEP HEVES and ELIZABETH HEVES, 1671, a dish. Chester Museum.

JAMES JOHNSON, 1694, a dish. Nottingham Castle Museum.

JOSEPH KING, 1664, a dish. British Museum.

RICHARD MEIR, a posset cup. Liverpool Museum.

JOHN MEIR, 1708, a posset pot, inscribed, "GOD BLESS THE QUEEN AND PRENCE GORGE." British Museum.

MARGERE NASH, a dish. British Museum.

MARY PERKINS, 1704, a dish. British Museum.

MARY PARVISH, a posset pot, inscribed, " MARY PARVISH : HER POT. 1714." British Museum.

ROBERT SHAW, 1692, a posset pot. British Museum.

MARY SMITH, posset pot, inscribed " MARY SMITH, HER CUP." British Museum.

RALPH TURNER, 1688, a posset pot. British Museum.

JOHN WENTTER, 1686, a jug. British Museum.

Museum specimens are drawn from many places, and they are sometimes wrongly located on account of the places where they have been found ; the circumstances under which many pieces are discovered are misleading, and cause mistakes being made as to their origin. Some museums, however, possess fine examples of mediæval pottery.

The London Guildhall Museum is particularly rich in examples. There are many authentic relics of well-assured periods arranged and tabulated in proper order, ranging from the twelfth century onward. Practically all the exhibits in the Museum have been found in London : some found during excavations, others were secured from old houses when they were pulled down, and some have been given by owners in whose families the relics have been from the time of the Great Fire, and in some instances earlier. These pieces, although all found in London and probably always used in the city, are placed as having been made in many different known seats of famous potteries, and are distinguishable by their peculiar characteristics. The group of manufactures known to collectors as "{Metropolitan pottery," referred to in another paragraph in this chapter, is well represented in the Guildhall collection, but scarcely more so than some of the potteries of wide repute.

In one of the cases containing pieces of the earliest English pottery in the Guildhall Museum there are many fine examples of thirteenth and fourteenth-century jugs and pitchers, mostly tall shapes, some labelled " Made in the reign of Edward III." ; these latter are of very common clay and unglazed. Nearly all these very early pieces take the form of tall jugs, some being of coarse red clay and others of buff, all more or less covered with lead glaze which has been coloured with green by copper oxide. Among the thirteenth and fourteenth-century wares are many quaint, grotesque pieces, the necks of the jugs being shaped like human heads or faces.

To particularise some of the specimens, mention may be made of a jug of pale buff clay, with large, narrow spout added after the rim was formed ; the base expands slightly, and the body is somewhat straight-sided from near the base. This vessel is decorated with bands of colour round the neck and base. Near the handle there is an ornament not unlike a fleur-de-lys, in brown colour ; it was found in Bishopsgate Street. Another curious piece found in the same street is a bulbous yellow pitcher covered with a light glaze ; there is another example of similar appearance, but ornamented with a band of yellow-brown glaze down the front, brown glaze on the base, and a grooved band running round the upper portion of the body. A jug of pale buff clay, the upper portion in the form of a human face, attracts special notice. The body of the vase is ornamented with vertical bars of yellow, chocolate, and green glaze ; on the sides are small yellow bosses ; that also was found in Bishopsgate Street. Among the representative pieces of fourteenth-century ware are several jugs ornamented with mottled green and yellowish glaze, the spout of one being in the form of a ram's head. There are very many jugs, but the greater part of them are covered, or partly covered, with yellow-green or green glaze ; these and the red ware being the two chief types of pottery of that period, as already explained.

Time passed on without any marked change being apparent in the characteristics of the wares in the pottery used in London, for even those vessels which were made in the fifteenth century do not present any great distinctive changes in form. Jugs continued to be the chief vessels of account. The colouring of the glaze became a little darker, for among the specimens of that century are some splashed with olive-green, and some are speckled and mottled with greater regularity than formerly, showing some little advance in the potter's art, or perhaps indicating greater pride in the work shown by the workmen. At this period costrels or pilgrims' bottles made their appearance. In the Guildhall collection there are several of these interesting pieces. One is of green glazed ware of flattened form, with three loops for suspension ; the body is decorated with deeply incised bands. Another costrel is of marbled ware, and it has an expanding base with lion's mask loops for suspension.

The variety of objects began to increase as the fifteenth century advanced, for among the domestic wares of that period are drinking cups and even dishes and a few porringers, all, however, of very coarse ware. In the case at the Museum in which there are many examples of the minor objects of interest of the fifteenth century, there are several watering pots with the bases perforated, the flow of water being regulated by the use of a thumb hole at the top. A charming little pipkin of glazed green is of somewhat unusual form ; the base is extremely slender, but the rim is wide and flanged. Another insight into the changing conditions of society and the homes of the people is given in the money-boxes of earthenware made at that time, one of which is illustrated in Fig. 18. Needless to say, the examples of such " savings banks " which have come down to us are mostly in a damaged condition, for their contents have been extracted.

The Tudor ware of the sixteenth century is again more varied; most of the examples in the Guildhall Museum are of Farnham ware. In this group are some choice examples of unusual types. There is a toast bowl, many jugs covered with delicate pale green glazes, the odds and ends including a bird-call of buff ware and a feeding bottle ; there are also cups, costrels, vases, jugs, salt-cellars, and bed-pans.

Candlesticks then made their appearance, and some are very gracefully fashioned, being well made, with conical bases and sockets. There is a fuming pot or stove with a cover of coarse red clay, the body urn-shaped, with overhanging rim and two horizontal loop handles. The chafing-dish became a domestic appliance for which the potter found some sale. One of these on view in the Guildhall Museum is described in the catalogue as a " chafing-dish, buff ware, yellow-glazed, consisting of a shallow bowl, with pedestalled base ; the bowl is orna-mented with incised lines, and bosses project from the rim ; the base of the bowl is perforated, and the foot has an arched opening on one side ; it was found in Fore Street." See Fig. 18 (top left-hand corner) for an example already mentioned. Ink-wells soon became common, and most of them were of red ware with greenish splashed glaze.

A century passed, and we are brought face to face with the rapidly developing industry which was springing up all over the country ; the making of pottery became more general, especially after the Civil War. The Guildhall collection of pottery used in London, but drawn from all over the country, includes a variety of seventeenth-century cooking vessels, pots, porringers, saucers, basins, bowls, dishes, pipkins, jars, candlesticks, tygs, and Delft and Lambeth wares.

The slip-decorated wares, especially tygs and posset pots, are associated with Staffordshire, but they rightly come within the scope of the collector of mediæval wares, for they are earlier than the true pottery for which the Staffordshire Potteries afterwards became famous. Tygs were made before the days of Toft and Simpson (*see* chapter xviii), and those vessels they made were based upon still older patterns. The slip-decorated wares of the seventeenth century had frequently several handles, such as the inscribed ware of Wrotham and elsewhere.

Mr Charles Lomax, in *Quaint Old English Pottery*, mentions old Somersetshire slip ware made at Donyatt or Crock Street near Ilminster, which he describes as " of a salmon-pink coloured body with an engobe of yellowish-white freely splashed with green and reddish spots."

The decoration of this seventeenth-century ware was incised ; describing the method of decorating it Mr Lomax says : " The ware was first coated with a deep orange slip. This was subsequently covered with a yellowish-white slip, the whole being lead-glazed, in which there are splashes of green varying in size from minute specks to broad patches. A red colour is occasionally found associated with the green, but to a minor extent. The yellowish-white coating having been applied, the design was roughly incised with some instrument, probably a pointed stick, so as to expose the underlying orange colour."

A curious feature of this Somersetshire ware, the manufacture of which extended from the seventeenth century onwards, is that little or no change was made in style or finish during the production of that pottery. There are some examples in the Taunton Museum, among them some pieces evidently made by the earlier potters from their dates, two of the inscriptions reading, " THREE MERY BOYS 1697," and "BE MERY AND WIS."

METROPOLITAN AND OTHER WARES.

The seventeenth-century ware made in or around London has been termed " Metropolitan slip ware " by the late Sir A. W. Franks. It is unlike the Wrotham ware in that the slip decoration used was very thin. Some of this is dated and often inscribed with mottoes. In the British Museum there is a jug inscribed, " WHEN THIS YOU SE, REMEMBER ME. OBAEY GOD'S WOURD."

In connection with Metropolitan ware Thomas and Abraham Cullyn, merchants of the City of London, obtained a patent in 1626 which gave them the sole right to make "stone pottes, stone jugs, and stone bottells, for the term of fourteen years." Most of the Metropolitan ware, correctly so-called, was made between the years 1630 and 1670, and was probably mostly made at the same pottery. After that period a distinct advance became noticeable, for it was in the year 1671 that John Dwight of Fulham obtained a patent for " transparent earthenware," and again in 1674 Dwight secured a further patent, conferring upon him the right to manufacture " fine stone gorges and vessels, never before made in England " (*see* chapter xi.).

Reference is made in chapter xviii. to Thomas Toft, who was probably one of the most renowned potters of his day. " Toft " dishes are rare and valuable ; wonderful conceptions in yellow, red, amber, and brown they were !

Toft worked at Tinker's Clough, near Hanley.   Such dishes so far removed from earlier and even contemporary pottery won much fame and were preserved with care ; they were the show pieces on the oak dressers of the seventeenth century.

A contemporary Staffordshire maker producing wares very similar to those made by the members of the Toft family was Ralph Simpson, upon whose dishes were representations of royal personages, his usual signature, " RALPH : SIMPSON," running on the rim.

The style of this quaint old pottery best known to collectors is that so fully exemplified in the Wrotham ware, made at Wrotham, in Kent, although there is no proof that the potters of that town had any special monopoly of manufacture of that particular ware, or of the form of decoration adopted.   The examples given in the accompanying illustrations are exceptionally fine pieces and show the type of decoration then prevailing.   They are reproduced by the courtesy of the authorities of the Maidstone Museum.

The place-name, added in slip as a decoration, is often found on these vessels ; other ornament, although occurring in different forms, may be defined as lozenges of clay on which have been stamped devices, such as rosettes, fleurs-de-lys, shields of arms, and initials—in most cases promiscuously scattered over the surface.

Fig. 20 is a double-handled vessel described as a jug or mug, decorated in yellow slip with rosette and star-shaped ornament and panels, and is inscribed " I. E." Fig. 21 is dated 1657, and is inscribed with the initials " H. I." (Jull) ; and Fig. 22 is dated 1656.

The bellarmines, which took their name from Cardinal Bellarmine, who died in 1621, form almost a connecting link between the early mediæval stoneware and that which was made under more advanced conditions at Lambeth,

FIG. 23.—TWO BELLARMINES OF THE 17TH CENTURY.

FIG. 24.—TWO COLOGNE JUGS.
From the Manor House, Hitchin.

[To face page 66.

F<small>IG</small>. 25 (A).

S<small>TAFFORDSHIRE</small> B<small>UTTERPOT</small>,
yellow glaze.

F<small>IG</small>. 25 (B).

T<small>UDOR</small> W<small>ATER</small> P<small>OT</small>,
deep green glaze.

To face page 67.]

Fulham, and other places. Some of these "greybeards," as they were often called, were excellently modelled and extremely decorative. The earlier ones, made during the second half of the sixteenth century, were chiefly Flemish. Cardinal Bellarmine was bitterly opposed to the Reformation, and it is said that the Protestants to show their dislike to him, caricatured his face upon the bellarmine jug or jar. Ben Jonson describes the bellarmine of his day as " a jug faced with a beard that fills out to the guest." The Fulham bellarmines of 1671 were salt-glazed, and, along with other wares produced at Fulham potteries by Dwight, were imitations of the stoneware of Cologne and Flanders. Two fine Cologne jugs are shown in Fig. 24.

There are examples of both the foreign bellarmines and those made in the neighbourhood of London in the Guildhall Museum. Some are ornamented with several coats-of-arms, many having excellent masks. They were evidently very plentiful in London, for vast numbers have been found and often in excellent preservation. (*See* Fig. 23.)

In concluding this chapter reference may be made to the London Museum, which has been arranged so that in rooms devoted to household objects of well-defined periods representative pieces of pottery made in or near London, and pottery which was used in London, although made, probably, elsewhere, can be seen in proper sequence. In this collection there are some beautiful examples of decorated slip ware found in Swan Street, Borough, the cross-hatching and raised slip ornament being especially effective. The chequered lattice of green and chocolate on the body is well done, better, perhaps, than the brown bands around the neck of the vessel. Another pitcher of slip ware found in Smithfield is covered with yellow ornament and coloured spots.

Many of the green-glazed jugs represent the usual types

of pottery made from about 1400 to 1500. There is a curious " fuddling " cup of grey ware (a group of three) found in the " Town Ditch," near Newgate, and much pottery for domestic purposes.

One of the exhibits in the London Museum is the pottery sign of the " Bell Inn," found in Bell Alley, London Wall. The " Bell," and the bell in combination, was a favourite sign from quite early times. Bell-ringing was an amusement much favoured in the country, and the bell soon became a sign of welcome. It is related that a German traveller in the time of Queen Elizabeth described the English people as being " fond of noises in the air, such as firing of cannon, beating of drums, and *ringing of bells*." The " Black Bell " was a sign of an inn which in the time of Edward III. stood on the site of the Monument.

Grouped among larger and more prosaic things it is interesting to note the pretty little toys in the London Museum collection, including children's whistles. There are also pipe-clay figures of saints, and a staff head of pipe-clay which was found in Chiswell Street.

The tygs of black-brown " Cistercian " ware, and costrels, are in excellent order, so are the bellarmines. A case of Tudor green-glazed pottery, in many cases a brilliant green, includes a few unusual pieces, among them a standing-salt found in Little Britain, a flower-bowl discovered in Smithfield, stove tiles, bird-calls, curious ale jugs, toy costrels, candlesticks, and a two-lobed dish found in Marshalsea Road.

In the " Commonwealth Room " there are tygs of brown-glazed ware and a case of Metropolitan slip ware ; on some of the pieces there are typical Puritan inscriptions, such as, " FAST and PRAY," and " HOLD FAST THE TRUTH."

In Figs. 25 (A, B, and C) are shown examples of Tudor pottery, the tall piece (Fig. 25A) being of Staffordshire

make, of the form commonly known as a " butter pot ";
the water pot (Fig. 25B) and the jug (Fig. 25C) are of
ordinary types.

For a time such pottery as has been described as
mediæval continued to serve the purposes of English
households, even until the eighteenth century, although
there must have been a growing distaste for the rough
wares which were no longer absolutely necessary. Improved conditions of society were gradually making an
impression on manufacture, and especially upon the trade
of merchants and those who were getting rich by the
importation of the more highly finished goods their ships
were bringing over to this country. The closer intercourse
with continental nations, and especially the introduction of
so much Dutch pottery during the reigns of William and
Mary and Queen Anne, and an altogether different class of
ware from Oriental countries, paved the way for the potters
of England to make goods on similar lines, and to produce
more beautiful wares than they had at one time thought
they could make, or had any idea would sell. The story of
the progress made by English potters is told in the succeeding chapters. The wealth of beautiful ceramics still
treasured in English homes and in museums demonstrates
how well they succeeded.

CHAPTER VII

Early experiments—The qualities of Bow china—Domestic porcelain
and figures—Bow marks.

In the previous chapter mention has been made of early
English and mediæval pottery. A great change came over
the scene towards the middle of the eighteenth century,
when, in consequence of greater facilities offered to china
merchants by quicker and better transport and improved
shipping conditions, so much beautiful Oriental porcelain
was brought over to this country. It was then that there
was a great awakening in many parts of England; the
potting industry seems to have attracted the attention of
many clever men, some of them chemists who delighted in
analysing the materials of which the old Oriental pottery
had been made, and in trying to discover the ingredients
of which the hard Chinese porcelain was composed.
Another class of men consisted of skilled artists, some were
modellers, others painters and enamellers who delighted to
beautify the decorative objects which the modellers had
fashioned. Improved kilns made firing easier, more even,
and productive of better results. Better road transport,
so much accelerated by the almost philanthropic action of
Staffordshire potters and others, made it possible to obtain
clays from distant counties. It was no longer necessary to
work local clay.

In the story of English potters of the eighteenth century

there is a vivid picture to be drawn of the rapid uplifting of the industrial classes, and the transforming of the workmen who had hitherto been engaged in the rougher potting craft into artists whose very touch was sufficient to mould and fashion things of beauty and ornament.

In this chapter, and in succeeding chapters, the story of English potters is recorded. It will be found that in nearly every one of the towns and separate districts referred to there were individualistic traits of character seen in the master potters and those they employed. Local conditions to a very large extent moulded the industry and provided the outlet for the products of the pot banks. Taking these different works in alphabetical order, the famous porcelain of Bow comes first. There have been differences of opinion as to the date of the earliest pottery at Bow, or Stratford-le-Bow, and also as to the actual ware made at that early period. The site of the Bow Works was, however, definitely located as in Bell Road, St Leonard's Street, Bromley-by-Bow, when some excavations were made in 1868. At that time several important fragments of pottery, together with saggers and part of a kiln, were found.

EARLY EXPERIMENTS.

The first authentic records of the Bow Works refer to a patent dated December 6th, 1744, taken out by Heylyn & Frye. The partners in this firm were Edward Heylyn, a merchant of Bow, and Thomas Frye, of West Ham, a painter. The patent rights they secured gave them the monopoly to produce a porcelain made of various specified ingredients, among which was " an earth, the produce of the Cherokee nation in America, called by the natives unaker " ; the other ingredients specified included potash and sand. The North American clay was first washed to remove the mica and other extraneous properties. In connection with this mixture which formed the body of the paste, a glaze containing seven parts of potash-glass to one of unaker was specified.

Thomas Frye took out another patent in 1749, for " a new method of making a certain ware, which is not inferior in beauty and fineness, and is rather superior in strength, to the earthenware which is brought from the East Indies, and is commonly known by the name of China, Japan, or porcelain ware."

Frye was the practical man, and retained the position of active manager of the works from the foundation until 1759, his death occurring in 1762. The actual ownership of the factory after it had been started and got into full working order seems to have been vested in two merchants, James Weatherley and John Crowther, the former dying in 1762.

The commercial instinct seems to have been strong in the management of the Bow Works, for quite early we find the products of Bow advertised in country local papers, especially so in Birmingham and Derby. During the early years of the Bow Factory useful rather than ornamental porcelain was made. In Aris's *Birmingham Gazette*, under date November 5th, 1753, there was an interesting little advertisement for a modeller. It read : " A person is wanted who can model small figures in clay neatly." In 1757 there appeared an advertisement in the public Press setting forth very clearly the class of goods made at Bow, and indicating the method by which they were retailed at the firm's warehouse in Cornhill. The announcement was as follows : " At the Bow China Warehouse in Cornhill are great Variety of useful and ornamental Wares of that manufactory greatly improved. And for the convenience of the Nobility and Gentry, their warehouse on the Terrace in St James's Street is constantly supplied with everything

new where it is sold as at Cornhill, with the real Price
marked on each Piece without abatement."

From an early dated piece inscribed " Edward Vernon
Esqr. 1742 "—an inkpot ornamented with under-glaze
flowers—it has been thought that the works at Bow were
founded earlier than the date on the inkstand, and therefore, that the date usually assigned to the foundation of
the Bow Works was not quite in order, but the discrepancy
is slight, and of no material importance.

The works were continued with more or less success
until 1776, when Duesbury of Derby purchased the plant,
and removed the moulds and models to his own works.

THE QUALITIES OF BOW CHINA.

From the fragments discovered on the site of the old
works at Bow, and from other authentic pieces in well-
known collections, it would seem that a soft paste was
always a feature of the ware ; the glaze with a yellowish
tinge was heavily charged with lead, and where it has been
unusually thickly laid on, it shows an iridescence and
often much discoloration. That also is a feature of
importance. Many of the fragments discovered in 1868
were of unglazed porcelain, some of them being painted in
blue. There were some pieces of broken dessert plates
and stands which have enabled collectors to determine
similar pieces which were formerly assigned to other
potteries.

The white biscuit ware made at Bow was decorated in
blue, laid on in " smalt or saffer " before glazing. The
glaze was then composed of saltpetre, red lead, sand, and
flint or other white stones. The gilding was put on over
the glaze, and afterwards fixed in a muffle kiln.

The glaze used at Bow was thick, and in some cases ran
down the pieces before they were fired, imparting an

unevenness to the surface which can readily be felt by running the fingers over the piece. This is very noticeable in some Bow figures, which, although quite smooth, show indications of the glaze being of double thickness in certain parts. When the glaze was thus coated on cups and embossed work the design of the embossing was impaired in parts by the thickness of the glaze. It may also be pointed out that in some instances tiny black spots are noticeable on the surface, due, probably, to the incomplete combustion of the wood which was used for firing purposes.

Domestic Porcelain and Figures.

As it has been suggested, much inexpensive domestic porcelain was made at Bow, as well as the more ornamental objects. From records existing some of these pieces were copies of patterns designed and first made at Chelsea and other factories. Transfer printing was at one time used extensively at Bow for ornamenting both over and under the glaze. Tea-sets, dinner services, sauce tureens, butter boats, small jugs, and all kinds of household china were made. One of the favourite patterns at Bow was the " Mayflower " or hawthorn, and embossed acorns and oak leaves, floral festoons and sprays of roses, were commonly printed or painted upon Bow china. Then again, there were the Chinese landscapes and other Oriental patterns extensively used.

Bow figures are a special study and of exceptional interest to the connoisseur of art. Some peculiarities of Bow figure modelling are noticeable, such, for instance, indications that the modeller or artist often touched up the figures with a knife-shaped tool after the moulding had been completed, but before firing. Bow figure painting was generally inferior to that of Chelsea, and the figures themselves were worse proportioned, although some of them are very elaborate, and show great expenditure of labour in carrying out the detail of the modelling. Many noted subjects are recorded, such, for instance, " Harlequin," " Columbine," and " Pierrot." There is a set of four seated figures representing " The Seasons " ; a seated " Venus and Cupid " ; a pair representing a boy and girl dancing, and various other designs, some of them being made to serve the purpose of candlesticks, a candle-socket being concealed in a portion of the design. There are a number of examples in the Victoria and Albert Museum, also in various local exhibitions and collections.

Bow Marks.

Most of the Bow porcelain was unmarked. The best known mark is an anchor and a dagger, generally painted in red. Another mark is an arrow, with an annulet on the shaft. A small crescent in blue is sometimes regarded as one of the marks of Bow. Thomas Frye signed engravings with the monogram composed of the letters T and F conjoined ; a similar mark is seen on some of the Bow porcelain under the glaze, in blue.

CHAPTER VIII

ENGLISH—BRISTOL

Early beginnings—Champion's porcelain—Other Bristol potters—Characteristics of Bristol porcelain—Representative pieces—Bristol marks.

THERE are many old associations in connection with Bristol, which was at one time one of the chief ports of the kingdom. Situated a few miles inland on the banks of the Avon a large shipping and export and import trade was done at Bristol in the days before steamboats and large liners. Trading vessels then brought much merchandise from foreign parts. In those days the beautiful porcelain out of which tea was drunk came from China, and was the envy of those who had hitherto worked in the coarser clays of the district, ornamenting their products with crude devices.

Bristol had for years been a place where earthenware had been made. The first potteries of which there are any authentic records were at work in the reign of Edward I., and many fragments and relics of those old works have been discovered. Their authenticity has been confirmed authoritatively, for in the Pipe Roll it is recorded that fragments of pottery of the reign of Edward I. were at one time discovered on the site of the House of the Carmelites in Bristol.

There was a well-established pottery in Bristol during the reign of Elizabeth, the chief wares produced being brown or grey pottery, and some vessels shaped not unlike the Staffordshire tygs.

The pottery industry was continued for some time in the neighbourhood, and many wares were produced there during the reign of James II. Quite early in the eighteenth century there appears to have been an important pottery at Redcliffe Backs, where tiles after the Dutch Delft style were made. Some of these have been discovered at different places, many of them dated, the earlier ones dating back to 1703 ; others were not made until the second half of the eighteenth century was well advanced, from their dates proving that the manufacture of tiles lasted in Bristol fully half a century. Some of these were illustrative of well-known architectural features, the more important buildings pictured on them being the Church of St Mary Redcliffe ; others exhibit the arms of Bishop Butler (1738-1750). Fragments of these tiles and of the still earlier pottery have been turned up during excavations near the river banks between Bristol Bridge and Redcliffe Pit.

Early Beginnings.

About the middle of the eighteenth century there was a well-conceived plan to make Bristol one of the chief centres of the potting trade. Pococke, in his Diary, writing from Bristol on November 22nd, 1750, recorded : " I went to see a manufacture lately established here by one of the principals of the manufacture at Limehouse which failed." He then tells of his visit to what he terms a glass-house or " Lowris China House." He says they had two sorts of ware, one called " old china, which is whiter, and, I suppose, is made of calcined flint and the soapy rock at Lizard Point." Describing the products he had seen, and the different wares made at these works, Dr Pococke says : " They (the manufacturers) make very beautiful white sauce-boats, adorned with reliefs of festoons, which sell for 16s. the pair." Such sauce-boats are not unknown to collectors ; most of them are marked with the name " BRISTOLL " in raised letters underneath the glaze.

To many there is a peculiar attraction about the Bristol Delft which was made at two different factories. One was owned by the Frank family ; at first it was founded at Redcliffe Back, afterwards removed to Water Lane ; the other belonged to Joseph Flower. In the Guide to the Bristol pottery in the British Museum some information about the differences between the Bristol Delft and other kinds are given. The Bristol Delft, it is said, " has a greenish-blue colour : a sprinkled ground of blue or manganese-purple with panels reserved for painted ornament occurs in several places ; the use of a pure white over the tin enamel (*bianco sopra bianco*) is supposed to have been confined to Bristol among the English factories."

The three pleasing examples illustrated in Figs. 26 (A and B) and Fig. 27 are in the British Museum, and are reproduced by the courtesy of the authorities. They are as follows : Fig. 26 (on left) (A) a plate painted by Bowen, diameter 9 in. ; (B) a plate by Michael Edkins ; and Fig. 27 a posset cup, inscribed " A. G. Bristol 1741."

Champion's Porcelain.

The collector's interest in Bristol ware centres chiefly in the beautiful porcelain which was for a short time made there. This industry, which resulted in the production of many beautiful works of art, was founded by Champion, a well-known Bristol merchant. He commenced operations in 1768, having received some financial assistance from his friends, among whom was Joseph Fry, who advanced £4,500, adding another sum, amounting to £1,500, later.

FIG. 25 (C).—LARGE SUSSEX WARE 16TH CENTURY JUG,
with mottled green glaze.

In the Author's Collection.

[To face page 78.

FIGS. 26 AND 27.—BRISTOL CHINA.

FIG. 26 (A).—A BRISTOL PLATE, painted by Bown.
FIG. 26 (B).—A BRISTOL PLATE, painted by Edkins.
FIG. 27.—POSSET CUP, inscribed "BRISTOL."

In the British Museum.

To face page 79.]

Thomas Frank is also said to have financed the under-taking to the extent of £1,000.

A little later W. Cookworthy removed his works at Plymouth to Bristol, and his patent rights were eventually acquired by Champion in 1773. From that time on to 1781 Champion was the owner of the Castle Green Works. It is a little uncertain to what extent porcelain had been made by Champion before he bought Cookworthy's patent ; it is clear, however, that some exceptionally fine pieces had been turned out. On March 30th, 1771, an advertisement appeared in *Felix Farley's Journal*, in which it was stated that a sale of pottery would be held at Taylor's Hall, and that many beautiful dessert services, ornamental figures, candlesticks, and valuable articles of the Bristol manufactory would then be sold. The sale took place, and was apparently satisfactory. It was followed by another sale during the summer of the following year. On that occasion the sale consisted chiefly of speci-mens of ornamental Bristol china, including " very elegant figures, vases, jars, and beakers, with all kinds of useful china, blue and white and enamelled."

In the *Bristol Journal* of November 28th, 1772, some description was given of the Bristol porcelain, which throws light upon the characteristics of the wares then being made as they were regarded at that time. The porcelain was described as being " wholly free from imperfections in wearing, which English china usually has, and its com-position equal in fineness to the East Indian, and will wear as well. The enamelled ware, which is rendered nearly as cheap as the English blue and white, comes very near, and in some pieces equal to Dresden, which this work more nearly imitates." It is quite true that much of the Bristol china conforms to the style of Dresden ornament. More-over, the Bristol potters then used the crossed swords in blue, under the glaze, as a distinguishing mark of that type of porcelain which resembled Dresden in form and decoration. Sometimes the mark was used in conjunction with the letter " B," making it a little confusing.

In 1775, not long after Champion had purchased Cookworthy's patent, he applied for a further extension, hoping to secure the monopoly of Cookworthy's invention for another fourteen years. The Staffordshire potters opposed his application, and Josiah Wedgwood, who had allowed some of his own inventions and discoveries to be freely copied, opposed the extension of the patent as being in opposition to the public good. He held that the use of natural productions of the soil ought to be the right of all. He also pointed out in reference to his own Queen's ware that very many makers were producing similar goods and shipping them to all parts of the world. Champion prepared a few beautiful examples which he submitted to the Committee of the House of Commons, by whom Champion's Bill for the extension of his patent was being considered. As a result of the application the extension of the patent was granted in 1775. The Act of Parliament conferring this benefit was entitled : " An Act for enlarging the term of Letters Patent granted by his present Majesty to William Cookworthy, of Plymouth, Chymist, for the sole use and exercise of a discovery of certain materials for making Porcelain, in order to enable Richard Champion, of Bristol, merchant (to whom the said Letters Patent have been assigned), to carry the said discovery into effectual execution for the benefit of the public."

The keynote of Champion's production was excellence of quality. Unfortunately then—as oftentimes now—those objects upon which the greatest care had been lavished and many hours of patient labour expended did not pay the artist as well as those objects of lesser importance made for the sale room. Apparently many of the very fine vases made at Champion's works were show pieces, or manufactured as gifts to friends. In the first instance when Champion commenced his pottery he had made useful products, chiefly blue and white ware. and success seems to have attended his efforts. He then became enamoured with Oriental designs, and made some very beautiful tea- and coffee- sets and dinner services, also jugs and mugs. His Chinese designs were excellent, and the blues he used were of superior colour. He excelled in plaques of white biscuit enriched with floral wreaths in full relief, such beautiful frames often surrounding portraits and coats-of-arms. Champion was at that time a public man, and probably adverse to his own interests gave too much attention to political questions, thus preventing the full development of his business.

Incidentally some of Champion's works throw light upon his family concerns, such, for instance, a dated piece made in October, 1779, which, in the form of a symbolic figure of "Grief, leaning upon an urn," commemorated the death of his eldest daughter.

We now come to an eventful time in the products of the Bristol potteries, marking a change in ownership. It was in 1781, after a series of efforts to dispose of his business, that Champion sold his patent rights to a company of Staffordshire potters, practically the same firm who had founded a business at New Hall, near Shelton, where they had taken advantage of Champion's hard paste, until it was superseded by soft paste.

For some months after Champion had sold his patent, he rendered assistance to the company, taking up his residence there for a time, apparently until April, 1782. Until then he London warehouse in which Champion had been interested remained open, but in May of the same year the remaining stock of china was sold by auction.

It was shortly after Champion severed his connection with the potting industry that we hear of him making use

F

of his political friends. Edmund Burke, who in 1774 had been nominated for Bristol and returned as the member, after a fierce contest in which Champion took part, procured for him the appointment of Deputy Paymaster General to the Forces. On the dissolution of the Ministry a year or two later, in 1784, Champion emigrated to America, and became a planter in South Carolina, his death occurring in 1791. A notification in which reference was made to his former occupation appeared in *The Gentleman's Magazine* of December, 1791, as follows: " 7th Oct. 1791, near Camden, South Carolina, Richard Champion, Esq., late Dy. Paymaster General of His Mys. Forces, and proprietor of the china manufactory formerly carried on at Bristol." Champion, who died in his forty-eighth year, was, like Cookworthy of Plymouth, a member of the Society of Friends.

Many persons have marvelled at the marked changes in Champion's career and occupation. He had undoubted ability, but he was somewhat dependent upon others, and lacked the practical knowledge so necessary to make his business a success. What the general opinion of the leading potters of his day in reference to him was may be gathered from a letter Wedgwood wrote to his partner Bentley, August 24th, 1778, in which he said: " Poor Champion, you may have heard, is quite demolished. It was never likely to be otherwise, as he had neither professional knowledge, sufficient capital, nor scarcely any real acquaintance with the materials he was working upon. I suppose we might buy some growan stone and china clay upon easy terms." It is said that Champion himself, when he became the proprietor of a pottery, confessed that he had no knowledge other than that he had acquired as a merchant, but he counted on the experience of Mr Cookworthy, the inventor, who was one of the most able chemists in the kingdom. The manager he employed, too, was an experienced man, and he depended upon him somewhat.

Other Bristol Potters.

Before considering the characteristics of Bristol porcelain as a whole, and referring to examples of the different porcelain manufactured in that city, it would be well to note that Champion had not the sole monopoly of the potting industry in Bristol town. Joseph Flower had a small pottery there in 1750, and for some years he continued to make plates and dishes of Delft ware. They were excellently enamelled in white, and well painted, although perhaps somewhat gaudy in their colourings. On his wares parrots and other birds were painted.

Joseph Ring gained some notoriety in 1784, and produced ware consisting of a whitish paste covered with a dark yellow glaze. Ring was afterwards in partnership with Taylor and Carter. It was at this firm's works that printing on porcelain was introduced in 1797. In 1813 we hear of a new partnership being arranged between Joseph Ring, son of Ring who had died some years before, and Henry Carter and John Pountney. Unfortunately, the deed of partnership was not signed when Ring junior died. Mr Carter remained in the business until 1816. Then the concern became Pountney and Allies, until 1835, when Allies retired, and Gabriel Goldney became a partner, retiring, however, in September, 1850. Mr Pountney died in 1852, the business being continued by Mr Clowes until 1872, eventually the concern passing into the hands of the Bristol Victoria Pottery Co.

Characteristics of Bristol Porcelain.

The characteristics of Bristol porcelain are, of course, two-fold, the distinguishing factors being the composition of the paste and glaze, and the decoration. Champion's porcelain, made chiefly according to recipes and the patent acquired from Cookworthy, is almost identical with Plymouth porcelain in its composition. In colour it is almost milk-white. If broken it is slightly flaky and exceedingly hard. When examined carefully spiral lines or ridges will be seen on the surface, and when broken the surface looks greasy. A pale blue tint is observable about the commoner wares, which are slightly bubbled. There is a high percentage of silica in the composition of the paste, and its hardness and density are due chiefly to alumina, which is present in considerable quantities. The china made by Champion varies somewhat in that the composition was not always identical in its proportions. It has been pointed out that whereas Dresden or Oriental china is characterised by the distinctiveness of the body and clay, the glaze used by Champion at Bristol adds a close affinity with the body, entering into its composition, and therefore the Bristol china did not present quite the same glassy surface noticeable in some wares. This to some extent may be accounted for by the method adopted, which was that of dipping the biscuit into the glaze and then firing it in one operation ; and this involved exposure to a very great heat in order to properly fuse the hard glaze. It has been pointed out that the presence of bubbles and pin-holes in the glaze of so much Bristol china was caused by the escape of gas from the material during firing.

Of the characteristics of the wares much might be written in that they are so diversified both in shape and ornament. Champion, as it has been stated, made all kinds of objects, and in his earlier days some of the commoner wares. Bouquets of flowers and festooned ribbons characterise the ornament of many tea- and coffee-sets. It is noticeable, too, that comparatively few colours or tints were employed, the chief favourite colours being pale blue, lilac, green, and red, with very little gilding. Undoubtedly Bristol decorators were fond of festoons or laurel, and they made a free use of greens, which in some instances made a very pleasing setting to the patches of colour introduced in the finer bouquets of flowers.

It is said that the originality in the shape and beauty of design is a striking characteristic of the Bristol vases and flower plaques. By many they are considered to be equal if not superior to Dresden, to which there was a strong resemblance. Then, again, there are the delightful oval and round plaques of biscuit porcelain, overlaid with boldly relieved flowers and foliage, also in biscuit. Some hexagonal vases made in Bristol, with open or perforated work round the neck, are special features, as well as the salmon scale-grounds enamelled in blues and greens with birds and sprays of flowers.

Bristol statuettes and figures are of some special interest, and, as in the work of other potteries, some importance must be attached to workmen's marks as individual characteristics ; these, which are so conspicuous in the work of some of these artists, should be carefully noted. Some of the statuettes made in Bristol were modelled by a man who is said to have been named Tebo ; the mark he used was " To," and as this mark has been found on statuettes made in other places it is assumed that Tebo worked for other potters.

William Fifield, who was born at Bath in 1777, was an enameller and a painter working at the Water Lane Pottery in Bristol, said to have been one of the chief artists of his day. Some examples of his work may be seen in the Victoria and Albert Museum at South Kensington.

Henry Clarke was also employed at the Water Lane Pottery for nearly half a century. He was a noted painter of flowers and landscapes during the first half of the nineteenth century. Another Bristol painter of repute was

Thomas Pardoe, who lived in Bristol between 1809 and 1815. He was a painter of porcelain, and a glass stainer and enameller, purchasing some of his wares from Staffordshire and afterwards painting and decorating them in his own peculiar way.

REPRESENTATIVE PIECES.

It is always interesting to learn of the masterpieces of leading artists. Such exceptional works, however, are sometimes far from representative, and in order to obtain a true knowledge of the average skill expended upon certain artists' work, and upon characteristic productions of a certain pottery, it is even better to examine less important examples, and especially so sets or pieces which have evidently been reproduced many times, owing probably to their exceptional popularity. Champion aimed at producing something of which he might be justly proud, and we can well understand that he strove to put some of his very best work before the Committee of the House of Commons at the time he was applying for an extension of Cookworthy's patent which he had purchased. Writing to his friend Edmund Burke in reference to some of the pieces he had sent up for exhibition he said : " There are two sets of beautiful tea china, one from Ovid's ' Metamorphosis, different subjects to each piece, an exact copy of the Dresden set ; the other Herculaneum antiquities, each piece a different subject : also two pairs of curious vase with festoons of fine flowers, and as it is treason to make a new king, we only have made his representation." Of such sets of beautiful tea china referred to in the previous paragraph was a set known as the " Burke china," called after his friend, and presented as the joint gift of Champion and his wife to Mrs Edmund Burke. It was most elaborately decorated with the arms of Burke, impaling Nugent

On it were emblematical figures and dedicatory inscriptions, bearing date November 3rd, 1774. Each piece of this remarkable service had a border of arabesque gold, and a Byzantine pattern on a canary-yellow coloured ground.

Another important tea-set was known as the " Smith set." It was a commission from Edmund Burke to be given by him to Mrs Smith, the wife of Joseph Smith, a merchant with whom he resided during his Bristol election campaign in 1774. This remarkable set was taken from a Dresden model. Each piece bore the arms of the Smith family, and a monogram composed of Mrs Smith's initials. It was highly decorative, being covered with blossoms, wreaths, and festoons, very handsomely gilded.

Bristol figures include some important and well-known sets ; one of the most notable is a set of four representing the four quarters of the globe, standing on scroll plinths. Europe, personified, is represented holding a book in one hand, and a palette in the other ; at her feet are trophies of war, and a horse. Asia is seen holding a vase, full of spices, at her feet a kneeling camel. A young negress typifies Africa ; in the group being a lion, crocodile, and an elephant's head as attributes. The last of the set, America, consists of a figure holding in her left hand a bow, and in the act of drawing an arrow from her quiver in her right hand ; at her feet is a prairie cat.

Another interesting set of four groups represent the Elements. Earth is shown as a husbandman leaning on his spade, his attribute being a basket of fruit. Air is a winged goddess resting on a plough. Water, a nymph, with fishes at her feet and a water-urn ; while Fire is well represented by Vulcan in the act of forging a thunderbolt.

Of public collections there are many ; some very beautiful specimens of Bristol porcelain being seen in local museums. One of the most famous of such collections is that which was presented to the Bristol Museum by Mr

Robert Lang in 1875. There are also fine examples in the Victoria and Albert Museum, and in the British Museum. In the last-named collection are two tumblers of fine Bristol porcelain made in 1775 for exhibition in the House of Commons.

The manufacture of true porcelain came to an end with the closing down of Champion's factory.

BRISTOL MARKS.

Bristol marks, which are, unfortunately, rarely found on ordinary pieces, are somewhat confusing. Those used on porcelain of the usual types are as follows : (*a*) the alchemic sign for tin (used also at Plymouth), found sometimes associated with a cross ; (*b*) an imitation of the Meissen mark, the crossed swords often being seen with a letter B added, and sometimes a number ; (*c*) the letter B and a number ; (*d*) a cross and number. These marks are frequently accompanied by workmen's marks and numbers. Mark " b " is usually in blue under the glaze, but sometimes incised on biscuit figures. Many of the marks are in colours, or gold under or over the glaze.

CHAPTER IX

Early days—Association with other potteries—Royal patrons—Paste and glaze—Ornament and decoration—Typical examples—Chelsea marks.

THE collection of high-class Chelsea porcelain has long been regarded as essentially the hobby of the wealthy. The more beautiful productions have become increasingly rare and valuable, and the examples which are from time to time offered for sale in the establishments of the West End dealers are brought under the notice of advanced connoisseurs and patrons who freely open their purses to secure examples of this much-talked-of pottery. The porcelain works at Chelsea owe much of their fame to the quality of the workmanship, and to the peculiar characteristics which at the different periods of the works were so apparent under the separate management of different owners and artists ; for as in the case of many other fine porcelain works, the artists contributed much to the success of the works, and their skill brought their products under Royal and other notice, resulting in important commissions being placed. Briefly, then, before entering into the details of the work carried on at Chelsea, and the fine porcelain produced, it may be pointed out that Nicholas Sprimont, artist and director of the works, is of greater interest to collectors than the actual founders or owners of the pottery in early days. His retirement, however, in 1769, brought William Duesbury of Derby on the scene, and it was under his judicious management that the works prospered, and the period of Derby-Chelsea porcelain attained notoriety. The dual management does not appear to have been altogether satisfactory, and in 1784 the Chelsea factory was closed and the plant removed to Derby.

EARLY DAYS.

Long before the fine porcelain works at Chelsea were brought into being, there had been attempts to produce porcelain in the neighbourhood.   At a still earlier date, in 1676, Venetian workmen under the patronage of the Duke of Buckingham had established a factory for the making of glass at Chelsea.   According to a book published by Dr Martin Lister, in 1698, the glass-makers very nearly approached fine porcelain in the opaque glass they were then making.   Their product has been considered by some as a sort of connecting link in British glass and British fine porcelain, a stage in the transition of glaze from glass to porcelain.

The origin of the factory, which is believed to have commenced in 1745, is somewhat obscure.   Here and there, in and around London, and in other places, there was a gradual approachment to the manufacture of finer wares than the common earthenware which had been hitherto made in England.   John Dwight of Fulham had already studied many of the problems associated with pottery, stoneware, and even some of the finer materials, but when Chelsea was being founded he had retired.   But the discoveries he had made in reference to " transparent earthenware " had borne fruit, and there were men who realised what could be done by the production of an artificial porcelain, constructed of a glassy body or paste not unlike Oriental.   Indeed, in many of the experiments

Oriental china was broken up and powdered and mixed with white clay. At quite an early date Chelsea wares had gained some degree of notoriety, some quaint figures having been produced. It is possible that the real date of the commencement of the Chelsea Works was earlier than has been stated, for in the *London Tradesman*, of 1747, it is stated that imitations of Chinese and Dresden china were then being made.

Apparently the management of the Chelsea Works in early days was under Charles Gouyn, but in 1750 he was superseded by the Flemish artist Nicholas Sprimont, who became director or manager of the works. Roquet, writing on the art of England at that time, referred to the Chelsea Works, then under the management of Sprimont, the Flemish or French artist, who was also a silversmith of some repute, saying : " In the neighbourhood of London there are three or four manufactories of porcelain ; that of Chelsea is the most considerable. A rich patron bears the expense of it, and an able French artist furnishes or super-vises the models and all that is manufactured there." The works seem to have progressed under the management of this able man, and the financial assistance and support given by the Duke of Cumberland brought the Chelsea Works into greater notoriety, and no doubt contributed to the success of the undertaking, and to the valuable com-missions given for important services of porcelain. Ap-parently, according to old records, the Duke of Cumberland subsidised the work by making an annual grant.

Nicholas Sprimont was fortunate in obtaining the assistance of Louis François Roubiliac, the great French sculptor, who was closely associated with English eighteenth-century art, and contributed to the success of the Chelsea Works, and to the beauty of many of the fine pieces which are still extant. Roubiliac studied under a Saxon modeller in Dresden, entering the studio of Nicholas

Couston, in Paris, where he won the second Grand Prize for sculpture in 1730. His first visit to England was in 1744, where he secured the patronage of the Walpoles. After a brief visit to Rome he returned to England in 1746, and very soon became actively engaged at the Chelsea Works. His association there marked the commencement of the greatest period of old Chelsea porcelain. Roubiliac died in 1762, after working for about eighteen years in England, during which time he had executed many fine works, not only in porcelain but in sculptured monuments, some of which are in Westminster Abbey, others in the University of Cambridge.

We learn much of the doings of the old potteries from the often-times quaint advertisements which appeared in the newspapers of that day, although they were limited in number, and the area of their circulation very restricted. An advertisement appeared in the *Public Advertiser* of December 17th, 1754, and from that announcement we learn that the Chelsea owners adopted the popular method of disposing of some of their wares by auction. In that year, one Hughes, an ironmonger, of Pall Mall, dealt in china and glass, and retailed some of the products of Chelsea. He advertised under date 1754: " Compleat services of plates and dishes, tureens, and sauce-boats, etc. several elegant epargnes for desarts, several figures and the greatest choice of branches with the best flowers." This points very clearly to some of the characteristics of the decoration then employed, and indicates that some of the goods then offered by Hughes of Pall Mall, possibly at quite small cost, included some of the now very rare and valuable Chelsea porcelain modelled from nature, the flowers so realistically coloured. Hughes recommended them for table decoration, and sold flower-pots and other trinkets.

It is not altogether clear where these works, which became so notorious in after years, were located. According to Faulkner the Chelsea porcelain works were situated at the corner of Justice Walk, occupying the upper end of the street. The ovens, however, appear to have been close by in Lawrence Street. In the eighteenth century Justice Walk, which is said to have been named after a noted Justice of the Peace who lived in the neighbourhood, was an important thoroughfare, an avenue of stately lime-trees. In *Old and New London* it is recorded that several houses at the corner of Justice Walk and Lawrence Street were formerly used as a showroom and manufactory of Chelsea china, and that the whole of the premises were pulled down towards the close of the eighteenth century, new houses being erected on the site. From Faulkner's book we learn that the Chelsea Porcelain Works under Sprimont employed a great number of hands, but the original proprietor having acquired a large fortune retired from the concern, and his successors, wanting his spirit and enterprise, did not so well succeed.

Previous to the dissolution the proprietors presented a memorial to the government requesting protection and assistance, and saying " the manufacture has been carried on by great labour and a large expense ; it is in many respects to the full as good as the Dresden ; and the late Duke of Orleans told Colonel Yorke that the metal or earth had been tried in his furnace, and was found to be the best made in Europe. It is now daily improving, and already employs at least one hundred hands." Chelsea was then a fashionable suburb, and close to the porcelain factory was the stabling for the old Chelsea stage-coaches, the fare to London being then one shilling and sixpence, and yet many came and went from London to the Chelsea showrooms to see the fine porcelain. So great was the prosperity of the Chelsea factory between 1750 and 1765 that dealers, it is said, surrounded the doors of the works, waiting to purchase the porcelain as it came out of the oven.

Nicholas Sprimont continued manager of the works until 1768, but owing to the long illness that he had between 1757 and 1758 the output of the works diminished, showing how important was his personality. Apparently efforts were being made to dispose of the works for several years before their transfer was effected, and the stock was much reduced, so much so that when Mr Cox bought the concern in 1769 he secured the stock and plant, materials and goodwill, for £600, a sum which would have been more than realised in the present day for a single article of the fine Chelsea porcelain, much of which was no doubt to be found there, notwithstanding the diminished stock.

Cox soon disposed of the works to William Duesbury, who carried them on until 1784, when the kilns were pulled down. But the short time while porcelain was being made at both Chelsea and Derby under the Duesbury's management was an important period for collectors. As is recorded in another chapter, Duesbury obtained possession of the Bow Works, and also acquired other works at Vauxhall. He continued to employ some of the old Chelsea workmen, among whom were Gauron, Boarman (a painter of landscapes and sea views), Wollans, Askew, Snowden, Boyer, and Barton.

Association with other Potteries.

The work of the Chelsea potters must have been peculiarly influenced by the association of Chelsea with other famous potteries and porcelain works. There is no apparent founder of a new industry there, and the story of Chelsea does not include the tale of some great discoverer of a new process, or of a worker in clay, who after having acquired the knowledge of routine work at some other works, was determined to found a new enterprise and to make for himself a name as the result of his expert skill or discoveries. Indeed, all through the career of the Chelsea porcelain works and its owners and workers, an outside influence was being brought to bear as the result of connection with other works. The first manager, Nicholas Sprimont, brought over the art of Flemish workers ; then Roubiliac, as a French sculptor studying in Germany and in Paris, introduced the art of those places intermixed with Italian influence gathered during his visit to Rome. Later there was the acquirement of the works by Duesbury of Derby, who would not only assimilate the products of Chelsea and their methods of production to those employed at Derby, but would later add whatever distinct characteristics there might have been at the contemporary works at Bow.

The very fact that the success of the Derby Works was the chief cause of the closing of those at Chelsea, suggests that before Duesbury had decided to close the Chelsea kilns he would, as a good business man, have incorporated in his Chelsea works the principles of manufacture and trading, and even the styles and patterns, which had been found successful at Derby, although of course they would be, and were, individual characteristics in form, colour, and decoration. For instance, at Chelsea were made some very beautiful biscuit wares, and charming figures representing classic subjects, such as the " Three Graces," " Cupids," " Mars and Venus," and " Bacchus and Ariadne." Then there were Royal figures and historic characters, including among them George II. and William Shakespeare. Some very beautiful vases show from their decorations the Italian influence which Roubiliac had brought to bear, such, for instance, the painting of Eneas meeting Venus before he entered Carthage seen upon one of these vases.

Continental characteristics were introduced by the foreign artists, Sèvres influence predominating. Indeed, this evident Continental type of decoration was cultivated

and admired, for in catalogues issued from the Chelsea
Works, Sèvres services are referred to as "the very beautiful
Sève pattern," or " the very elegant Sève pattern." So
nearly were these imitations of Sèvres porcelain that it is
very difficult indeed to distinguish some of the old Chelsea
ornament. Much of the decoration of these characteristic
pieces was hand work, very often the delicate outline only
was applied by the transfer, the colour and the gold
ornament being applied by hand.

Another outside influence may be referred to in connection with Chelsea in that close by were the Battersea
enamel works. As mentioned in the chapters dealing with
Staffordshire pottery, when transfer printing was first
introduced the process was patented and chiefly understood
by Sadler & Green, of Liverpool, and porcelain was sent
from Staffordshire and other places to be so printed, and
returned for firing. At Battersea, however, a similar
process of printing was going on, and the workers at
Chelsea and Bow were able to obtain any assistance they
required near at hand·

Royal Patrons.

It is necessary to point out the importance of royal
favour and patronage bestowed on the different potteries
and porcelain works in olden time. Manufacturers in the
twentieth century value very highly patronage which
brings them notoriety. They regard royal patronage as a
valuable publicity asset, but, in olden time, royal patronage
and favour and that of wealthy patrons sometimes carried
with it financial support, and in nearly every case furnished
important assistance in that it found employment for
skilled artists. The very costly services of porcelain which
were made at Chelsea and other works enabled the owners
to employ the very best men they could obtain. In very

many cases they would not have had sufficient remunerative employment for artists of repute, nor would they have attracted such men to their works had it not been for royal patronage. It is said that we owe much of the support given to manufactures and works during the eighteenth century by English kings to the practice among German princes of engaging to some extent in art production. The patronage of royal princes is probably due to a survival of feudal customs, where the overlord was the direct patron of the craftsman. We know that on the Continent of Europe some of the most important art factories, both in porcelain and textiles, were associated with royal palaces.

George II. of England seems to have taken an interest in the Chelsea Works, which were founded during his reign ; so much so that he went to some trouble to secure models, materials, and some workmen from the Duchy of Brunswick, and from Saxony. He took an interest in the attempt which was being made to produce in England porcelain equal to that of Sèvres and Dresden. Then the Duke of Cumberland assisted in the reorganisation of the works, and gave Chelsea his patronage and support. When George III. came to the throne in 1760, he too continued to support the factory at Chelsea, and gave some large orders which found employment for skilled artists. Among the earlier commissions, however, was one for £600 which had been placed by the Duke of Cumberland. Then in the first year of George III.'s reign a commission was given for a large table service in mazarine blue, crimson, and gold, the cost of which was £1,150. That very beautiful set was destined to find a place in the palace of the Duke of Mecklenburg, where it would appear as a testimony to the quality of Chelsea porcelain, and probably be used in conjunction with services of Continental make. Referring to this service Horace Walpole, in a letter to Sir Horace

Mann in 1763, wrote: "I saw to-day a magnificent service of Chelsea china, which the King and Queen are sending to the Duke of Mecklenburg. There are dishes and plates without number, an epergne, candlestick, salt-cellars, sauce-boats, and a tea and coffee equipage. In short, it is complete."

Orders were also given for services for use in the English royal palaces.

Paste and Glaze.

It is said that the Chelsea porcelain was regarded with jealousy by the manufacturers of France, who petitioned Louis XV. to concede to them exclusive privileges, thus bearing testimony to the quality of both materials and decorations, which, owing to foreign influence, had been brought into such close competition with foreign products ; many magnificent pieces as the result of royal patronage had been produced equal to choice pieces of Sèvres porcelain. The collector, always desirous of ascertaining the source of materials, and of the constituent parts of paste and glaze, is naturally anxious to discover something about the soft milky-white paste used at Chelsea. The body is thick and comparatively heavy and readily chipped. It can quite easily be cut by a file, and even indented with the finger-nail. The glaze is thinner than that used on Bow china. Another characteristic is found in the tiny black specks in the paste, almost recognisable by touch. The glaze was often irregularly imparted, and there are frequently inequalities noticeable. The larger pieces, such as dishes and plates, were supported in the kiln, and often show marks of three points, which are free from glaze. It has been pointed out that little flakes or pieces of Chelsea porcelain when held up to the light show translucent spots which have been called " moons," caused by imperfect grinding, which has left small glassy substances in the paste.

As regards the raw material there are differences of opinion as to the origin of the soft paste. At first some of the clay used was secured from Poole in Dorset, but afterwards the kaolin or china stone from Cornwall was employed; the same was brought from Alum Bay. Some say that shippers sailing from the Thames brought back China clay as ballast, when trading with the East, thus enabling the potters of Chelsea and Bow to produce a similar paste to that of the Oriental pottery. Dr Johnson seems to have taken a great interest in the Chelsea Works, and even to have studied the chemical constituents of porcelain, and in common with some clever men of his day turned his attention to the improvements of china manufacture. These experiments resulted in many visits to the Chelsea Works, but the tests he made do not appear to have been successful, commercially, and he soon gave up the series of experiments. When Duesbury took over the Chelsea Works the materials he employed were similar to those he was using at Derby.

ORNAMENT AND DECORATION.

The influence exerted by artists, workmen, and others is more conspicuous in the decoration and ornament of the Chelsea porcelain than in the raw materials and the methods of firing. The position held in the works by Sprimont, and afterwards by Roubiliac, naturally influenced the modelling of the Chelsea figures and groups to a very large extent. Roubiliac had a free hand, no doubt, hence it is that there is a foreign type about his models, and the home connoisseur who does not pretend to be an expert in such matters finds it difficult at times to distinguish between the figures modelled at Dresden and

Sèvres and those of undoubted English make produced at Chelsea, and even the figures of Derby and elsewhere.

The different influences brought to bear at each successive period of the Chelsea Works explains the variety of type, and the difference between the early specimens and those made at the best period and others modelled when a change had set in. Then again the quality of the workmanship differed, for naturally the modelling of Roubiliac bore little or no comparison with that of those unskilled artists who were studying there, and perhaps copying his style. Early specimens of Chelsea are rude in form, and show a great want of finish.

The beautiful groups of the later period are very different indeed to the early figures, like the shepherd shearing sheep, harlequins, birds, lambs, sheep, cupids, and boys catching squirrels and bird's-nesting. Again, those beautifully modelled groups so richly coloured and painted have little or no kinship with the Derby biscuit. The early figures were mostly white, relieved with a little colour and some gilt. The Chelsea-Derby figures reached their best period between 1770 and 1784. Some of Roubiliac's figures were almost identical copies of Dresden groups. Many of the figures which have been noticed in leading collections, and which have been seen in the London sale-rooms, are very simple in composition and yet are strikingly effective. One simple figure is that of an itinerant musician with a pack on his back, apparently singing while he plays a quaint-looking instrument—a somewhat ragged, uncouth-looking figure, but choice in its rarity. Then there is the well-known pair of harlequin dancing with a maiden with long plaited hair, harlequin wearing a broad-brimmed cap and a masque. Far more important, however, is a famous group of Chelsea, made from 1750-1760, consisting of a gallant, Isabel, and harlequin, taken from an Italian comedy. Isabel holds a toy spaniel in her lap, and is gaily apparelled with a yellow underskirt, richly painted with flowers, and a green overskirt with white lining, her bodice being lined with crimson. Her lover, the gallant, wears a yellow coat lined with purple, and a white waistcoat contrasting with the crimson breeches tied with green bows. In a very important collection of Chelsea figures, recently exhibited by a noted firm of London dealers, a garniture of three groups of figures by Roubiliac, formerly in the possession of a nobleman, were exhibited. This magnificent and marvellously beautiful set of old Chelsea, masterpieces of this famous artist's work, represented pastoral idylls in the style of Watteau. The central group represented " The Music Lesson." Seated under a bower of white jasmine in full blossom was a damsel with a youthful musician. There was a small dog dressed in man's attire dancing on a marble stool, the lady evidently teaching the dog to step to the music. This group is a splendid demonstration of the colouring and decoration adopted by this master artist; the damsel in a white gown richly brocaded with gold and colours was shown wearing a pink cap and blue shoes, the gold and other ornaments being strikingly characteristic. This truly splendid piece, now in the London Museum, is shown in Fig. 29 (centre of page); Fig. 28 (left) and Fig. 30 (right) are the two groups known as the Four Seasons—one group representing Winter and Spring, and the other Autumn and Summer. Here again the colouring is simply magnificent, and typical of the highest period of Chelsea art. Winter wears a scarlet jacket, figured with black and gold and edged with ermine, also a yellow tippet of fur, a pink cap and pink shoes. Spring is charmingly arrayed in a green bodice and a white skirt, figured in gold and rich colours. She carries in her apron a profusion of flowers, symbolic of the season. Perhaps Summer in the companion group presents a greater wealth of colour, and shows how well the artists of Chelsea knew how to blend vivid tints, for Summer wears a dress of rose crimson and a blue bodice, her attire being overlaid with many gold pencillings.

From such rich and glorious groups and figures of old Chelsea works of fame we may turn to the more utilitarian porcelain, of which there are many examples in exquisite tea-services, and also vases, although more ornamental than useful, yet similarly ornamented with delightful paintings. At that time there seems to have been an almost conflicting influence exerted between the Continental paintings produced under foreign influence of the artists, and the common desire to imitate Oriental porcelain. The Oriental porcelain, which had for some time past been imported into this country, had gained a strong following, and those who were making pottery in England had to copy as far as possible some of the Oriental porcelain and introduce in English wares Chinese taste. Some of the Chelsea porcelain was like the Chinese enamelled in reds, blues, and green, relieved by matt gold and pencilled in black. Then again the Chinese powdered blue, mazarine blue, and apple-green ground, with Oriental ornament, were much copied. Some of them were moderated in design, and gradually characteristic treatment of birds, flowers, and classical subjects distinguished the Chelsea porcelain from the Oriental. Chelsea fell under a series of influences, chief, however, of which were those of China, Dresden, and Sèvres.

In the very interesting collection of old English porcelain exhibited some little time ago at the King Street Galleries of Stoner & Evans, where the Chelsea figures already referred to were then to be seen, there was a very early Chelsea tea and coffee service of octagon shape, decorated on a white ground, with illustrations from Æsop's Fables. The rims of the cups and plates were edged with red-brown, every piece bearing a rare mark, a

FIG. 28.   FIG. 30.

FIG. 29.

THREE GROUPS OF THE FINEST PERIOD OF CHELSEA PORCELAIN.

The centre group is "The Music Lesson" (now in the London Museum).
The two groups (on the right and left) represent "Winter and Spring," and "Summer and Autumn,"

Photo by the courtesy of Mr. Albert Amor,

[To face page 102.

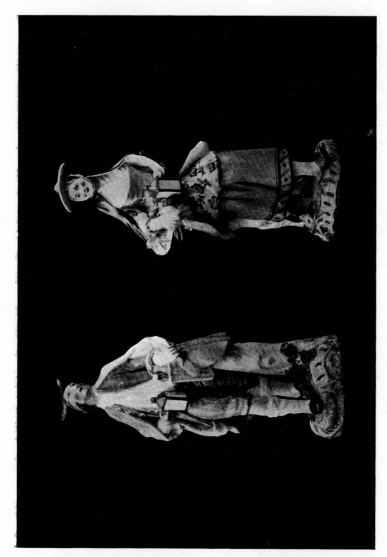

Fig. 31.   Fig. 32.
"The Night Watchman" and Companion Piece.

In the possession of Mr. Albert Amor.

raised anchor upon an oval tablet. This service consisted
of tea-pot and ewer of hexagon shape, and cream-ewer,
sugar-bowl, six tea-cups, six coffee-cups, and six saucers of
octagonal form. The curious fables represented on every
piece were supplemented by miniature landscapes, sprays
of flowers, and insects on the flange of the plates and the
interior of the cups. Truly a unique set !

In the same gallery was a tea and coffee service almost
entirely covered with somewhat large sprays of moss-roses,
painted on a delicate canary ground. There was a profusion of burnished gold, that represented a later period,
perhaps 1756-1770 ; another exhibit was a magnificent
dessert service. The Derby-Chelsea period was represented by a tea service, finely decorated with a border of
brilliant turquoise edged with gold. The white ground
was divided into eight spaces by narrow radiating bars of
crimson, inclined trellis-wise with separate gold scrolls, the
compartments thus formed being painted over with green
foliage and red berries. Such services are, of course,
among the rarities, but many home connoisseurs possess
odd cups and saucers, and certainly nothing can look better
than a cabinet of different pieces representing the various
periods of the Chelsea Works, and selected on account of
the variety of styles, decoration, and ornament represented.

Typical Examples.

The very remarkable pieces already referred to are
indeed typical examples of the finer works of art made
at Chelsea. In the London Museum at Lancaster House,
where the splendid group shown in Fig. 29 may be
seen, there are quite a number of exceptional pieces ; and
there others too, while not so magnificent and costly
are more typical of the Chelsea porcelain found in private
collections. Some of these have been handed down as

precious heirlooms ; others have been acquired after much search by purchase.

The collection of fine porcelain is no new hobby, for there are records of many large collections which have in many instances been dispersed.   Horace Walpole in his remarkable collection at Strawberry Hill had some fine cabinet specimens.   In his catalogue mention was made of two white salt-cellars with crayfish in relief, and also of two white barrels with vines and grapes, as well as of Chelsea porcelain.   The late Lord Dudley possessed four Chelsea vases, for which it is said he paid £10,000.   One of those remarkable pieces was formerly the property of the Foundling Hospital, presented to that institution by a Dr Garnier, who had purchased a set of three at the Chelsea Works in 1763.   The remaining pair were presented by Dr Garnier to the trustees of the British Museum shortly after he had procured them.   They were entered in the Donation Book of the Museum on April 15th, 1763, and described as " two very fine porcelain jars of the Chelsea Manufactory."

Among some of the exceptional pieces of which there is historical record was the figure of Shakespeare modelled after the monument in Westminster Abbey, there erected from the design of Kent. Under the figure is the following inscription :

> " The cloud cap't towers and gorgeous palaces,
>   The solemn temples, the great globe itself,
>   Yea, all which it inherit, shall dissolve,
>   And, like the baseless fabrick of a vision,
>   Leave not a wreck behind."

There is a companion figure of Milton, under which is the inscription :

> " Into the heaven of heavens
>   I have presumed, an earthly guest,
>   And drawn empyreal air."

In addition to those already described there are many fine pieces which have passed through the hands of Mr

Albert Amor, to whom we are indebted for several of the Chelsea illustrations. Fig. 31 and Fig. 32 represent " The Night Watchman " and a companion piece. The pair of Chelsea figures illustrated in Fig. 33 and Fig. 34 are of rather more than ordinary interest. They represent two actual personalities then well known. One of the pieces may also, from its associations, be of even greater interest than the other. The tablet on the warlike figure is inscribed : " DAVID GABARISCO, PRUSSIAN DWARF." The companion piece, Fig. 34, is " IOHN COAN, ENGLISH DWARF." The " Dwarf Tavern " was kept in Chelsea Fields by John Coan, a Norfolk dwarf. The death of the inn-keeper was recorded in the *Daily Advertiser* of March 17th, 1764, thus : " Yesterday died at the Dwarf Tavern in Chelsea Fields Mr John Coan, the unparalleled Norfolk Dwarf."

The " Shepherd " and the " Shepherdess " are another well-known Chelsea pair. Less important pieces but bearing similar characteristics are easily recognisable by comparison with authentic and marked examples.

Size is not much criterion of value in old china, for many of the choicer bits are quite small. The collection of miniature figures and trinkets is a pleasing hobby and one which appeals to some. Unfortunately many of these beautiful objects have perished, or been broken and lost or discarded by their owners in years gone by. Some delightful little figures, however, are met with occasionally. There are also beautiful little scent-bottles, miniature seals and charms, and pipe-stoppers. Some are undecorated, others profusely ornamented.

CHELSEA MARKS.

The Chelsea triangle and the anchor marks are known to most collectors. The anchor was not exclusive to

Chelsea, for it was used sometimes at Bow, and was common as a Venetian mark, but it is familiar to English collectors as typical of Chelsea, and, in combination, of the early period of the Chelsea-Derby porcelain. The incised triangle was one of the early marks, followed soon afterwards by an embossed circle with an anchor inside. The anchor points of the later issues differ, being sometimes barred and at others in the form of an annulet. The cable ring is, however, conspicuous in all of them. The mark in gold is generally typical of the finest pieces, especially those richly decorated in gold pencilling. In the less important specimens the colour or one of the colours used in the decoration of the piece was employed in making the mark. Generally speaking, however, those marked in colours are of an inferior quality to the rarer examples marked in gold. When Duesbury purchased the Chelsea Works in 1769 he added the " D " in script, using the crown over the " D " from 1773 to 1784, the latter addition being commemorative of an important visit of the King and Queen to the works at Chelsea.

Unfortunately not all Chelsea porcelain is marked, and it is further to be regretted that none of the marks of the English porcelain works have been fabricated to a greater extent than the Chelsea anchor by copiers, or those who are engaged in the somewhat doubtful occupation of producing modern replicas of old porcelain.

FIG. 33.

CHELSEA FIGURE,
"The Prussian Dwarf."

FIG. 34.

"The Norfolk Dwarf."

By the courtesy of Mr. Albert Amor.

[To face page 106.

Figs. 35 and 36.—Pair of Old Derby Biscuit Figures, representing George III, and Queen Charlotte and the Royal Children.

By the courtesy of Mr. Albert Amor.

CHAPTER X

ENGLISH—DERBY

Owners of Derby potteries—Some trading methods—Characteristic features
—Artists employed at Derby—Notable examples—Derby marks.

THE beautiful and now priceless china and figures—useful
and ornamental—which collectors treasure so much, were
made chiefly at the Derby Old Works during the last half
of the eighteenth century and the first few years of the
nineteenth century. During the period when so much that
was delightful and of exceptional interest in household
porcelain was made in England, Derby stood out conspicuously. It is of the products of the Derby Old Works
that collectors desire to know, and in the history of them
many celebrated men who worked there are necessarily
mentioned ; indeed, in those days of personal influence and
craftsmanship, the artists frequently made the fame of the
works with which they were associated ; and when they
removed to other places they carried their trade secrets
and special methods of working with them.

It will clear the ground before beginning a sketch of
Derby china—such as was turned out from the works before
the days of the modern Royal Crown Porcelain Company—
to admit at once that it is difficult to disassociate the china
of Bow and Chelsea from a collection of Derby china, for
the removal of the potteries at both Bow and Chelsea
resulted in their incorporation in the Derby Old Works.

The introduction of Chelsea and Bow characteristics,
and a continuation of work produced by the same artists

who had worked there, have helped to give sufficient
individuality to certain periods of work at Derby to
distinguish several of those periods by the names of the
two lesser works as indicating the peculiarities of the
porcelain then being made ; thus it is that we speak of
" Chelsea-Derby " and of " Bow-Chelsea-Derby " porcelain.

Owners of Derby Potteries.

It is somewhat curious that so little is known about the
early management and control of the potteries at Derby.
It is clear, however, that Duesbury was from the beginning
associated with the foundation and actual work carried on
there.   The date, a year more or less, when the first
" figgars " and other porcelain were made in Derby, is
really immaterial.   As an approximate date 1751 has been
named, although it has been proved that William Duesbury
was in that year working in London as a modeller.   It
has also been ascertained that he was then twenty-six
years of age.   Apparently he went to Longton in Staffordshire soon afterwards, and finally settled in Derby in 1755.
During his career as an enameller of pottery, he either
worked at, or was familiar with, the Bow and Chelsea
Works which he subsequently acquired.   It may also be
assumed that Duesbury undertook the enamelling of
unglazed porcelain for the proprietors of Bow and Chelsea
and other works.   Such inference is derived from his work-
book, which clearly indicates the charges he made for the
different pieces he executed.   Assuming that his work-
book records his own personal efforts, Duesbury must have
stuck very close to his work, for there is a record showing
several pieces finished daily ; and although the prices
appear comparatively low, and colours and gold were then
expensive items, it is evident that the profits realised were

satisfactory. To take an example of a representative day's entry, the following extract will serve ; and it must of course be assumed that the charges were for decorating or finishing: " May 22nd. Two pairs of sitting men, 4s., a group of large figgars, 4s., a pair of phesants, 3s., 2 pairs parrots, 5s., and one pair of birds, 2/6."

The works at Derby, which had been built on the Nottingham road, were doubtless small, and of but little importance as judged by modern standards. It is probable that Duesbury was the real founder of those works, and it is clear he was the mainstay of the business. A deed was drawn up (but never signed) in which the names of Andrew Planché and John Heath as well as Duesbury appear. It has been suggested that John Heath was the capitalist ; William Duesbury was, of course, a skilled enameller ; and Planché had gained some reputation as a maker of china.

As it has already been shown, Duesbury was acquainted with the Bow and Chelsea Works, quite intimate with their owners, and familiar with their products. Apparently he saw the rare beauty of their porcelain, and possibly understood its popularity ; he therefore seized an opportunity which presented itself of acquiring the Chelsea Works, which he took over in 1769 ; in 1775 he further extended his operations by securing the works at Bow.

The Chelsea factory was kept going until 1784, when it was closed down, and the patterns and some of the men who worked there transferred to Derby, where for some time the work which had been in operation at Chelsea was continued. It was not very clear when or how Duesbury became possessed of the entire group of works in his own right, but apparently Heath and Planché withdrew, for there is no mention of their names in the transfer to Duesbury's son, William Duesbury the younger, at the time of the founder's death, which took place in 1786. William Duesbury, junior, was soon afterwards joined in partnership by Michael Keen, who was a designer and a miniature painter.

William Duesbury the younger only lived to enjoy the partnership for a few years, but the business was carried on by his widow and his partner, who eventually married her. Then, after the retirement of Keen, a third William Duesbury, a grandson of the founder, continued the works until 1811.

The business was then sold to Robert Bloor, who for many years had been an employee of the firm. It was Bloor who cleared some of the accumulated stock of " seconds," and thus released a considerable amount of locked-up capital. But in doing so he incidentally placed upon the market many inferior objects ; and it was probably due to this action of Bloor that the tone of the productions of the Derby Old Works was, at any rate for a time, lowered. Owing to Bloor's illness the works were carried on for some years, probably from 1828 to 1844, by his manager, Thomason, who was eventually superseded by Thomas Clarke, who had married Bloor's daughter.

To sum up the periods to which the products of the Derby Old Works may be assigned, the following dates are given :

Duesbury	-	-	-	- 1751-1769
Chelsea-Derby	-	-	-	- 1769-1775
Bow-Chelsea-Derby	-	-	- 1775-1786
Crown-Derby	-	-	-	- 1786-1796
Duesbury and Kean	-	-	- 1796-1811
Bloor	-	-	-	- 1811-1848

SOME TRADING METHODS.

The methods adopted by the owners of the Derby Works whereby their trade could be promoted are of interest to collectors. As early as 1756, indeed shortly after Duesbury must have founded the enterprise, he adopted the plan of disposing of his goods by occasional auctions in London. This method he continued for some time, holding one very important sale in 1763. There are marked catalogues extant from which the then market values in open competition may be gauged. The practice of disposing of the surplus products of the Derby factory by auction in London does not appear to have given satisfaction to retail traders, by whom some of the wares were sold, and it was discontinued in 1785.

When Duesbury had decided to give up the auctions, and to confine his distributing methods to sale at fixed catalogue prices to retail shopkeepers, a Mr Hewson, on behalf of the London traders in porcelain, wrote to Mr Duesbury as follows :

" SIR,
    " The Gentlemen of the China Trade have directed me to inform You that your promising to discontinue your Spring Sales to the Nobility has met their approbation. They have desired your acceptance of the thanks of the Society for the same, and have unanimously agreed to assist the Derby Manufactory by forwarding the Sale of its Manufactures ; hoping at the same time Mr Duesbury will never lose sight of the Interests of the Members of the China Society.
    " I am, Sr, your most obedient humble Servant,
                                    " WM. HEWSON.
" *Aldgate*, 19*th Oct.*, 1785."

Previous to that date Duesbury had opened " a commodious Warehouse in Bedford Street, Covent Garden," and had issued a catalogue or list. From the title page of that little book we learn something of what was made for or by Duesbury & Co., as the proprietors were then styled at their warehouse, where they were said to have had a selection classified as " ornamental " and " useful." The ornamental

part chiefly consisted " in jars, vases, urns, tripods, altars,
etc., designed in the antique and modern taste with great
choice of richest and most elegant decorations of figures,
emblems, and histories, taken from ancient history and
mythology, adapted for the embellishment of chimney
pieces, cabinets, toilets, consoles, etc." ; and " the useful
part furnishing an extensive variety of rich and select
table and dessert services, elegant tea, coffee, and chocolate
equipages, caudle and cabinet cups and dejeunes from new
patterns in the most approved present taste. To which
are also added for dessert surtouts great choice of biscuit
groups and figures in a grotesque style from accurate
designs elaborately finished, even to the minutest imitation
of lace."

CHARACTERISTIC FEATURES.

Most of the Derby porcelain was of soft paste. In its
preparation Cornish steatite was used until 1779, when
bone ash was substituted, and afterwards the same ingredients as were then used in other potteries were employed.

The opinion as to the late introduction of bone ash
expressed by some writers does not appear to have been
borne out by modern research, which places the use of bone
ash at Chelsea, Bow, and Derby at a much earlier period.
Many authorities consider that the early body used at
Derby before 1769 was a frit porcelain, containing Dorset
clay ; then came the introduction of bone, and finally
china clay and china stone, the latter being used in Bloor's
day.

The collector tells much from the glaze, especially so
in the case with old Derby china, which was coated with an
easily fusible glaze which left many small cracks in the
process of firing. The glaze, too, is very soft and easily

filed, and the filings may be readily reduced to a very fine powder. The characteristics of colouring and ornament are important. The ground colours of the beautiful tea-sets and other fine Derby china include apple, olive, and pale green, lapus lazuli, turquoise, and light blues; also rose, salmon, brown, and yellow.

The collector finds much to delight in the beautiful figures of Derby, and many admire the biscuit figures, the best of which were made at the Derby Works from 1770 to 1810; the biscuit china paste is soft and white, almost wax-like in touch. In the modelling of the figures many clever artists were employed, notably Coffee, Spengler, and Stephan. Some figures were made from parian, a composition which was discovered by John Mountford, who was one of the Derby modellers, afterwards being employed by Copeland and Garrett, of Stoke-on-Trent.

Derby figures were much sought after at that time; indeed, they were specially referred to at the auction held in London in December, 1756, which was advertised as being held by the order of "the Proprietors of the Derby Porcelain Manufactory." In the catalogue of that sale some Derby figures were said to be "as good as those made at Dresden."

It is helpful to study the shapes of porcelain when desirous of distinguishing the work of certain periods, and especially those of some porcelain made in factories where individualistic treatment and characteristic design were followed. There were some very characteristic designs made at Derby, among them the Greek krater vase; also the "Hydria" patterns upon which the decorations were chiefly exotic birds and landscapes in medallions. There were also several varieties of the so-called Japan style, distinguished as "Derby-Japan," "Rock-Japan," "Grecian-Japan," and the "Witches-Japan."

Transfer printing originated at the Derby China Works in 1764, having been introduced by Richard Holdship, of Worcester, who had obtained an agreement with the firm to give him a regular engagement, or a contract for sufficient work to keep him occupied for a stated time.

It has been pointed out that some amateur painting was done at that time, sent to various kilns to be fired, and in some instances decorated and finished off. That may account to some extent for inferior specimens, which, although obviously Derby in finish or paste, do not appear to be up to the usual standard of quality.

It has been pointed out that the old pattern books of eighteenth-century traders and manufacturers are the best guides to the actual objects being sold at the time they were published. No doubt illustrated catalogues used for selling purposes are very helpful indications of the chief characteristics of the work of the firm by whom they were issued, and also of the popular taste of the period. One of the catalogues of the Derby Old Works issued in the eighteenth century contains about 770 patterns. Some of these show very neat borders on coloured ground. Festoons of laurel and sprays of flowers, and ribbon tied and festooned, were of frequent occurrence. Many of the cups illustrated in that pattern book were fluted, and some were embossed with a narrow leaf running part way up the cup. The coffee cans were about $2\frac{1}{2}$ in. in height, and of similar diameter ; many were made in pairs, and beautifully painted. Among notable commemorative pieces made at the Derby Works was a cup, on the one side of which the figure of Peace was represented standing on a rock by the seaside ; in her right hand, which is extended over the waves, is a wreath ; with her left hand she supports a medallion of Nelson, round which is inscribed : "Europe's hope and Britain's glory," and round the whole design is the legend : " Rear-Admiral Lord Nelson of the Nile." On the reverse of the cup are views of the battle of the Nile, with the inscription : " VICTORY OF THE NILE, AUG. 1, 1798." Notwithstanding this, the catalogues of specialists and illustrations of novelties like the Nelson memorial cup are not always sure guides to the everyday things then in daily use.

ARTISTS EMPLOYED AT DERBY.

There is much importance attached to the quality of the work of the artists who decorated Derby porcelain. These men contrived to impart distinct characteristics to their work, and much of the value which attaches to this beautiful china is found in those pieces conspicuous for their specialistic treatment. These workers in clay and painters and enamellers in colours and gold were for the most part artists, that is, they were men of character and touch, as well as of individuality—not merely operatives, that is, painters following designs prepared by someone else and multiplied indefinitely. As a rule each vase or set of vases differs materially in its decoration, and often in its style. Still more is that special treatment seen in one of the many tea-sets and other wares of differing shapes, in which the same design and colouring is carried out on every piece, although the adaptation of the design or the introduction of a different painting or picture gives it a distinct appearance. Some of the artists then employed undoubtedly showed great genius, such, for instance, Billingsley, referred to in connection with several notable potteries, a man who had a remarkable career and worked at many places, but probably did most of his work, if not actually his best, at Derby. He was born at Derby, and apprenticed to Duesbury in 1774, continuing to work at the Derby Old Works until 1796, when he left to establish a factory of his own at Pinxton in conjunction with John

Coke. In 1801 he left Pinxton and became a decorator of porcelain at Mansfield, from which town he removed in 1803. In 1805 we find him decorating porcelain at Torksey in Lincolnshire. Then in 1808 he was in Worcester, from whence he went to Nantgarw in 1811. He was a restless man, for in 1814 he removed to Swansea, but returned to Nantgarw in 1817. Two years later he sold his recipes and moulds to W. Young, and took service with J. Rose of Coalport in 1819; there he continued until his death in 1828.

William Pegg followed Billingsley, and was employed by Duesbury as leading hand. He was a member of the Society of Friends, and was locally known as " Quaker Pegg." His work has been described as naturalistic, for he painted flowers with wonderful precision and very true to nature; especially remarkable was his treatment of roses, passion flowers, and asters.

Curiously enough there was another William Pegg who also worked at Derby at a somewhat later date. This man, whom we may call Pegg the younger, left Derby in 1817, and went to Nantgarw, where he joined Billingsley. At the time of his removal there was no railway communication, so he elected to walk all the way. He, too, was an excellent painter of natural flowers, and was evidently an admirer of the lily (*Lilium testaceum*) with which he was very familiar, and that flower was undoubtedly the best thing he did, for it would bear examination under a magnifying glass. William Pegg the younger eventually gave up work as a decorator of porcelain and became a textile designer.

Moses Webster, who was born in 1792, living on until 1870, was a one-time decorator and painter of porcelain at Derby, but the greater part of his work was executed at Worcester, and some of it at Mortlock's in London.

James Turner may be mentioned as a Derby artist.

Thomas Steele, too, was a noted painter of porcelain slabs on which he grouped flowers and fruit. He worked at Derby from 1815 until 1848, when he went to Staffordshire and became a painter, first at Davenport's and then at Minton's. Among other artists whose work is known upon the finer pieces of old Crown Derby are R. Askew (figure painter), Bancroft, Z. Boreman (landscapes), Brewer, Geo. Hancock (flowers), J. Hancock (flowers), J. Haslem (figures), M. Keene, G. Mellor (insects), J. Mountford, and E. Withers.

Most of the leading decorators and painters of the later period at the Derby works marked the pieces they made with distinctive numbers. These, as far as it is known, were as follows : (1) Thomas Soar ; (2) Joseph Stables ; (3) William Cooper ; (4) William Yates ; (5) John Yates ; (6) *not known ;* (7) William Billingsley ; (8) William Longdon ; (9) William Smith ; (10) John Blood ; (11) William Taylor ; (12) John Dewsbury ; and (13) Joseph Dodd. The rules applying to numbers were extended to the use of specific colouring, which indicated the colours the artists employed in printing or painting patterns and ornaments : thus the workers in blue used blue, but other colours were indicated by an orange-red mark ; for gold or gold pencilling the number was painted in puce.

NOTABLE EXAMPLES.

The varieties of useful and ornamental porcelain manufactured at the Derby Old Works are exceedingly numerous, and in all the more important collections of Derby china it is quite evident that the owners of the works not only catered for wealthy patrons, but supplied quite a number of figures, tea-sets, and ornamental china at moderate prices. Nevertheless it is evident that the greater portion of the products of these works consisted of high-class goods. Boswell mentions Dr Johnson's visit to the Derby factory in 1777, in connection with which the worthy Doctor said that the " china was beautiful but too dear, for they could have vessels of silver of the same size as cheap as what were here made of porcelain."

Among some of the choicer works were several sets made for royal patrons, including a splendid dessert service of 120 pieces, made for the Prince of Wales in 1788. The Duke of Devonshire commissioned a magnificent set covered over with paintings, among which were views of Chatsworth, Hardwick, and elsewhere. The Earl of Shrewsbury had a Derby service, the decoration being fruit upon a green ground.

As regarding well-known authentic pieces there are some beautiful specimens in the South Kensington Museum, some of which were formerly located in the Jermyn Street Museum. One very noted example is a group by Askew, representing some country children and a few sheep taking refuge under the trees during a thunderstorm. At the time when the best productions of the Derby Works were being made sauce-boats were much in vogue, and many " blue-fluted," " sage-leaf," and " fig-leaf " boats were made. There were also caudle cups, butter tubs, honey-pots and beakers, as well as the very decorative tea- and breakfast-sets, so richly ornamented with a wealth of reds and blues. Most of such pieces are found marked with the Crown Derby mark in red.

Curious little figures, already referred to as " figgars," were modelled by Andrew Planché, who was an undoubted adept at figures, and such animals as dogs, cats, and sheep. The old cupids of Chelsea and Bow were afterwards reproduced at Derby, and made during both the Derby and the Chelsea-Derby periods. They may frequently be distinguished by the numerals hand-scratched into the paste on the rim of the small pedestals.   Most of the Derby-

Chelsea cupids are highly coloured. Their hair is often represented reddish, and the flowers and greenery bright in colouring. Among oddments of Derby china may be mentioned small figures, smelling-bottles, charms, and seals. There are also some portrait medallions, notably one of Mrs William Duesbury, the wife of the second William Duesbury.

The accompanying illustrations, reproduced by the courtesy of Mr Amor, represent two very fine white Derby biscuit groups made about 1775 and copied from the picture of Zoffany. Fig. 35 is a portrait of King George III. standing in the characteristic attitude of the period. Fig. 36 is a group somewhat stiffly posed, representing Queen Charlotte and her children, George Prince of Wales (after-wards George IV.), and Frederick, who was afterwards created Duke of York.

DERBY MARKS.

The marks commonly met with on Derby china are illustrated in Figs. i., ii., iii., iv. (page 120) ; a plain script D was used before 1769 ; it was either printed in red or scratched in the paste. When Duesbury took over the Chelsea Works he altered his mark and combined the Chelsea anchor with the Derby " D." Then about 1788 the script D was surmounted by a crown, which was divided from it by crossed batons and three dots (*see* Fig. iv.). The colouring of the marks varied ; thus, there are gold, blue, puce, and vermilion.

Other marks of minor importance, chiefly painters' marks, used at the Derby Old Works are met with, especially on the rarer pieces ; among those calling for special notice is the potter's stool, a mark which was also used at other places, and of ancient origin. Bloor substituted his own name for the older Derby mark about 1825.

It may be further explained that the use of the crown is said to date from a visit of George II. to the London warehouse of the Derby potters, which was situated in Bedford Street. The marks indicated, although generally followed, were not always used with correctness. As an instance, in the catalogue of the Victoria and Albert Museum it is recorded that sometimes a suite of five vases and beakers will be found to have four of them marked with the Chelsea-Derby mark, whereas the fifth may have only the Chelsea anchor upon it. Whether that indicates that the sets were made up of pieces painted at different times, and possibly by different artists, or whether they had been carelessly marked, is not quite clear.

The earliest marked statuettes of Derby were made about 1770; on some of these the fashion of the times is faithfully represented, thereby assisting in fixing the period. Upon the dresses worn was beautiful lace, similar to the lace found on old Dresden statuettes; moreover, such figures were often marked with crossed swords in imitation of the Dresden mark.

Of the lesser Derby firms whose names are mentioned in old records in connection with the manufacture of Derby china there is that of Locker & Co.; also Stevenson & Co., which afterwards became Stevenson and Hancock, a firm who also used the Crown Derby mark.

Fig. i.   Fig. ii.   Fig. iii.   Fig. iv.

DERBY.—A few of the many marks used at the Derby Old Works previous to 1815.

The later productions of the Royal Crown Derby Porcelain Works do not come within the scope of this work, which deals only with *old* china. The very beautiful productions of the firm, which still maintains the traditions and high reputation of the Derby Old Works, are in many instances cabinet specimens of great beauty and value, but however beautiful they may be they have not the same interest to the connoisseur of the antique as genuine old porcelain.

CHAPTER XI

ENGLISH—FULHAM AND LAMBETH

Early accounts of the works—Some examples of Fulham wares— Lambeth pottery.

As recorded in a previous chapter, the good folk of Old England in the sixteenth century, and at an earlier date, received their supply of pottery vessels, such as then served all their needs, from local potters. Little pot banks were to be found in many parts of England in Tudor times and in the seventeenth century, chiefly, of course, where the local clay sufficed. Many of these old potteries have been carried on intermittently for centuries, in some instances almost on the actual sites of potteries worked in the seventeenth century, fragments of old pottery and indications of much earlier pot banks being constantly dug up. The exceptionally fine array of ancient pottery, such as served the purposes of Londoners throughout the many centuries which intervened from that far-away period when Roman London came into being to the London known to us through historians, as it was until the close of the eighteenth century, has already been referred to. It is at the Guildhall Museum, and also at the London Museum in Lancaster House, we find so many of the curiosities of Old London, none of them more interesting than the old pottery.

EARLY ACCOUNTS OF THE WORKS.

Although there are records of potteries which have been

worked quite close to the City, such as the Lambeth
Potteries, and those at Bow and Chelsea, the Fulham
Pottery, which was in the days when it was first worked far
removed from the centre of the City, presents an exceptional
story of great interest and value.   It was there that one of
the oldest manufacturing concerns of the Metropolis was
to be found.   In the days of Charles II. John Dwight, of
Fulham, had a well-established pottery.   In olden time
men of learning took up the potter's art.   There were
mysteries and trade secrets associated with the industry,
the discovery and possession of which seem to have appealed to men of research.   John Dwight was such a man,
for he was an M.A. of Christ Church, Oxford, and had held
an appointment of secretary to more than one bishop.
The well-known Dr Plot wrote of him in 1677 as " the
ingenious John Dwight, formerly M.A. of Christ Church
College, Oxon," who " discovered the mystery of the stone
of Cologne, wares (such as D'Alva bottles, jugs, noggins)
heretofore made only in Germany, and by the Dutch
brought over into England in great quantities," and who had
" set up a manufacture of the same which (by methods and
contrivances of his own, altogether unlike used by the
Germans), in three or four years " had " brought it to
greater perfection than it has attained where it hath been
used for many ages, insomuch that the Company of
Glass-sellers of London, who are the dealers for that
commodity, have contracted with the inventor to buy only
of his English manufacture and refuse the foreign."

Dr Plot further mentions in this account of the Fulham
Pottery that Dwight " hath discovered also the mystery
of the Hessian wares, and vessels for retaining the pene-
trating salts and spirits of the chymists, more serviceable
than were ever made in England or imported from Germany
itself.   And hath found ways to make an earth white and
transparent as porcellane, and not distinguishable from it

by the eye, or by experiments that have been purposely made to try wherein they disagree. To this earth he hath added the colours that are usual in the coloured china ware, and divers others not seen before. The skill that hath been wanting to set up a manufacture of this transparent earthenware in England, like that of China, is the glazing of the white earth, which hath much puzzled the projector, but now that difficulty is also in great measure overcome. He hath also caused to be modelled statues or figures of the said transparent earth (a thing not done elsewhere, for China affords us only imperfect mouldings), which he hath diversified with great variety of colours, making them of the colour of iron, copper, brass, and partycoloured, as some Achat stones." But before Dwight had gained such notoriety he had struggled on, testing his discoveries, experimenting, and when they were completed obtaining a patent right. It was in the year 1671 that John Dwight presented a petition to the Merrie Monarch stating that he had discovered " the mystery of transparent earthenware, comonly knowne by the names of porcelaine or China and Persian ware, as also the misterie of the stoneware, vulgarly called Cologne ware, and that he designed to introduce a manufacture of the said wares into our kingdome of England, where they have not hitherto been wrought or made," and praying that a patent might be granted to him to secure for him " the sole benefitt of the manufacture of the said wares for fourteene yeares, according to the statute in that behalfe made and provided."

The petition was favourably received, and on April 23rd, 1671, the patent prayed for was granted. Its terms are of sufficient interest to deserve somewhat lengthy reference. After reciting the character of the application, the document proceeds :

" Know yee, that wee, being willing to cherish and

encourage all laudable endeavours and designes of such of our subjectes as shall find out vsefull and proffitable artes, misteries, and invençons, by granting and appropriating vnto them for some term of yeares the frvite and benefitte of their industry, whereby their labours and expenses in the attainmt thereof may be recompensed and rewarded vnto them, of our especiall grace, certaine knowledge, and meere moçon, have given and granted, and by theise presentes, for vs, oure heires, and successors, doe give and grant vnto the said John Dwight, his executors, adminis- trators, and assignes, speciall lycense and full and free libertye, priviledge, power, and authoritie, that he, the said John Dwight, his executors, administrators, and assigns, by him and themselves, or by his or their deputies, ser- vantes, workemen, or assignes, and none other, shall and may, from time to time, and at all and everie time and times hereafter, dureinge the terme of fourteene yeares next ensueinge the date of these presentes, att his and theire owne proper costes and charges, vse, exercise, practise, and enjoy the said mistery and invençon of makeing transparent earthenware, comonly knowne by the names of porcelaine or China, and Persian ware ; and alsoe the mistery and invençon of makeing the stoneware, vulgarly called Cologne ware, within any convenient place or places within our realm of England, dominion of Wales, or towne of Berwick-vpon-Tweed, in such manner as to him or them in their discreçons shall seeme meete ; and shall and may have and enjoy the sole benefitte and advantage from, by, or vnder the said misteries, invençons, or manufactures of the said wares, or either of them, by him, the said John Dwight, found out and discovered, as aforesaid, ariseing or groweing from time to time dureing the tearme hereby granted, to have, hold, and enjoy the said lycenses, priviledges, powers, and authorities, benefitt, advantages, and other the premisses in and by these presentes granted or mençoned to be granted, and everie of them, vnto the said John Dwight, his executors, administrators, and assignes, from and dureing the tearme of fourteene yeares from henceforth next ensueing and fully to be compleat and ended, yielding and paying therefore yearely and every yeare during the said tearme into the receipt of our Exchequer att Westminster, to the vse of vs, our heires, and successors, the yearly rent or sume of twentie shillinges of lawfull money of England."

It then went on to " require and streightly comand and charge all and everie person and persons, bodies politique and corporate, of whatsoever qualitie, degree, name, or condiçon they be, that neither they nor any of them, dureinge the tearme hereby granted, either directly or indirectly doe or shall use or putt in practise the said misteries and invençons or manufacture of the said wares, or either of them, soe by the said John Dwight found out or discovered as aforesaid ; nor doe or shall counterfeite, imitate, or resemble the same ; nor doe or shall make any addiçon therevnto, or substracçon from the same, whereby to pretend themselves the inventors or devisors thereof, without the lycense, consent, and agreement of the said John Dwight, his executors, administrators, or assigns, in writing vnder his or theire handes and seales first had and obteyned in that behalfe," under pains and penalties.

Dwight seems to have been very successful, and to have found a ready market in and around London for the Fulham stoneware made in the pottery near Putney Bridge. To a certain extent it took the place of Cologne ware, which was so extensively imported into this country during the sixteenth and seventeenth centuries. Dwight made grey mugs, jugs, and butter pots, and as each successive monarch sat on the English throne Fulham stoneware was ornamented with medallions or initials signifying the name of the king or queen then ruling. Thus there are

examples known on which are the royal cypher " C. R."
(Charles II.), " W. R." (William III.), " A. R." (Queen
Anne), and " G. R." (George I.). The ornament and
enamelling consisted of raised and incised bands, leaves, and
flowers. In Fig. 39 we show a stoneware mug of Fulham
make on which is the characteristic ornament and the
cypher " G. R." Fig. 40 is on a little older date, for it is
after the manner of the *gres-de-Flanders*, and has upon it
the initials of William III., " W. R."

In due course the grey stoneware gave place to the
brown stoneware. The collector of antique pottery,
however, aims at securing some of the specimens of the
earlier patent, for there were two patents; the first one
having expired and the manufactory of the pottery having
been a commercial success, Dwight applied and obtained a
grant of a second patent, which was dated June 12th, 1684.
In that document it was set forth that " John Dwight, gentl,"
has " by his owne industry, and at his owne proper costes
and charges," " invented and sett vp at Fulham, in our
County of Middx, ' severall new manufactures of earthenwares, called by the names White Gorges, Marbled
Porcellane Vessells, Statues, and Figures, and Fine Stone
Gorges and Vessells, never before made in England or
elsewhere ; and alsoe discovered the mistery of Transparent Porcellane, and Opaçons, Redd and Dark coloured
Porcellane or China and Persian Wares, and the mistery of
the Cologne or Stone Wares,' and is endeavouring to settle
manufactures of all the said wares within this our United
Kingdom of England ; and hee having humbly besought
Vs to grant unto him our Letters Patents for the sole vse
and exercise of the same for terme of fowerteene years,
according to the Statute in that case provided, Wee are
gratiously pleased to condescend to that his request."

What a wonderful old pottery that must have been,
outside London and yet so near, easily accessible, and

situated on the banks of the Thames, and in a position to
send down the river boatloads of stoneware to London
Bridge ! Although the works have been rebuilt within
the last century much of the old Fulham Works remain,
and the owners manufacture brown stoneware of excellent
quality, in some instances making replicas of antique
ware, such as the Fulham Pottery was noted for centuries
ago. To the present firm we are indebted for the later
history of Dwight's venture as well as the earlier. They
tell us that, as he deserved, Dwight obtained an extensive
market for his wares, which were held in great regard by
the appreciative public of his day. His success attracted,
as it was sure to do, the attention of rivals, and as a well-
informed writer on the subject puts it, he was " watched
by hungry imitators who waited for the day on which his
patents expired in order that they might reap the benefit
of his labours." Dwight, however, was not the man to be
easily circumvented by trade competitors. He enrolled no
specification as to his materials or processes, and left his
recipes a profound secret. It is even said that he buried
in some part of the Fulham Works his models, tools, and
moulds, in order that descendants or others should not
be able to carry on that branch of the trade which he
was first to invent. Colour is lent to this story by the
circumstance that a good many years ago some workmen,
while employed in digging foundations for some new
erections at the pottery, came across a walled-up vaulted
chamber which, on being opened, was found to contain a
number of characteristic specimens of Dwight's work,
including " greybeards " or " bellarmines," and ale pots
which answer to the designation of " stoneware, vulgarly
called Cologne ware."

It is not possible to state with certainty the date of John
Dwight's death. There is, however, a record of the demise
in 1737 of a Dr Samuel Dwight, who is pronounced to have

been the famous potter's son. He was a well-known writer on scientific subjects, and is described in obituary notices as " the first who found out the secret to colour earthenware like china." Presumably, therefore, he maintained the family interest in the pottery. It, at all events, remained in the family, for there is evidence that about the time of Dr Dwight's death the establishment was carried on by a Margaret Dwight, in partnership with a certain Thomas Warland. The association does not appear to have been a fortunate one, for after a few years the pair had to seek refuge from their difficulties in bankruptcy. Subsequently, Margaret Dwight married a Mr White, or Wight, who continued the works. White was a man of some ingenuity, and he obtained in 1762 a patent for the making of " white crucibles or melting potts made of British materials," for which in the previous year he had obtained a premium from the Society of Arts.

The White interest in the pottery continued for many years, in fact, quite down to modern times. The last representative of the family was a Mr White, who died in 1862. On the realisation of his estates the pottery was acquired by Messrs MacIntosh and Clements, who worked it for a short time and then transferred their interest to Mr C. C. Bailey. Mr Bailey introduced steam machinery and in other ways greatly improved and extended the works, and they remained in his hands for a good many years. Ultimately they were acquired by their present owners, the Fulham Pottery and Cheavin Filter Company, Limited, the filter business having hitherto been carried on at Boston in Lincolnshire, and the filter cases being manufactured at Fulham. In 1891 the two firms were amalgamated, and under the present ownership the Fulham Pottery has attained a state of prosperity and renown which could never have been conceived by its original founder in his wildest imaginings.

I

Some Examples of Fulham Wares.

As already stated, there is a very fine collection of
Fulham and contemporary pottery in the Guildhall
Museum, London.   No doubt many of the objects shown
there without labels of identity were made at Fulham, but
with exemplary caution there is a query mark placed
against some even of the objects labelled Fulham ware.
Of those about which there can be but little doubt, there is
a delightful small seventeenth-century jug, marked with a
" W. R. " and crown ; there is also a jug of mottled stoneware of the ordinary greybeard form, an early eighteenth-
century jar of Fulham ware, and several bellarmines of light
brown glaze which are undoubtedly Fulham.   One of these
is embellished with a medallion on which there is a thistle
surmounted by a crown, and on either side the royal
initials " C. R." (Charles II.) ; it measures 8 in. in height,
and was discovered some years ago in Leadenhall Street.
There are other bellarmines of Fulham ware differently
marked, one ornamented with a rose medallion.

Some beautifully shaped bottles of grey-glazed ware
were made at Fulham in the seventeenth century ; several
of them are in the Guildhall Museum, one being pear-
shaped, with a short, slender, tapering neck and a side
handle ; on the shoulders of the vessel are scrolls in light
blue, the measurement being 12 in. in height and 7 in. in
diameter.   There is a similar bottle of smaller size, and
porringers, too, one a beautiful little cup of brown stoneware with a band of incised ornament, a genuine seventeenth-century specimen, found in Basinghall Street.   In
the same collection are a number of grey stoneware vessels,
labelled " Grès de Flanders," but some of those, too, may
have been made at Fulham.

The chief exhibits of Fulham ware at the British

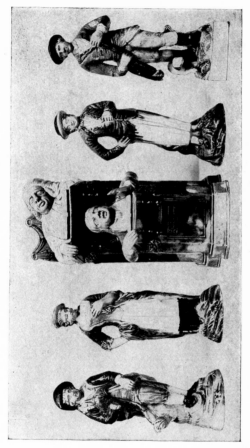

FIG. 37.—"THE VICAR AND MOSES."

FIG. 38.—SET OF FOUR FIGURES.

In the British Museum.

[*To face page* 130

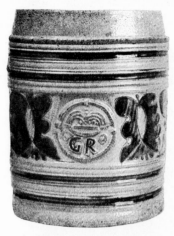

FIG. 39.
FULHAM STONEWARE MUG.

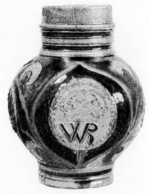

FIG. 40.
GRES DE FLANDERS JUG.

Mr. Phillips, Hitchin.

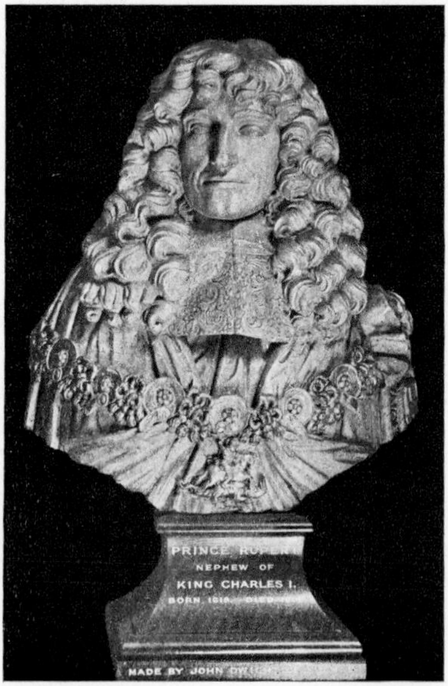

FIG. 41.
FULHAM WARE, Bust of Prince Rupert.
In the British Museum.

To face page 131.]

Museum are the bust of Prince Rupert (*see* Fig. 41), and several figures of Dwight's stoneware. Referring to the dinner-set made by Dwight for Charles II. it is said that there was a dish among the specimens retained by the Dwight family dispersed at a sale in 1862 which was originally made as one of the set. A description of this piece appearing in the *Art Journal* at that time was as follows : " It is of round form and large size, being 64½ in. in circumference. The groundwork is a rich blue approaching to the ultramarine. It is surrounded by a broad rim, nearly 4 in. wide, formed by a graceful border of foliage and birds in white and shaded in pale blue. The whole of the centre is occupied by the Royal Arms, surmounted by its kingly helm, crown, and lion crest. The arms themselves are encircled with a garter, on which is inscribed the well-known motto : '*Honi soit qui mal y pense.*' The arms and supporters rest upon a groundwork of foliage, in the middle of which is the motto : ' *Dieu et mon droit.*' The workmanship of this piece is of a very superior quality, and a dinner-set of similar ware would make many a modern one look poor." One rare piece is the half-length figure of an apparently lifeless child inscribed : " LYDIA DWIGHT, DYD MARCH 3, 1672."

Many of the old records of the Fulham Works are still extant, and references are made in them to the different clays then used, and also to the slips and glazes. So tenaciously did John Dwight cling to his instincts as a commercial potter that it is said he destroyed many of his recipes, trusting to memory for their use. As already stated he buried models and moulds to prevent his successors from pursuing what he had found an unprofitable branch of the business. He found some sale in the eighteenth century for some remarkable grotesque pottery, among which may be classed jugs and mugs, ink-stands, and brandy bottles, the latter consisting of humorous, well-modelled figures serving the purpose of spirit bottles, and of others decorated with hunting scenes in relief.

Unfortunately, specimens of Fulham ware are scarce, and it is difficult to meet with well-authenticated stoneware of this pottery. Collectors before paying extravagant prices are advised to examine the few examples in our national collections, from which they will learn something of the characteristics of the grey stoneware of Fulham.

One of the most important pieces of Fulham Delft or stoneware is the famous West Malling jug, which was sold at Christie's in February, 1903. The curious part about this vessel is that it has upon it a rim of silver, hall-marked in 1581. Needless to say, this silver-gilt mount was probably one of an earlier date placed upon the jug, which is of old stoneware splashed purple, green, orange, and other colours. This curious vessel, known as a " stoup," is associated with the village of Malling in Kent, and possessed more than the mere interest usually associated in old stoneware even as rare as authenticated pieces of Dwight's early pottery in Fulham. The price realised was 1,450 guineas.

Mention is made of yet another pottery at Fulham in old records. It appears to have been carried on by one James Roel towards the close of the eighteenth century. It ceased to exist in 1798.

LAMBETH.

The greatest interest in Lambeth pottery centres in the old Delft ware. It is well known that in the seventeenth century a great deal of this curious ware was imported into this country from Holland, and also that many Dutch potters settled in the neighbourhood of London, chiefly in Lambeth. In 1676 John van Hamme and other Dutch potters there carried on the " art of makeinge tiles and porcelane and other earthenwares, after the way practised in Holland." Hamme obtained Letters Patent which protected his recipes and gave him some monopoly ; but he was by no means the first to make Delft ware in England. The earlier Delft pottery made in Lambeth was, however, very crudely ornamented with figures and landscapes painted in blue. There are wine jugs and platters bearing dates between 1650 and 1680, the earliest known piece being dated 1631 ; that, however, is an exceptionally early specimen.

Many of the old Lambeth wares were intended as bottles or jugs for wine, and were branded " CLARET," " SACK," and " WHIT." Then again apothecaries' vessels were made in Lambeth, some bearing the arms of the Apothecaries Company. Hamme made tiles after the pattern of the Dutch Delft tiles, many waste tiles and broken pieces having been found in the neighbourhood.

Apothecaries' jars and pots form almost a separate class, and have a special interest for some collectors. There are good examples of drug-pots in the Bethnal Green Museum. Mr Jewell, perhaps, is one of the best known collectors, and his fine collection may be seen at Heppell's, the chemists, in Piccadilly (*see* chapter xxxviii. and Figs. 93 and 94). Although drawn from many sources, that collection includes quite a number of Lambeth Delft jars and small pots used for unguents. The sack-jars or jugs of Lambeth Delft are, perhaps, the most interesting specimens. They were made for light-coloured Spanish wine, but they were afterwards used for other purposes, in the days when " CLARET " took the place of " SACK." Similar vessels were originally made for the wine imported into England from France.

There are various early specimens of Lambeth pottery and Delft ware in the British Museum and in the Victoria and Albert Museum at South Kensington, including Delft plates, of which there is a set bearing inscriptions which must be read together, the inscriptions of the six plates reading thus :

(1)   What is a Merry Man ?
(2)   Let him do What he can.
(3)   To Entertain his Guests.
(4)   With wine and Merry Jests.
(5)   But if his Wife do frown.
(6)   All merriment Goes down.

Eventually the old Delft ware made at Lambeth was superseded by the brown stoneware, such as was then being made at Fulham. At those works, which were founded in the eighteenth century, the brown stoneware at first formed the chief output. Although there have been several potteries in the neighbourhood of Lambeth and Vauxhall, the one which has gained the greatest notoriety is the large works now owned by Doultons. The Lambeth pottery founded by Mr John Doulton, early in the nineteenth century, was transferred to a small pottery which he founded in conjunction with Mr J. Watts in Vauxhall Walk, in 1815. The works were removed to High Street, Lambeth, in 1826, when the present enormous undertaking was begun in a very small way, the firm of Doulton & Watts then employing about twelve persons, working one kiln a week. Mr Doulton had learned the mysteries of his trade at Fulham, where he had been apprenticed at Dwight's factory. Although gaining world-wide notoriety as makers of works of art, the art pottery of Lambeth scarcely comes within the purview of the connoisseur of old china and pottery. Mention, however, may be made of some of the early productions, such as those commemorative pieces on which Nelson and Wellington figure, and also of the bottles made at the time of the passing of the Reform Act of 1832, when at Lambeth, and in other places, jugs and bottles, the upper portion of which resembled William IV., Earl Grey, John Russell, or some other celebrity of the day, figured. It is noteworthy that salt glaze as applied to decorative pottery was revived at Lambeth, but it died out in other parts of England.

A very fine collection of old Lambeth ware can be seen at any time in the Guildhall Museum, among other objects jars, pitchers, jugs, vases, mugs, posset cups, sack bottles, and barbers' bowls. In the same collection there are many good examples of drug jars on which is highly decorative scroll work, apothecaries' signs, and abbreviated labels.

CHAPTER XII

History of the pottery—The chief wares made in Leeds—Collections
and choice specimens—Marks and characteristics.

THE pottery made in Leeds in the eighteenth century was
in part a continuance of an industry which had been
practised in the neighbourhood for centuries. Indeed,
there are indications that the coarse pottery used chiefly
locally was made in the district in quite early times. It is
probable that the Romans worked clay in the district and
made pottery. Then in mediæval times the wares commonly made in other parts of England, wherever there
were suitable beds of clay, were produced in the neighbourhood of Leeds. The Wortley bed, near Leeds, is peculiarly
well suited to the manufacture of stoneware, and such of
the commoner kinds of earthenware as were then used.
The potters of Leeds would produce similar vessels to those
being made in Staffordshire and other parts of England
where the clay was of a similar nature. It would be
earthenware coated with lead glaze. Mention is also made
of pottery like the black-glazed Jackfield ware having been
made in Leeds. The Wortley clay is by no means ex-
hausted, and in modern times brown stoneware drain-pipes,
sanitary wares, and other specialities have been produced.
All these stonewares, however, are, of course, of not much
importance to the collector of fine pottery and porcelain,
and must not be confused with the pottery of the eighteenth
century made by the firm who founded the noted Leeds
Works somewhere about the year 1760.

HISTORY OF THE POTTERY.

Writers on Leeds pottery take different views about the actual foundation date of the works there; one writer points out that there are much earlier pieces of fine ware extant than pottery which would have been made at a time the works were established by the two brothers Green. It is safe to assert, however, that the actual date of the founding of the pottery at Leeds in the eighteenth century was not later than the year 1760. The works were apparently carried on at first by the two brothers Green; but the Greens sought the assistance of others, and there were several changes in the personnel of the firm; these changes came in rapid succession, and in various ways brought about changes in the class of goods made there, and also in the business relationships of the firm and method of marketing their wares.

In 1774 the firm style of the owners was Humble, Green & Co. Then William Hartley joined John Green and his partners, and some further progress was made. It was during the years immediately following the changes in ownership that some splendid pieces were made, and great improvement was effected in the wares turned out, as may be judged from comparison when examining several pieces of known dates, such, for instance, coffee-pots and jugs, some of which not only bear names of owners but the dates when they were made. Incidentally it may be mentioned that at that time some of the decorated goods known as Leeds ware were made in Staffordshire and finished off in Leeds. It may be pointed out here, too, that in addition to the better-known potters there was at an early date a firm in Leeds who were enamellers and decorators. In the *Leeds Intelligencer* of October 8th, 1760, the following notice appeared :

" Robinson & Rhodes in Briggate, Leeds, undertake to enamel and burn in gold and colour on foreign and English china, and to enamel stone ware which they sell as cheap as in Staffordshire."

It has been pointed out that the best pieces were made at Green's works about 1783 ; at that time the firm's style was Hartley, Greens & Co. The owners threw considerable energy into the enterprise and made much of that very excellent cream-ware which equals if not excels the greater part of the contemporary Staffordshire cream-ware. Leeds potters also succeeded in producing other types of pottery then being made in Staffordshire. These they imitated —it would not be correct to say copied, for there is a distinctive style and appearance about much of the Leeds ware of that day which shows that the Leeds potters were able to strike out in some new directions.

They extended their business, for at that time a considerable export trade was done by them with some continental countries, principally with Russia and Germany. To enable them to successfully handle and develop the foreign trade, Hartley, Greens & Co. published an important catalogue, giving copious descriptions of their goods in English, German, French, and Spanish. This must have had good results, for the catalogue passed through several editions ; the first was printed in 1783, the second in 1785, another edition appeared in 1794, and in 1815 there was a reprint with some additions.

William Hartley was a keen business man and possessed the necessary capital ; these qualities and financial status, in conjunction with Green's practical technical knowledge, helped the firm to bring out many new designs and to produce some of those exceptional pieces now so much sought after.

Mr Humble had retired in 1781, and Hartley died in 1820. The loss of such a sound business man as Hartley was the cause of the decline of the concern, which, however, was continued by the other partners until 1825, when it was disposed of to Wainwright & Co. Wainwright died in 1834, and for a time the works were owned by Stephen and James Capel ; more changes followed, and eventually the works were closed. It is, however, not in the later days of the Leeds Pottery that collectors are interested, for it is the beautiful ware of the eighteenth century they seek to procure. The proprietors of the Leeds Pottery during its best days were also associated with other potteries, a point of some importance to the connoisseur. John Green and other partners in the Leeds Works were part owners of the Swinton Works, afterwards known as the Rockingham Works (*see* chapter xvi.); indeed, both works are said to have been under the same management.

We find that the Greens as a family were also associated with some other undertakings. It was John Green, probably a son of John Green, senior, of Leeds Works, who was one of the proprietors of the Don Pottery. This John Green, or a namesake of his of the same family, commenced business at a small pottery at Kilnhurst, near Rotherham, towards the end of the eighteenth century. He was joined in his undertaking by a man of the name of Clarke, and we find that the works were carried on under the title or firm style of Green, Clarke & Co.

This, briefly recorded, is the story of the founding of the Leeds Pottery by the Greens, and their long connection with the undertaking and similar undertakings in the neighbourhood ; it will enable collectors to understand to some extent the controlling influences which operated in the manufacture of Leeds ware.

THE CHIEF WARES MADE IN LEEDS.

As it has been suggested, much of the work carried on

at the Leeds Pottery was identical with that of many potters in Staffordshire. Perhaps one of the earlier types of pottery made in Leeds was the mottled or tortoiseshell ware, much of which was slip-decorated, the clays being coloured with various oxides. The groundwork of this ware consisted of a cream-ware body, ornamented with coloured slip. The agate ware, which was then made of different coloured clays, a speciality favoured so much by Wedgwood, was produced in Leeds, the mottled pattern popular there appearing in bands, some of the decoration having evidently been applied by a feather, and possibly combed over.

Black Egyptian ware, similar to some of the Staffordshire wares, was made in Leeds. The articles produced were chiefly teapots, cups and saucers, sugar basins, slop bowls, butter pots, and some very fine coffee-pots. It was not until about 1790 that blue-printed ware was made at Leeds, but soon after its introduction it became one of the chief products. Enamel printing and water gilding were applied to cream-coloured ware with excellent effect, and it has been suggested that some of the Leeds cream-ware was sent to Liverpool to Sadler & Green, who were at that time decorating by their patent process printed wares for Staffordshire potters.

About the year 1800 some of the Leeds ware resembled Wedgwood's " Pearl," and much of it is extremely decorative. Lustre ware was a special feature at Leeds, where the potters appear to have been very successful with their metallic compounds, using platinum for their silver ware. The process is described as platinum dissolved in *aqua regia*, added to three parts of spirits of tar, applied with a brush over brown earthenware and then fired. The ware then received a second coat, which gave it a full and rich appearance, oxide of platinum produced by sal ammoniac being applied. After the application the ware was fired in a muffle kiln at a low heat. Silver lustre was also used on a cream body, and in that way some very attractive tea- and coffee-sets were produced. Again, copper lustre ware was a speciality at Leeds, chiefly employed about 1820 to 1825, the copper used being amalgamated with a small quantity of gold, producing a fine copper colour. Another speciality is known as purple lustre, a tint almost approaching rose colour (*see* chapter xxxviii.).

Much of the Leeds ware was essentially utilitarian, and druggists' jars, and drug pots and other vessels for traders' use, were made.

COLLECTIONS AND CHOICE SPECIMENS.

It is very difficult to judge correctly of the chief features noticeable in Leeds ware from the isolated examples found in general collections; and even the national collections of ceramics in public museums do not adequately represent Leeds ware. Fortunately there are a few enthusiastic collectors who have specialised on this ware, and have secured representative examples as the result of careful search, hunting up choice specimens and representative pieces wherever they could be met with. Illustrations Figs. 4 and 5 represent a portion of the very large collection of Leeds ware gathered together by Mr A. E. Clarke, of Cambridge. It will be noticed from the illustrations that while these objects are almost essentially utilitarian, consisting of tea china and useful table ware, they possess more than ordinary interest on account of the curious mottoes, historical references, legends, and inscriptions upon them. Many are inscribed with the names of the persons for whom they were originally made. Thus, on a teapot in this collection, illustrated, may be seen, " Mary Marten, Let Virtue be the Fair One's Guide. I. B. 1776." On another, " John & Mary Wheeldon, 1772."

Another curious-looking teapot has for its central inscription, " Love and Live Happy." One mug is inscribed, " Clarke for Ever." Another teapot has the usual Grace inscribed upon it :

> " Be present at our table, Lord,
> Be here and everywhere adored,
> Thy creatures bless, and grant that we
> May feast in paradise with Thee."

Some vases are known, but they are very scarce, and few of them authentic. Some statuettes and busts were undoubtedly made at Leeds, one well-known pair being " Air " and " Water," and there is a famous group entitled " Grief." The figures have been described as of three types, those of plain cream-ware, figures with a white body and a bluish uneven glaze, and painted figures. The Leeds firm issued an important catalogue from which some of their wares are named and recognised, and curiously enough a similar catalogue, almost identical, was published in connection with the Don Pottery at Doncaster, with which Mr John Green was connected. Indeed, some authorities have regarded the Don Pottery as a branch of the Leeds Works.

MARKS AND CHARACTERISTICS.

There are two ways of identifying pottery ; one, the easiest, of course, is by the marks, the other, relied upon chiefly by experts, is the characteristics of paste, glaze, and decoration, and to some extent of form. The Leeds marks vary, but consist chiefly of the name of the pottery or the name of the firm. In the form indicated the two words, " LEEDS POTTERY," impressed twice, crosswise, may be regarded as the earliest. Most of the pottery made during the ownership of Hartley, Greens & Co. was marked " HARTLEY, GREENS, & Co. LEEDS POTTERY," in two lines.

Among the characteristics which should be regarded as indicative of the peculiarities of Leeds ware, it is pointed out that the black basalt ware was engine-turned after having been completed, the mark being impressed while the paste was in a soft state, consequently the turning sometimes completely removed the mark, or defaced a considerable portion of it. Many of the black basalt teapots are marked under the rim, and sometimes under the spout or handle, where the impress would be out of the way of the tooling which black basalt ware was frequently subjected to. Characteristic of some of the Leeds ornament was the diamond or heart-shaped piercings, effected by a hand punch in the soft clay.

The Leeds cream-ware was of a rich cream colour, and not as yellow as some of Wedgwood's earlier wares. It was also very glossy, and the glaze was hard. It has been stated that under certain lights there is a peculiar greenness about the cream shade, contrasting with the yellowness of some cream-ware. The hard glaze has helped to preserve the appearance of Leeds cream-ware, whereas much of the Staffordshire cream-ware is badly scratched owing to its softer nature. As it has been suggested, most of the Leeds ware was utilitarian. From the catalogue issued, and also from some of the finer examples in noted collections, it is evident there were exceptions to the rule. There are some very fine centre-pieces ; and Leeds candlesticks are noted for their beautiful decoration. The different objects were carefully designed, something very light and graceful in appearance, the decorations often consisting of fluted bands and feather-edged moulding.

CHAPTER XIII

ENGLISH—LIVERPOOL

Local Potters : Shaw—Chaffers—Pennington—Barnes—Herculaneum
Pottery—Sadler—Other potters.

COLLECTORS of Liverpool wares have to consider and
classify their specimens according to the several potteries
with which they were associated, for the potters of Liverpool worked independently of one another, and there were
several distinct factories.

It is true there are specimens of seventeenth-century
earthenware, known as " cupps and muggs," which were
at that time made in considerable quantities, but there
are few in collectors' cabinets.

The great wave of potting enthusiasm which was experienced in Staffordshire was felt in Liverpool, and in the
eighteenth century, when so many works were being
established in other parts of the country, quite a little
group of Liverpool potters left their mark on the industry.
Although they were established for the most part in the
neighbourhood of Shaw's Brow, where Shaw's Delft Works
were first erected, they worked independently, and like so
many of the Staffordshire potters on different lines, concurrently. According to the *Liverpool Directory* of 1769,
there were at that time fully twenty proprietors of pot
works.

The Liverpool potters and potteries to which special
reference must be made include Chaffers, Shaw, Sadler,
Pennington, Christian, and the Herculaneum Pottery,

FIG. 42.—PLATE made at the Herculaneum Pottery, Liverpool.
(Part of the Town Hall Service.)

FIG. 43.—TRANSFER-PRINTED DISH (View of Lord Street, Liverpool).
Herculaneum Pottery.

In the Liverpool Museum.

[To face page 144.

FIG. 44.
PORCELAIN PLATE,
Liverpool.

FIG. 45.
BAT-PRINTED
ENAMELLED JUG.

FIG. 46.
BLUE PRINTED PLATE, by Pennington.
In the Liverpool Museum.

To face page 145.]

the last named surviving until 1836, when it was closed down.

The Free Public Museums of Liverpool contain a very representative collection of Liverpool pottery and porcelain, some of the most important pieces of which are illustrated here by the courtesy of the museum authorities. Several of these are the products of the Herculaneum Pottery. Fig. 42 is one of the plates of the celebrated Town Hall service; it is a fine porcelain plate, in the centre of which are the Arms of the City, the whole of the ground and rim being covered with a handsome pattern; this service was made at the Herculaneum Pottery. Another fine transfer printed dish, also from the Herculaneum Pottery, is shown in Fig. 43; the centre view represents Lord Street, Liverpool, as it was when the plate was made. Fig. 44 is an excellent example of a service printed with scenes; in this instance there is a picture of a waterfall in the centre and pretty little scenes at the sides. Fig. 45 is a bat-printed enamelled jug; both these pieces were made at the Herculaneum Pottery. Fig. 46 is a plate showing quite a different style of decoration and one which is associated with the pottery made at seaport towns. It shows a ship of the period in full sail, the legend reading, " SUCCESS TO THE R. BIBBY "; the plate, which is of blue printed porcelain, was made by Pennington.

SHAW.

The Delft works at Shaw's Brow were founded by Alderman Shaw in 1710. He occupied his attention chiefly in the manufacture of so-called Liverpool jugs, made of a ware which was much inferior in quality to the Delft ware made at Lambeth as regards the enamelling; but the transfer decoration on the Liverpool Delft ware contrasted favourably with most of the contemporary

K

decoration. A considerable portion of the output of Alderman Shaw's works consisted of tiles, which differed from the original Dutch tiles in that the edges were almost invariably bevelled to grip the cement, whereas collectors of tiles will have noticed that the old Dutch tiles are always square on the edges (*see* chapter xxxiv.).

Another important section of Shaw's works was devoted to the manufacture of domestic wares, among which jugs and bowls were very prominent. These were chiefly ornamented with picture scenes, rendering them peculiarly interesting to local collectors, in that the scenes chosen were taken from pictures and engravings of then familiar objects in the neighbourhood, including buildings and scenery.

It is evident that a very determined effort was made by Alderman Shaw about the year 1716 to improve upon the older crude English wares for which Liverpool had been noted at an earlier date. This is abundantly evidenced by the pictorial ornamented Delft ware already referred to, a good example of which is found in an enamelled Delft plaque on which is a landscape entitled, " West Prospect of Great Crosby." This and other similar pieces are dated and marked.

Connoisseurs of collections of Liverpool ware will have noticed that some of Shaw's pieces were large and imposing. These, needless to say, attract the attention of the collector, especially those beautiful punch bowls, some of which were covered with local scenes; others, emblematical of the town, represent nautical views and ships of olden type like the plate illustrated. Some of these bowls, too, were presentation bowls and inscribed. In the Mayer Museum there is a bowl bearing the following inscription, " Made for Captain Metcalfe, who commanded *The Golden Lion,* which was the first vessel that sailed out of Liverpool on the whale fishery and Greenland trade, and was presented to him on his return from his second voyage by his employers, who were a company composed of the principal merchants of Liverpool, in the year 1753."

In those days fish seems to have been one of the special delicacies for which special plates and dishes and other vessels were made. Thus Delft char-pots, or dishes for a char—a variety of the salmonoid family—were made in Delft, coated with tin enamel. Another variety of Liverpool ware is found in the drug-pots which were made at the works of Alderman Shaw and other manufacturers; many of these old apothecaries' jars, in blue and white enamel, and appropriately lettered, are among the collectable objects of the present day, unfortunately getting more difficult to obtain every year. Yet so slow has been the change in many of the chemists' shops in out-of-the-way country towns that it is quite possible to come across an apothecary's shop in which some of the old Liverpool Delft ware jars are still in use, containing the drugs indicated by the exterior lettering (*see* chapter xxxviii.).

CHAFFERS.

Richard Chaffers, who was born in 1731, served an apprenticeship to Alderman Shaw, and at Shaw's Brow Works learned his trade. At the early age of twenty-one years he commenced in business as a potter on his own account. At first he tried his hand at the manufacture of white earthenware, such as was then being brought into Liverpool from the Staffordshire Potteries. He met with much opposition, however, and was not able to compete successfully in the manufacture of common earthenware with the larger firms who had greater facilities, and were producing it in much larger quantities. He then turned his attention to producing a better class of ware, and found that which suited his needs in porcelain. Unfortunately, however, the supply of Cornish clay ran short. Cookworthy of Plymouth had at that time obtained a lease of the only Cornish mine where the right clay was known to exist. For a time therefore the enterprise of Chaffers was defeated by the monopoly Cookworthy had secured.

Chaffers, nothing daunted, determined to discover a new vein of soap rock which would serve his purpose, and with that object in view he set out on a journey on horseback to Cornwall, a by no means easy undertaking in the middle of the eighteenth century. Having accomplished his journey without any untoward accident, he at once engaged the services of several miners, and with his small force set out on his prospecting expedition.

At first Chaffers met with nothing but disappointment; indeed, it was only when he was on the point of returning somewhat disheartened, without having found the much-needed material, that one of the men with him struck an excellent vein. Chaffers was not long in securing the rights of excavation, and with mining rights in his possession he soon obtained a sufficient supply of the raw material. In due course this was transported to Liverpool, and some excellent china resulted.

Chaffers did not follow stereotyped lines, and seems to have been always devising some fresh product to put on the market. One of his best known novelties was a sand box of hour-glass shape, which was dubbed " Dick's pepper-box." It was decorated in blue enamelled ornament, the border being of chequered design, the name of the maker in large type appearing round the box, reading thus, " RICHARD CHAFFERS 1769." In the present day such an article would have been deemed an excellent advertisement. Whether that was Chaffers' object we cannot tell, but certain it is that " Dick's pepper-box " has made Richard Chaffers very familiar to connoisseurs of ceramic art in the twentieth century.

Richard Chaffers not only showed enterprise in obtaining the materials he needed from a new source, and in designing curious objects and using novel ornament, but he gained much notoriety as an expert colour mixer. His fame spread, for the great master potter of Staffordshire, Josiah Wedgwood, wrote of his successes thus : " This puts an end to the battle. Mr Chaffers beats us all in his colours, and with his knowledge he can make colours for two guineas which I cannot produce good for five."

The dates to be remembered in connection with Chaffers may be briefly enumerated. His works were established in 1752 ; in 1756 he obtained soap rock from Cornwall ; and he died in 1767.

With so much promise of a successful career it was sad that Richard Chaffers caught a fever, from which he died, through visiting a workman who was ill with a malignant and infectious disease. At his death the concern was broken up. Many of the workmen who had been employed by Chaffers emigrated to America ; a few of the more skilled operatives went to Staffordshire, where they obtained employment with Wedgwood and others.

PENNINGTON.

Another well-known manufacturer in Liverpool was John Pennington, who commenced business in 1760, his career there terminating in 1790. His chief products were punch bowls, tea-services, and some vases. He worked in soft paste, using for his china body bone ash and Lynn sand. He seems to have favoured Oriental decorations, some remarkably fine Oriental-like china being made and decorated in a beautiful blue. So closely did these products imitate Oriental porcelain that they are often mistaken for it. He possessed a recipe for a rich blue, which he jealously guarded. So highly was this colouring appreciated by other potters who recognised its beauty, that on one occasion it was said he was offered 1,000 guineas by a well-known Staffordshire House for the recipe. This he refused. Unfortunately Pennington's brother, who had learned the secret, when the worse for liquor gave it away to one of his companions, and thus for a comparatively small sum the recipe became known in Staffordshire. So the story runs. It was probably due to the secret of his rare colouring having become known, and, therefore, the monopoly he possessed having been destroyed, that Pennington determined to close his pottery. This, however, was not before many remarkable pieces had been produced. One of the most noted was a large punch bowl measuring upwards of 20 in. in diameter, the painting upon it having been executed by John Robinson. This celebrated bowl was ultimately presented to the Pottery Mechanics' Institution at Shelton.

Comparatively few of Pennington's wares were marked. Some, however, are marked " P " in gold or colours.

BARNES.

Zachariah Barnes was born in 1743 at Warrington. He commenced business as a potter in the Old Haymarket, and specialised on several different classes of goods; making china and also Delft ware. Among the latter were many druggists' pots and large dishes. The quality of his ware was rather coarse, coated with a thick tin glaze. He seems to have cultivated a trade in North Wales, and also in the English Lake District, to both places sending supplies. It was his custom to attend the annual fairs at Chester, and there to dispose of a considerable quantity of china and Delft ware to the Welsh people who came down from the mountain districts to buy on those occasions. His decorations were chiefly flowers and landscapes and ships, usually painted in blue.

Barnes was also a tile maker, producing tiles on the Dutch pattern about 5 in. square, very thin, but remarkably hard and very suitable for lining walls and fireplaces. These, too, were well ornamented. Zachariah Barnes died in 1820, when his works were given up.

HERCULANEUM POTTERY.

Richard Abbey, in conjunction with a Scotchman named Graham, founded a pottery on the south shore of the Mersey about 1790, and there made some excellent pottery. It is said that Abbey caught the idea of naming his works " Herculaneum " in that Josiah Wedgwood had then named his works near Stoke " Etruria." The pottery was situated on the site of an old copper works, and the fact that much of the ware made during the early years of the pottery had a greenish tinge is attributed to that cause, for it is said the buildings, ground, and even the neighbourhood were impregnated with tiny particles of copper.

Apparently Abbey had no great love for the industry, his interests tending towards rural occupations rather than manufacture and trade ; therefore, he soon abandoned the business, and sold the works to Worthington & Co., who for a time used the same mark adopted by Abbey, which was a crown, above which in a semicircle was " HERCULANEUM."

The Company, which at first continued the blue painted wares, soon began to make china, introducing it about the year 1800. They produced some very pretty pieces covered with flowers and birds, the enamelled colours being enriched with much gilding. Worthington & Co. also made wares transfer-printed in black. In 1833 the Company sold their interests to Thomas Case and John Mort, by whom the works were carried on until 1836 ; afterwards the firm became Mort & Simpson, until 1841, when the works were closed, and the site was used for the construction of the Herculaneum Dock.

The marks used at the Herculaneum Works were somewhat varied. After the earliest marks already referred to the crown was enclosed within a garter, on which was inscribed " HERCULANEUM " ; then for a time the name only was used, that being printed in blue. Throughout the closing years of the career of this enterprise the firm used an impress of the liver, the bird from which Liverpool took its name, the memory of which is still retained in the arms of the city. Another mark of occasional use was " LIVERPOOL," and beneath it an anchor.

SADLER.

John Sadler, who founded a small pottery in Harrington Street, Liverpool, was the son of a painter, and he laid claim to the discovery of the art of printing upon pottery, an invention which he worked out in conjunction with a Mr Green. They kept their invention secret without taking out patent rights. Wedgwood, ever keenly alive to any improvements, sent some of his ware to Sadler & Green to be decorated by the new process they had adopted. It was conveyed to Liverpool by wagon, and returned again by the same conveyance to Burslem. This somewhat laborious method of producing earthenware decorated by the printing process discovered by Sadler & Green was continued by Wedgwood until his death in 1795 (*see* chapter xxii.).

It is interesting to recall the source from which Mr Sadler obtained his first idea of the possibilities of printing pottery. It is said that he noticed that some children to whom he had given waste prints placed portions of them upon broken pottery, thus giving him the idea, which after some unsuccessful attempts enabled him to discover how to transfer a print to an enamelled surface. The colours used were black, purple, red, puce, and sometimes green. The subjects chosen for transfer decoration were public characters, including actors and actresses. There were also some caricatures, and some quaint little pictures drawn from Æsop's fables. Examples of Sadler & Green's wares include mugs, teapots, and jugs; the mark used by this firm was first " SADLER " and then " SADLER & GREEN."

OTHER POTTERS.

There were a few other potters in Liverpool, of which mention should be made. One of these was Philip Christian, who at one time had a pottery at Shaw's Brow. It was he who purchased Chaffers' lease of the vein of soap rock in Cornwall, selling it again, however, to the owners of the Worcester Works in 1775. Christian made some ornamental china, including large vases, also producing some excellent tortoiseshell ware.

George Drinkwater was a noted Delft ware potter, who had a factory in Pothouse Lane, but unfortunately there are no marks or any distinctive characteristics by which his pottery can be distinguished from that of contemporary potters in Liverpool at that time.

William Reid & Co. were makers of blue and white china in Liverpool from 1756 to 1760. Their works were situated in Castle Street. The ware they made was similar to Staffordshire goods, and there does not appear to have been any distinguishing mark by which collectors could identify it.

CHAPTER XIV

ENGLISH—LOWESTOFT

The site of the old works—Discoveries of importance—Museum examples—Typical illustrations.

ONE of the most vexed subjects of porcelain collecting is that which surrounds Lowestoft china. Although the excavations on the site of the old pottery which took place some years ago threw light upon much that had been obscured, it by no means solved to the satisfaction of all the problem as to what wares were actually made at Lowestoft, or the full extent of the decorations carried out there. Until those discoveries were made in 1902 there were many who had collected so-called Lowestoft china—but now known to be Oriental—because of its beauty, its decorative effects, and pleasing representations of the old English rose and of sprays of flowers, which appeared to many conclusive evidence that the decoration was effected in England by English artists. The custodians of our national collections never admitted these features as being conclusive evidence, and contented themselves with labelling a few examples of undoubted Lowestoft as such, now and then indicating, in deference to the opinions of some collectors, certain examples in the collections that might possibly have been decorated at the Lowestoft Works.

THE SITE OF THE OLD WORKS.

It seems curious that in a little place like Lowestoft so little was then known about the old works or their

FIG. 47.—THREE LOWESTOFT MUGS decorated in underglaze blue,
Oriental taste.

In the Collection of Mr. Merrington Smith.

FIG. 48.

INKSTAND, inscribed "A Trifle
from Lowestoft."

In the Collection of Mrs. Benger.

FIG. 49.

A rare LOWESTOFT MUG.

*In the Collection of Mr.
Merrington Smith.*

[To face page 154.

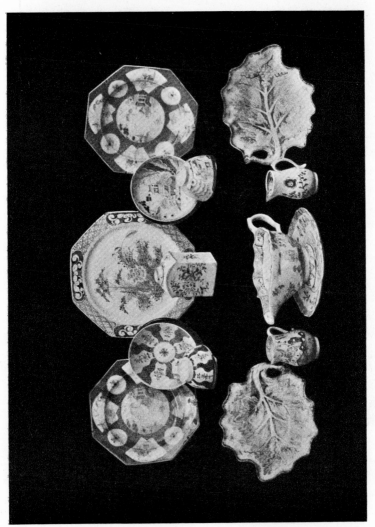

FIG. 50.—BLUE AND WHITE LOWESTOFT, some marked pieces.

In the Collection of Mr. Cecil G. Taylor.

To face page 155.]

productions. Research into records, in addition to the discoveries made in 1902, have revealed perhaps all that will ever be known of the true story of the Lowestoft potteries and of the china made there. It is an admitted fact that some very interesting pieces were produced in Lowestoft, useful and in some instances very ornamental. The genuine authentic specimens of tea china, mugs, cups, and inkstands are few enough, but there are sufficient to indicate the class of ware turned out from the old potteries, and also to show that many of them were intended as gift pieces, souvenirs of Lowestoft. As the result of recent research it is now pretty well agreed that the pottery was founded somewhere about 1756, and that its career ended about 1802—curiously enough, just one hundred years before the discoveries were made which led to a more satisfactory statement of the disputed works and their output.

Apparently Mr Hewlin Luson found clay on his estate which he believed would be suitable for the manufacture of fine porcelain or china. Mr A. Merrington Smith, of Lowestoft, whose name is closely associated with the discoveries subsequently made, in a very pleasing booklet he issued some time ago, gives a photograph of the Warren House, Denes, North Lowestoft, where clay for the manufacture of Lowestoft china was discovered. It appears that Mr Luson was not altogether successful in the steps he took to put to practical use the clay he had carefully analysed. Soon afterwards, however, a company was formed, the partners being Walker, Browne, Aldred, and Rickman, and they were fortunate in securing some clever workmen. We learn that about 1770 Robert Browne & Co., as the firm was then styled, opened a warehouse in London, and were then in a position to manufacture and supply a considerable variety of pieces. They succeeded to so great an extent that their productions came under the notice of Wedgwood, who procured specimens, and evidently was interested in what was going on in the little pottery so far removed from his own works.

The Lowestoft china actually made by this firm, when compared with Oriental porcelain, such as was once commonly called " Lowestoft " or " Oriental Lowestoft," is very different indeed, although there are some similar characteristics in the style of decoration. It may be mentioned here that the Chinese, who were then manufacturing for the English market, did their best to produce goods acceptable to English buyers, and very cleverly painted English roses and other flowers. The success of their tea china was acknowledged by all the potters, and the Lowestoft makers seem to have specially endeavoured to copy the Oriental, those Oriental designs or sprays of flowers which were particularly acceptable in the English market. To some extent they succeeded, and therefore, although there does not appear to be any actual proof of such work, it is quite possible that some of the plainer Oriental pieces of hard paste porcelain were further ornamented at Lowestoft, and finished in a muffle kiln.

DISCOVERIES OF IMPORTANCE.

It was not until 1902 that Mr A. Merrington Smith, in consequence of some alterations going on at the brewery occupying the site of the old pottery, learnt from the workmen employed there that some pieces of moulds and scraps of pottery had been discovered. It was then that, in conjunction with one or two others, Mr Smith obtained permission to further examine the floor of the malt kiln, which was evidently in an undisturbed portion of the old pottery. The result of extensive excavations brought to light quite a number of moulds and fragments. The moulds were in a bad state, having been buried so long—

Fig. 51.—Small Service of Lowestoft Ware, Oriental taste.

In the Collection of Mr. Merrington Smith.

FIG. 52.—LOWESTOFT FIGURE in colours; subject, "Winter."

In the Collection of Mr. Cecil G. Taylor.

To face page 157.]

practically a hundred years—but by careful handling many were secured intact. The moulds, which were made of plaster of Paris, were those which had been used in the making of cups, basins, cream-jugs, sauce-boats, and tea-pots, representing just those pieces which have been treasured in public and in private collections as undoubted Lowestoft. There were some fragments of Oriental porcelain which it is thought may have been used as examples from which to copy. A few fragments of figures, too, were found, indicating that probably some ornamental pottery, as well as the utilitarian, was made at Lowestoft. The fragments, which were numerous and represented a number of different broken pieces, were of soft paste. In that they differed from Oriental china, and from any of those pieces which were at one time thought to have been made, or at any rate decorated and finished, at Lowestoft. The soft paste of Lowestoft was produced by the introduction of soap rock or bone earth, and not China clay added to the local clays.

It may be of interest to collectors to have before them the exact analysis of fragments found at Lowestoft in 1902, which was as follows : Loss on ignition, 0·18 ; silica, 42·02 ; alumina (with a trace of iron), 6·56 ; lime, 26·44 ; phosphoric acid, 22·21 ; magnesia, 0·62 ; soda, 0·82 ; and potash, 0·70.

The genuine Lowestoft specimens have a creamy appearance and colouring, but the glaze seems to have been used with a view to hiding that tint and giving the Lowestoft china an Oriental appearance. Most of the soft paste was softer than the soft-paste china made in other potteries. Again, it should be remarked that there is often a green or bluish-green tinge in the glaze, but that does not apply to all specimens. It was a clear glaze, however, though sometimes applied rather thickly. It has been pointed out that as a characteristic of the methods of manufacture adopted at Lowestoft, the lids of teapots were glazed all over the flange, whereas in Worcester portions were left unglazed.   There is no doubt from the styles of ornament found on some of the china that the decorations, especially the floral decorations at Bow, Bristol, Caughley, and other potteries, as well as those on Oriental china, were copied, there being very little originality noticeable in the Lowestoft designs.   There are few marked pieces, and, as there have been many forgeries, no reliance can be placed upon so-called Lowestoft marks.

MUSEUM EXAMPLES.

The examples which are reproduced through the courtesy of Mr Merrington Smith are taken from his own collection and those of a few well-known connoisseurs of Lowestoft china.   They are characteristic of the different kinds of decoration adopted, and also represent the typical inscription, " A Trifle from Lowestoft."   Visitors to the ceramic galleries at the Victoria and Albert Museum at South Kensington will recall the few examples there, the inscribed mug and the inscribed inkstand, and a few other pieces, all of similar types.   There is the ribbon and wreath decoration and the sprays so characteristic of much of the silversmiths' ornament used at that period.   Many pieces decorated in blue, although differing from the Worcester wares, remind the collector of the decoration used at Worcester.   The dated jugs, mugs, and other pieces mostly give the names of local families, and were probably made as presentation cups for persons either interested in or connected with the works, or with their friends.   Among early dated museum pieces recorded there is one, " ABRM. MOORE, 1765 "; and another, " JOHN MOORE, YAR- MOUTH, 1782."

In reference to form, there are so few examples on view in

the public museums that it is difficult to obtain an accurate opinion as to the characteristic shapes, but those who have had opportunities of examining some of the old moulds found under the floor of the malt kiln will be able to realise special types. Some of these moulds are in very good preservation. There is a case of casts taken from them shown in the British Museum, the originals being in the possession of Mr F. A. Crisp. Mr A. Merrington Smith, too, has some of the originals.

The scarcity and even rarity of genuine Lowestoft china makes it almost prohibitive as a popular hobby, and the pitfalls that beset the unwary when collecting make it exceedingly difficult for any but experts who have studied Lowestoft in every possible way to make sure that they are obtaining genuine or authentic pieces. Dealers have for so many years been accustomed to label Orientally decorated hard-paste porcelain with the floral sprays associated with Lowestoft as genuine Lowestoft china, that they still continue, sometimes in a very barefaced way, to assure buyers that the objects they are offering them are genuine Lowestoft, whereas when such pieces and Lowestoft pottery or porcelain are put side by side the difference both in texture of paste, in glaze and in colouring, is quite obvious.

Typical Illustrations.

The exceptionally choice examples of Lowestoft china illustrated are taken from the collections of Mr Cecil G. Taylor, Mr Merrington Smith of Lowestoft, and Mrs Benger of Colwyn Bay, and are as follows : Fig. 47, three mugs decorated in under-glaze blue with red and gilt over-glaze, all very rare and most brilliant in colour ; Fig. 48, an inkpot inscribed, " A Trifle from Lowestoft," in blue and white ; Fig. 49, a mug, in colour, decorated with cornflowers, and inscribed like Fig. 48 ; Fig. 50, a group of blue and white ; the centre plate has a workman's number on the back, and the tea-caddy has a copy of a Worcester mark upon it ; Fig. 51, a small service in red and gilt (blue under-glaze) ; it is of Oriental taste and of the design known as the " Cock " pattern ; Fig. 52, a figure, the subject being " Winter," is decorated in colours ; and Fig. 53, a group of blue and white, including pickle dishes, cream-boats of dolphin form, sauce-boats with raised chrysanthemums corresponding with moulds discovered, and a large bowl decorated in the Oriental style.

Mr Merrington Smith's collection is varied and includes many choice examples. There is a sauce-boat in blue and white with raised fruit decoration, illustrated in Fig. 54, an unusual piece. Some of the pottery is richly coloured, as the two bowls shown in Fig. 55.

FIG. 53.—GROUP OF BLUE AND WHITE LOWESTOFT WARE.
In the Collection of Mr. Cecil G. Taylor.

[To face page 160.

FIG. 54.—SAUCEBOAT in blue and white, with raised fruit decorations.

FIG. 55.—TWO BOWLS in colours.
In the Collection of Mr. Merrington Smith.

To face page 161.]

CHAPTER XV

Curious Nottingham pottery—Cookworthy's Plymouth china.

MANY writers on old pottery are almost silent about the Nottingham potteries, and yet, although there is not much to relate, that little is of great interest, not only to local collectors, but to collectors as a body.

Local records tell us clearly that there was a prosperous industry in the manufacture of pottery carried on at Nottingham from 1641 onwards. It was, however, not until the early years of the eighteenth century that the Nottingham pottery acquired any great notoriety. We learn from *The Annals of Nottinghamshire*, written in 1757, that Charles Morley was a maker of brown stoneware mugs and jugs. The author of the annals says : " Mr Morley was a maker of brown earthenware carrying on his work in the lower part of Beck Street on the road to St Ann's well, and by this business he amassed a very considerable fortune." The writer then proceeds to point out that Nottingham was celebrated at an earlier date for its brown earthenware, for he says : " The ware was at one time of great celebrity throughout the whole of the Midland Counties, especially its famous brown mugs for the use of public houses ; and the appellation of Nottingham ware is still in many remote villages attached to the better and more highly finished class of earthenware pots of every description. In 1726 Charles Morley carried on an extensive business, making jugs and mugs of brown stoneware, some exceedingly smooth.

Their rich warm brown tint, sometimes ranging from red to yellow, being noticeable in the examples which may be seen at the Castle Museum at Nottingham. The memory of the old works was long maintained in the name of Mug House Lane." The salt glaze Nottingham stoneware had a slightly lustrous appearance. It was very hard, the metallic lustre being ornamented with double and triple incised bands. As regards these old wares there are some very fine stoneware punch bowls; one remarkable bowl long exhibited in the Museum of Practical Geology in London was a splendid example. Then there are mugs, tobacco jars, and puzzle jugs.

Curious Nottingham Pottery.

The tobacco jar made in Nottingham was a curious vessel in the form of a bear; the coat of the bear was roughened by fragments of potsherd sprinkled over the surface. There are several varieties of these old bear jars and jugs, all of which are now scarce. It is said one of the rarest varieties represents a Russian bear hugging Napoleon Bonaparte, who wears a plumed hat. The clay for the Nottingham stone pottery came partly from the East Moor in Derbyshire, and the finished ware is of darker tint than the stoneware made in Fulham and Lambeth. The best examples are found in the local museums; an excellent Nottingham jug is on view in the Lichfield Museum.

Plymouth China
(Cookworthy's Porcelain).

The porcelain which was produced so successfully in Plymouth was the result of discoveries made by William Cookworthy, who, although not a potter by profession, was a keenly observant chemist, and a man of much natural ability.

Cookworthy, who was born in Devonshire in 1705, settled in Plymouth and engaged in business as a chemist and druggist. When on a visit to Cornwall this observant chemist noted the peculiarity of the china clay he saw, and discovered " china stone " in Tregonning Hill. He secured some of the Cornish ingredients and set about making experiments with the clay, which he found to be infusible, and also with the fusible felspar stone. As the result of numerous experiments in china making and firing in a small kiln he had set up, William Cookworthy secured patent rights and began to manufacture porcelain, after the manner of the Chinese porcelain he sought to copy. The paste he compounded proved satisfactory, as well as the special glaze he used, his kilns being heated with wood— then a fuel plentiful in the neighbourhood.

When Cookworthy's business grew he sought financial aid, Thomas Pitt, afterwards created Lord Camelford, becoming his patron and assisting him with money.

Cookworthy, describing the china earth he had dis- covered, said it was in every way equal for the purposes of china-making to that used by the Chinese and other Asiatics. At that time, about the year 1768, Cookworthy had had no experience as a potter, and knew little of the business of china-making or how to conduct such an enterprise pro- fitably. He built works at Coxside, Plymouth, and employed clever workmen, who assisted him in throwing much originality into the design and in the decoration of the pieces he produced. One of the most noteworthy of the artists he employed was Soqui or Sequoi, a French painter.

The leading scheme of ornament used was an arrange- ment of sea-shells resting upon coral. Some very beautiful centre-pieces, salt-cellars, and vases were made, both in white and coloured. The white ware is chiefly unmarked, but the blue and white is often marked in blue, the distinguishing mark being the chemist's sign for tin, usually painted in blue, and occasionally in red and in other colours, under the glaze.

Cookworthy, under the style of Cookworthy & Co., carried on the china factory until the year 1773, when Richard Champion, who had been experimenting in porcelain for some time before, acquired Cookworthy's patent, the works being eventually transferred to Bristol, on Castle Green. Genuine Plymouth porcelain is undoubtedly rare, although it does not fetch quite the high prices commanded by some of the better known and much admired porcelains of English make.

Fig. v.   Fig. vi.   Fig. vii.   Fig. viii.

PLYMOUTH.—A few of the commoner marks used at Plymouth.

The Plymouth marks are curious; most of them were taken from the chemical signs for metals. Those shown in the accompanying illustrations (*see* Figs. v., vi., vii., viii.) indicate those frequently seen upon early specimens. There are some, however, which are of a more elaborate type, in which are incorporated date and place-name, together with the arms of the town, the letters " C. F." in script indicating their origin (Cookworthy's Factory).

CHAPTER XVI

Rockingham ware—Some remarkable examples—Rockingham marks.

THE estates of Charles, Marquis of Rockingham, in York-shire, were in the neighbourhood of Swinton, near Rother-ham. It was there that Edward Butler established a pottery and worked the clays which he had obtained on the adjoining common lands. That was in the middle of the eighteenth century, the pottery produced at those works gaining more than local reputation.

The works were afterwards tenanted by Mr William Malpass, who worked them in 1765; and he continued them some years, but transferred the ownership to Thomas Bingley in 1778, under whose management the works were found too small for the then improving business, and Bingley built new kilns and otherwise added to the works. He increased the variety of his wares, and although he continued to make common pottery, began to produce better dinner- and tea-services. The colouring used at that time was chiefly blue and white.

There was another change in proprietorship in 1790, when the style of the firm became Greens, Bingley & Co. They continued to make the commoner wares, as well as the blue tinted patterns, but they produced some highly glazed black earthenware, similar to that which was then being made at Jackfield.

The rich brown Rockingham teapots, copied in after years in Staffordshire, became very popular. The basis of the ware was a species of cream-ware dipped in glaze of heavy lead, a richly coloured brown. The best teapots and similar vessels were made between 1796 and 1806. There are shades varying from dark chocolate to lighter colourings, presenting a great variety of teapots which at that time came very much into favour, owing to the peculiar properties which were attributed to them, in that it was believed—rightly or wrongly—that they were especially valuable in extracting the full flavour of the tea. Tea was becoming a popular drink, but it was still costly, and the Rockingham teapots gained the credit of producing the best results and effecting household economy in the consumption of the beverage.

There were various goods of a domestic character, such as mottled tea- and coffee-services and jugs, for which there was a ready sale in many parts of the country, and in London, Mortlock & Co., of Oxford Street, did much business in them.

There were some freak pottery wares made at Nottingham including the "Cadigan" teapot ornamented with a Chinese pattern, which was a curious puzzle pot filled at the bottom.

John and William Brameld became the proprietors of the Rockingham Works in 1806, and the porcelain they made at that time and onwards (the best period was about 1820), is the china now sought after by collectors. It is said that although the workmanship of the Rockingham china was of the best, and the gilding and colouring beautifully executed, the shapes and designs were not artistic. Admirers of Rockingham, however, find much to please in the delightfully quaint wide open-topped cups so rich in soft colours, and with their profusion of gold pencilling. Many of the tea-sets and dessert services are florally painted as well as heavily gilt. The work of the artists was supervised by the owner, for J. W. Brameld was himself an excellent painter of flowers.

SOME REMARKABLE EXAMPLES.

There are some remarkable examples of Rockingham china, and many beautiful tea-sets which have been preserved complete for close upon a hundred years, although the most beautiful examples are not quite so old. The Rockingham works were patronised by Royalty. William IV. had a most gorgeous dessert service made there at a cost of £5,000. This magnificent service of 144 plates and 56 large pieces is still carefully preserved in Buckingham Palace. It is said that it was used for the first time at the Coronation of Queen Victoria, by whom it was always greatly valued. The scheme of decoration was a dark border of oak leaves in dull gold and turquoise blue. In the centre of each piece the Royal arms were emblazoned, and special decorations embellished the larger fruit baskets and central dishes. In 1830 H.R.H. the Duchess of Cumberland ordered a service consisting of three dozen plates, painted with shells, fruit, birds, landscapes, and marine views, all elegantly ornamented. The price of the service was 250 guineas. A few years later the Duke of Sussex purchased a set, including 40 pieces and 72 plates ; the cost of this very elaborate service was 860 guineas. The designs were made by J. W. Brameld, and in some instances executed by him, and at others by painters like John Creswell, a clever painter who in 1826 engaged with the firm for five years. Shortly after that time, in 1830, the title " Royal " was used as a prefix to the Rockingham Works.

In 1838 some new departures were made in the firm's work, a novel feature being the manufacture of bed posts of earthenware. They also made cornices, candelabra, and many large objects, but few have survived. The Rockingham Works were closed in 1842.

ROCKINGHAM MARKS.

Much of the early Rockingham china was unmarked, and many of the little rustic cottages, as well as the tea-sets without marks, no doubt are wrongly assigned to other works. The Bramelds had sought the financial assistance of Earl Fitzwilliam in 1826, and were enabled to continue their works longer than they would otherwise have done. It was through the aid they received from Earl Fitzwilliam that they used his crest—the griffin mark—upon some of the later porcelain (*see* Fig. x.). This mark is printed in red. There are examples in the Bethnal Green Museum of figures, plates, and vases, on which are the griffin marks. In other well-known collections, too, there are authentic examples, but unfortunately the average collector has to be content with locating his Rockingham from the general characteristics of colour and ornamentation, rather than from the mark which is so often absent, even from well-known sets which are known to have been purchased from the Swinton Works.

Brameld.

Fig. ix.   Fig. x.

ROCKINGHAM.—Marks used at Swinton Works near Rotherham, 1757 to 1842.

CHAPTER XVII

ENGLISH—SALOPIAN POTTERIES

Distinctive characteristics—Marks used at Caughley—Coalport and Coalbrookdale—Some notable features—How the porcelain was decorated—
Jackfield pottery—and Broseley.

THE story of the rise and fall of Salopian pottery and china
is short compared with that of the larger potteries. It is,
however, full of interest and romance, for it was at the
Salopian Pottery that one of the best-known patterns
originated.

Earthenware was made in Salop from 1750 to 1775 by
Browne, but the greater interest centres in the porcelain
which was destined to be decorated with the famous
willow pattern, which was in after years—and is still—
repeated upon the more inexpensive common earthenware
for which Staffordshire in course of time became so justly
celebrated.

Thomas Turner, whose name is associated with the
willow pattern and with Caughley, married the niece of Mr
Browne in 1772, and settled down to bring his talents to
bear upon the output of the works. He came from
Worcester, and was familiar with the manufacture of
porcelain, and he was specially noted for the peculiarly rich
dark blue colouring he used for his under-glaze decorations.

DISTINCTIVE CHARACTERISTICS.

The collector seeks to distinguish between the products
of Broseley and Caughley and the other Salopian potteries.

169

This he is enabled to do by realising the peculiar constitution of the wares and their characteristic ornaments. At first Turner devoted his attention entirely to printing in blue under the glaze, following the methods with which he had been familiar during his experience at Worcester. The best period of his work was about 1793, when Turner had secured the services of Lucas, a clever engraver, and Richards, a printer, both of whom ultimately left him and entered the employment of Josiah Spode.

It may be convenient here to explain the process of decorating porcelain by the printing then in vogue. The pattern having been engraved upon a copper plate, it was transferred on tissues to the biscuit ware, thus differing from the enamel printing on a glazed surface. The earlier engravings were in line only, but they were afterwards shaded by stippling. Some of Turner's printed wares are in black and in red, but the blue, most generally in use, was much more effective, and when it was glazed the glaze added a soft and rich toned appearance to the pattern.

Turner gradually increased the beauty of his wares by adding much gold, the patterns in the latter part of his time being gilded. Some of the most beautiful decorated wares for which the Salopian potteries became famous were, however, made after 1799, in which year John Rose of Coalport took over the Caughley Works.

The greater portion of the porcelain found in collectors' cabinets consists of the tea china and other objects covered with printed and gilded patterns. Many finely modelled figures were, however, made by Turner, some being rather large and in detail not unlike the best quality of Staffordshire figures. The subjects selected for these figures were numerous; among one of the best pairs known is " Prudence holding a mirror," and " Fortitude," a companion piece, both being modelled from classical designs.

In 1780 Turner visited France, and gained some further

knowledge of how the finer wares were then being decorated in that country, and when he returned he was successful in securing the services of several French workmen whom he brought over with him to Caughley.

It was shortly after that time that Turner began to favour Chinese taste, which he introduced into several of his more important designs. It was then that he designed the " Willow " pattern, about which there is such a pretty romantic legend. It is said that this wonderful design was almost entirely copied, although varied, from the Oriental. (For a description of the " Willow " pattern *see* page 175.)

Another famous pattern made at the Caughley Works was known as the " Blue Dragon," and was probably engraved by Hancock. The " Chantilly Sprigs " was a design much favoured, and one which showed French influence. Thus Turner added to the variety of his products, and a year or so later he found it necessary to employ as many as four printing-presses. He engaged the services of many additional artists, among whom were T. Randall and a decorator who worked in a style characteristic of Sèvres porcelain.

Turner sent some of his wares to Worcester, where they were decorated by Chamberlain ; indeed, there is a difficulty at times in determining to which pottery such pieces should be assigned—Caughley or Worcester.

MARKS USED AT CAUGHLEY.

The marks used between 1772 and 1799 were an " S " or " C," printed or painted in blue under the glaze. The crescent mark was also employed, and more rarely " SALOPIAN." Some pieces are marked with Arabic numerals, in their forms almost resembling Chinese characters. Many of the marks are strikingly similar to those used at Worcester and Bow.

The accompanying illustrations are the marks frequently met with on specimens of Salopian porcelain and on some pottery. Figs. xi., xii., xiii., xiv. are all marks used by Turner at Caughley between 1772 and 1799. Fig. xv. is the mark used at Coalbrookdale from 1785 onwards; the name is sometimes given in full.

Fig. xi.   Fig. xii.   Fig. xiii.   Fig. xiv.   Fig. xv.

SALOPIAN.—Figs. xi., xii., xiii., xiv. are marks used by Turner at Caughley, 1772-1799.

Fig. xv. is one of the commoner marks used at Coalbrookdale, 1785 onwards.

COALPORT AND COALBROOKDALE.

The story of the Caughley Works becomes merged in that of Coalport and Coalbrookdale in the year 1799, when the Caughley Works were purchased by John Rose of Coalport. The story of the several potteries is somewhat mixed, in that not only did the ownership of the Salopian potteries change, but the workmen, and especially the leading artists, removed from one town to another. This frequent removal of artists in clay, and painters and decorators on porcelain, was not confined to Salop, for such men frequently removed long distances and sought employment elsewhere, perhaps to a greater extent than is usually attributed to the methods of workmen in those early days.

The constant interchange between master potters, the transfer of works, and the perpetuation of a paste, glaze, decoration, pattern, or shape is shown up very conspicuously in the history of the Shropshire potteries.

The story of the commercial career of John Rose is necessarily a prelude to an account of Salopian wares, and to the history of their places in manufacture. Together with Thomas Minton of potting fame, John Rose learned the arts and mysteries of his craft at Caughley, where Thomas Turner was already established. Then for a time John Rose made pottery at Jackfield—that was in 1780. His small pottery was in the neighbourhood where for years before a common class of earthenware had been made.

In the chapter dealing with South Wales porcelain, it is related that John Rose bought up the famous Nantgarw Pottery, and a little later he secured the larger pottery at Swansea.

With increasing facilities for a larger output Rose found his trade increasing. He was then employing some notable artists, among them Billingsley, whose fame as a clever painter of roses and other flowers had brought him much notoriety. He followed his new employer to Coalport, where Rose had his works, at the time he removed the plant and businesses of Nantgarw and Swansea to Shropshire.

The year 1799 was an eventful one in the life of John Rose. Indeed, it was so throughout the whole of the Salopian potting industry. The events which transpired were startling, for it was then that Turner died and Rose became the purchaser of the Caughley Works. In October of that notable year there was a disastrous accident on the River Severn, for a ferry boat full of workmen employed at Coalport was upset in crossing to Broseley, on the other side the river; upwards of thirty persons, among the number many of Rose's best men, were drowned. This was a great loss to Rose, for his leading hand Walker was among the number.

Here it will be convenient to interpolate a brief account of the career of Thomas Turner, whose works Rose had acquired. Turner had been an engraver at Worcester, but in 1772 he journeyed to Caughley, and there he found employment with a man named Brown, who was a maker of common earthenware. Promoted to the position of manager Turner made many improvements in the works, and new premises were built in order that the manufacture of porcelain might be introduced, the alterations being completed in 1775. A few years later the works passed into Turner's hands, and in 1799 Rose, who was then trading as John Rose & Co., at Coalport, took over the Caughley Works, continuing them until 1814, when they were abandoned, Rose thenceforward carrying on all his business at Coalport. In 1820 Rose obtained a gold medal from the Society of Arts for a glaze which consisted of felspar, borax, sand, Cornish china clay, nitre, and soda, a welcome substitute for that formerly employed, in that it did not contain either lead or arsenic. Rose continued to carry on a successful business until his death in 1841.

Some Notable Features.

The paste used at Coalport is of importance, as it helps the connoisseur to distinguish the products of the works there. The Caughley body which was employed at Coalport for some years was like the Worcester paste. The Nantgarw body which was at one time used at Coalport was soft, and differed somewhat in that it was white and almost transparent. A change in the appearance and substance of Coalport china came with the improved glaze, which was used until about 1820. In regard to the earlier pieces it should be noted that Turner was a practical man, and the mixing of the materials was carried out by his own hand, or by his sister, who is said to have assisted him. Many of the pieces severally spoken of as Caughley or Coalport wares were made during Turner's management of the works.

How the Porcelain was Decorated.

Turner's career was remarkable for the distinctive following of the Oriental style, which he imparted to his wares. As the inventor of the " Willow " pattern already referred to he became famous.

There are few, if any, designs which have appeared on pottery and porcelain connected with the romance of life to a greater extent than the well-known " Willow " pattern, first designed by Turner, and copied by so many makers until in its numerous forms and slightly varied design it became of world-wide repute, commonly called " the Broseley pattern." The earliest examples are marked " C," the Caughley mark, or distinguished by the Salopian mark " S." As applied to tea-services and old cup-plates of either earthenware or porcelain, the latter frequently enriched with gold ornament, the " Willow " pattern is found in its earlier and truer representations. There are many varieties, so much so that collectors specialising on old blue and white can surround themselves with quite a number of types, distinctive enough to those initiated into the mysteries of the love story which forms the basis of the " Willow " pattern legend.

The story is such a charming one that it may well be repeated. The scenic view is drawn from Old Shanghai, where it is recorded there was a small lake, once spanned by a delightful crooked bridge leading to a tea-house. A curious building, too, it must have been, with latticed windows, surrounded by orange-trees, so-called, in reality trees of persimmon. There are willow-trees, a little boat, a bridge, and the lovers. Li-chi, a mandarin's daughter, and Chang his scribe, loved one another, so the story runs. The lovers eloped to the home of Chang, having first been concealed for a time in a cottage over the bridge, seen on the " Willow " plates. Chang's home was on an island to which he safely took his bride in a little boat. Alas! their happiness was shortlived, for the mandarin pursued them and was about to take vengeance, when, according to the legend, the gods looked on with a kindly eye, and changed them into two turtle doves, so that they escaped and flew away.

The chief differences in the interpretation of the story lie in the arrangement of the island, the bridge, and the dovecote. Different painters altered the peach blossoms and enlarged or decreased the so-called orange trees, and varied the catkins of the willows. All these minor differences are pointed out by the enthusiastic collector as he discovers them.

The "Blue Dragon" pattern, too, was, like the "Willow," an excellent exponent of the taste which had been brought into being by the importation of Oriental wares into this country.

The illustrations given in Fig. 56 are from the British Museum collection of Caughley porcelain. Fig. 56 (a) is a mustard-pot in blue; Fig. 56 (b) a cup and saucer; and Fig. 56 (c) a milk-jug, in colours. The group shown in Fig. 57 includes some varieties of the "Willow" pattern and shades in blue; several of the pieces are marked "S"; others, among them the sucrier or sugar-box, are unmarked; this latter and the teapot stand are very richly gilt with a large pattern over the glaze.

In the later period of the Coalport and Coalbrookdale potteries other patterns of note were introduced—some of them by John Rose, who showed a strong leaning towards so-called "Japan" patterns. "The Indian Tree" was one of them, long continued at Caughley and the Salopian potteries. Like the "Willow," the "Indian tree" is still a well-known design copied by modern makers.

The markings of Coalport china are few, indeed very many pieces are without any indication of origin. The

(A) (B) (C)

FIG. 56.—COUGHLEY PORCELAIN.

(A) Mustard Pot in Blue.
(B) Cup and Saucer.
(C) Milk Jug in enamelled colours.

In the British Museum.

FIG. 57.—A SELECTION OF SALOPIAN WARE,
various.

[To face page 176.

Fig. 58.—Coffee Pot and Cover, decorations emblematical of the Seasons. Mark, "Adams," impressed.

name "COALPORT" is, of course, the surest identification mark ; a rose is another mark, less frequently met with. Later examples of Coalport and Coalbrookdale potteries were generally marked in script, "John Rose & Co. Coalbrookdale." Another mark prepared soon after Rose won the gold medal in 1820 was round, and fully 2 in. in diameter. The legend upon it reads, "Coalport Improved Felspar Porcelain," in a laurel wreath surrounded by "Patronised by the Society of Arts. The gold medal awarded May 30th, 1820."

JACKFIELD POTTERY.

Reference has been made to the works at Jackfield, near Iron Bridge, in the Salopian pottery area. There are traces of pot works existing there as far back as 1560. The first authentic account of a Jackfield pottery, however, is met with in 1713, when Richard Thursfield, a potter of Stoke-upon-Trent, settled there. He began by making tea-sets and jugs of "red earth," using a black glaze, which was occasionally relieved by painted flowers and scroll work, the vessels thus made gaining some notoriety as "black decanters."

The works at Jackfield were carried on by a son of the founder until 1772. They then changed hands, and in 1780 were purchased by John Rose of Coalport.

BROSELEY.

John Thursfield established a pottery works at Benthal, near Broseley, in 1772, and there made black glazed ware. After Thursfield's death, which occurred in 1818, the Broseley Works were taken over by W. Pierce & Co.

Tiles have been extensively manufactured at Broseley in more recent years ; the neighbourhood, too, was at one time famed for the manufacture of pipes—"churchwarden" clay pipes.

M

CHAPTER XVIII

Early wares—Discovery of salt glaze—Old Staffordshire—Improved
ornament—Staffordshire figures.

SOME mention has already been made of the early pottery
for which Staffordshire was famous—in the days before the
potting industry became more than one of local interest.
In the chapter on " Prehistoric Pottery " (chapter iv.), it is
pointed out that the barrows, which at one time were
numerous in the county, when opened, were found to
contain examples of ancient pottery. Such ware may,
therefore, be regarded as indicating the first types of
earthenware known to have been made in the district which
was afterwards to become famous as the Staffordshire
Potteries. They were, doubtless, fashioned from local
clays and shaped by hand, the ornamentation, which was
very crude, being imparted by the finger and thumb, by a
small piece of stick or bone, or some other primitive tool.

EARLY WARES.

The geology of this country is exceedingly varied, and
it is to that cause that Great Britain owes so much of her
prosperity, in that metals, minerals, and other natural
products have enabled workers from very early times to
produce a vast variety of objects, and to gain proficiency
in manufacture and craftsmanship which could not have
been acquired at an early date had it not been for the gifts
with which Nature had endowed them. The mud deposits

and clays of this country have throughout the ages proved of the utmost use. The clays of Staffordshire were valuable even in prehistoric times, and in the Middle Ages they were far more so than was then imagined by the humble dwellers in the few hamlets and scattered villages of that thinly populated county. Native talent displayed itself in many ways, in no instance more than in the fashioning of raw materials, such as were obtained locally. The workers in clay in Staffordshire kept on producing common earthenware with very little variation in pattern or form until the sixteenth century. Up to that time they seem to have had no thought or knowledge of the possibilities of manufacture, or of the brilliant future of the Staffordshire trade and the beautiful wares the county was destined to produce.

The " peasant pottery " of the sixteenth century and earlier was intensely utilitarian, but it served, no doubt, all local requirements, and no one seemed desirous of obtaining any improved fabric or of using the material to better advantage. The inhabitants of that part of England were quite satisfied with what they could obtain ready at hand. Progress was apparently made when one or two specialities of manufacture gained more than local fame.

The Staffordshire butter-pots gradually won renown throughout the surrounding counties, and local pedlars began to carry them on the backs of horses and mules " over the ridge " into Cheshire, and even farther afield. As time went on the usefulness of the butter-pot was acknowledged. It gained still wider reputation, for in 1661 it was recognised, in that an Act of Parliament was passed whereby the size of the Staffordshire butter-pot was ordained to be such as would hold 14 pounds of butter. Here again we have in that Act of Parliament of 1661 an honest attempt to secure quality of workmanship and reliability of material in British productions, for it was enacted that the butter-pot should be made of hard material, properly fired and baked so that no moisture might be imbibed. The size of the pot was regulated, too, in order that uniformity might be obtained ; the height was fixed at 14¼ in. and the diameter at 6½ in. The material of which the butter-pot was made was what we should now term coarse, and it was without glaze. It was not a thing of beauty, but it had its good points, and the few unbroken specimens which remain are interesting mementos of old Staffordshire ware.

The Staffordshire tyg was another important speciality which became notorious. It was a recognised local vessel until other cups were in course of time standardised and the varieties of Staffordshire wares became far from restricted. The collector of old pottery is always anxious not only to locate his specimens, but as far as possible to obtain representative pieces so that the different potters of renown may be represented in his collection. Among the most notable of the seventeenth-century makers of Stafford-shire pottery—a period during which many collectable pieces were being made—were Richard Cartwright and his son, both of whom were noted makers of butter-pots and similar vessels, their period of work extending from 1640 to 1715.

In 1670 the famous Toft dishes were made. They were made of " firebrick " clay, and were glazed with brown slip. The chief characteristics of the Toft dishes are the yellow or buff ground and the ornament of rudely-drawn heraldic devices, figures, and scroll-work with which it is covered. The maker's name and date are generally attached, in some instances the figuring and letters being larger proportionately than is warranted by the decoration. Prominence has been given to the Toft dishes in that several of them have been illustrated by different writers on old English pottery. One of the best known

examples frequently sketched is a dish by Thoma
the centre of which is a lion rampant, crowned, a
emblems, which was formerly in the Museum of
Geology, but which may now be inspected in the
and Albert Museum; there are also examples of Toft
pottery in the British Museum.

DISCOVERY OF SALT GLAZE.

In 1680 a new glaze was invented, destined to be known
in the future as " salt glaze." It was an accidental
discovery, but it led to quite a revolution in the pottery
trade. The process which was involved by this accidental
discovery was simple in the extreme, common salt (chloride
of sodium) being thrown into the hot kiln; the salt then
volatised and decomposed, and the soda combined with the
free silica of the clay, producing a hard silicate of soda.

The legend of the discovery of salt glaze, true or
untrue, may be related, for it is typical of some of the most
important discoveries in science. It is said that a female
servant of Mr J. Yale, of Stanley, near Bagnal, was preparing a salt lye for pickling pork in a common unglazed
earthenware vessel. During her absence the liquid boiled
over on the fire, at a time when the sides of the pipkin were
red-hot. When the accident had been remedied and the
vessel had cooled down, it was found the pipkin was
covered over with a rich glaze. This was pointed out to
Mr Yale, and after a series of experiments salt glaze became
an acknowledged feature in earthenware manufacture, and
was very generally adopted in Staffordshire.

OLD STAFFORDSHIRE.

The Staffordshire Potteries, such a densely populated
centre of a thriving industry in the twentieth century,

was in the seventeenth century but an assemblage of small villages and hamlets, separated from one another by a few miles, more or less, of wild, uncultivated land. Burslem was the mother town, the centre of the district, and had in the seventeenth century become famous for its wares. In order to arrive at a true estimate of what they were, it is necessary to look up old authorities, and to discover what contemporary writers had to say about it. Platt, who wrote the " History of Staffordshire," which was published in 1686 says :

" The greatest pottery they have in this county is carried on at Burslem, near Newcastle-under-Lyme, where for making their different sorts of pots they have as many different sorts of clay, which they dig round about the town, all within half a mile distant, the best being nearest to coals, and are distinguished by their colours and uses as follows :

" Clays for the Body of the Pottery—
(1) Bottle clay, of a bright, whitish-streaked yellow colour.
(2) Hard fire clay, of a dullish whitish colour ; and fuller intersperst with a dark yellow, which they use for their black wares, being mixed with the
(3) Red blending clay, which is of a dirty red colour.
(4) White clay, so called, it seems, though of a blewish colour, and used for making yellow coloured wares, because yellow is the lightest colour they make any ware of.

" All of which they call throwing clays, because they are of a closer texture, and will work well on the wheel. Which none of the three other clays, they call sips, will any of them doe, being of looser and more friable natures ; these mixed with water, they make into a consistence thinner than a syrup, so that being put into a bucket it will run through a quill, this they call slip, and is the substance wherewith they paint their wares ; whereof the

(1) Sort is called orange slip, which before it is worked is of a greyish colour mixed with orange balls, and gives the ware (when annealed) an orange colour.

(2) The white slip, this before it is worked is of a dark blewish colour, yet makes the ware yellow, which being the lightest colour they make any of, they call it (as they did the clay above) the white slip.

(3) The red slip, made of a dirty reddish clay, which gives the wares a black colour.

" Neither of which clays or slips must have any gravel or sand in them ; upon this account, before it is brought on the wheel, they prepare the clay by steeping it in water in a square pit, till it be of a due consistence ; then they bring it to their beating board, where with a long spatula they heat it till it be well mix't ; then being first made into great squarish rolls, it is brought to the wageing board, where it is slit into flat thin pieces with a wire, and the least stones or gravel pick't out of it.   This being done, they wage it, *i.e.*, knead or mould it like bread, and make it into round balls, proportionable to their work, and then 'tis brought to the wheel, and formed as the workman sees good."

The potters of Staffordshire began to make improvements, not only in the form of the vessels they fashioned, but by introducing different constituents into the materials employed, and using more artistic ornament.   An advance was made by John and David Elers, who in 1690 had a little factory at Bradwell Wood, near Etruria, where they distinguished themselves in the blending of clay.   Their red ware is now among the rarities of Staffordshire pottery.   It resembled some of the Oriental ware then being imported into this country from Japan ; the ornamentation consisting chiefly of imitations of the branches of the tea-plant, to which some disconnected scroll-work was added.   The potters Elers quickly discarded the commoner objects, and began to make tea- and coffee-sets, the price of which was very high, even in those days. The Elers gave up their works in Staffordshire in 1710 and removed to London. Soon afterwards they appear to have disassociated themselves with the pottery trade, and we hear of them at a later date as connected with the manufacture of Venetian glass, which was then being made in this country.

From that time onward Staffordshire gave birth to many potters of renown, none of greater fame than Josiah Wedgwood, whose name seems to stand for all that is beautiful and rare amidst eighteenth-century ceramics. Little by little the importance of the Staffordshire pottery became recognised, and each fresh discovery or new process introduced added to the greatness of the district, and to the eagerness with which tea-sets, ornamental vases, and figures were purchased in London and in many parts of England.

Improved Ornament.

One of the earliest processes of ornamenting pottery adopted by Staffordshire potters early in the eighteenth century is now distinguished as " scratched blue " salt glaze. The decoration was produced by scratching the pattern or design upon the clay vessel. Glass powder, coloured with cobalt, was then dusted into the incisions, and the simple decoration was complete, ready for the firing under the salt glaze method.

Many strange devices were scratched on these early wares, and a great deal of misspelt script was introduced, oftentimes the date being added.

It is obvious that to the ordinary man the material of which Staffordshire ware was made was an obstacle in decoration, although men of genius like Josiah

Wedgwood and some of his contemporaries overcame that difficulty. The patent rights which had been granted to Champion, who had bought the early patent rights of Cookworthy of Plymouth, whereby he gained some proprietary right to the manufacture of porcelain, had an important bearing upon the products of the Staffordshire potters, who had unsuccessfully opposed the patent. It caused the Staffordshire potters to concentrate their efforts upon earthenware instead of trying to copy Oriental porcelain, and it led them to perfect pottery and even to rival china in the beauty of their cream-ware, to which they added the Cornish kaolin and the growan stone.

It was then that the need of improved transport was so acutely felt, for the only way Cornish clay could be brought to Staffordshire was by sea to Chester, and then by transport overland to Staffordshire. The makers of pottery were well satisfied with the new materials they had obtained by dint of careful and costly research, and they set about improving the quality of their wares. The ornament upon the quaint drinking cups known as tygs, and posset cups, had a beauty all its own, with its brown and yellow slip decoration, sometimes covered with dark brown glaze ; but still such ornament failed to be a successful competitor with the Oriental porcelain which was being copied at the Plymouth Pottery, and the different makers who had up to that point been making similar goods gradually evolved specialistic characteristics, which are treated of more fully in the following chapters, which refer to the individual productions of the more notable works in the Staffordshire Potteries. Fortunately there are many examples of most of the old firms extant, not only in private collections but in public galleries. There is an important representative collection at the Wedgwood Institute in Burslem. There are also museums in most of the chief towns in the neighbourhood. Many of the manufacturers own private collections which are in many instances on view at their works, one of the most notable being the museum belonging to the Wedgwood firm at Etruria. In the years 1905 and 1906 there were some important discoveries of genuine antiques, and some trial pieces which then threw considerable light upon the story of old Wedgwood, and resulted in the formation of the museum at the works. That gave rise to other makers being desirous of perpetuating the memory of some of the old pottery upon which the founders of their firms built up extensive businesses, and in some instances accumulated large fortunes.

Those collectors who have visited the Potteries have no doubt carried away with them mixed views of the places where some of the finest pieces of china which now command such high prices have been made. The Staffordshire Potteries look bright enough in the sunshine, but when clouds of smoke and driving rain are the dominating factors in the outlook the appearance of a typical factory in the Potteries is not inspiring. Many of the best known works have changed little for years, and the makers of ceramic treasures and useful pottery have rarely rebuilt. They have preserved the original appearance of the works as left by the founders, or at most have added to them as modern needs required. Fortunately there are some old concerns in the hands of the original firms; the picture reproduced in Fig. 1 (*frontispiece*) will serve; and surely it is representative, for it is the pottery of Josiah Wedgwood & Sons, whose works at Etruria were founded and built up by that prince of master potters, old Josiah.

STAFFORDSHIRE FIGURES.

There is one important group of collectable objects which cannot very well be referred to, to any extent in a general way in association with an account of the products of any one firm. It is that remarkable group commonly designated " Staffordshire figures." There are specialistic collectors who confine their attention to such figures, and there are some museums where large collections have been got together so that collectors can familiarise themselves with the different figures collectable. Most of them, however, are without any special mark, and it is very difficult to define accurately the origin of these sometimes crude and not very life-like figures. There is, however, a peculiar interest in them, although the colourings of the commoner kind are vivid and not at all pleasing ; but in the best figures the tints are softened, and the glaze gives a finish which must be " felt " to be fully appreciated. The glaze upon the earlier specimens is often irregular, and not infrequently some portions of the figure are uncovered. The glaze was put on by hand with a brush, and it was sometimes carelessly done ; it often overlapped, giving irregular effects ; this is especially noticeable in some of the earlier pieces made by Wood and by Whieldon. Many of the figures or groups faithfully portray rural life in the district at the time they were made. Rustic figures represent lovers in various attitudes and in all grades of life ; others picture the landlord and his dame, one very interesting pair being lettered on their respective stands, " LAND LORD " and " LAND LADY."

Designers and modellers were often copyists, for the figures produced by famous artists and sculptors were copied and modelled in inferior clay figures. Those which caught the popular fancy were duplicated, in some instances the later reproductions being very inferior in modelling and in finish. The quaint and at that time much-sought-after " Cupids " of Bow, Chelsea, and elsewhere, were copied in Staffordshire, some being attributed to Ralph Wood. Of the figures modelled in the form of cups and jugs like the

" Toby " jugs, special reference is made in another chapter.
It may be mentioned here, however, that although not
actually figures, the grotesque characters which were made
to serve the purpose of receptacles of table condiments are
among the curiosities of Staffordshire ware ; notably
there is the set of grotesque figures, six in number—two
salts, two mustards, and two peppers—after the style of
the " Toby " jugs.

Several interesting pieces in the British Museum are
illustrated in Figs. 37 and 38. The large piece in the
centre of the group (Fig. 37) is shown as " The Vicar and
Moses." Those shown in Fig. 38 include sportsman
and bagpiper. They are reproduced by the courtesy of
the Museum authorities.

FIG. 59.—ADAMS TEAPOT of blue jasper.

FIG. 59 (A).—ADAMS BOWL of blue jasper.

In the Collection of Mr. Jesse Haworth, of Bowden.

[To face page 188.

FIG. 60.—ADAMS CREAM JUG of blue jasper.

FIG. 61.—ADAMS SUCRIER of blue jasper.

In the Collection of Mr. Jesse Haworth, of Bowden.

To face page 189.]

CHAPTER XIX

STAFFORDSHIRE—ADAMS

The famous potter—Some Adams wares—Characteristics summarised—
Methods of trading—Marks and stamps.

THE name of Adams has been linked with the pottery
industry of Staffordshire for many generations. Quite a
number of these famous men bore the same Christian name,
and William Adams was a common designation of many
potters in the villages of the county.

It may clear away some of the cobwebs—for there are
many difficulties in the way of collectors anxious to date
and locate their specimens—to tabulate those who bore the
name of William Adams and worked as master potters
during the latter half of the eighteenth century. Most of
these men were related, the two mentioned last in the list
being father and son. They are as follows:

William Adams of Greengates, Tunstall, 1745-1805.
William Adams of the Brick-House, Burslem, 1748-
1831.
William Adams of Stoke-upon-Trent, 1772-1829.
William Adams of Greenfield, 1798-1865.

THE FAMOUS POTTER.

The William Adams in whom collectors of old pottery
and china are chiefly interested is the William Adams who
is said to have been one of the favourite pupils of Josiah
Wedgwood, and learned much of his art under the great
master, and in after years followed closely in his footsteps,

189

imitating many of the wares for which Wedgwood had already become famous, in some instances effecting improvements and developing processes with which he was familiar.

According to the records still in possession of the Tunstall firm of potters bearing the honourable name and so worthily maintaining the family reputation, there was an earlier William Adams, who lived in Burslem in 1617, and he was a potter also. He had inherited his potting skill from a still earlier ancestor, for there was a William Adams of Tunstall, living in the year 1307, a Richard Adams in 1487, and a Nycolas Adams who owned a pottery and a colliery in Burslem in 1568.

John Adams founded the Brick-House potteries in 1657, and a hundred years or so later Josiah Wedgwood became the tenant of the same potteries, occupying them for about ten years. It was when young William Adams had learned the art of potting and acquired some skill in decorating the choicer wares under the tuition of Josiah Wedgwood, that he was first initiated in the mysteries of jasper ware, which Wedgwood was then experimenting with, and perfecting. William Adams seems to have taken considerable interest in this particular class of ware, and when he commenced to make pottery on his own account he effected some important alterations in the blue jasper body, giving his wares an almost distinctive appearance. His attention was, however, chiefly given to fine stoneware, Egyptian black or basalt, and blue printed and painted wares.

SOME ADAMS WARES.

The chief objects in Adams wares were jasper vases, plaques, scent bottles, jardinières, candlesticks, wine coolers, lamps, tea-sets and table furnishings, and some very beautiful cameos and medallions. The colourings adopted by Adams were chiefly blue, green, black, and some other coloured grounds, relieved in white ; the subjects chosen were chiefly classical, and were drawn principally from Grecian and Roman mythology. In the eighteenth century there were quite a number of men working upon similar models, and sharing in what might then have been justly termed the specialities of Staffordshire ; but although many of them worked on similar lines, producing the same class of wares and drawing their inspirations from the same or common sources, they were very particular to impress an individuality all their own upon the objects they created. Thus it is that the expert, when comparing several specimens, although many may not be marked, sees traces of some minor peculiar characteristics which enable him with a very good chance of correctness to group them together.

The accompanying illustrations represent some choice examples of old Adams wares, some of them in the possession of one of the members of the present firm still carrying on business at Greenfield, and claiming to be the successors in the original business founded in 1657 ; other pieces, selected from well-known collections and reproduced by the courtesy of their owners, give some little idea of the decoration of the cameo and jasper wares, which, as it has been already stated, embrace quite a number of useful pieces of domestic pottery, as well as ornamental wares.

As has already been intimated, there is a great sameness in design, or style of design, but a distinctive difference in detail. It has also been suggested that the similarity is accounted for in that the origin of the designs is found in the same subjects. The potters of the eighteenth century practising their art in Burslem, Tunstall, and the surrounding villages of Staffordshire, made use of the masterpieces of Italian sculptors, and had to resort to the same drawings and engravings of pictures for their inspirations, and to use similar models in their studies. The chief difference in the jasper of Wedgwood, Adams, Turner, and others lies in the separate rendering of the same thought and idea.

Adams was himself a clever artist, and he employed skilled workmen. Among his staff was a Swiss artist of considerable merit, and some of the pieces he modelled are now much sought after by collectors and command high prices, for they had a peculiarity which does not appear evident in the works of any other artists of that period. High figures have been reached at Christie's and other sale-rooms for examples of his artistic skill. Of late years William Adams & Co. of Tunstall have revived the manufacture of jasper ware, and have reproduced some of their earlier designs; but of course there is a marked difference between the reproductions and the genuine antiques, which not only bear signs of age, but show indications of the picking out and touching up by hand, the result of so much laborious labour expended by the early potters and their workmen in perfecting their models, and in producing perfect figures. Such labour would be exceedingly costly at the present day, and only moderate prices are paid for the best copies of former antiques. Among the favourite reproductions, reflecting the popularity of the genuine antiques of those types, are " The Seasons," " The Sacrifice of Apollo Belvedere," " Diana," " Artemis," and other classic subjects.

CHARACTERISTICS SUMMARISED.

The chief characteristics of the Adams wares (so many of which have recently been reproduced as modern works of art) are as follows :

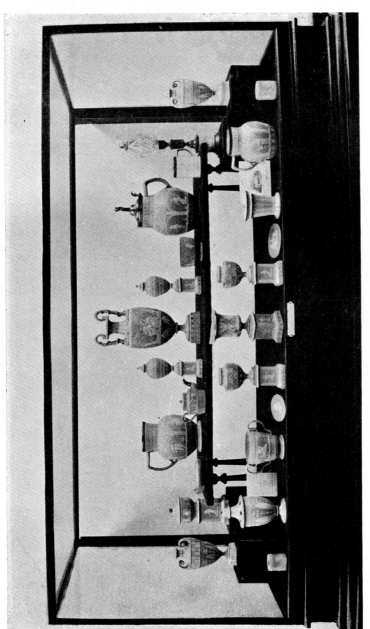

FIG. 62.—ADAMS JASPER WARE, period 1780.

In the Tunstall Museum.

[To face page 192.

FIG. 63.—TEAPOT of blue and white jasper ware,
marked "ADAMS."

In the Hanley Museum.

FIG. 64.—TANKARD, mounted in silver, period 1780.

(*a*) Jasper ware, described as " an opaque porcelain bisque of great beauty and density."

(*b*) Egyptian black, a reproduction of the art made by the Egyptians ; black throughout, of great density.

(*c*) Vitreous stoneware of pale ivory colour, relieved with brown glazed bands, ornamented by hunting scenes, as made by Turner and others, as well as Adams.

(*d*) Ivory ware, including many beautiful perforated museum pieces.

Among the specialities made during the earlier period by Adams at Tunstall, other than jasper ware, was " Mocha " ware. It has been described as white or cream ware, " rudely decorated with seaweed or tree-like effects in black or dark brown, on a coloured zone of pale blue or light brown, outlined with narrow bands of dark colours." The name was derived from a kind of moss agate stone, found near Mocha, in Arabia.

It is claimed that William Adams was the first to introduce blue printed wares in Tunstall. This he did in 1787. Another William Adams is said to have been the first to attempt copperplate printing in Staffordshire, the art being introduced in 1775. This method soon became a popular way of imprinting a pattern upon the wares and was quickly adopted by other manufacturers. As regards the business of William Adams of Greengate, who died in 1805, his works were carried on by Benjamin Adams until 1820.

METHODS OF TRADING.

The methods of marketing goods in olden time are always worth investigating, in that they often have some bearings upon the actual form and use of the goods, and not infrequently impart some local element in decoration. Local surroundings frequently suggest new

N

models, some of them commemorative in design and decoration. Mr William Turner, F.R.S., in his work on *William Adams, an Old English Potter*, says : " From what can be gathered from general sources, it would seem that a great many persons called at the works and made purchases direct, and high prices were obtained, especially for vases and plaques. Many ladies and gentlemen of quality purchased in this way when paying visits to their friends in Staffordshire."

There was also a warehouse in Fleet Street, London, kept by a Mr A. Mist, who sold large quantities of Adams vases and other wares. As Mr Turner puts it : " There, and at other warehouses, the ' grand dames ' would make their purchases of choice pieces, for in spite of the competition of Wedgwood and other makers, the name of Adams ware was well known in the Metropolis at the close of the eighteenth century."

Collectors of antique furniture will recall the frequent use of jasper plaques and medallions in some of the beautiful art furniture of the eighteenth century ; many of them were made by William Adams. This same manufacturer received orders from the aristocracy for the beautiful cameo gems which he designed. They were used for a variety of purposes ; set in gold they made pleasing objects of jewellery to wear. They also became fashionable as buttons and clasps. Among the many special commissions received by William Adams during his somewhat lengthy career was one from his Majesty King George III., for whom he made a set of jasper buttons, pierced for the reception of precious stones for their further ornament and enrichment.

The illustrations given in this chapter include an exceptionally fine coffee-pot of tall, vase-like shape (*see* Fig. 58). The subjects are emblematical of the seasons, and are divided by inverted acanthus ornament. It is marked (impressed) " ADAMS." Figs. 59, 59a, 60, and 61 are four very remarkable pieces forming a set, consisting of a teapot, bowl, sucrier, and cream-jug of blue jasper with white relief, highly decorative and ornamented with the initials " A. D." in script letters which occupy much of the space on the sides of the vessels.

The group of Adams jasper ware shown in Fig. 62 consists of a few pieces forming part of a large case in the Tunstall Museum ; the period represented is 1780. Fig. 63 represents a blue and white jasper teapot of the same period ; it is marked " ADAMS." Another piece similarly marked is a jasper tankard with silver mount (*see* Fig. 64).

MARKS AND STAMPS.

The old marks on Adams ware (some of them still used) consisted of name stamps, impressed, and printed marks. The mark best known is " W. ADAMS " used by him until his death in 1804.

CHAPTER XX

STAFFORDSHIRE—ASTBURY, BYERLEY, DAVENPORT, ELERS, AND OTHERS

Astbury's discoveries—Thomas Byerley, a maker at Etruria—Davenport of Longport—Elers red ware.

THERE were many smaller and lesser known makers of pottery in Staffordshire, contemporary with those who won lasting fame and left behind so many beautiful examples of their handicraft. Yet many of those lesser known men were clever potters, and some of them made discoveries which proved of the utmost advantage to the industry as a whole. To many of these men the potting industry owes much, for they laid the foundation of future developments, perfected in some instances by larger firms who had more capital and greater opportunities to make use of the discoveries which had been made by their more modest competitors. The collector of Staffordshire pottery should not neglect these lesser known makers, and whenever opportunity occurs should secure a few specimens of their productions, and wherever possible marked pieces.

ASTBURY'S DISCOVERIES.

It was Thomas Astbury, the son of a potter who made red ware at Shelton, who had a pottery at Lane Delph in 1725. He found out the secret of readily grinding flint to powder, having ascertained how it might be done from one

196

Heath, of Shelton, who had learned it from an ostler who had so made a powder with wh'ch he treated horses for eye trouble.

The discovery led to quite a revolution in the trade, for instead of breaking the flint by laborious methods it was found that by heating a nodule of flint until it was red-hot the calcined stone was quite easily reduced to powder. Another important advance was made when Thomas Benson discovered the process of wet grinding, which did away with much of the dangerous inhaling of flint particles during the process of crushing dry.

Astbury appears to have gained some reputation in his day. In the British Museum there is a very famous punch bowl, known as the " Portobello bowl," which was made to commemorate the victory of Admiral Vernon in 1739. About that time there was quite a rage for military as well as naval commemorative pottery, among the best known military figures being that made by Astbury, designated " the Grenadier," a very fine specimen of which is also in the British Museum collection. Astbury died in 1743, but his business was continued by his son, who succeeded him, the pottery being carried on until it was finally closed in 1780. The Astbury mark consisted of letters, each one of which was stamped separately, the whole forming the name " ASTBURY."

THOMAS BYERLEY, A MAKER AT ETRURIA, AND OTHERS.

Thomas Byerley, who was a nephew of Josiah Wedgwood, made soft paste porcelain at Etruria early in the nineteenth century. His chief products were tea-sets, mugs, plates, and other domestic wares. They were ornamented by a process of transfer printing. His subjects were view prints, chiefly reminiscent of many of the then little known features of interest in Wales and Devonshire. Some of his wares were also printed with Irish scenery. Byerley continued to work from 1808 to 1816. Most of his pieces are stamped " Wedgwood," in red.

Among the lesser known potters of the beginning of the nineteenth century was the firm of J. and R. Clewes, of Cobridge, who made cream-coloured ware in 1814, and gave up business in 1836. Clewes, the founder, was one of those men who subsequently settled in America and founded the India Pottery Co.

A few pieces of pottery are met with marked, " Warranted Staffordshire," impressed, " CHILD." They are of cream-coloured and Queen's ware, the former being chiefly busts ; they were made by Smith Child at Tunstall, *circa* 1763. The business afterwards passed to a man named Clive.

Some pottery is met with marked " H and R DANIEL." It was the product of a business started by Henry Daniel, who had been an enameller and modeller at Spode's at Shelton, in 1826.

DAVENPORT OF LONGPORT.

The founder of the firm of Davenport & Co. began in a modest way as a potter in Longport, Burslem, in 1793. He made common earthenware of the blue printed type ; but after a visit to France, towards the close of the eighteenth century, Davenport introduced the manufacture of fine porcelain. The chief feature of the decoration of the earlier Davenport wares consisted of beautifully painted flowers and fruit, and some remarkably well executed landscapes. Steel was employed by him, as well as several other artists of note, who decorated plaques, and painted wares with fruit and flowers and scenery.

Fig. xvi.   Fig. xvii.

DAVENPORT.—Fig. xvi. and Fig. xvii. are marks used by John Davenport of Longport from 1793 onward.

The early mark consisted of the name " DAVENPORT," printed in red. Later, an anchor beneath the name was added ; on stoneware the words " STONE CHINA " were printed on the base of the mark, upon which was erected two columns, supporting a scroll on which was the name " DAVENPORT " (*see* Figs. xvi. and xvii.).

The stoneware made by the firm of Davenport was not unlike that generally attributed to Mason. Unfortunately only a small proportion of Davenport china or stoneware was marked. Consequently there is some uncertainty as to the origin of many beautiful pieces which were in all probability produced at the Longport works. In the early years of the nineteenth century Davenport was very busy executing some important commissions from the aristocracy and nobility ; perhaps the most important commission secured at those works was for a coronation service for William IV.

As an indication of where the distinguishing line between old china and new porcelain may be drawn, collectors gladly secure any of Davenport's wares manufactured prior to 1835. More recent than that time china cannot be called " old," although there are many very pretty dessert sets and tea services of a slightly later date, well worthy of being placed in a cabinet of "old china."

ELERS RED WARE.

Among the rare pieces of old Staffordshire ware are examples of red ware made by Elers late in the seventeenth century. In 1688 two brothers, John Philip and David Elers, settled at Bradwell Wood, near Burslem. Their aim was to produce a red ware similar to that which had been imported into this country from Japan. They made use of the ochreous clays of the district, and ornamented them with scroll and leaf work. The decorations were pressed on the surface from copper moulds. The products consisted chiefly of tea-sets. As it has been intimated, the red paste and its peculiar decoration constitutes the chief characteristics of Elers' products, but in addition the Elers made some early basalt ware from a black paste, which they obtained by mixing clay and ironstone. The secrets which the brothers Elers long preserved became known to Astbury, who used the same recipe for the manufacture of red ware. As intimated in an earlier chapter, Elers left Staffordshire in 1710 and became associated with the manufacture of glass in London.

The very fine specimens illustrated in Figs. 65, 66, and 67 are examples of Elers ware from the British Museum. Figs. 65 and 67 are mugs decorated with sprigs of prunus. The coffee-pot (centre of picture), Fig. 66, is a beautiful piece.

The Museum authorities remind us that the term " Elers ware " is somewhat generic, being applied to much of the red ware made in Staffordshire at different periods and by various makers.

FIG. 65.　　　　　FIG. 66.　　　　　FIG. 67.

ELERS' WARE.

FIG. 65.—Mug.　FIG. 66.—Coffee Pot.　FIG. 67.—Mug.

Typical examples of the ware made in Staffordshire by the
Brothers Elers early in the 18th century.

In the British Museum.

FIGS. 68, 69 AND 70.—LONGTON HALL PORCELAIN.

P... of D.... marked in blue : and florally decorated Vase

CHAPTER XXI

STAFFORDSHIRE—LAKIN AND POOLE, LITTLER, MASON, MAYER, MINTON, NEWHALL, SPODE, TURNER, WHIELDON, AND WOODS

Lakin and Poole—Littler of Longton Hall—Mason's stoneware—Mayer—
   Minton's early porcelain—Newhall pottery—Spode, afterwards Copeland—Turner of Lane End—Walton of Burslem—Thomas Whieldon
   of Fenton—Woods—Other Staffordshire potters.

CONTINUING the story of the makers of earthenware and porcelain in the Staffordshire Potteries, it cannot be too clearly set forth that although the names of the makers are not always distinguishable, nor are their marks found upon examples of their wares, these, perhaps lesser known makers, produced some very beautiful wares, and the collector of Staffordshire pottery must perforce try to secure authentic specimens of all known makers within the district in order that he may make his collection at once beautiful and representative.

LAKIN AND POOLE.

About the year 1770 a firm named Lakin and Poole made some excellent cream-coloured wares at their pottery in Hanley. They also made black basalt after the style of Wedgwood and other better known manufacturers of eighteenth-century fame. The printed designs for which Lakin and Poole became famous at that time took the form chiefly of ruined landscapes, and some excellent patterns were produced. They also gained some notoriety for their figures and groups, and now and then their mark, usually

" LAKIN & POOLE," impressed, may be noticed on the stands and bases of Staffordshire figures and groups. This firm's business appears to have ceased about the year 1800.

LITTLER OF LONGTON HALL.

Although the founder of the Longton Hall pottery is but little known to collectors, considerable interest is shown in the beautiful works produced at the pottery, now distinguished as Longton Hall Pottery, the " Hall " being Littler's residence. Mr William Bemrose, in his book entitled *Longton Hall Porcelain*, gives some very pleasing details of many exquisite examples of Longton Hall ware with which he illustrates his book, many of them being reproduced in colours.

William Littler is said to have been one of the first, if not actually the first maker of porcelain in the Staffordshire Potteries. Together with his brother-in-law Aaron Wedgwood, William Littler commenced to make porcelain in the year 1752. His wares differ considerably, some of them resembling old Chelsea and Bow porcelain, some very beautiful vases and ornamental porcelain having been made at Longton Hall. Mr Lichfield, in his work *English Pottery and Porcelain*, points out the peculiar blue which Littler used as a ground colour, especially for his vases. He also calls attention to the unusual scroll ornament of the bases. An examination of a good collection of English porcelain in which there is a fair representative selection of Longton Hall, Chelsea, Bow, and other English potteries, shows that there is a difference in encrusted flowers, the use of which may be regarded as a strong characteristic of Littler's decoration, in that they are usually larger than those met with on vases and ornamental porcelain known to have been made at Chelsea or Bow. There are some very fine examples of Longton

Hall wares in different museums, especially so in the local museum at Hanley.

Some idea of the scope of the Longton Hall Potteries may be gathered from an announcement which appeared in Aris's *Birmingham Gazette* of July 27th, 1752, which ran as follows : " This is to acquaint the public that there is now made by Littler & Co., at Longton Hall, near Newcastle, Staffordshire, a large quantity, and great variety of every good and fine ornamental Porcelain or China ware, in the most fashionable and genteel taste. Where all persons may be fitted with the same at reasonable rates, either wholesale or retail." The general excellence of Littler's wares as set forth in the foregoing public announcement is well borne out by museum specimens. Among the exhibits in the British Museum are a butter-boat and cover, decorated with overlapping leaves, alternately enamelled on white panels with flowers, and on cobalt blue panels with scrolls in tin-white enamel. There is a teapot of globular shape with crabstock handle and spout, and three claw feet with masks, stamped floral ornaments, applied, and the whole coated with a deep blue glaze, showing traces of gilding on the reliefs.

In the Victoria and Albert Museum, at South Kensington, there are two fine jugs with a broad blue border at the base of the neck which have a gold marbled design on a blue band, which is enamelled with flowers. Littler improved the salt glaze ware by dipping it while in a clay state into a bath of carefully " lawned " slip. Burton says that : " Ultimately by adding to the slip a small proportion of the ground zaffres or cobalt glass, they produced a blue dip, which under the salt glaze developed a tint of exceeding richness and brilliance."

It appears that Littler, then trading as Littler & Co., in 1757, following the approved method of trade practice at that time, offered his surplus stock of porcelain at a

London auction mart.   The announcement which appeared
in the newspapers in reference to the contemplated sale
intimated that Mr Ford would sell at " his great room at
the upper end of St James' Hay Market, a quantity of new
and curious Porcelain or China both useful and ornamental
of the Longton Hall Manufactory, which has never been
exposed to public view."   A further announcement, which
makes this sale notice of such importance to collectors
specialising on Longton Hall porcelain, gives a list of
objects included in the sale.

This supplementary notice intimated that the contents
of the sale were to " consist of Tureens, Covers, and
Dishes, large Cups and Covers, Jars and Beakers, with
beautiful Sprigs of Flowers, open-worked Fruit Baskets,
and Plates, Variety of Services for Deserts, Tea and Coffee
Equipages, Sauce Boats, Leaf Basons and Plates, Melons,
Colliflowers, elegant Epargnes, and other Ornamental and
useful Porcelain both white and enamelled."

Unfortunately, but a very small portion of the Longton
Hall porcelain was marked.   The mark when used was
two L's intertwined.   As a means of identification it may
be further pointed out that the paste of this porcelain is
rather vitreous and translucent.   It is not as good as
the latter period of Chelsea, but closely resembles the
earlier specimens of that pottery ; and there are many
imperfections due to indifferent firing.   From the use of
the pure cobalt the colouring has a very brilliant appearance, but very dark.   The characteristic work of the gilt
scrolls on the base has already been referred to, but for
such decoration Littler frequently used white enamel
instead of gold.

The illustrations given here are of two distinct types.
In the centre of the page, Fig. 69 represents a Longton
Hall vase.   Figs. 68 and 70 are a pair of typical dogs with
white and brown spots ; all these pieces are marked in blue.

MASON'S STONEWARE.

Miles Mason was a man of some notoriety and influence in the pottery trade, having been a retailer of such goods before entering in business as a manufacturer. In this way he had acquired considerable knowledge of the wares then in demand. Long before "Mason's China" became popular the china sold by Mason was known, and the taste of the dealer fully appreciated. Mason learned that there was a strong leaning towards foreign wares, and he considered that the abilities of British makers, and the qualities of their productions, were not recognised sufficiently. In his emporium in Fenchurch Street, London, he had sold much "Indian" porcelain, but heavy duties levied upon the importation of these goods from abroad made it difficult to sell them at a profit. With characteristic energy and enterprise Mason established a pottery works at Lane Delph, near Newcastle-under-Lyme, and there he commenced to make pottery after the "Indian" fashion. The pottery was popular and other dealers took it up. The speciality was sold as "British Nankin," and Mason claimed that it possessed all the good qualities of the Oriental and was more beautiful in design and decoration. He claimed that it was very durable, and not liable to break, a quality much appreciated. As a good trader he knew that it was no use making an inferior substitute, and the wares he produced were soon acknowledged as very satisfactory, dealers admitting that they were saleable and in every way equal to, if not better than, the Oriental they had previously sold. Mason stamped or printed his name on most of his wares; thus it is that collectors have in marked specimens a guarantee of genuine pieces.

It is with ironstone china that Mason's name is chiefly associated. In conjunction with his partners Mason took out a patent in 1813, under which he made some very beautiful wares, some of them of considerable size. There were many large punch bowls, octagonal-shaped jugs, broad on the base and very substantial, with characteristic dolphin handles. There were many richly painted dinner-services and noted granite china vases. Mason also made " Cambrian-Argil," another variety, and some porcelain in imitation of Chinese wares. He seems to have been mixed up with the importation of Oriental as well as in the manufacture of ironstone china, in the designs of which he introduced Chinese taste. In 1780 he opened a shop in Fenchurch Street, London, and at that time appears to have placed on the market chiefly copies of the Oriental style, but a little later he turned his attention chiefly to English wares.

After the death of the founder the works at Lane Delph, near Fenton, were carried on for a time by his sons, under the firm style of " Mason & Co."

" MASON'S PATENT IRONSTONE CHINA " is the brand which collectors quickly recognise. The earlier pieces were simply marked, " MILES MASON," then a cartouche with the legend, "C. J. MASON, LANE DELPH," was used ; from 1813 onward the words " MASON'S PATENT IRONSTONE CHINA," surmounted by a crown, were employed, the name of the pattern being sometimes added.

In 1851 the old pottery formerly belonging to Mason was purchased by Francis Morley, and became incorporated with the firm of Ridgway, Morley, Wear & Co.

The examples of rich ironstone china shown in Figs. 71, 72, 73, and 74 are all exceedingly well decorated in blues and greens and reds, and profusely decorated in gold. Fig. 71 is a plate, one of a dinner-set, each piece of the service being marked with one of the Mason marks. Fig. 72 is finely pencilled with gold, and is from a dessert-

FIG. 71.—IRONSTONE CHINA PLATE (Mason's).

FIG. 72.—IRONSTONE CHINA PLATE (Mason's).
In the Author's Collection.

[*To face page* 206.

FIG. 73.—IRONSTONE CHINA JUG.

FIG. 74.—IRONSTONE CHINA VASE AND BOWL.
In the Author's Collection.

service that is marked, "MASON'S PATENT IRONSTONE CHINA." The jug, Fig. 73, is of a type well known to collectors, and the one shown is the largest of a set of three. Fig. 74 is rather exceptional ; it is a vase and bowl (of which there are two pairs) very highly coloured and heavily gilt, the bowl being decorated all over, outside and inside.

MAYER.

Elijah Mayer gained some notoriety for his black basalt ware which he produced from 1786 to 1813. He was also a maker of unglazed cane-coloured wares. The pottery was founded by Elijah Mayer at Hanley, in the year 1770, the founder dying in 1813, when the firm style was changed to Joseph Mayer & Co., under which name it was carried on until 1830.

The marks by which specimens of this pottery may be distinguished are divided into those pieces made in or before the year 1820, most of which are impressed, "E. MAYER" ; then for a time the mark "E. MAYER & SON" appears to have been used. From about 1824 on to 1830 the mark was, "Joseph Mayer & Co., Hanley," in script type.

MINTON'S EARLY PORCELAIN.

The firm of Minton's of Stoke have gained almost world-wide fame for their beautiful decorated wares. Collectors, however, although they recognise that countless objects with varied schemes of decoration made in more recent years by this well-known firm are welcome cabinet pieces, must pass most of them by when confining themselves to the really antique. The *early* period of the Minton wares, however, is readily included in a collection of old china. Thomas Minton founded this firm in 1790,

and the time during which his wares now recognised as
" old china " were made dates from that year onwards
until 1810. It is interesting to recall that Thomas Minton
was in his early days associated with a well-known
eighteenth-century potter. He was apprenticed to Thomas
Turner of Caughley, his attention being chiefly taken up
with the engraving of copper plates for the printing of porcelain. Minton when he founded his pottery at Hanley, in
conjunction with Pownall and Poulson, made both porcelain
and earthenware. The early " MINTON " mark was used
for some years, until superseded in 1836, when Herbert
Minton joined Boyle in partnership, and the mark they
adopted then was " M. & B." for their felspar china.

NEWHALL POTTERY.

An exception must be made in this paragraph to the
method followed in the previous chapters on Staffordshire
potteries, namely, that of describing them under the names
of their owners. To follow this rule in this instance would
be misleading, or at any rate confusing, in that few collectors are familiar with the names of the owners of the
Newhall Pottery, whereas the wares themselves are well
known to connoisseurs of ceramics, and are usually classified
as the products of the Newhall Pottery without mention of
its ownership.

The Newhall Pottery was founded in 1777 by a
company consisting, according to Shaw, of S. Hollins, of
Shelton ; Anthony Keeling, of Tunstall ; John Turner, of
Lane End ; Jacob Warburton, of Hot Lane ; William
Clowes, of Port Hill ; and Charles Bagnall, of Shelton.
The works were situated at Shelton, and noted in that it was
there that kaolin and porcelain granite were first introduced.

The owners of Newhall Works purchased the patent
rights of Champion of Bristol, using the same paste as that

of which Bristol china had been made for many years ; but about 1800 they began to use bones, which were then being extensively employed in other contemporary potteries.

The Newhall Works were continued for a quarter of the nineteenth century, but during that time several important changes were made in the constitution of the firm. Unfortunately none of the older porcelain was marked, although it is well known that much excellent china was made. In the year 1820 the wares were stamped or printed in red, over glaze, " NEW HALL," within a double circle. Then for a time the same mark was imprinted. In 1825 the Newhall Works were given up.

SPODE, AFTERWARDS COPELAND.

Josiah Spode received some of his early training with Thomas Whieldon. He commenced business for himself at Stoke-on-Trent in 1784, chiefly confining his attention to blue printed, cream agate, red terra-cotta, jasper, and stone wares.

Josiah Spode the elder was succeeded by his son in 1797, and Josiah the younger very soon turned his attention to the making of stoneware, for which he became famous. He is said to have been the first to use bone ; he was certainly the first Staffordshire manufacturer to introduce felspar into the making of English china. He was a man who believed in specialising upon certain wares, and in 1805 devoted most of his attention to opaque china. His death took place in 1827, but the works were continued. Copeland became a partner, and the style of the firm was altered to Spode, Son & Copeland. The works then passed into the hands of the junior partner, who was eventually joined by Garrett, until 1847, when the firm style became Copeland & Sons.

O

There are many of this firm's specialities with which collectors are familiar. Perhaps one of the best known is the blue and white wash-basins and jugs, which were used in connection with tripod stands which were made during the period of popularity of Chippendale furniture. Some very delightful miniature jugs and bowls were produced in the early days of Copeland, that is, soon after he joined the firm, and some well-known painters decorated some of the sets turned out at the works.

It is very comforting to know that nearly all genuine Spode is marked. The name " SPODE " is associated with felspar porcelain, and often impressed on the earlier specimens. Then came the circular brand, " SPODE, SON & COPELAND." During the time that Alderman Copeland was in partnership with Garrett the brand was chiefly " C AND G." Then when the works were controlled by Alderman Copeland alone the mark was two " C's," back to back, intertwined, below, " COPELAND."

TURNER OF LANE END.

John Turner, of Lane End, was contemporary with Wedgwood, and at one time his friendly rival. His name is of some note, in that he was the pioneer of printing under glaze. He founded his works in Lane End in 1762, and appears to have devoted much of his time to export business, doing a large trade with the Low Countries; indeed, some of his plates were decorated at Delph, where he had a depot.

Some of Turner's patterns were very curious, especially those derived from Biblical subjects. Unfortunately, few pieces were marked, although some were impressed, " TURNER," one such plate being on view in the National Museum of Wales at Cardiff.

WALTON OF BURSLEM.

John Walton had a pottery in Burslem from 1790 to 1839. His work is chiefly known to collectors in " Toby " jugs and rustic figures. It is said that Walton was originally a maker of marbles, and then began by making quite simple figures. Very unnatural, too, they were, stiff and formal, giving one the idea that neither Walton nor the modellers he employed (if any) had much knowledge of Nature. The modelling of Walton's sheep and other animals, too, was very inferior. Among some of the best known pieces are " The Shepherd " and " Shepherdess," and some quaint-looking animals, said to represent lions and tigers. Walton also modelled figures representing Saint Matthew, Saint Mark, Saint Luke, and Saint John. On marked pieces the name " WALTON " appears on a scroll.

One of John Walton's " Toby " jugs, which is in the British Museum, bears Walton's mark on the base, and it certainly is very distinctive in its modelling, being well described by a writer on the subject as " full of life and movement." Two very interesting groups, representing respectively " The Hairdresser " and " The Shoemaker," have been attributed to Walton, in that there is a striking sameness between them and a known marked piece entitled, " The Widow." There are marked groups, entitled, "The Flight to Egypt " and " The Return from Egypt," said to be among the best of Walton's productions.

THOMAS WHIELDON OF FENTON.

Thomas Whieldon, of Fenton, gained some notoriety from his connection with Josiah Wedgwood, with whom he was associated in partnership from 1753 to 1759.

Of the wares in which Whieldon excelled there are

some possessing very striking characteristics ; very remarkable were the little teapots and other articles of table use, looking so much like real cauliflowers and other vegetables, being shaped to give them the right appearance.   Whieldon must have been a very observant man and ready to grasp great possibilities when modelling his choicer objects.

The solid agate ware introduced by Whieldon was skilfully formed from two layers of clay placed one over the other, until one might easily imagine that the earthenware vessel was cut from solid agate.   From this material Whieldon made jugs, teapots, and knife handles.

Whieldon's tortoise-shell ware was another attempt— very successful, too—to imitate something quite different from what had hitherto been copied.   Of this ware he produced some very beautiful dessert-sets, introducing clever markings.   Another speciality of this maker consisted of figures, many of which now command fairly high prices in the sale-rooms.   Whieldon's mark was his name, impressed.   The pottery he established in 1740 was continued until his death in 1798.

The Woods, and other Staffordshire Potters.

In referring to old pottery attributed to makers of the name of Wood, we must treat such wares on general lines as belonging to a famous family of potters, rather than to any individual maker.   Briefly, Ralph Wood worked in Burslem, making some excellent wares between 1735 and 1740.   His son Aaron Wood seems to have been a specialist, for he is described in old documents as a cutter of moulds for salt-glazed stoneware.   At one time he worked for Thomas Whieldon and others, but about 1750 he commenced business on his own account.   Aaron Wood has some claim to be acknowledged as the inventor of cream-ware, which under the master hand of Josiah

Wedgwood was eventually improved, and in course of time became known as " Queen's " ware.

The business belonging to the Wood family became the property of Enoch Wood, a son of Aaron, in 1770, who achieved some fame as a sculptor, and produced well-modelled figures and busts.

From 1790 to 1818 the business was carried on as Wood & Caldwell, who were the successors of Enoch Wood, and it is probable that very many of the best pottery figures which are to be seen in museums and private collections may justly be ascribed to the period during which Wood & Caldwell conducted the business. The figures are well modelled, and the colouring is somewhat distinctive.

The earliest marked pieces bear the name of " Ra. Wood," Burslem. The name of " Aaron Wood " appears about 1750, followed by " Enoch Wood," in 1784. Then " WOOD AND CALDWELL " between 1790 and 1818, and finally some figures are marked, " E. WOOD & SONS."

.   .   .   .   .

There are a few products of other Staffordshire potteries occasionally met with in collections, some being marked. For instance, John and George Rogers had works in Burslem in the eighteenth century, their pottery being established at Longport in 1780. The mark used on tea-services and other china was " ROGERS," accompanied sometimes by an arrow. Some " Willow " pattern and Broseley blue wares were made there, the pottery being continued for some years afterwards by James Edwards & Son.

Another firm, Hilditch & Sons, of Longton, gained some notoriety in the closing years of the eighteenth century, producing very beautifully decorated tea-services, some in imitation of Indian designs. Some of their patterns were floral and drawn from Nature.

CHAPTER XXII

Josiah Wedgwood, the potter—Wedgwood's wares—Celebrated examples—
Designers and modellers—Collections of Wedgwood ware—Marks.

It is probable that no name is better known to collectors of
English pottery than that of Josiah Wedgwood. The
productions of the famous potteries established by the
great pioneer founder have been admired, collected, and
valued almost from the moment they left the kiln, for they
were unique and claimed notice ; they arrested the
attention of the art critic, and became objects of interest,
in that so many of them were commemorative. In some
instances they revived long-forgotten styles of decoration,
at other times they memorialised men and events, and in
some few cases were replicas of still more famous triumphs
of art—such, for instance, the justly celebrated copies of
the Portland vase.

Probably more than in any recorded instance of great
achievements in ceramic art the personality of Josiah
Wedgwood, and his undoubted skill as a potter, had much
to do with the artistic effects produced at his works. The
influence he had in every branch, and the personal supervision he exercised over his workpeople, secured for his
wares uniform quality and a general acknowledgment of
their exceptional merit as works of art. The superiority
of modelling is conspicuous, and the delicate touch of the
master hand very apparent when examples are examined.
Yet even in a works founded and carried on under the

214

control and guidance of such an exceptional personality as that of Josiah Wedgwood a passing tribute must be paid to the skill and genius of some of those who were employed by him, notably such men as Flaxman, whose work is referred to later, and Hackwood and Webber.

JOSIAH WEDGWOOD, THE POTTER.

Much has been written of the personal history of Josiah Wedgwood, and the story has been told again and again of his life, spent for the most part in his native county. This book deals with the actual achievements of the potters rather than of their careers, or of those motives which led up to the success which attended the efforts of so many of them. Josiah Wedgwood, however, was an exceptional personality, and one which cannot be passed over lightly. His whole career was one of discovery and improvement. Little by little he advanced in the arts. He took first one piece and then another, and studied its composition and its scheme of ornament, and then determined to produce something like it, only better ; or to make a new paste, a design, or a novel form of decoration, which, whilst having some semblance to what was already popular, far exceeded it in grandeur, and consequently commanded a greater and wider market.

Wedgwood was commercial as well as artistic, a fact evidenced throughout his career. He began with a few pounds and ended a wealthy manufacturer. That is a fact which should be borne in mind when examining specimens of Wedgwood's wares, for although as an artist he aimed at producing a perfect object, he always considered its suitability for actual use, and rarely, if ever, produced pieces of pottery for which there would be no demand. Even when designing and planning his scheme of reproduction of the celebrated Portland vase, Josiah

Wedgwood determined to make each one object a master-piece; but he wisely limited the number of his replicas, by which he was able to maintain their price both at that time and in the future. They were a commercial success as well as a triumph of art.

It is pleasing to record that the great Josiah Wedg-wood, F.R.S., S.A., who was destined to bring fame to the Staffordshire Potteries, was born in Burslem, the mother town of the Potteries, in the year 1730. Unlike so many famous potters and artists, he does not seem to have possessed roaming tendencies, and throughout his studies, progress, and the gradual upbuilding of his works at Etruria, he lived on his native soil; and while planning and discovering new processes was unconsciously helping on the development of that group of towns and villages which are now linked together in one vast commercial whole.

How different the country was when young Josiah learned the art of potting, to the district when, in a good old age, he died. Still greater was the contrast between Etruria in the eighteenth century and the Staffordshire Potteries in the twentieth century, although the business Josiah Wedgwood founded continues and prospers, and is still carried on by those who bear the worthy name of the founder.

Wedgwood's ancestors had been workers in clay; in-deed, they, in common with others, had long before dis-covered the value of the local clays, and recognised that the neighbourhood in which they dwelt was exceptionally well suited by Nature to the practice of the potter's art.

The early history of the Wedgwood family takes us back into quite early days. So numerous were its members that one writer calls them a clan. Its founder, from whom the family took its name, lived at Weggewood, a little hamlet near Newcastle-under-Lyme, the first whose

FIG. 75.—CREAM-COLOURED VASE, made at Burslem, 1760-7.
In the Wedgwood Museum at Etruria.

[To face page 216.

FIG. 76.—FIVE PLATES, forming part of the Service made by Josiah Wedgwood for Catherine II of Russia, period 1772-4.

To face page 217.]

name is recorded in history being Thomas de Weggewood, in the time of Edward III.

It was Gilbert Wedgwood of Burslem who in 1612 may be said to have founded the long line of potters. He was a maker of Staffordshire butter-pots, and no doubt also made basins, jugs, and porringers. In 1691 a John Wedgwood was a maker of Delft ware in the neighbourhood, and gained some repute for his puzzle jugs. We then learn of the grandfather of the great Josiah, who was a master potter in 1715. Those were the days of small things, for although occupying a position of some importance, this worthy potter employed but three workmen, who were remunerated with the by no means princely wage of four shillings per week ; he employed some apprentices, too, but they received much less—perhaps nothing at all.

Young Josiah was only nine years of age when he left school. When fourteen years old he was apprenticed to his brother Thomas, who was then in business as a potter. The boy Josiah seems to have possessed a remarkable aptitude as a copyist, for he delighted in modelling things he saw around him. Alas ! he was destined to suffer much physical pain, for as the result of an attack of small-pox when very young it was found necessary after a time to amputate one leg. For aught we can tell it may have been a blessing in disguise, for it caused him to devote more attention to modelling than " throwing," and it also prevented him taking part in the active sports of his day which then occupied so much of the attention of the youth of Staffordshire.

Some of young Josiah Wedgwood's earliest efforts when he began to strike out in a new line of his own were directed towards modelling such small objects as knife handles, plates, and even snuff boxes, which he cleverly made in imitation of agate, marble, tortoise-shell, and porphyry. He became an expert in colouring the clays which he handled.

In course of time Josiah Wedgwood contemplated working on his own account, and doubtless saw visions of the future when he might put into practice the new ideas he had conceived. His first venture was taken in co-partnership with John Harrison of the Cliffe Bank Pottery, at Stoke-on-Trent. It is said that Harrison provided the capital and Wedgwood the brains. Wedgwood appears to have come in contact with Whieldon, and Thomas Whieldon evidently recognised the unusual ability shown by young Josiah. When Harrison retired Wedgwood joined Whieldon, the partnership existing for about five years. It was after the dissolution of that partnership that Wedgwood commenced alone in a small pottery in Burslem; that would be in 1759. He was then thirty years of age and had already studied chemistry and learned a great deal about the native clays of the county in which he lived. His work at that time seems to have borne fruit, for his business grew and very soon he found it necessary to take over larger works, the site being that which at the present day is occupied in part by the Wedgwood Institute, which many years after his death was built to his memory.

In achieving great successes Wedgwood found that he must pay attention to details of production, and to better effect that end he improved the tools used in his work. Up to that time the potters' tools were very primitive, but, as was the experience of many pioneers in those days, it was no easy task to teach the workmen to use and appreciate improved lathes, although by their use better results were achieved and more economic working resulted. As an indication of the trade Wedgwood hoped to secure it is interesting to note how he applied his very modest capital; when, according to *The Burslem Dialogue*, "he started i' bizness fust, he made spewnes, knife hondles, and smaw crocks at the Ivy hahs."

In the biographical notes given in the catalogue of the

Wedgwood Museum at Etruria, it is stated that at the time of Wedgwood's advent the pottery industry was gradually undergoing a change. The general use of tea and coffee demanded suitable vessels, which had been hitherto indifferently supplied by importing expensive porcelain from China and Japan. Staffordshire makers were producing salt glaze pottery, copying the Oriental models, practically the only patterns they knew, and they lacked originality. Wedgwood threw himself with energy into the work of improving local designs, and began at once upon useful objects. Although not physically strong he was full of activity. His wares were essentially distinctive. His new departures, in which must be included his tortoise-shell, agate, mottled, and other coloured pieces, followed one another in quick succession. He improved the potter's lathe, and actually discovered or invented no less than twenty new bodies or pastes.

Wedgwood, when in partnership with Whieldon, distinguished himself as a man of business as well as of art ; he found time to supervise the practical manufacture of pottery, and also to conduct much of the business procedure.

At that time he visited the chief towns and secured markets for his wares in London, Birmingham, Sheffield, Manchester, and Liverpool.

The London show-rooms which afterwards brought Wedgwood and his firm much business were opened in Newport Street, on the advice of his wealthier patrons, among whom was the Duke of Marlborough. The opening of the London depot was the means of popularising Wedgwood's jasper ware, upon which he was then concentrating so much attention. It was about that time that Wedgwood brought out his first catalogue ; it was indeed a comprehensive affair, and was printed in several different languages.

No story of Josiah Wedgwood and his doings would be complete without reference to his public career, and to the efforts he made to secure better conditions in order that not only might he himself benefit thereby, but that the trade of the Staffordshire Potteries might be extended. The roads in Staffordshire were indeed bad, and it was on these tracks that he and others depended for transport. In the year 1760 the only method of transport was by pack-horse train, and it was some miles to the nearest main road. Wedgwood favoured the idea of introducing waterways as well as improving roads, and he was instrumental in the promotion of the Grand Junction Canal, which proved of such value to Staffordshire potters.

Some of the greatest men of the nineteenth century paid tributes to the memory of Josiah Wedgwood, and pointed to his ability to unite art and commerce—for his artistic tastes and talents are undisputed, and his potting industry was successful, securing him a fortune. Lord Lytton, in his *England and the English*, of Wedgwood says : " How did Wedgwood manage without a public school for designers ? In 1760 our porcelain wares could not stand competition with those of France. Necessity prompts, or, what is quite as good, allows the exertions of genius. Wedgwood applied chemistry to the improvement of his pottery, sought the most beautiful and convenient specimens of antiquity, and caused them to be imitated with scrupulous nicety." This confirms the opinion formed by ceramic experts of his work, all of whom testify to the excellence of Wedgwood's productions. He never cheapened his wares, and was always willing to employ the highest talent obtainable. The best artists of the day found employment at his works, and he had no difficulty in finding talent, for he was willing to pay for it.

The late William Ewart Gladstone, when opening the Wedgwood Institute in 1863, said : " Wedgwood was the greatest man who ever, in any age, or in any country, applied himself to the important work of uniting art with industry." Continuing, Mr Gladstone said : " Wedgwood completely revolutionised the character of the fabric made in England at that period. He recalled into existence the spirit of Greek art. Before his time we may say of the earthenware and porcelain manufacture that it has never risen to the loftiness of the spirit of Greek art. If you compare the famous porcelain of Sèvres, the vases of Sèvres with the vases of Wedgwood, I don't hesitate to say they are greatly inferior. If you pass your eye along this line of productions in eighteenth-century England, although there are very good forms in others, those of Wedgwood stand pre-eminent. Though in all his productions you are reminded of Greek art, they are not mere reproductions. His style is strikingly original." Such a tribute coming from so keen an observer and a connoisseur of art of exceptional ability places Josiah Wedgwood upon a unique platform, and should call particular attention to his productions.

Wedgwood's business enterprise led him to open a London warehouse, which was placed under the care of his brother John. He had also a resident agent in Liverpool. Wedgwood sent wares to Liverpool, where they were printed by Sadler & Green from 1760 until his death in 1795. It was when on a visit to Liverpool that Wedgwood, suffering from his old leg trouble, met with a slight misadventure by the way, and on that occasion he met Thomas Bentley, a merchant, who afterwards became his close friend and partner for many years.

Josiah Wedgwood was married in 1764, and by that time he had become a prosperous man. It has been pointed out that Wedgwood took a keen interest in improving transport service, and he numbered among his patrons the Duke of Bridgwater, who was the proprietor of the great waterway between Manchester and Liverpool, and the Staffordshire Potteries. He received some important commissions from the Duke, for writing to his London agent on July 6th, 1765, Wedgwood said : " His Grace gave me an order for the completest set of table service of cream colour that I could make." The commission for Queen Charlotte's set came through the good offices of Miss Chetwynd, and he gave his personal superintendence to " the burning in of the gold and the illumination of the borders with flowers " of a beautiful breakfast-service. This so pleased the Queen that further orders were forth-coming. Wedgwood also made a service for the King on which was painted and gilded, " The Royal pattern."

WEDGWOOD'S WARES.

Wedgwood's connection with Whieldon led him to take in hand the cauliflower ware, and to improve it. Indeed, that was one of his first efforts when in 1759 he com-menced business for himself. Wedgwood had in mind the beautiful red ware of Elers when he introduced his red terra-cotta or unglazed ware. This he termed *Rosso antico*. He also improved the cream-ware ; indeed, it would appear that whatever kind of ware Wedgwood deter-mined to imitate he did so without any slavish regard for either form or colouring of what had gone before, but he approached his object with the avowed intention of making his ware an improved adaptation of the older design or type. After his first few attempts he succeeded in showing a decided advance, greatly adding to the beauty of glaze and body.

The breakfast set already alluded to, made for Queen Charlotte, was beautifully painted by David Steele and Thomas Daniel, two well-known artists. That resulted, as it has been seen, in further orders, and also to Wedgwood's

FIG. 77.—WEDGWOOD'S COPY OF THE PORTLAND VASE,
period 1790.

In the possession of Messrs. Josiah Wedgwood & Sons, Ltd.

[To face page 222.

Fig. 78.—Red Ware Spill Cup, coloured decorations,
part of a set of five pieces.

(Wedgwood ware.)

To face page 223]

appointment as " Potter to Her Majesty." It also turned cream-ware into " Queen's ware." In this ware there is a remarkable likeness to the work of the silversmiths of the eighteenth century. About 1775 Wedgwood experimented with cream-ware, making it whiter by the use of more china clay and flint, resulting in what became known as "pearl ware." The decoration he adopted for his new ware consisted of shells, models from specimens in Josiah's own collection, for in his moments of leisure he was somewhat of a conchologist. Cream-ware ground was used for many objects, including well-modelled figures, among the best known being those representing " Juno," " Ceres," " Charity," " Prudence," and " Fortitude."

The celebrated jasper ware is the most typical of Wedgwood's great triumphs. Its characteristic ornament was drawn from Greek models ; both the design and ornament seem to have been surrounded with a classic atmosphere. At that time Wedgwood was in partnership with Bentley, who is said to have been a scholarly man, and to have influenced Wedgwood in his tastes. The ground colours of jasper ware were sage and olive greens, blue, lilac, and black. The two varieties are distinguished as " solid jasper " and " jasper dip," the latter giving more delicate and translucent reliefs, very appropriate to the drapery of the classic figures. Many of the tea-sets and other objects made in this delightful cameo ware were quite useful. Others, however, were purely ornamental, such as plaques and medallions. Some charming cameos suitable for jewellery and the ornamentation of furniture, inlays, and similar purposes, were also made.

The old green glaze made by Wedgwood, according to Miss Meteyard, was made on the following formula : Flint glass, 6 parts ; red lead, 2 parts ; white enamel, 4 parts ; vitrefied ; and one-twelfth part calcined copper, the blue-green produced requiring much yellow ground to make it grass green. This ware was afterwards much imitated by different makers. Genuine Wedgwood examples of dishes, trays, and finely modelled wreaths of flowers, fruit, and strawberries are collectable. It is said that very large quantities of this ware were shipped to America, where dealers in the eighteenth century handled it successfully. One such dealer's announcements, made in the *New York Morning Post* of November 7th, 1783, was as follows : " Just arrived in ' The Iris ' from London, and to be sold low by Robert Loosely In Water Street, between the Coffee House and Old Slip, A Great variety of Goods, Amongst which are a few Books, Gold Rings, Lockets and Pins, Very fine and fresh French and English hard and soft Pomatums, Fine plated and high finished steel spurs, a parcel of very neat Wedgwood Ink stands, Cream Ware, etc."

Whieldon had won some notoriety for his mottled, marbled, or agate ware. Wedgwood made it, too, and applied the liquid clays to cream-coloured ware foundation, calling it " surface agate " to distinguish it from the " solid agate."

Of the increasing popularity of Queen's ware after the manufacture of Queen Charlotte's set, Wedgwood wrote : " The demand for a cream colour, alias Queen's ware, alias ivory, still increases. It is really amazing how rapidly its use has spread almost over the whole globe, and how universally it is used."

Another important feature in Wedgwood's productions was the black basalt ware, which might have been termed a revival of a lost art, for even in Pliny's time the old Etruscan art of painting vases with durable colours burnt in by fire was regarded as an ancient craft then forgotten. Summarising Wedgwood's chief discoveries, they may be taken in order as : (1) TERRA-COTTA, coloured to resemble porphyry and other stones ; (2) BASALTES or

EGYPTIAN, a black biscuit, nearly resembling natural stone, and when fired extremely hard ; (3) WHITE POR-CELAIN, of smooth, waxlike surface ; (4) JASPER, a white porcelain biscuit capable of being coloured by metallic calces; and (5) CANE-COLOURED BISCUIT.

As a guide to the variety of sundry ornamental objects of Wedgwood ware collectable, although by no means exhaustive, the following objects given by Miss Meteyard in her admirable work on Wedgwood, may be useful :

" Fish drainers, oval and round, Root dishes with pans to keep them hot, Covered dishes, Soup dishes, with covers, Dishes for Water Zootjes (Dutch fish), Herring Dishes, single and double, Ice pails, Pickle stands, Leaves and shells of different kinds, Epergnes for the middle of the table, Egg baskets to keep boiled eggs hot, Egg Cups with or without covers, Oil and Vinegar Stands, Egg Spoons, Table Candlesticks of different patterns, Bread Baskets, oval or round, Cheese Toasters, with Water Pans, Oval and round Potting Pots, Pudding Cups, shapes for Blancmange, Asparagus pans, Monteiths for keeping Glasses cool in water, Curvettes, Cheese Plates, Beer mugs and Jugs with or without covers, Large soup Ladles, Fruit Baskets with or without covers, Sweetmeat Baskets, Croquants or Sweetmeat Dishes, Glacieres (for ice-cream), Ice-cream cups and covers, Ice-cream bowls, Strawberry Dishes and Stands, Custard Cups, Tartlets, Dessert Spoons, Water Plates with covers to keep toast and butter warm, Gondolas for Dry Toast, Butter tubs and stands, Wash hand basons and ewers, Shaving Basons, Punch bowls, Spitting pots, Sauce Pans for cooking, Night Lamps to keep any liquid warm all night, and Table and toilet candlesticks with extinguishers."

According to the catalogue of Wedgwood & Bentley, 1773, so numerous were the various goods made that it was

P

found necessary to divide them into no less than twenty divisions as follows :

" *One*.—Intaglios and Medallions or Cameos, accurately taken from antique gems and from the finest models that can be procured from modern artists. In 1787 there were 1,032 designs of these objects.

" *Two*.—Bas-reliefs, Medallions and tablets, etc. Of these there were 300 designs.

" *Three*.—Medallions, etc., of Kings, Queens, and Illustrious persons of Asia, Egypt and Greece. In 1787 there were over a hundred of them.

" *Four*.—A set of sixty medals, from Dassier, illustrating ancient Roman history, from the founding of the City to the end of the Consular Government including the age of Augustus.

" *Five*.—Heads of Illustrious Romans. Forty of these were produced.

" *Six*.—The twelve Cæsars made in four sizes, and their Empresses which were made in one size only.

" *Seven*.—Fifty-two medallions showing Emperors from Nerva to Constantine the Great.

" *Eight*.—Heads of the Popes, 253 medallions.

" *Nine*.—A series of 102 heads of Kings and Queens of England and France.

" *Ten*.—Heads of Illustrious moderns.

" *Eleven*.—Busts and small statues, boys, and animals. Eighty busts and forty animals.

" *Twelve*.—Lamps and Candelabra in marbled ware or basaltes and jasper.

" *Thirteen*.—Tea and coffee services, including chocolate pots, sugar dishes, cream ewers, cabinet cups and saucers, in bamboo, basaltes, plain and enriched ; also in jasper of two colours polished within like the natural stone.

" *Fourteen*.—Flower pots and root pots.

" *Fifteen*.—Ornamental vases of antique form in terracotta.

" *Sixteen.*—Antique vases of black porcelain or artificial basaltes, highly finished with bas reliefs.

" *Seventeen.*—Vases, tablets, etc., with encaustic paintings.

" *Eighteen.*—Vases, tripods, etc.

" *Nineteen.*—Inkstands, paint-chests, eye-cups, mortars and chemical vessels.

" *Twenty.*—Thermometers for measuring strong fire or the degree of heat above ignition."

CELEBRATED EXAMPLES.

Reference has already been made to the Royal orders which resulted in the production of " Queen's ware." The sets made for George III. of England and his Queen, may, of course, be regarded as celebrated examples of Wedgwood's wares. They were eclipsed, however, by the service of " Queen's ware " made for Catherine II., Empress of Russia, in 1774. It was a most costly service, upwards of £3,000 being expended upon it. According to Wedgwood's catalogue it was : " A complete table service for fifty persons, ornamented with various views of Great Britain, country seats of the nobility, gardens, landscapes, and other embellishments, all painted and enamelled, and executed according to the orders and instructions of the most illustrious patroness of art, the Empress of All the Russias, by her Imperial Majesty's very humble and grateful servants Wedgwood & Bentley, London, 1774."

The service consisted of 952 pieces, with no fewer than 1,282 views painted upon them. Describing those views Wedgwood wrote : " They were views of rural cottages and farms to the most superb palaces, and from the huts of the Hebrides to the masterpieces of the best known English architects." The body of each piece was of a pale brimstone colour, the view being painted in purple. The border was an ornamental wreath of oak leaves, and in the place of a coat-of-arms was painted a frog, a subtle allusion to the Empress's palace of La Grenouillère, the name of which indicated " a marshy place full of frogs." This wonderful service was long hidden from view in the Russian palace, discovered a few years ago by Dr C. N. Williamson, a well-known authority on miniatures, with the result that some of the pieces were for a time on exhibition in London by permission of the Czar.

Wedgwood's triumph of art was the reproduction of the celebrated Barberini, or as it was afterwards called, the Portland, vase. The original, which is in the British Museum, is of glass, a relic of an unknown art, discovered in the seventeenth century in a marble sarcophagus near Rome. Sir William Hamilton secured it for £1,000, but it was eventually bought by the Duke of Portland. The copies made by Wedgwood, limited in number, were far superior to the numerous reproductions which have since been made, but they fell short of the unique treasure which, although years ago injured by the hand of a lunatic, is still preserved as one of the most valuable possessions in the Gem Room of the British Museum.

DESIGNERS AND MODELLERS.

As in other potteries, and indeed in a greater degree than in many, the artists employed by Wedgwood contributed to his success. Chief among the sculptors, modellers, and workers in clay of his day was John Flaxman, who was born in York in 1755. He must have inherited his skill from his father, who was a sculptor and modeller, working for Roubiliac and others.

Whilst of tender years Flaxman was brought to London, where his father settled in New Street, Covent Garden. There he acquired a taste for designing, and after studying for a short time at the Royal Academy won a silver medal, although at that time only thirteen years of age. Soon afterwards, in the same year, he exhibited his designs in competition for prizes offered by the Society of Arts, winning a gold " pallett " inscribed, " Given to Mr John Flaxman, aged 13, New Street, Covent Garden, for model in clay, Class 100—1769." A year later he was again successful, and took the first premium for a basso-relievo in clay.

Wedgwood first made the acquaintance of young Flaxman in January, 1775, in which year a commission was given him by the firm—Wedgwood & Bentley—amounting to £15 9s. 3d. He modelled the " Nine Muses," receiving in payment half a guinea each. Shortly afterwards he executed four basso-relievo groups, " The Seasons "; he also modelled figures of " Jupiter," " Juno," " Minerva," " Justice," and " Hope," in each case receiving half-a-guinea remuneration.

Flaxman married Anne Denman, and lived in 27, Wardour Street, London, from 1781 to 1787, at that time holding office as a parish officer and rate collector. The soul of the artist then gained the ascendancy, and Flaxman set out for Italy, remaining in Rome nearly seven years. There he acquired his great inspirations, and designed, if not actually modelled, his best works. All the time he was working for Wedgwood. Shortly after his return in 1797 his genius was acknowledged, and Flaxman was elected an A.R.A. His greatest monuments are those erected to Nelson, Howe, and Reynolds in St Paul's, and to Lord Mansfield in Westminster Abbey. Flaxman died in 1826, and was buried in the Church of St Giles-in-the-Fields ; on the tablet erected to his memory is written, " John Flaxman, R.A., P.S., whose mortal life was a constant preparation for a blessed immortality ; his angelic spirit returned to the Divine Giver on the 7th of December, 1826."

Among other artists employed—and Wedgwood surrounded himself with the best when producing his gems of classic modelling—were, in addition to John Flaxman, James Tassie, Thomas Stothard, and George Stubbs, Wm. Hackwood, Henry Webber, and John de Vaere. Wedgwood was also assisted in his designs by his patrons and some amateur artists, among whom was Lady Templetown, who designed some of his works of art.

COLLECTIONS OF WEDGWOOD WARE.

Although some provincial museums contain very charming groups of Wedgwood ware, the collection of ceramics in the Victoria and Albert Museum at South Kensington is peculiarly short of representative pieces. The British Museum is better supplied, and there may be seen some fine vases, as well as an exceptional collection of medallions and other small objects, chiefly jasper ware.

In the Wedgwood Institute in Burslem there are some cases of exhibits including beautiful examples. Other local museums where excellent collections can be seen are at Glasgow, Liverpool, Birmingham, and Nottingham.

The museum at the Etruria Works of the Wedgwood firm is peculiarly interesting and instructive, for not only are the exhibits authentic specimens, but there are many moulds and wax models, and some relics of the old work. There are eleven original wax reliefs, prepared for the reproduction of the Portland vase, modelled by Henry Webber, who died in 1826. There is also a series of 126 wax portraits and classic medallions used by Wedgwood's modellers as guides for their designs; some of them are signed "J. and M. Gosset."

In the Wedgwood Works' museum there are figures and groups, including " Orestes and Pylades," and " Penelope and her Maidens," both in original wax designs, modelled by

Flaxman. Another splendid wax design is " Mercury join-
ing the hands of England and France," an original also by
Flaxman ; and a companion piece entitled, " Peace
preventing Mars from opening the Temple of Janus."
They were modelled in 1787 in commemoration of the
commercial treaty between France and England, an early
indication of the *entente cordiale*, now so fully exemplified ! The first copies of these pieces in jasper ware
were given by Wedgwood to Lord Auckland, who was
appointed Envoy Extraordinary to Paris.

The beautiful plaquettes or tablets already described,
of which Wedgwood wrote to his partner Bentley, " My
tablets only want age to make them valuable," are fully
represented in the collection.   There are basalt tablets and
a curious oval plaque, representing Zeno, upon a red
coloured ground, intended for mounting upon a wainscot
panel, or fixing on a plaster wall.   The jasper plaques in
the museum include examples of the Wedgwood & Bentley
period.   There are many models, too, including a pattern
model for the " Apotheosis of Virgil," which design was
selected as the model for the head emblematic of the Repub-
lic as it appears on the coinage of France on and after the
Franco-German war of 1871.

Medallions, portrait medallions, and pattern models,
representative of persons of notoriety then living, are fully
exemplified ; especially interesting are the pattern models
of medallions of Josiah Wedgwood and Mrs Wedgwood,
also one of Thomas Bentley, who was partner with Wedgwood from 1768 to 1780.   The collection further includes
medallions of Flaxman and his wife, modelled by Flaxman.

The vases with portrait medallions upon them are of
special interest, particularly those on which are portrait
medallions of Admirals Nelson, Howe, Jervis, and St
Vincent, on the cover of the vases being a well-modelled
figure of Britannia, accompanied by nautical emblems.

In Wedgwood's catalogue of 1787 he refers to jardinières and flower-pots thus : " Of *root-pans*, as well for bulbous as other roots, and of *flower-potts*, or *bouquetiers*, there is a great variety, both in respect to pattern and colour ; and the prices vary accordingly.   Some of the bulbous root-pots are finished higher, with bas reliefs, enamelling, etc. and the prices are in proportion."   In the museum there are some charming examples of these old flower-pots, some of them called "bough pots."   There are also choice bits which the home connoisseur would delight in possessing, such as candlesticks, ladles, inkstands, lamp vases, and even jasper chessmen.

MARKS.

There are some collectors who express disappointment at the long series of Wedgwood marks, all bearing strong resemblance to one another, with little to distinguish the old from the comparatively new.   The modern firm, lineal descendants of the great Josiah Wedgwood, continue to use his marks, his moulds, and his designs.   Their modern replicas are good—some very good—but there is a some-thing, indescribable, that tells the connoisseur almost intuitively the difference between the old and the new. The marks, however, are a guide, especially when taken in conjunction with minor marks and other indications of potters' customs practised at certain periods.

The round stamp mark, " WEDGWOOD AND BENTLEY," was one of the earliest used.   Afterwards the simple name-stamp " WEDGWOOD " in several sizes was impressed in the soft clay.   The old marks were carefully impressed and were easily read.   Such stamps are often accompanied by letters, numbers, or signs, workmen's indications, scratched or impressed.   It is of value to note that some pieces were stamped with letters

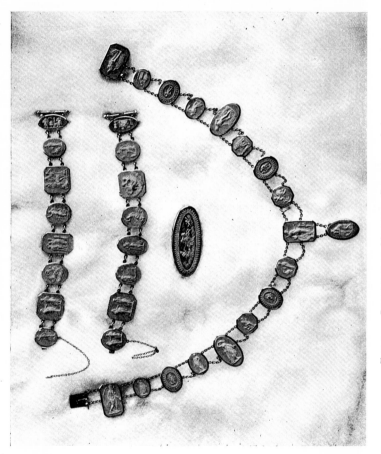

FIG. 79.—SPECIMENS OF MOUNTED CAMEOS, period 1790.

In the Works Museum of Messrs. Josiah Wedgwood & Sons, Ltd.

[To face page 232.

FIG. 80.—FOUR CAMEO PLAQUES, representing
(top) Byerley, who died 1819;
(left side) Thomas Bently, 1730-80;
(right side) Josiah Wedgwood, F.R.S. and S.A., 1730-80;
(bottom) Mrs. Wedgwood, 1734-1795.

In the Museum at the Wedgwood Works.

To face page 233.]

such as "A N O"; such marks, the present firm point out, did not occur before 1846, so that they should be absent from all collectable pieces of genuine antique china. In explanation of the use of such marks in more recent days, it is stated that the first letter was the workman's mark, the second letter indicated the month, and the third letter the year of manufacture. Thus, as a key to some of these marks used in more recent days it may be mentioned " O," as the date letter of the year, meant 1860, and " P " would be used for 1861, and so on.

The "WEDGWOOD & BENTLEY " mark is found only upon basalt and crystalline agate or imitation stone vases, plaques, medallions, and portraits of the same period ; it is not found upon the blue.

The illustrations shown in this chapter are mostly given by the courtesy of Messrs Josiah Wedgwood & Sons, Ltd., and are taken from specimens in their private museum at the works. That museum is of special interest to visitors in that there are many trial pieces and special examples of pottery and effects in which the great founder was experimenting. There are many fine models there too. The vase shown in Fig. 75 is cream-coloured and represents the early period, 1760-1767.

Reference has already been made to the remarkable service made for Catherine II. of Russia, ornamented with so many interesting landscape views and pictures of English scenery. Fig. 76 represents five plates which were part of the service, the period of which may be given as 1772-1774. Fig. 77 shows one of the remarkable copies of the Portland vase made by Josiah Wedgwood in 1790 ; it is a photograph of the authentic vase preserved in the Works Museum at Etruria. Of quite a different kind is the red ware spill ornamented with enamelled colours and richly gilt ; this piece is similar to a tea-set in the collection from which this was taken (*see* Fig. 78).

The love of detailed miniature work led Wedgwood to devote much time to the production of fine cameos, so many of which represented classic subjects, and in the excellence of their workmanship rivalled almost the ancient cutters of gems and cameos from which they were taken. Many of these gem-like cameos were mounted in gold and set in various ways. The illustrations in Fig. 79 are all specimens of mounted cameos of the period 1790.

The last of this short series of Wedgwood porcelain is a series of lifelike portrait gems (*see* Fig. 80). They represent respectively Josiah Wedgwood, F.S.A., S.A. (1734-1815); Mrs Wedgwood (1734-1815); Thomas Byerley (died 1810); and Thomas Bentley (1730-1780).

CHAPTER XXIII

SWANSEA AND NANTGARW

Some distinguishing features—Other Swansea attributes—The Nantgarw works—The porcelain and its decorators.

IT will be convenient to refer to the pottery and porcelain made in South Wales in one chapter, in that the different works, their separate ownerships, and the products made there are somewhat intermixed, notwithstanding that the potteries of Nantgarw (a small village some eight or nine miles from Cardiff) and Swansea were quite distinct.

It is probable that at a much earlier date than that when the beautiful ceramics for which Swansea, and afterwards Nantgarw, became famous, crude pottery and earthenware were made in the neighbourhood. The first pottery in modern times was the Cambrian, which was leased from the burgesses in Swansea, in 1764, to William Coles, of Cadoxton, near Neath. This was at a time when the new impetus to the potting industry was gaining ground in Staffordshire, Worcester, and other parts of England.

At first the Swansea potteries produced chiefly earthenware, but a great advance was made when George Haynes acquired the works in 1790. He soon found that the premises were too small, and their arrangement and kilns were behind the times, for already progress had been made by competitors in other towns. The real advance in Swansea china, however, was made when Haynes discovered or introduced a method by which he was able to make a fine hard paste, resulting in the production of "opaque china." Another development came when Haynes produced cream-coloured ware, using china clays from Bideford, and from Poole in Dorset.

Another phase passed over the pottery industries of South Wales when the Swansea Works changed hands in 1801-1802. At that time William Dillwyn, of Ipswich, and his son Lewis Weston Dillwyn, became the enthusiastic proprietors, and set about developing several schemes for the improvement and advancement of the works, effecting considerable alterations in their products. More extensions were made as their opaque china became popular. Again a great stride onward was accomplished by the altered character of the decorations and ornaments used. It appears that Mr Lewis Dillwyn was a Fellow of the Linnæan Society ; he was also author of several botanical books. That, perhaps, may have had something to do with the character of the ornament and the decoration and colouring of the china which eventually obtained such a marked predilection for botanical and natural history subjects.

The whole of the Swansea Works were at that time remodelled, it is said after the plans of the works which had been established so successfully by Josiah Wedgwood at Etruria.

The Dillwyns were fortunate in having the experience of Mr G. Haynes, who continued with them as manager until 1810. In that year Timothy Bevington became manager, and was assisted by his son. A few years later both father and son acquired shares in the concern, the apportionment of their joint interests and of those of the former owner being in the proportion of seven shares held by Dillwyn, two by Timothy Bevington, and one by his son John Bevington. The concern does not appear to have been altogether a success under the altered scheme of management and control, for it was discontinued in 1820, when the whole of the moulds and apparatus were acquired by John Rose of Coalport, who soon afterwards removed them to his own works in Shropshire.

SOME DISTINGUISHING FEATURES.

As already mentioned, the characteristic feature of the composition of the Swansea china was its hard paste. It was a compact fracture paste, differing from the granular nature of the Nantgarw paste. The chief charm of Swansea porcelain lies in the delightful paintings and exquisite ornament, rather than in the composition of the paste or in the form of the object. This peculiar charm and beauty was due, no doubt, to the decorators employed. We learn that in the year 1810 William Weston Young became chief decorator of the Swansea Works, and that he executed some remarkable paintings. The name of Billingsley, whose work is so frequently referred to in connection with other potteries, also became familiar at Swansea. He brought fame to the Swansea Works, where he was more commonly known as Beeley. Billingsley's somewhat changeful career is referred to at some length in the chapter on Derby porcelain (*see* page 115), and also in this chapter, in connection with the Nantgarw Works (*see* page 240).

Walker was another artist of note who left his mark upon Swansea porcelain. It should be remembered that the works at Swansea were founded at a time when most of the English potteries were paying more attention to porcelain than to the coarser earthenware. Therefore it is not surprising that the earthenware made during the first few years when the pottery at Swansea was gradually developing and being improved, was soon discarded for the more valuable and much-sought-after porcelain, and when opaque china was introduced it gained popularity with great rapidity.

The Swansea porcelain so much sought after by collectors was of a somewhat later date than the choicer ceramics of Derby and Worcester. It was made chiefly during the early years of the nineteenth century, prior to the close of Bevington's lease, which terminated in 1824. This very beautiful porcelain was alike celebrated for its excellent paste of undoubted quality, and for its unique decorations. The Swansea hard paste had a peculiar greenish hue when viewed in a strong light, a characteristic attribute which is helpful to collectors, who may with a little practice recognise this peculiar colouring of the paste.

It would appear that Mr Dillwyn, who had been appointed by the Board of Trade to report upon the work of the Nantgarw potters, who had applied to the Government for aid in September, 1814, was so favourably impressed with their work that he persuaded the owners of the Nantgarw pottery, and most of the operatives, to leave the little works and go to Swansea, which they did, and for a time worked for him. The arrangement did not last long, for these men returned to Nantgarw in 1817.

W. Young excelled as a painter of flowers, and his ability to paint birds, butterflies, insects, and shells true to Nature appealed to Mr Lewis Weston Dillwyn, who not only employed Young in the works as a painter of china, but engaged him to illustrate several books on botany and natural history which Mr Dillwyn was then preparing. Young, therefore, appears in his dual character as a painter of china and a book illustrator, working in colours and painting from natural objects, drawn chiefly from Mr Dillwyn's own collection.

Baxter, a clever painter on china, worked at Swansea for upwards of three years. He had previously been employed at Worcester, and after his engagement at Swansea terminated he returned to the Worcester Works. He was an artist possessing considerable skill; some of his decorations upon the choicer porcelain were reproductions of several of Sir Joshua Reynolds' pictures. Baxter was also successful in his original work.

Other painters of note contributing to the fame of Swansea china were Morris, a painter of fruit, and Beddoes, a noted heraldic painter. Morris, along with another painter named Pollard, had been pupils of Billingsley, whose style they copied closely.

OTHER SWANSEA ATTRIBUTES.

Some few special pieces were made at Swansea, but the bulk of the wares followed well-known styles and patterns of that period. Now and then departures were made, such, for instance, the manufacture of black basalt ware in imitation of the Egyptian ware of Wedgwood. Then again some very beautiful cameos in white on a black ground, similar to the cameos then being made in Staffordshire, were attempted with considerable success. Some of the figure subjects made at Swansea give evidence of having been copied or modelled after the fashion of old Staffordshire figures. There is, however, a distinguishing mark which it is useful to remember. It is that round the pedestal of Swansea figures will generally be found a line in chocolate or orange.

Then again the connoisseur notes the paste as a distinguishing feature of some importance. The granulated porcelain has already been referred to, and also the paste producing a greenish hue when held to the light. There are some pieces which have a very similar appearance to Sèvres china. The wonderfully translucent body of which they were composed made them resemble Sèvres; it was one of Billingsley's recipes, a paste he often used at Nantgarw.

Much Swansea china is unmarked. When the mark occurs it is usually " SWANSEA " stamped or printed in red, a trident being added to the name and in some places used separately (*see* Figs. xix. and xx.).   It is rather an unusual procedure in works practice to find the name of " BEVINGTON," who was works manager, on some of the pieces.   It is the opinion of some authorities that all the granulated porcelain stamped " NANTGARW," and perhaps decorated there, was made at Swansea.   That also is a point worthy of note.

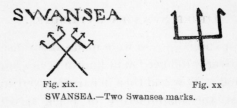

Fig. xix.   Fig. xx
SWANSEA.—Two Swansea marks.

The Nantgarw Works.

The works at Nantgarw were founded in 1811 by William Billingsley, who emigrated there from Worcester.   According to a well-known authority he was accompanied by his two daughters, Lavinia and Sarah ; the latter's husband, Samuel Walker, also formed one of the party.   The works at Nantgarw were on a very moderate scale, but some very charming pieces were made there, as is evidenced by the beautiful examples in the Cardiff and other museums. Financial troubles disturbed the progress of the Nantgarw Works, for Billingsley was short of capital.   It is said that the sum he had available was about £250, supplemented from time to time by assistance rendered by his friends. The work he achieved was good, and there was a market for it, so that Billingsley was hopeful of securing Government aid, for which he applied in September, 1814.   Apparently the Government of that day was not unwilling to give help to British manufacturers, and was evidently desirous of promoting useful industries, for Mr Dillwyn of Swansea was commissioned to report upon the prospects of the kilns. It does not transpire in what way Dillwyn fulfilled his mission, or the tenor of the report he made. Apparently he favoured the products of the little works, and was satisfied with Billingsley's skill as an artist, for, as it has earlier been pointed out, he persuaded Billingsley and his family, and some of his men, to take service with him at Swansea. In less than three years this family party of potters and decorators returned to Nant-garw, and once more commenced to manufacture and trade independently. Again Billingsley was in monetary difficulties, and in 1819 he left Nantgarw and found employment with Mr Rose of Coalport.

The Nantgarw Works were at that time taken over by Mr W. Weston Young, from whom Billingsley had borrowed money. Thomas Pardoe of Bristol was appointed manager; but the concern was not a success, and was closed down in October, 1822.

The Nantgarw Works were reopened by the Pardoes— father and son—about ten years later, and there they made some earthenware, quite a different class of work to that which had been carried on under Billingsley's artistic supervision. We also learn that the Pardoes became well-known makers of tobacco pipes.

THE PORCELAIN AND ITS DECORATORS.

The paste of the Nantgarw porcelain is very fine, and presents a somewhat glassy appearance. Some of the pieces look as if the glaze had been cracked according to design, not much unlike Chinese "crackle" ware.

It has been observed that when Nantgarw porcelain is held up to the light the body shows small pinholes or air bubbles in its composition. Then again, although the

Q

owners of the Nantgarw Works were exceedingly clever decorators and painters of porcelain, they do not appear to have been experienced potters, for many of the more fragile objects, like cups, are irregular in shape, having been carelessly fired through want of proper arrangement in the kiln. Even some of the most beautifully decorated cups have been thus indifferently fired.

The Nantgarw marks were sometimes impressed, at others painted, stencilled, or transfer-printed in red or other colours, and now and then the name appears written in gold.

It is evident to all who have followed the story of the founding of the Nantgarw Works, the somewhat chequered career of the owners, and the failure of the business commercially, notwithstanding the exquisite beauty of the porcelain, that the chief standard of quality and excellence of Nantgarw lies in the work of the artists, of which Billingsley was the chief.

The life history of Billingsley has already been sketched in connection with Derby, where this artist was employed as a flower painter. Owing to financial difficulties he found it convenient to change his name to Beeley, as already intimated. Some of his migrations may have been due to a similar cause, for we have heard of his short residences in Mansfield, Torksey, and Worcester. It is recorded that he made a flying visit to Coalport, where with his son-in-law Walker he put up a new kiln, which Walker had devised. He worked intermittently at several places in the West of England, and at Worcester, before settling at Nantgarw and commencing his little pottery on the banks of the Taff.

There is no doubt that Billingsley had a wonderful mastery of the brush and palette. He delighted in roses, and the distinctive character of the Billingsley rose seems to have found him employment anywhere. The china he so charmingly painted sold well, but it was almost too good, and its production rarely remunerated either artist or potter. This is not surprising when we examine with a magnifying glass the exquisite flowers on some of the Nantgarw porcelain. In every group rose, tulip, auricula, and nasturtium are true to nature, every botanical feature being correct. Indeed, so wonderfully are these flowers painted in the minutest detail, that the old china painted by Billingsley is said to be more attractive to the botanist than to the connoisseur of porcelain. Thus, in admiring old Nantgarw, the microscopist joins hands with the connoisseur of ceramics.

Of other artists there is not much more to add; the following, most of whom have been mentioned before— William Weston Young, Thomas Pardoe, John Latham, and William Pegg—were, however, artists of no mean repute.

The impressed stamp used at Nantgarw Works was " NANT-GARW " in small type, to which was often added " C W," which stood for " China Works."

The examples given in this chapter are specimens selected from the splendid collections of Swansea and Nantgarw in the National Museum of Wales, and are reproduced by the courtesy of the Director of the Museum.

Fig. 81 is a porcelain pot-pourri vase decorated with garden flowers, and is marked " SWANSEA." The very beautiful porcelain sucrier shown in Fig. 82 is also marked " SWANSEA." The entire set of which this forms a part is decorated with Bourbon sprigs in blue and red and gold enrichments. The plates shown in Figs. 83 and 84 are Nantgarw : the former is richly decorated with flowers and the border is embossed ; the latter plate (more correctly described as a dish) is ornamented with a cruciform pattern and marked " NANTGARW," impressed.

CHAPTER XXIV

ENGLISH——WORCESTER

The owners of the potteries—Paste and glaze—Some noticeable features—
Processes of decoration—Worcester marks—Some examples—Other
Worcester factories.

THE story of the manufacture of Worcester china is
coincident with that of Derby china, in that it began in the
same year Duesbury is said to have begun his enterprise at
Derby. There are difficulties in the way of definitely
locating some of the pieces assumed to have been made in
Worcester; on the other hand there are some special
characteristics of form and ornament which make the china
of certain periods indisputable ; moreover, much of the
finest porcelain is marked—not all, however, unfortunately.

THE OWNERS OF THE POTTERIES.

As in the case of Derby, the Worcester potteries changed
hands many times. The respective owners were, however
not all practical men like Wedgwood, Duesbury, and other
potters of personal fame, and much of the work produced in
Worcester consequently gained its great reputation from
the artists and decorators employed there. Indeed, the
personal craftsmanship of the decorators, which was of
such excellent quality, must have had much to do with the
commercial success of the owners ; for there was a well
maintained sameness in form and quality of colouring and
ornament throughout the earlier productions.

FIG. 81.—SWANSEA PORCELAIN POURRI VASE,
decorated with garden flowers.

FIG. 82.—PORCELAIN SUCRIER, marked "Swansea."
Decorations, Bourbon sprigs and gold enrichments.

FIG. 83.—NANTGARW PLATE, embossed border,
richly decorated with flowers.

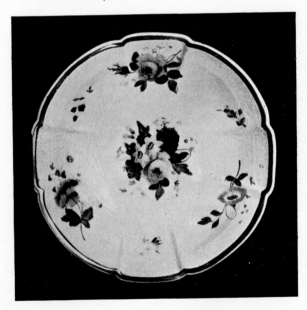

FIG. 84.—PORCELAIN DISH of cruciform pattern,
impressed mark "NANTGARW."

In the National Museum of Wales.

To face page 245.]

The founders of the works were Dr J. Wall, a medical man, and an experienced chemist, too, and W. Davies, who was an apothecary and presumably associated with Dr Wall professionally. The works were located in a house belonging to the Earl of Plymouth, the building being, in fact, an old mansion, known as Warmstry House.

The venture, which began in 1751, was a partnership concern in which there were fifteen joint owners or proprietors, Dr Wall retaining chief place. Among the better known partners in addition to Dr Wall were the Rev Thomas Vernon, William Davies, and Richard Holdship. In 1772 the lease of the works expired, and a new company was formed to continue the business, but Dr Wall retained the premier position. Among others brought in to the company at that time were Richard Cook, of London, and Robert Hancock, a clever engraver. The management remained in the hands of W. Davies until 1783, when the works were sold to Joseph and John Flight for the sum of £3,000. The transfer brought about many changes in management and in production. The period was marked by many alterations in the general character of the Worcester china, and also in the marks by which the porcelain of the different periods can be identified.

Some ten years after the transfer of the works to Joseph and John Flight, Martin Barr became a partner, and the style of the firm was changed to Flight & Barr—that was in 1793.

Again another change was made when the son of Martin Barr was admitted as a partner, an event which took place in 1807, the signature and mark of the firm at that time being altered to "Barr, Flight & Barr." In 1813 another son of Martin Barr came into the firm, the senior partner having withdrawn; that alteration in ownership necessitated a further change in signature and marks, which became "Flight, Barr & Barr."

Such frequent changes as those recorded are naturally confusing to the connoisseur of art porcelain, but they ought to be fully understood by collectors, as they are of material importance, assisting in understanding the marks and fixing definitely—within a measurable period—the time of manufacture of any marked piece, or of a piece having the same characteristics as well-known marked specimens.

In 1786 Robert and Humphrey Chamberlain, who had formerly worked at the old works, commenced in business for themselves in High Street, Worcester.   Their products were, of course, quite distinct, although possessing many of the old firm's characteristics, and should not be confused with the output of the works founded by Dr Wall, although made in Worcester.

The Chamberlains' mark during the period when they manufactured as an independent firm was either "*Chamberlains*," or "*Chamberlains' Worcester*," in script.   The script type used resembled the so-called copperplate writing of that day.

The connection of the Brothers Chamberlain with the old works began in 1840, when they were acquired by the Chamberlains and amalgamated with their own works under the trade style of Chamberlain & Co.; at that time name stamps being used as marks.

Another change was made in 1848, when the proprietors of the works were Walter Chamberlain and John Lily.   In 1850 the owners are stated to have been Walter Chamberlain, F. Lily, and W. H. Kerr.   Then two years later, in 1852, W. H. Kerr in conjunction with R. W. Binns purchased the works, which in 1862 passed into the hands of the Worcester Royal Porcelain Co., Ltd.

Collectors' fads include not only the collection of things of artistic merit and objects of beauty, but many things incidental to and associated with the manufacture of the curios collected. A collection of old trade cards is of considerable interest ; many are pictorial and illustrate works as they were at the time when curios, antiques, and "old china " were being made. Fig. 84A is an old trade card of the Worcester Works as they were in the days of Flight & Barr, whose firm name is seen on the card. It is reminiscent of transport and methods of despatching goods in the " good old times," and also of the boats which brought the clay and afterwards took away manufactured products.

The changes which came about at Worcester are more marked and more easily defined than in many other works ; this is due to the definite dates on which there were alterations in the firm style, and in the partners and management. And each succeeding owner or manager made great changes in the products for which the works at the different periods became famous.

The changes in the proprietors of the Old Works may, therefore, for the convenience of reference, be tabulated as follows :

1751.—Founded by Dr Wall.

1783.—Flight (who had been the London agent of the firm).

1793.—Flight & Barr.

1807.—Barr, Flight & Barr.

1813.—Flight, Barr & Barr.

1840.—Chamberlain & Co.

1862.—The Worcester Royal Porcelain Co., Ltd.

PASTE AND GLAZE.

Paste and glaze are of vital importance in identifying specimens of porcelain. No doubt many experiments were made and different ingredients tried by the respective owners of the Worcester Works before the full beauty and quality of their china was achieved. If a number of pieces were analysed they would yield different results, and show that many alterations were made in the recipe used throughout the greater portion of Dr Wall's period of control. The recipe which was at that time formulated and largely used was as follows : Sand, 120 parts ; gypsum, 7 parts ; soda, 7 parts ; salt, 14 parts ; alum, 7 parts ; and nitre, 40 parts. The glaze then used consisted of red lead, 38 parts ; sand, 27 parts ; brown flints, 11 parts ; potash, 15 parts ; and carbonate of soda, 9 parts.

There are many ways in which the pastes may be distinguished ; thus frit paste is dense, and shows a greenish shade of colour when viewed by transmitted light ; soap rock body is, however, less dense, and is yellowish in tint.

It was soft paste that was chiefly used at Worcester, and most of it can be scratched with a knife or a file without difficulty. The glaze is considered to be much thinner than that employed at Chelsea or Bow. The colour is not always pure, due, probably, to the use of too much lead. These are points of importance which the connoisseur of Worcester china may regard as essential features in distinguishing not only the origin of their specimens, but the particular period to which they must be assigned.

SOME NOTICEABLE FEATURES.

There are features which may be regarded as distinguishing marks of many of the potteries. In previous chapters it has been seen how in Staffordshire and other places the leading potters sought to give independent characteristics to their several productions, and how the artists employed in the different works were able to stamp their individuality upon the works they carried out. It has been the same in many potteries. In Worcester, however, perhaps the noticeable features are even more striking, for there are some distinctive points which collectors know full well, and are able without hesitation to point to them as certain characteristics which cannot be mistaken. At Worcester when a good thing had been discovered and the design or specific colouring adopted, it was retained very tenaciously. Many of the earlier objects were repeated in later years, often the same moulds being used, although a different scheme of decoration was adopted. Hence it is that collectors have two sets of noticeable features to keep in view, namely, the Worcester moulds, and the Worcester patterns and decorations.

There were tea- and dessert-services and compotiers, cider-mugs, punch-bowls, and butter and sauce-boats. These were goods which were at that time made at many places, but most of those produced at Worcester can be picked out at once by the notable features of either form or decoration. Then again, Worcester jugs are distinctive, especially those made during the transfer period. Very many beautiful vases were made at Worcester, the hexagonal and other Chinese forms and schemes of ornament being especially interesting and distinctive. Mugs with portraits upon them were made in great numbers ; and during the period when Flight was in control some magnificent sets and services richly embellished with armorial bearings were made, and some important commissions carried out.

As regards decoration it is worthy of note that many of the best artists of the day worked at Worcester as decorators. Many of these men gained notoriety for special forms of decoration. Some devoted the whole of their time to the study of Nature, and very realistically painted flowers, shells, and birds and other creatures. Others again preferred to follow the old masters, and copied classical subjects. Among the artists who are notorious for their distinctive treatment of the objects they decorated are the following : Astles (flowers and insects) ; Baxter (classic subjects) ; Barker (shells) ; Billingsley (flowers) ; Brewer (landscapes and flowers) ; Cole (groups) ; Davis (birds) ; Donaldson (groups) ; Pennington (groups) ; Pitman (groups) ; Rogers (landscapes) ; Stanton (insects and flowers) ; and Webster (groups).

PROCESSES OF DECORATION.

The ornamentation upon Worcester china at certain periods was, as it has already been stated, very distinctive ; especially is this the case in the earlier types like the old panel decorations. In the earlier days some remarkable exotic birds and insects in white compartments on deep blue plain or scale ground, constituted a special process or method of ornament. In rarer instances this decoration was enriched by the use of finely executed gold pencilling.

Most of the older forms of ornament and decoration were introduced from purely artistic motives. The artists desired to gain fame, and comparatively few of them looked to the commercial side or the owner's view point. Now and then, however, even in days gone by, an inventor of more than ordinary calibre either purposely or accidentally introduced some new feature which proved an immense commercial success, and pushed forward, as it were, the business capacities of the works where the invention was taken up and the discovery put into practice. Great inventions have often created a commercial epoch distinct and without parallel. One of these periods began when transfer printing was invented. Indeed, the value of the process cannot be over-estimated, because it enabled makers to vastly increase their output without additional labour and at reduced cost, in that by the simple device of transferring the pattern from the copper plate upon which it was engraved to a piece of unfinished pottery or porcelain, much of the hand labour of former days was done away with, and much time was saved.

The beginning of transfer printing in Worcester is placed in 1756, and there is a saucer printed in black with a portrait of Frederick the Great of Prussia, dated 1757 ; there is a similar saucer in the British Museum collection.

Dr Wall early realised the value of transfer printing, and introduced the process in Worcester ; the plates he used were executed mostly by Robert Hancock, who had at one time been a copperplate engraver at Battersea. The printing of transfers became a separate branch of the business, and we hear of Josiah and Richard Holdship, who were noted printers of transfers at Worcester ; their initials are found on some specimens in conjunction with those of Robert Hancock. Many of these original plates are still in the possession of the Worcester Royal Porcelain Co., Ltd., and may be seen at the Works Museum by visitors interested in these old relics.

Of the Worcester printed ware made in 1757 two of the best known lines are Hancock's " Tea Party," and the " King of Prussia." Other well-known subjects are " Queen Charlotte," the " Marquis of Granby," and " William Pitt." These printings were transferred to jugs and mugs and similar objects. The method adopted was almost invariably under-glaze printing. The process, at first confined to Worcester, Derby, and Battersea, soon became known, and very quickly spread until it was generally adopted throughout the Staffordshire Potteries.

The colours in which the Worcester designs were printed were black, red, or puce (an old-fashioned colour often mentioned in reference to china marks), printed, as it has been stated, under the glaze, although some of the earlier pieces were evidently printed over the glaze, and then fixed by another firing.

The causes which lead to public appreciation of pictures, engravings, and other schemes of ornament are varied, and sometimes a little uncertain. It is often a matter of speculation as to how it came about that much of the porcelain in China and other Oriental countries was distinctly according to European taste. In connection with transfer printing it has been pointed out that during the years when what we now regard as old china was being made, efforts in social and religious matters helped to influence in some way design and taste in porcelain. Just as merchants of olden time brought back in their trading vessels cargoes of china, and thereby introduced the Chinese taste in so many branches of art in this country, so missionary enterprise exerted an influence upon Oriental taste, and assisted them in their commercial success. The first missionaries from Europe to China carried with them engravings of European subjects, both religious and mythological. These the Chinese copied, and painted them by hand upon cups and saucers and bowls and plates made for the European markets. The little pictures, faithful copies of English engravings, became popular in this country, and English potters at Worcester and elsewhere began, in consequence, to transfer similar subjects to the wares they were making. Having learned the art of transferring and engraving without the cost and trouble of an original painting or hand-made copy, they were able to satisfactorily compete with Oriental competitors. The method of transfer printing on porcelain became known as "jet enamelled," under which head such pictorially decorated wares were described in old trade catalogues.

Bat-printing was another process by which pictorial ornament could be transferred from an engraved or etched copperplate prepared after the designs of pictures and engravings by Angelica Kauffmann, Cipriani, Bartolozzi, and others. The *modus operandi* was as follows : Upon

Fig. 84 (A).—Scarce Trade Card used at Worcester by Flight & Barr, 1793-1807, affording a pictorial view of the pottery as it was at that period.

the plate was placed a thin coating of linseed oil, which was then cleaned off from the service, leaving the engraved portion of the plate susceptible to the bats of glue on which impressions were taken, and afterwards dusted over with colour and transferred to the china. The printing of the well-known floral designs in blue, which was used at a somewhat later period at the Worcester Works, was put on under the glaze.

WORCESTER MARKS.

Marks are highly prized by collectors, and especially by the home connoisseur, who is naturally wishful to point out to his friends the authenticity of the pieces he displays. They are, however, of lesser importance—although of material advantage, and to some extent a factor, in market value—to the expert who understands the true test of paste, glaze, and other indications of genuine specimens of stated periods.

Marks are not always a true test or indication of quality, for the intrinsic value of a piece must be judged by the touch of the master potter, the decorator, or enameller, as well as that of the modeller, and not by the stamp or mark of the place of origin and the date of manufacture. It is well known that many of the finest pieces are not marked. Moreover, the scarcer the mark, the more its genuineness should be tested, for the forger knows quite well the amateur's predilection for marks.

The script and sometimes the Roman letter " W " is seen on some of the older pieces made during the time of Dr Wall. The crescent marks, open and filled in, are to be found on a great variety of Worcester wares made between the years 1751 and 1800. The crescent may be regarded as the true mark of the first Worcester pottery, in that it was one of the emblems in the family arms of Warmstry.

(It will be remembered that the works at Worcester were established by Dr Wall in Warmstry House, an old family mansion.)

Dresden and Sèvres marks appear to have been extensively copied at Worcester, and were no doubt used on pieces decorated in the characteristic styles of those celebrated Continental potteries. Some explanation of the monogram " R H " found on some pieces is necessary. This monogram is probably more in the nature of a workman's mark, for it was used by Richard Holdship in conjunction with an anchor and a place name. Some of the transfer pieces made between 1756 and 1774 were marked, " R. Hancock."

The greater part of the Worcester porcelain was made during the ownership of the Flights and their partners. " FLIGHTS " has been found impressed between 1783 and 1791 ; and during the same period " *Flight*," in script, was used in blue under the glaze. In a few instances the name in combination with a crown or crescent was used, notably on a service made for the Duke of Clarence. The crown is supposed to have been added to the Worcester marks after the visit of George III. to the works in 1788.

During the years intervening between 1793 and 1800 a capital "B " was scratched in the clay ; that was after Mr Barr had been admitted to partnership. Concurrently, and on to 1807, the firm's name surmounted by a crown was used.

From 1807 to 1813 the mark was frequently "B F B," above which was a crown. Sometimes, however, the style and address of the firm was given in full, thus, " Barr, Flight, and Barr, Royal Porcelain Works, Worcester."

From 1813 to 1840 the name or initials of the altered style of the partnership, which was then Flight, Barr and Barr, appear on most of the china. That brings to an end the period of *old* Worcester china ; afterwards various marks of origin were introduced until the present-day mark of the Royal Porcelain Works was adopted.   The marks shown on this page are the commoner varieties, yet they include the "square marks" for which there is such keen competition in the sale-rooms.

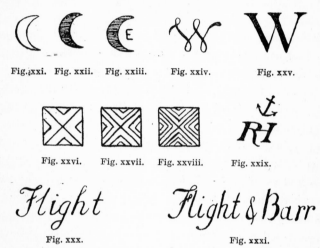

Fig. xxi.   Fig. xxii.   Fig. xxiii.   Fig. xxiv.   Fig. xxv.

Fig. xxvi.   Fig. xxvii.   Fig. xxviii.   Fig. xxix.

Fig. xxx.   Fig. xxxi.

WORCESTER.—Figs. xxi. and xxii. are found on Worcester china made from 1751 to 1800.   The crescent was taken from the Warmstry arms.   Fig. xxiii. is a scarcer mark used occasionally on blue ware. Figs. xxiv., xxv. (the W in script and in Roman—Dr Wall, proprietor) are found on early specimens.   Figs. xxvi., xxvii., and xxviii. are the commoner variations of the "square" mark. Fig. xxix. is a transfer mark of Hancock.   Fig. xxx. is an under-glaze mark used 1783 to 1791.   Fig. xxxi. was the mark chiefly in use from 1793 to 1807.

Figs. xxi. and xxii. are the two crescent marks (open and filled in) used extensively on porcelain made between 1751 and 1800.   The crescent mark, as has already been stated, was a part of the Warmstry arms, on whose family estates the works were erected.   A scarcer variety is that given in Fig. xxiii., and is found occasionally on blue wares.   Figs. xxiv. and xxv. indicate the script Roman and the "W" used in several forms and minor differences during the period of Dr Wall's proprietorship.   Following these are the three well-known varieties of the square mark, Figs. xxvi., xxvii., and xxviii.; of these, too, there are many minor varieties.   Some of the transfer-printed wares have the signature of Hancock the engraver; others a combined monogram, as in Fig. xxix. Figs. xxx. and xxxi. are marks indicating the introduction of Flight, and afterwards of Barr, as already indicated.

SOME EXAMPLES.

There are many fine specimens of transfer-printing in the Victoria and Albert Museum at South Kensington, including a jug, which was for many years in the Museum of Practical Geology in Jermyn Street, which has upon it a portrait of Frederick the Great of Prussia, representing the monarch as being crowned by an angelic figure. On the other side is an allegorical engraving of Fame, which is signed "R. H. Worcester." This jug is of further interest in that it is dated 1757, and inscribed "King of Prussia." We are reminded by an authority on the subject that the well-known Liverpool jug, which is inscribed "The Prussian Hero," must not be confused with the Worcester jug, which was printed from quite a differently engraved plate. Many very fine services were made in Flight's time at Worcester, including a service for Prince William Henry, who became Duke of Clarence and St Andrew. The design incorporated the rose of England and the Scotch thistle, which were painted in panels on the different pieces, the central device being the arms of the Prince.

Many fine historic pieces were at that time produced, such, for instance, the Royal portrait series, which includes portraits of George III. and Queen Caroline, and of George III. and his sons the Dukes of Sussex, Kent, York, and Clarence, some of the later pieces having upon them portraits of William IV. and Queen Adelaide, and of Queen Victoria as quite a young girl. Another variety of Worcester porcelain was that ornamented with masonic emblems. They were, however, of an earlier period than the portrait jugs just referred to. Dr Wall was a freemason, and most of the masonic jugs and mugs, of which there are many fine examples, were produced at the Worcester potteries during his lifetime. Some of the most notable examples are those still treasured in the Freemasons' Hall, in Great Queen Street, London.

Added to the portrait series, and those covered with emblems, were commemorative and ornamental porcelain souvenirs made soon after the battle of Trafalgar. Busts of Nelson and other naval heroes were also made at Worcester, and are met with in collections of Lambeth and Swansea pottery.

The modern works at Worcester well maintain the traditions of the old potteries, from which they rightly claim direct descent. It is in keeping with the long and honourable connection with the potter's art in this country that they keep in memory green the traditions of the Worcester potters in the eighteenth century, by the excellent collection of old china in the museum associated with the works. It is appropriate, too, that they should show by way of introduction a case of Roman pottery ; and it is especially suitable, in that the pottery has been found in the immediate neighbourhood, and is, consequently, literally " Worcester pottery." The collection includes specimens of Upchurch ware, and also some examples of Roman Samian ware (*see* chapter v.). There are also some bottles and vases of yellowish clay which have a distinctive form as well as colour.

Worcester pottery was not unknown in the Middle Ages (*see* chapter vi.). Kilns have been found on lands formerly belonging to the Priory of Malvern, and some very interesting tiles (*see* chapter xxxiv.) were discovered there. In the museum belonging to the Worcester Royal Porcelain Co., Ltd., are several of the tiles, which formerly were part of the floor tiling of Malvern Abbey, one having upon it emblems of the Crucifixion. In the Worcester Works Museum there is a jug of yellowish clay partly covered with a green glaze, probably a fourteenth-century piece. There is also a two-handled tyg of brown ware, with glazed black decoration.

The Museum begins its real purport, however, with the beautiful specimens of Dr Wall's day, and includes some Oriental pieces from which the early Worcester china was copied. In the introductory notes to the catalogue of the Museum it is stated that "the original company confined themselves principally to making blue-and-white ware in imitation of the Nankin." This gives the cue to the reason why blue-and-white ware of the early period has been made such a special feature in the exhibits at the works. The examples arranged in proper sequence show the varieties of the paste which was at first so very like the Chinese paste ; but some of the early Worcester porcelain could readily be mistaken for Oriental. The connoisseur who goes about with a hard file, testing pieces he comes across, finds out the difference, for Oriental ware was true porcelain made of natural clays, coated with a glaze of fleurspar, whereas the Worcester paste was artificial, and much lead was used in the glaze. The paste was cleverly composed, and showed the genius of a skilled chemist, such as Dr Wall assuredly was ; in his day suitable natural clays had not been discovered.

The collection at the Worcester Works includes many cups and saucers, typifying nearly all the main varieties of the Chinese taste. They are mostly marked specimens, represented by the square mark and the various forms of the crescent. The specialist who desires to understand the industry finds much of interest in the old moulds, picture blocks, and cut-outs which are shown. There is the usual range of obsolete articles, such as sauce-boats and artichoke cups of flower-shape, fancy dishes, pierced basket-work stands, leaf-shaped and shell-shaped comports, and egg drainers, mostly crescent marked. The range of tea-sets with handleless cups, many of extreme beauty, is supplemented by similarly decorated tea canisters, cream jugs, and knife handles.

Processes of manufacture in the early days are illustrated by exhibits of some of the original copperplates, notably those by Hancock representing Queen Charlotte and George III.

The set of Worcester china shown in Fig. 85 is indeed a splendid example of the best period of Worcester porcelain, and of the finest types of decoration still extant. It was made in Dr Wall's day and is painted with exotic birds, butterflies, and insects in panels upon a rich blue scale ground, the gilding being exceptionally good. The set comprises a teapot, cover and stand, cream jug and cover, basin and spoon tray, two large dishes, butter-dish, cover and stand, five plates, six tea-cups and saucers, six coffeecups and saucers, one sucrier and cover, and a ginger jar and cover.

A few other pieces of Worcester china are found in the groups illustrated in Figs. 88, 89, and 90, notably one of the well-known scarce and very beautiful fan pattern plates; also a dish with shield-shaped ornament of the Chippendale type, both pieces being marked with the square mark. The other pieces in these groups, including Crown Derby china, are more fully described under the illustrations.

Other Worcester Factories.

It is clear that although reference has been made to Chamberlain's connection with Worcester Old Works of world-wide fame, the factory which was founded by Robert Chamberlain and others in 1786 was a distinct concern, and should be treated separately.

It was when Flight took over the Old Works that Robert Chamberlain, in conjunction with his brother Humphrey Chamberlain and Richard Nash, founded Diglis Works. Some ten years later they secured the Old Works, with which their name was henceforth associated, for the two concerns were amalgamated.

Although many clever artists were employed at that time at Worcester, the personal skill of the proprietors no doubt contributed to the success of the business, and helped to maintain a high standard of quality and artistic merit. Robert Chamberlain had been a clever painter in his earlier days, and his son Robert took after him. Perhaps one of his greatest successes was the portrait of the Princess Charlotte, which was afterwards imprinted on many of the Worcester jugs.

Mention must be made of the works established in Worcester in 1808 by Thomas Grainger, a nephew of Humphrey Chamberlain, who secured the assistance of a Mr Wood as a partner, the firm then becoming Grainger & Wood. In 1812 the partnership was dissolved, and Mr Lee took his place ; at that time the name of the firm was changed to Grainger & Lee. Again another change, when Grainger & Co. became the proprietors of the works.

The chief feature of Grainger's china was its heavy body. In most examples the painting is over the glaze and there is a good deal of gilding.

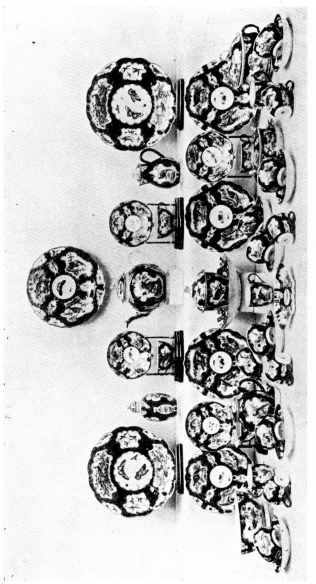

Fig. 85.—A Fine Worcester Tea Service of the best period of Dr. Wall.
Rare square mark.

Photo by the courtesy of Mr. Albert Amor.

[To face page 260.

FIG. 86.—DELFT PUNCH BOWL.

FIG. 87.—PUNCH BOWL in colours and gilt.
in the Oriental taste.

In the Author's Collection.

To face page 261.]

CHAPTER XXV

ENGLISH—LESSER KNOWN POTTERIES

Banksea — Bolsover — Bournes — Brampton — Brentford — Brislington—
Cadborough—Castleford—Chesterfield—Church Gresley—Cockpit Hill—
Don—Ferry Bridge — Isleworth — Mortlake — Pinxton — Wadhurst —
Wrotham—and Yarmouth.

As will have been seen from the stories of English potters in mediæval days, the potting industry was carried on locally by the many small manufacturers until quite recent times. Indeed, at the present day there are isolated potteries in Devonshire and other places, far away from those great centres where manufacturers of pottery and porcelain have for so many years congregated. In nearly every instance the establishment of a local pottery has been the result of someone on the spot having found suitable clay for making earthenware vessels. As time went on, however, it was found that other materials were needed in order to produce acceptable wares, and as the great waterways of a century or more ago were directed towards those towns and districts where the pottery trade flourished, manufacturers in those places were better able to secure raw materials from Cornwall and elsewhere than were those potters in out-of-the-way towns and villages far removed from canals and main thoroughfares. Hence it was that so many of the smaller potteries dwindled away and were finally closed down, and only in a very few instances were they continued on modern lines or reconstructed.

BANKSEA.

Many years ago a small pottery was worked on Banksea Island, opposite Poole, in Dorsetshire. The local clays there were suitable for common wares, but of not much use for better class porcelain. That district affords an object lesson of the resuscitation of an old industry on modern lines, and the manufacture of goods suitable for present-day requirements; for some years past an important industry has been carried on at Poole by Carter & Sons for the manufacture of fine hearth and architectural tiles.

BOLSOVER.

Prior to the middle of the eighteenth century there was a pottery in the Market Place, Bolsover (Derbyshire), at one time owned by T. and W. Robinson and T. Robinson, junior. The works, at the request of some of the townspeople, who appear to have objected to the pottery in the centre of the town, were closed down in 1750.

The ware made in Bolsover was of the ordinary bright brown-glazed type, with mottled or light slip decoration. There are but few specimens known; some, however, are owned locally, authentic relics including a sugar basin, a dish, and a mustard pot.

BOURNES.

Stoneware was made at Bournes potteries, at Belper, another pottery at Denby being worked by the same owners. The ware produced was mostly sold locally, and was without any special interest. An exception, however, must be made in favour of the "brandy bottles" of stoneware made at these potteries about the time of the great

Reform Bill of 1830. They took the form of figures representing William IV., Earl Grey, and others associated with the Government of the day. The inscription on the base or bottom half of the bottle was, " WILLIAM IV TH'S REFORM CORDIAL." The ware was mostly marked, "BELPER and DENBY, BOURNES POTTERIES, DERBYSHIRE."

BRAMPTON.

The stoneware vessels made at Brampton, Tickenall, and Codnor Park, in Derbyshire, gained some local notoriety. The names of local potters in the district were Blake, Luke Knowles, John Wright, and William Bromley. The clay they worked was obtained locally, the chief products being useful stoneware jugs, bottles, and kitchen utensils. The Brampton potteries were famed for their posset-pans and puzzle-jugs.

BRENTFORD.

There is said to have been a pottery at Brentford, Middlesex, but little is known of its productions.

BRISLINGTON.

Richard Frank had a pottery at Brislington about 1800. His chief efforts were directed towards producing lustre wares, not unlike, but much inferior to, the old Spanish lustre ware.

Some of the Brislington ware may still be found in farmhouses and cottages, near the site of the old potteries.

CADBOROUGH.

There was a pottery at Cadborough, near Rye, in 1800, at that time owned by the Smith family, but it passed into

the hands of the Mitchells in 1840. The works were chiefly
noted for a curious red ware which was coated with green or
brown mottled glaze. The memory of this pottery has
been kept in mind by the drinking vessel known as the
"Sussex pig," made at the Cadborough pottery. The
special feature of the vessel is that when the head is taken
off it forms an ale jug, from which at country weddings it
was formerly the custom to drink a "hog's head" of beer
to the health of the bride; other quaint cups have been
used for a similar purpose.

CASTLEFORD.

There was rather an important pottery at Castleford,
near Leeds, between 1770 and 1790, where Queen's ware
and black Egyptian ware were made. The works were
closed in 1820.

Some few pieces of the Castleford pottery are found
marked with the name of the firm "DUNDERDALE &
CO." The chief wares made at Castleford were tea-sets,
teapots, candlesticks, and useful household objects.

CHESTERFIELD.

According to old records, there was a pottery at Walton,
near Chesterfield, in 1730; the family owning the works was
named Briddon. As early as the fifteenth century brown
pottery had been made in the neighbourhood; and in the
eighteenth century, and again in more recent days, the
chief products consisted of brown earthenware of utilitarian
forms.

CHURCH GRESLEY.

A porcelain factory was founded by Sir Nigel B. Gresley, near his residence, Gresley Hall, in 1795. He obtained

his clay from Devonshire and Cornwall, making excellent tea-, breakfast-, and dinner-services, also some well-modelled figures. The painting and gilding of the porcelain were special features, and the colouring of the birds, the chief form of decoration, was exceedingly striking. Church Gresley china may be said to closely resemble inferior Derby ware. Some first-class artists, however, were employed there, among them W. Coffee, a Derby modeller. The Church Gresley porcelain works were closed in 1808.

COCKPIT HILL.

Many years before Duesbury established the Derby china works, William Heath had a large pottery at Cockpit Hill. It flourished about the middle of the eighteenth century, some excellent ware, chiefly brown mottled, being produced. There was a striking resemblance between the brown stoneware of Cockpit Hill and that made at Fulham and Nottingham. Many of the jugs and mugs were well moulded, and ornamented with hunting scenes, some of them were inscribed, " WILLIAM HEATH," a date being often added.

The works appear to have been carried on until 1788, although in 1750 it was John Heath who entered into partnership with Andrew Planché of Derby and William Duesbury of Longton, resulting in the establishment of the famous works in Derby.

DON.

John Green, of New Hill, had a pottery near Swinton, on the river Don, in 1790. He produced much fine ware, not unlike Leeds pottery. The style of ornament consisted of pierced borders and designs. The firm subsequently became "Greens, Clarke & Co.," and they published a catalogue in which they gave some particulars of their products. The *old* pottery may be said to have ceased when the works changed hands in 1834.

FERRY BRIDGE.

Tomlinson & Co. had a pottery at Ferry Bridge in 1792. In the year 1796 a relative of Josiah Wedgwood became a partner, the business then being carried on as Wedgwood & Co. The name of the firm was stamped on some of the pottery, which at that time consisted chiefly of ornamental jasper and Queen's wares, after the pattern of the Wedgwood wares being made at Etruria.

In connection with the Wedgwood family, it may be mentioned that in the eighteenth century there was a maker of the name of Wedgwood at Yearsley, who make "pani-keens" (deep pans), and pitchers of coarse earthenware.

ISLEWORTH.

The pottery established by Joseph Shore at Isleworth was noted for cups and other soft-paste porcelain not unlike Worcester. Shore was assisted by Richard and William Golding; the works were opened in 1760 and closed in 1800. During that period no doubt much pottery was made, but very few authentic pieces are met with in collections. In the London Museum there are several specimens, mostly brown or chocolate glazed ware, the varieties including moulded dishes, spills, cups and saucers, match-stands, and teapots.

MORTLAKE.

In a small book entitled *A Short Account of the Mortlake Potteries*, by John Eustace Anderson, some interesting information is given about the little-known Mortlake pottery. The works intended for the manufacture of Delft ware were established at Mortlake between 1742 and 1752, by William Sanders, who was afterwards followed by his son John Sanders, of East Sheen. There were two kilns erected, one for firing white ware, the other for coarser pottery. The works passed into the hands of Wagstaffe & Co., of Vauxhall, about 1827.

Some claim has been made to a first "Toby " jug having been made at Mortlake. There is no doubt that some very fine specimens of these quaint jugs were produced there. The chief ware, however, was Delft. Some excellent Delft tiles were decorated in blue and white, and others with little picture scenes upon them, in colours.

There was another pottery at Mortlake, commenced in 1759 by Benjamin Kishere, who had been an employé of Sanders. Mr Anderson, the writer of the account of the Mortlake Works already referred to, owned several examples of Kishere pottery, which he says were stamped, " Kishere, Mortlake Pottery, Surrey." They consisted of four jugs and two mugs ; one of the jugs held three and a half pints, its upper part was brown, and its lower light-brown ; on the upper half were, according to the author, "a windmill and a cottage with a figure leaning on the half-door of the cottage looking at a woman leading up a donkey with a sack on its back, a small windmill by itself, two trees separate, and two men together, one sitting on a barrel drinking and the other sitting, leaning on a table on which stands a jug." On the lower half of the jug "are two horsemen with eight dogs hunting what looks like a fox : it appears too small for a deer."

PINXTON.

A porcelain factory was established at Pinxton in Derbyshire between 1793 and 1795. The porcelain was soft paste. The chief decoration was the "French sprigs," which consisted of a blue cornflower or forget-me-not with gold edge. William Billingsley, of Derby, rendered John Coke, the founder of the works, some assistance.

The Pinxton Works were noted for the issue of porcelain tokens for five shillings, seven shillings, and ten shillings, which were inscribed, " LET THE bearer have in goods, etc." ; on the other side was the inscription, "JOHN COKE PINXTON, DEC. 4TH. 1801." The only mark known was " P." Mr Coke was a younger son of the Lord of the Manor of Pinxton. During the short time he worked the Pinxton factory he turned out some excellent useful china, consisting chiefly of tea-services and dessert-sets. The earlier porcelain was of an exceedingly fine texture, somewhat transparent, and well glazed. There is a rather curious metallic tinge about the paste that is not noticeable elsewhere. Pinxton is not a much collected china, and apparently has never been copied, and not many examples come under the hammer. Occasionally, however, isolated specimens are seen. Some of the small mugs were ornamented with views of bridges, and the tea china is painted with landscapes. There are a few pieces in the British Museum, and others in the Victoria and Albert Museum. This china is often wrongly classed as " Derby " or " Worcester."

NEWCASTLE AND SUNDERLAND.

Several "pot banks," as they were locally called, were established in Newcastle, Sunderland and neighbourhood, in the eighteenth century. Sunderland wares have gained some notoriety from their mottoes, and verses of poetry very frequently addressed to the sailors to whom they would largely be sold, and also commemorative of ships and matters relating to the briny ocean. A common pottery

FIG. 88.—A TYPICAL CABINET OF OLD CHINA
owned by a "Home Connoisseur."

FIG. 89.

TWO WORCESTER PLATES and a
CROWN DERBY CUP AND SAUCER.

FIG. 90.

A SUNDERLAND BOWL and
CUPS AND SAUCERS.

[To face page 268.

FIG. 90 (A).—Basket with rope-twist handle.
marked "Castlepie Works, Comber."

In the Art Gallery and Museum, Belfast.

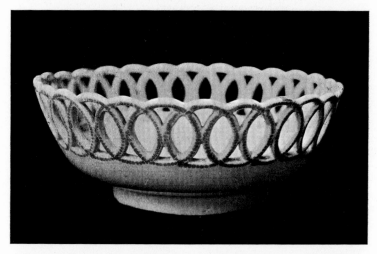

FIG. 91.—Irish Bowl (Dublin).

FIG. 91 (A).
View of bottom of Irish Bowl
(Fig. 91), showing mark.

FIG. 92.
Plate of Dublin Pottery,
Dublin mark.

In the Collection of Mr. Stopford Sackville.

To face page 269.]

was formerly made in the neighbourhood, for as early as 1730 a potter of the name of Warburton had a factory near Gateshead, making white ware until 1816.   In Newcastle Beyers had a pottery in 1755.   Samuel Dawson, of Staffordshire, opened a pottery in 1802 at Hylton, Sunderland. That pottery was noted for views of the iron bridge over the Wear, which commemorated what was then a great event, a bridge carrying a single span of 236 ft. 8 in. Nelson's victories were commemorated upon Sunderland jugs, too.   Again, we find a pottery near Sunderland, at Southwick, in 1789, which was established by Brunton & Co., who were followed by Moore & Co. in 1803.   Many bowls were printed with scenes like the "Sailor's Farewell."   The transfer decorations, which were on a creamy-white ground, had much the same appearance as those made in Liverpool, and seen on some of the Leeds ware. Sunderland lustre ware gained notoriety, too, gold lustre (see chapter xxxviii.) being sometimes used in conjunction with copper and bronze.   The " frog mugs " mentioned in another chapter were made at Newcastle.

The commemorative bowls already referred to present an interesting field to the specialist who is seeking motto inscriptions.   One of these is a quotation from Barton, and is entitled, " Forget-me-not."   It reads :

> The sailor tost in stormy seas,
> Though far his bark may roam,
> Still hears a voice in every breeze
> That wakens thoughts of home :
> He thinks upon his distant friends,
> His wife, his humble cot ;
> And from his inmost heart ascends
> The prayer " Forget me not ! "

Sewell & Donkin had a pottery at Newcastle in 1780, where they made Queen's ware and pink lustre.   Some of the pieces made at their works are marked " Sewell & Donkin." There was also a pottery at Sheriff Hill, near Newcastle.

WADHURST.

The earlier history of the potting industry in Sussex is referred to in chapter vi., " Mediæval Pottery " ; a new start was, however, made at Wadhurst in 1721, when an important pottery was founded.   This ware is interesting to collectors, too, in that many of the pieces are marked, and often dated.   The majority bear dates towards the close of the eighteenth century, those having been made in the earlier days of the pottery having probably perished.

The ornamentation used at Wadhurst was imparted by white or yellowish soft pipe-clay, applied with a quill in a very liquid state, in the form of dots or stars.   The objects consisted of a variety of useful wares, such as two-handled cups, teapots, and some very elaborate bowls.   For other Sussex wares see " Cadborough " and " Wrotham."

WROTHAM.

Some useful coarse earthenware was made at Wrotham in the middle of the seventeenth century.   That Kentish pottery was worked from 1656 until 1710.   There is a dish in the British Museum inscribed, " I. E :   WE 1699 : WROT : HAM " in enamelled beading, and decorated with an incised pattern of rosettes and geometrical design. There are also early tygs, and some very small mugs of Wrotham ware.   In the Maidstone Museum there is a piece dated 1666, which is probably the earliest example of this interesting ware.   For illustrations of Wrotham ware, *see* Figs. 20, 21 and 22.

YARMOUTH.

There was a pot bank at Yarmouth towards the close of the eighteenth century which went under the name of

" The Ovens." There are no authentic records of the
different wares produced there, neither do any of them
appear to have possessed any special merit. Indeed, most
of the Yarmouth earthenware or white ware was obtained
elsewhere, then painted and decorated at Yarmouth, and
fired in a gloss kiln. The mark found on such pieces is
generally," W. ABSOLON, YARM.," varied sometimes by,
"ABSOLON YARMD." On some of these pieces are
marine views, a picture of Yarmouth church, and the arms
of the town.

CHAPTER XXVI

Belfast—Dublin—Limerick—Rostrevor—Wexford and Waterford.

THERE is a peculiar interest in the collection of locally-
made pottery to any one resident in the neighbourhood,
especially when such a collection is not confined to the
products of one pot works or of any one given period.
Such a collection may very well be made of Irish pottery,
a comparatively little-known study, although there are
special features connected with the products of the several
potteries which have been established from time to time in
the Sister Isle. Mr M. S. Dudley Westropp, in a remarkably interesting paper read before the Royal Irish Academy
some little time ago, gave a very lucid account of his
exhaustive enquiries into the different potteries in Ireland,
and the various wares which have from time to time been
made. During early days, he tells us, a coarse kind of
pottery was made in Ireland, including food vessels, incense
cups, and cinerary urns. Large quantities of these ancient
vessels have been found in Irish crannogs. The dates of
the manufacture of such old pottery are uncertain, in that
the crannog in Ireland, although dating from the Bronze
Age, was constructed even in later periods, down to Elizabethan times.

Among the pottery of mediæval days must be included
encaustic tiles found on the sites of old Irish monasteries
and used as floor tiles in cathedrals. The finer kind of

pottery, such as was made towards the close of the seventeenth century and throughout the following two centuries,
was made in many parts of Ireland, the different localities
being for convenience' sake divided under the names of the
towns where they centralised.   The earliest mention of a
fine pottery in Ireland was one at Belfast.

BELFAST.

Mr Westropp recalls the story alluded to by Dr William
Sacheverell in *A Voyage to I-Columbkill in the year* 1688,
in which the worthy doctor tells how, owing to a gale, the
ship in which he was a passenger had to put into Belfast
Lough, and there he came into contact with a Mr Smith,
who had built a new pottery where Delft ware was made.
Not much is known of this pottery.   There is, however, in
the National Museum at Dublin a shoe of enamelled or
tin-glazed earthenware decorated in blue, bearing on the
sole the letters, " H M R " and " BELFAST 1724."

There was another pottery in Belfast towards the close
of the eighteenth century, where an attempt was made to
introduce a better class of ware, such as was then being
made in Staffordshire and other places.   The proprietors on
January 29th, 1793, petitioned the Irish House of Commons for aid, stating that :   " Taking into consideration
the many and great advantages which might arise from the
introduction of a manufacture of Queen's ware and other
kinds of fine earthenware, such as made in Staffordshire,
they conceive that many materials which have been
hitherto overlooked and neglected would be thus rendered
useful and important ;   and many workmen and children
would thus find employment.   With these views and from
these motives the petitioners have united themselves into
a company, and by their exertions have carried this manufacture to greater perfection in the County of Down, near

S

Belfast, than was ever known in this kingdom. That petitioners have been at great expense in searching for and making experiments upon materials for this purpose, the more important of which they have discovered in this country, and which are mostly prohibited from being imported from England. That petitioners have also been at great expense in erecting buildings, in importing machinery, and in bringing workmen from foreign places. That petitioners have found that the expense attending the introduction of this new manufacture and the difference in the price of coals from which they are in Staffordshire has greatly exceeded their expectations, and that several additional buildings are necessary to the greater extent and perfection of it."

The firm of Greg, Stephenson & Ashmore owned the pottery at Ballymacarrett, near Belfast, in 1792. In an advertisement they inserted in the *Belfast News Letter* they claimed to have brought to a high state of perfection cream-coloured or Queen's ware. They advertised again in 1793 a great quantity of cream-coloured and painted earthenware, as well as apothecaries' gallipots. Greg, associated with this firm in 1795, was awarded a premium which had been offered by the Dublin Society to the first person who should erect a proper mill for grinding flint.

Mr Westropp tells us that a potter of the name of Victor Coats set up a pottery in Belfast, in 1793, advertising for sale " a good assortment of butter-crocks and milkpans of different sizes, garden-pots, ridge, malt-kiln and flooring-tiles of a remarkable good quality, and also chimney-pots made to any shape at the shortest notice." His pottery was on the banks of the river Lagan, near to the china factory of Greg, Stephenson & Ashmore.

In the Public Art Gallery and Museum in Belfast there are very interesting exhibits of locally-made pottery and some examples of the products of early Irish wares produced in other parts of Ireland. There are some pieces which are said to have been made at Ballymacarrett about 1794 by Greg, Stephenson & Ashmore. They have also pieces which have been made at a somewhat later date than collectors of old china touch. Among these are some beautiful Larne ware made from 1850 to 1857; they have a plate of Rostellan ware made about 1852, on which are the arms of Cork. In Fig. 90 we show a basket in the Museum. It has a rope-like handle and splashed brown body; it is marked, " CASTLEESPIE WORKS, COMBER," impressed.

DUBLIN.

In the year 1739 John Chambers was busily engaged in pottery-making in Dublin. Chambers died in 1751, when his pottery was taken over by Crisp & Co., who made wares of Carrickfergus clay. An advertisement appeared in the *Dublin Courant* in 1748 as follows : " At the Irish delft warehouse on the North Strand near the Ship Building, Dublin, are made and sold by wholesale and retail a variety of blue and white delft ware, allowed by the Honourable the Dublin Society to be as good as any imported." The Dublin Society appear to have offered premiums at different times for the erection of a manufactory of earthenware in imitation of Delft. This premium was secured in 1754 by Captain Delamain, who petitioned the Irish House of Commons for aid to enable him to carry on the manufacture. He was voted the sum of £1,000, and afterwards appears to have made a decided effort to found the industry on the most satisfactory basis, employing skilled workmen and instructors to teach apprentices. The way in which he set about to do this will be best understood by the following advertisement, which appeared in *The Dublin Journal* of October 16th, 1753 : " The new Delft Manufactory on the Strand is almost built, the proprietor of which to endeavour to establish the earthenware manufacture in this kingdom has provided the ablest masters for making earthenware, and instructing youth in all branches, and will take 25 Charter Schoolboy apprentices every year, and as they will be masters of the trade in three years, several manufactories can be supplied with workmen ; and what it cost him large sums to discover, viz., inventing kilns to glaze delft with coals, grinding flint, glazing it, he will communicate all secrets of the trade to any person who will establish such works, and will supply them with workmen to carry it on, so that large sums of money will be saved that goes out of it for French delft. I am sure no nation has better or cheaper materials for it."

In an announcement made in August, 1755, addressed " To the Merchants of the Kingdom of Ireland," Delamain stated that he had brought his earthenware to such perfection that he had received great demand for it from Germany, Spain, and Portugal. He further stated that having discovered the method of burning his wares with coal, and having produced a good body and glaze, he was able to export his pottery and "undersell the French." After his death, which occurred in 1757, the Irish Delft manufactory was carried on by his widow, and later by his brother and other relatives. Their methods of export business seem to be somewhat novel, although perhaps in accordance with the customs of the times. They exported pottery to Jamaica and received its value back in rum !

The Dublin ware is very rare, one of the finest collections being in the hands of Mr S. G. Stopford Sackville, of Drayton House, Thrapston, through whose courtesy we are enabled to illustrate two pieces of Dublin Delft. One is a remarkably beautiful bowl (the bottom with the Dublin mark being also illustrated), see Figs. 91 and 91A. The other piece, a plate, is shown in Fig. 92. The mark is a large harp and crown, and the word " Dublin," also in blue, the same on both pieces. These once formed part of a set, made at Delamain's factory, presented to Lord George Sackville in 1753. Later records speak of the firm as " Wilkinson & Delamain," who were manufacturing Delft ware in 1769. Then the factory passed into the hands of workmen who had been employed at Delamain's. The quality and variety of the wares they made may be judged from an extract from the advertisement which appeared in a Dublin paper in 1770, which reads : " They acquaint the nobility, gentry, and public that they have opened a commodious shop in front of their delft factory in North Strand, where they intend selling their goods and no where else, and have now a considerable assortment of excellent wares, such as plates, dishes, etc., far superior and cheaper than any of the kind imported. They likewise do landscapes, coats of arms, crests, and views of gentlemen's country seats in the most elegant manner. They also make pots for grocers, apothecaries and perfumers."

A Delft ware pottery which was in existence in 1771 was owned by Edward Ackers and James Shelly, both of whom had formerly been earthenware manufacturers in Staffordshire, and at their works in Dublin made "Queen's ware," as they were careful to mention, out of Irish materials.

There is mention also of a Delft factory having been worked at World's End Lane, Dublin. Then for a time the pottery industry in Dublin ceased, to be revived again in the nineteenth century, when in several places pottery was made from Irish clay ; in this industry there has been a recent revival.

LIMERICK.

There was a Delft factory in Limerick in the year 1762, but Mr Westropp tells us that the only reference to it that he has been able to find is an award of £30 having been granted by the Dublin Society to John Stritch and C. Bridson, who had erected an earthenware factory in the city of Limerick. Bridson died in 1768, and it is supposed that the factory was closed shortly afterwards.

There was a pottery near the Limerick Gaol in 1818, where coarse ware was made by John Hanks & Co., the wares produced being chiefly garden pots and common domestic crockery.

ROSTREVOR.

There was a pottery in Rostrevor in the eighteenth century, where blue-and-white earthenware was made. The owners seem to have specialised upon sets and services, which they ornamented with coats-of-arms, expressing a willingness to ornament pottery " with any pattern desired."

WEXFORD AND WATERFORD.

Early in the eighteenth century a Quaker of the name of Chamberleyne, said to have settled there from Staffordshire, manufactured pottery, and afterwards introduced china, at Wexford. The old kilns were not cleared away until the year 1870, although the pottery had long been in disuse.

According to an advertisement which appeared in the *Dublin Journal* of 1755, some white transparent china was made there. Even the name of the potter appears to have been lost, although it was recorded, thirty-six years later than the announcement, that a potter of the name of John Williamson was then living in Waterford.

Among other potters to whom reference is found in old documents are Thomas Hardin, who made black crockery

ware, in 1767, at Portadown, using turf fuel; Thomas
Claugher, of Charlemont, who in 1793 made black glazed
ware; and William Robb & Co., who had " a crock
manufactory " at Derrybroughy, in 1803.

There is a very interesting collection of Irish pottery in
the Belfast Municipal Art Gallery and Museum, where also
may be seen some English stonewares. There is further an
excellent collection of clay pipes, which were formerly
made in considerable numbers in the neighbourhood of
Belfast. Although neither ancient pottery nor old china
in the strict sense of the term, tobacco pipes are very closely
allied to the pottery industries, and a collection of these
curious little objects, which became a necessity almost as
soon as tobacco was introduced, is an extremely interesting
adjunct to a collection of old pottery. We learn from the
Quarterly Notes of the Belfast Municipal Art Gallery and
Museum, that there is little doubt that the first clay pipe
bowl was merely a lump of clay, moulded into shape by
hand and baked in the household fire. It was Richard
Thursfield, of Broseley, who in 1575 became a noted maker
of pipes made of clay. The Pipemakers' Company, who
obtained a charter in 1619 from James I., was an important
body, consisting of a Master, four Wardens, and twenty-
four assistants. The pipes made at that time were usually
impressed with the maker's initials or some device on the
heel of the pipe, replaced later by a spur. Many romantic
stories have been told about the curious little pipes then
made, and which have been dug up and are now exhibited
as museum specimens; while in England they were thought
to have belonged to fairies, in Ireland they were believed to
have belonged to the *cluricannes*, a kind of mischievous
fairy demon. There was a fashion in pipe-making, and the
shapes changed from the barrel bowls of the reign of
James II. to the elongated bowl of the time of William III.

In 1682 there was a short-stemmed pipe used in Ireland, very different to the long " churchwardens " of later years. There was a clay-pipe works in Belfast in 1812, the old signboard of the shop where the pipes were sold being now in the Belfast Museum.

CHAPTER XXVII

CONTINENTAL—FRANCE

Palissy the Potter—The faience of Henry II.—Beauvais—Lille—
Moustiers—Nevers—Niederwiller—Rouen—Sèvres—Strasbourg.

THE mediæval pottery made on the continent of Europe, in many of the principal towns, was not only quite different to that which was being made in England at contemporary dates, but it was of a more artistic and altogether more advanced type. The renaissance of art which became so pronounced in Italy, and passed through the several continental countries in rapid succession, exerted a marked influence on Continental pottery. Some of the potters caught the inspirations of great artists, and learned from sculptors, painters, and modellers how to render minor articles, even domestic objects, beautiful and decorative by applying artistic form and colouring to the objects they were fashioning.

Taking the different countries, which in some cases included quite a number of independent Provinces and Duchies, and even States, in their grouping, France comes first on the list. The chief period during which objects of art were fashioned, and the foundations were laid for those remarkable collections of pottery which have been such distinctive features in Continental museums, and in our own museums and art galleries for many years past, was between the sixteenth and the late eighteenth centuries. Throughout the whole of that somewhat lengthy period there were, of course, many changes in the types and characteristics of

281

form and ornament.   During the sixteenth century there
seems to have been two distinct types.   First of all there
was that distinct and characteristic pottery modelled in
relief by Bernard Palissy, and those who copied his style.
The other pottery was the Orion ware or the faience of
Henry II.

PALISSY THE POTTER.

In the first-named group Bernard Palissy modelled in
relief some remarkable dishes, plates, and other vessels,
and then covered them over with a white tin enamel,
afterwards painting this extraordinary ware in many
bright colours.   Palissy was born about 1510 at La
Chapelle Biron, a small village in Perigord.   History tells us
that he was born of poor parents, and that he began his
career as a worker in glass.   One branch of his work was
associated with the cutting of glass for those richly stained
and painted windows which have since become the admiration of connoisseurs of painted glass, and which have added
so much to the beauty and quaint decoration of the old
Gothic churches.   Palissy spent much time in acquiring a
more accurate knowledge of geometry, and had a taste for
painting and modelling.   He became a distinguished
painter on glass, drawing his inspirations from the mediæval paintings of Italian masters.   He must have been an
artist of some repute, and his work must have been fairly
remunerative, for he travelled much, visiting Flanders, the
cities on the banks of the Rhone, and becoming familiar
with the chief features in French towns.   It is said that he
was at that time a land measurer or a student of geology
and chemistry.

In 1539 Palissy became a worker in the art with which
he was associated in after-life.   He achieved much success
in producing beautiful enamelled pottery ; but it was after

many privations and hardships. He began without any knowledge of how the enamel he sought to produce was made, and apparently was ignorant even of the firing of common earthen vessels. He lost most of his savings in these experiments, and it was only after he had, in his frenzy, burnt up the chairs and tables in his house for fuel —being without the wherewithal to purchase it—that he succeeded. Sixteen years had been spent in discovering the enamel which satisfied him and served as the coating for the rustic pottery which he had modelled by his remarkable skill. He lived in troublous times, and suffered much owing to having embraced the principles of the Reformation. He fled, however, to Paris, having been delivered by a direct order from the King, and there Catherine de Medici provided him with a workshop, and it is said often visited his potting-sheds and furnace, watching him model and colour his finest pieces. Yet, notwithstanding royal favour and personal visits from Henry III., who was desirous of giving him liberty, that weak monarch allowed him to be thrown into prison, where he remained until he died in the dungeons of the Bastille in 1589, refusing up to the last to give up Protestantism.

Palissy appears to have drawn his inspirations in modelling and in colouring partly from his study of natural history, and partly from religious subjects. His favourite scriptural scenic representations were Adam and Eve, the Sacrifice of Isaac, and the Holy Family. He also showed some knowledge of ancient mythology, for among other representations are " Venus, surrounded by Cupids," the "Birth of Bacchus," and "Neptune with his Seahorses." Palissy was indefatigable in his work, but he was assisted by two relatives, sometimes mentioned as brothers, at others as nephews. Palissy was an old man of over eighty years of age when he died, but his assistants survived him, and worked on during the reign of Henry IV.

Specimens of their art are extant, but they do not equal the originality of the founder of that peculiar style. Indeed, many of his imitators missed accurate reproduction by introducing modern shells and other objects of natural history, with which Palissy does not appear to have been familiar. Most of his modelling of such things consisted of reptiles, plants, and fossil shells, not those of a contemporary date.

There are some examples of Palissy's ware in the Victoria and Albert Museum at South Kensington, also in the Cluny and the Louvre Museums in France, and here and there examples in private collections, especially in France. The Palissy cistern in the Victoria and Albert Museum is one of the most noted examples of the exquisite work of Bernard Palissy at his best. It is described as having on the side the head of a marine deity. The ground of the scroll upon which it is placed is of a greyish blue, indented with wavy lines to represent water. On the other side is the head of a female with somewhat disorganised hair, two locks being tied under her chin. The festoons decorating the cistern are flowers, the rustic ground being of a rich, dark blue. Very rare indeed is a marked piece. Some of the initials upon undoubted Palissy vessels are probably the initials of workmen who may have taken part in the modelling or possibly the firing or decoration.

The Faience of Henry II.

The early faience ware or Orion pottery made during the reign of Henry II. takes its name, not from the potter, Cherpentier, who made it, but from his rich patron, Hélène de Hangest, who provided a workshop for her protégé at her château d'Orion between the years 1524 and 1537. This peculiar faience ware was chiefly ornamented with masks, frogs, shells, lizards, and shields, a kind of pink colour being much in evidence, described, however, by some writers as a delicate cream tint with a pinkish shade on it. This peculiar colouring is said to have been imparted by introducing a little yellow in the lead glaze. Many different objects are met with, chiefly ewers, salt-cellars, plates, and tazzas. There are some magnificent specimens of this work in the South Kensington Museum, especially several of the enamelled tazzas. It should be clearly understood that this faience ware was made of a true pipe-clay, fine and white, much harder than the paste of the Palissy ware. The ornaments, too, are more clearly cut, in that the pottery is covered with a thin, transparent, yellowish glaze differing from the thicker coating of enamel on most of the Italian majolica, which to some extent it may be said to resemble.

BEAUVAIS.

There was a factory or works at Beauvais as early as the twelfth century, where some commoner earthenware was produced, such as flat pilgrim bottles. Early in the sixteenth century, however, some rather remarkable dishes and ornamental pieces were made, inscribed with the name of the King, Charles VIII of France. On some of these are the arms of France and Brittany. Such vessels are said to represent contemporary pieces then being made in Nuremberg.

LILLE.

A porcelain factory was established in Lille somewhere about 1711 by a Frenchman named Barthélemy Dorez, the porcelain produced there being somewhat similar to St Cloud ware. The decorations were to a large extent copied from Chinese porcelain, the mark used being either " D " or " LL." Another porcelain factory was established in

Lille about 1784 by M. Leperre Durot, and over his door-way was painted, "Manufacture Royale." Beautiful white porcelain, richly decorated with gilded bouquets of flowers, was manufactured. There are also small biscuit figures. The mark on the Lille porcelain of that period was "A LILLE."

Faience was made at Lille towards the close of the seventeenth century, the decoration being chiefly in Delft style. There was another faience factory established in Lille in 1740 by Jean Baptiste Wamps, who died in 1755, the works then passing into the hands of another family.

MOUSTIERS.

Some choice pottery was made at Moustiers by a potter named Clérissy in 1686. During the first period of his work, assisted by several clever potters and artists, plates and dishes were ornamented with the claws and heads of lions, and with grotesque human masks. A little later sporting scenes were introduced. It is said that at that time Clérissy made a service costing 10,000 livres for Madame de Pompadour. Later, in the reign of Louis XVI., the art of Moustiers appears to have depreciated, and there is little to admire in the pottery made there after the Revolution of 1789.

NEVERS.

Majolica ware was introduced in France in the time of Catherine de Medici, and afterwards became the French faience. The pottery at Nevers prospered from about 1570 to the end of the seventeenth century, but most of the pieces made there were indifferent copies of Italian majolica. In the eighteenth century some vases of Chinese form, painted in blue with Oriental figures and flowers, not at all unlike Delft ware, were made there.

NIEDERWILLER.

A works was founded in Niederwiller in 1754. The pottery produced there consisted of (1) faience enamelled and coloured, (2) Japanese faience, (3) white or blue faience, and (4) pottery decorated with landscapes, some of this faience being much like Dresden in appearance. At the time of the ownership of the Niederwiller works by Baron de Beyerly the pieces were mostly marked with a " B "; afterwards, when owned by Count de Custine, the mark consisted of two C's interlaced.

ROUEN.

Francis I. founded works at Rouen in the seventeenth century, much of the pottery produced there being similar to Nevers ware, the seventeenth-century specimens being the finest examples. The colouring was chiefly red and blue, and some very carefully designed arabesques of geometrical form were introduced in the decoration. Examples of Rouen ware may be seen in the Victoria and Albert Museum, in the local museum at Rouen, and in the museum at Sèvres.

SEVRES.

The Royal Manufactory of Porcelain, which was ultimately settled at Sèvres, was first established at Vincennes by Louis XV. The King became a partner in the works, owning a third share of the property. The factory was soon afterwards moved to Sèvres, where many improvements were made, the finest examples being produced between 1760 and 1770. It is said that the King was induced to take up this venture after having seen the successful products of the two brothers Dubois, who had worked at the factory of St Cloud, and had discovered the secret of the manufacture of soft porcelain. One of their workmen, Grevant, continued the factory until the formation of the new company, in which the King had a share, and in which his Majesty became the sole proprietor in 1759. Until 1761 nothing but soft paste, an artificial compound, was used. Soon after that date hard porcelain like that made in China and Japan was introduced. It was then that two kinds of ware were made—soft and hard paste—calling for the distinctive phrases *pâte tendre* (soft paste), and *pâte dure* (hard paste). Those who wish to pursue this subject, and enquire more fully into the distinctive differences in the compounds used at Sèvres, should study M. Brongniart's book, *Traité des Arts Céramiques*. (For further reference to the pastes and glazes used at Sèvres, *see* chapter iii.)

Some very remarkable pieces, now of great value, have been made at the Sèvres factory, those decorated with floral ornaments upon plain coloured grounds being chiefly admired, especially those in the favourite colour *bleu de roi*. In 1752 a new blue colouring was introduced at Sèvres, generally known as turquoise or *bleu celeste*. Then a few years later came the pink or *du Barry;* other shades for which Sèvres porcelain has been noted, subsequently introduced, are jonquil, canary colour, apple-green, and grass-green. What is known as "jewelled Sèvres" is a form of decoration composed of small pieces of enamel in gilt or gold setting.

Sèvres has been much forged, and the marks have been copied with great accuracy. As a guide it is pointed out that on old Sèvres the gold has a dull appearance ; due to its being polished by hand ; whereas the substitutions or replicas of a later date shine more, having been polished with agate burnishers. The green of the old colouring was produced by an oxide of copper, whereas the imitations were made of an oxide of chromium, a chemical substitution not dis-covered until 1803.

| Fig. xxxii. | Fig. xxxiii. | Fig. xxxiv. | Fig. xxxv. |

SÈVRES.—Fig. xxxii., mark used during Royal period under Louis XV. Fig. xxxiii., Double letters used under Louis XVI., 1778-1793. Fig. xxxiv., marks of Republican era, 1792-1804. Fig. xxxv., mark without " R.F.," used 1792-1799.

Some of the Sèvres marks are interesting developments of the Royal cyphers of the periods when the porcelain was made. Fig. xxxii. is the mark used in the Royal period under Louis XV., and Fig. xxxiii., by its double letters, denotes the reign of Louis XVI., 1778-1793. The manufacture of porcelain was continued at Sèvres during the Republi-can era, 1792-1804. Contemporary with these marks " Sevres " surmounted by " R. F." was used, as in Fig. xxxiv., and also the place-name only, as Fig. xxxv. Again, under Louis XVIII., 1814-1823, the royal cypher came into vogue, the form it took being indicated in Fig. xxxvi. ; in the reign of Charles X., *circa* 1830, Fig. xxxvii. was used ; the circular mark shown in Fig. xxxviii. was the one in use in the time of Louis Philippe, 1831-1834, and later under the patronage of Napoleon III., *circa* 1854, Fig. xxxix. was in use.

| Fig. xxxvi. | Fig. xxxvii. | Fig. xxxviii. | Fig. xxxix. |

SÈVRES.—Fig. xxxvi., mark under Louis XVIII., 1814-1823. Fig. xxxvii., Charles X., *circa* 1830. Fig. xxxviii., Louis Philippe, 1831-1834. Fig. xxxix., mark under Napoleon III., 1854.

STRASBOURG.

A factory was established at Strasbourg in 1709 by Charles Hannong, of Holland, and in 1720 we read of him

T

making the name of the town famous by the table services
he produced. This noted potter died in 1739, and was
succeeded by his two sons. Although table services were
the chief things made by the Hannongs, they produced
some very beautiful porcelain clocks in rock-work style, as
well as decorated vases, an exceptionally fine clock of their
make being on view in the Cluny Museum. The marks on
Strasbourg ware during the different members of the
family's ownership were : " P H " in monogram
(Paul Hannong), " P I H " (Paul Hannong and his son
Joseph), and "J H," interlaced (Joseph Hannong). The
Potters Corporation of Alsace, Bâle, and Strasbourg was
regulated by statute, each of the master potters electing
three representatives from their number, the first for
Upper Alsace, the second for Lower Alsace, and the third
for the town of Colmar. At the time when Strasbourg ware
was being made the town was rightly classed among French
industrial towns ; the wares, now antique, of that period,
may therefore very fitly be classed as "French pottery."

CHAPTER XXVIII

CONTINENTAL—GERMANY AND OTHER COUNTRIES

Meissen or Dresden—Berlin—Fürstenberg—Höchst—and Ludwigsburg.

THE chief interest in the ceramics of Germany and those Continental towns whose industries are more or less associated with the products of the States and Duchies and Kingdoms now included in the German Empire, lies in the beautiful porcelain which was produced at the Royal factories, the handiwork of those potters who worked under distinguished patronage. Some interest is, however, shown by collectors in those early Continental wares, like the jars of Cologne, which are illustrated in Fig. 24.

Such early wares as those indicated were produced in great quantity in Germany and in Flanders; they were chiefly of grey stoneware, mostly coming under the denomination of "grès de Flandres." The ornament was chiefly Gothic, following the favourite style of that day. Other wares, made principally at Kreussen in Bavaria, of hard red clay, were finished to resemble closely enamelled metal work, many of the designs favouring Augsburg or Briot styles. Some of the examples in the Victoria and Albert Museum are highly coloured, the enamels being brilliant shades of red, green, and yellow. Best of all was the Cologne ware of the seventeenth and the early days of the eighteenth centuries; then there were beautiful wares decorated with white pipe-clay slip, followed by those more modern works of art referred to in the following pages.

The hard paste porcelain of Germany is exemplified in the Meissen china, that is, the porcelain of Germany made at the famous works on the Elbe, about fourteen miles from Dresden, the products of which are commonly known as "Dresden" china.

MEISSEN OR DRESDEN.

The discovery of how to make the hard paste for which the Meissen Works became famous is ascribed to Johan Fredrich Böttger, who was born at Schleiz, educated at Magdeburg, and apprenticed to a chemist in Berlin. He pursued alchemistic studies, which brought him under the notice of the King of Prussia, who kept Böttger in confinement in order that he might benefit by the discoveries it was thought the chemist had made.

Eventually Böttger became a potter, and devoted much attention to imitating the red stoneware of the Chinese. In order to make advantageous use of this discovery the King granted him the right to found factories, and supplied him with money. With others associated with him as experienced scientists and experts in the pottery craft, Böttger established a well-equipped factory in 1707, in Dresden. In 1710 the works were removed to Meissen. It was then that many improvements were made, and in a short time the products of the factories had multiplied both in extent and variety. They were then divided into several distinct classes, among which was what is termed "iron porcelain," the red-brown clay, of which the paste was composed, being coated with an opaque black-brown deposit which resulted from the iron oxide in the clay, brought out in the firing. There were also wares in which portions of the iron oxide coating were cut away and polished, giving a peculiar relief effect; and another variety which was coated with a black glaze composed of clay, lead, and tin. The colouring which was added imparted a striking beauty to these wares, the treatment being in two styles—Chinese, and German hunting scenes. This remarkable porcelain attracted the attention of Peter the Great, who ordered some of it in 1716, the service then made for him being heavily gilded.

The true porcelain of Meissen was made from 1710 onwards. Its chief ingredient was the white clay from Colditz. This ware without much change was made until the death of Böttger, which took place in 1719. This necessitated some changes in the management and also in the control of the works. The factory became to a large extent a royal enterprise, continuing under kingly patronage until May 19th, 1731, when the King took over the personal directorship, assisted by three commissioners. In the meantime, however, there had been a steady advance in the quality of the workmanship of the wares, and much delightful porcelain had been produced. At that time a conspicuous feature in the ware was the free use of colouring matter, which gradually superseded the more liberal use of gold ornament.

The collector is, naturally, much interested in the shapes of the earlier Meissen porcelain. In the earlier days Oriental forms had been copied. A further change both in style and in decoration came when, instead of the Oriental taste, typical European shapes were favoured. Changes in habits and customs of social life have ever exerted much influence upon commercial work. It has been so in porcelain at all periods.

In the Meissen wares it is found that the period 1720-1730 was characteristic of the greater use of breakfast-sets, a full service consisting of six cups and saucers, teapot, coffee-pot, sugar-bowl, tea-poy, and slop-bowl. As time advanced the chocolate-cup was added to the breakfast-set. The designs at that time may be described as favouring shell-shaped forms.

Another change came when paintings were introduced in the decoration of Meissen porcelain. That period dated from the time when Johann Gregor Herold, the painter, was first employed at the works. Eventually he became chief controller of the decorative department, then receiving a salary of 1,000 thalers per annum.

Another period in the history of the Meissen Works was reached about 1735, when the management of the works was in the hands of Graf Heinrich von Brühl. Kändlar had then become the chief designer or modeller of the porcelain. From that time onward there was a marked improvement in form, coupled with the gradual discarding of Oriental styles.

The life history of Kändlar is interesting ; this distinguished artist was born in 1706 in Saxony and educated under Thomä of Dresden, a sculptor. His first work in association with porcelain manufacture was that of modelling figures for the "Japanese Palace" the King was then erecting. He was not only successful with ordinary figures but achieved wonders with figures much larger than life. Then he turned his attention to the modelling of beautiful little objects, revelling in the curious and sometimes grotesque. After this fashion he made knobs, feet, and handles for quite ordinary articles. Kändler was diversified in his tastes and introduced several distinctive styles of ornament, one of the best known being that in which the chief attraction was those remarkable female figures wearing immense crinolines and wide skirts—a much copied style.

The rococo style which became so famous in French art was first employed at Meissen Works in 1740. Among the figures modelled after that style are the shepherds and shepherdesses of varied forms and represented by different emblems. The greatest achievement of Kändler was, probably, the equestrian statue of Augustus III., which he modelled but never executed. The model is still preserved in the Royal Collection at Dresden.

As regards the colouring of the earlier Meissen pieces, the under-glaze blue became famous and was advanced in 1745, when a separate department for blue painting was organised under the management of Carl Eggebrecht, a brother-in-law of Kändler. A school of art was established at Meissen under the directorship of C. W. G. Dietrich, the court painter ; that was during the minority of Augustus III. At the age of eighteen the King assumed the sovereignty and appointed Count Marcolini as chief of the porcelain factory.

During the long and continued prosperity of the works at the different periods during which special characteristic work was done, many wondrous colourings and striking departures were made in style and decoration ; perhaps, however, the colouring that will remain longest in the minds of collectors is the *bleu de roi* of Sèvres, which towards the close of the eighteenth century became the favourite blue of Meissen.

The marks on Dresden or Meissen porcelain are best understood as the " crossed swords." The marks on such pieces were usually under the glaze, in blue, sometimes in association with " K. P. M." (*Konigliche Porzellan Manufaktur*), the official mark as announced in the *Leipziger Post Zeitung* of April 7th, 1723, when it was ordered that the mark should appear on every teapot and sugar-bowl in a service. The crossed swords were not used regularly as a mark until 1725, but they became the sole mark in 1740. Other minor marks which have been used in conjunction with the crossed swords are now and then met with.

A few of the Dresden marks are given in the accompanying illustrations. Fig. xl. is the mark which was used from 1709 to 1726 on porcelain intended for the King's private use; that indicated in Fig. xli. was used during the period 1716-1720 ; Fig. xlii. was employed *circa* 1770, and Fig. xliii. *circa* 1796.

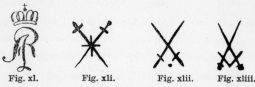

Fig. xl.   Fig. xli.   Fig. xlii.   Fig. xliii.

DRESDEN.—Fig. xl., 1709-1726, the mark used for Royal pottery only.   Fig. xli., period 1716-1720.   Fig. xlii., period 1770 (*circa*).   Fig. xliii., period 1796 (*circa*).

BERLIN.

The Berlin factory for the manufacture of porcelain was founded in 1750 by Wilhelm Caspar Wegeli, who used clay from Aue in Saxony. The works do not appear to have been very successful at first, for they changed hands several times; they were, however, eventually taken over by the King, and under Royal patronage became popular. The works in which King Frederick II. had in 1763 an interest became known as the " Royal Porcelain Manufactory " (*Konigliche Porzellan Manufactur*).

At one time the clay used at the Royal works came from Passau, but later kaolin from Silesia was employed. Many important commissions were executed, some of the best workmen from the Meissen Works being from time to time employed.

The mark during the Wegeli period was " W " in blue under glaze.   For a time, when the factory was controlled by Gotzowski (1761-1763), the mark was as shown in Fig. xliv., and from 1763 the mark was a sceptre (Fig. xlv.).

Fig. xliv.   Fig. xlv.

FÜRSTENBERG.

The factory at Fürstenberg was founded in 1746 by the Duke of Brunswick. The Seven Years' War was responsible for the cessation of work at Fürstenberg for a time. From 1770 onwards, however, some beautiful ceramic work was done. Among the specialistic works were many cameo portraits and medallions ; many fine busts of the princes were modelled and many artists employed were Rombrich, Lupau, and Schubert. Many of the older objects have been frequently reproduced from the original moulds.

The mark is in script ; the horse of Brunswick sometimes being used in conjunction on pieces of biscuit porcelain.

HÖCHST.

The pottery at Höchst was founded by Johann Christoph Göltz, Johann Feliciann Clarus of Frankfort-on-the-Main, and Adam von Löwenfinck, a painter, formerly employed at Meissen. The works passed into the hands of a company in 1765 and some headway was then made. But the chief progress was made when the Government took over the works in 1778 ; they were, however, closed in 1798.

In the earlier days of these works Oriental designs were chiefly followed. Then came rococo styles, and later the introduction of Watteau paintings. The distinguishing feature of marked specimens is the "wheel of Mainz," in blue, under the glaze, and in red, violet, or gold over the glaze. The mark of the wheel, a part of the arms of Mainz, had been granted by the Elector, who had also given up the Speicherhof at Höchst, which was a government building, to potters' use.

LUDWIGSBURG.

Among other German works there was a porcelain factory at Ludwigsburg, founded in 1758 by the Duke of Würtemberg, where figures and other objects were made. It was closed in 1824. The marks were the letter " L," and three stags' horns, which were a portion of the arms of Würtemberg ; the initials being crowned after the Duke had been crowned King.

AUSTRIA.

The Emperor Charles VI. of Austria followed the example which had been set by the King of Poland, and caused a pottery to be erected in Vienna under his patronage and direct support. One of the most successful members of his staff, in the early days of the factory, which was founded in 1718, was Konrad Christoph Hunger, who had been employed as a gilder and enameller at Meissen. It is said that when at Meissen he had obtained the confidence of Böttger and learned much from him about the secrets of the craft practised there.

Other workmen left Meissen to take up employment at Vienna, among them Samuel Stenzel. Almost from the first, and throughout the whole of the early years of the undertaking, indeed, until 1744, Claudius Innocenz Du Paquier controlled the works, and he was an ardent student of Eastern ceramics. In 1744 the Government were induced to take over the factory, but Du Paquier was retained as director of the works, the Government providing him with a residence and an income of 1,500 gulden per annum.

Authentic specimens of the first period of the Vienna Works are very rare, several of the best known being in the Austrian Museum, one of these being marked in red, " Böttengruber F. Viennae, 1130."

Franz Karl Mayerhofer von Grünbühel became director, and under his management the works were enlarged and the number of employés increased. Later other changes were made and Hofrath von Kessler, who had been appointed as director in 1770, made many unsuccessful attempts to imitate the porcelain of Sèvres and Meissen, resulting in much financial loss.

Again a change of management was made, and under Baron von Sargenthal in 1784 a time of prosperity came once more. At that time the products of the Vienna factory were very much the same as those of Meissen and Sèvres, although the hard paste of Vienna distinguishes it from the soft paste of Sèvres. So great was the advance made in the demand for the porcelain wares and figures of Vienna at that time, that in 1800 it was found necessary to open branch factories near Passau, from whence had been taken much of the clay which had been used at Vienna.

The ornament then employed was in some instances extravagant ; for four distinct classes have been pointed out, namely, historical, floral, blue ornament, and gilded designs. A marked change was made about that time, in that the rococo was superseded by the antique, which was then introduced with marked success.

The death of Baron von Sargenthal took place on October 17th, 1805, and his successor, as director, was

Matthäus Niedermayer, who had many difficulties to contend with. As the result of the war in 1809, Austria lost Passau and the clay beds, and the Vienna factory had to procure clay from Bohemia and Hungary. The war, too, caused changes in output, and a lower priced porcelain was mostly in demand. The retirement of Niedermayer in 1827 marks another change. His place was taken by Benjamin Scholtz, who controlled the works, introducing more economic methods and some machinery, until his death in 1833. The factory was eventually closed in 1864.

The marks at Vienna were chiefly composed of the Austrian shield. At first the shield was marked in blue, impressed; afterwards it was painted in blue under the glaze; from 1827 onward a wooden stamp was used (*see* Figs. xlvi. and xlvii.).

Fig. xlvi.   Fig. xlvii.

SWITZERLAND.

There was a factory at Zurich which was founded in 1763 by Heidegger and Korrodi, the principal artist being Spenglar. The products of that factory were chiefly of hard paste; they were German in character. The mark used at Zurich was the German " Z."

There was another Swiss factory at Nyon where articles similar to those produced at Zurich and at many German potteries were made. These works flourished during the closing years of the eighteenth century, but were shut down in 1813. The mark at Nyon was a fish, in blue, in outline, under the glaze.

DENMARK OR COPENHAGEN WARE.

One of the lesser-known Continental potteries is that from which emanated such beautiful Copenhagen ware in the eighteenth century. The factory was opened by a chemist, who, in conjunction with a French potter, had made many successful experiments, resulting in the founding of a factory in 1772. This enterprise was not altogether successful, and, like many other owners of potteries, the proprietors had to resort to an appeal to their Royal patrons. It is said that rather than that the industry should be abandoned, King Christian VII., of Denmark, gave the enterprise his support, and the ware made at that time became known as "King's Period." Then came fresh inspiration, when Thorwaldsen brought his influence to bear. He was a great sculptor and helped to raise the ware to a high standard. It is said, however, that it was by no means easy to reproduce in pottery the sculptures of the artist. The chief characteristics of Copenhagen ware of the eighteenth century and early in the nineteenth century consisted in the very remarkable blending of greys and soft pale shades of blue, green, and pink.

The mark used in Copenhagen consisted of three waving lines surmounted by a crown. These lines symbolised Denmark's three watercourses. The factory was closed in 1867. Modern attempts at reinstating Copenhagen ware have been very successful, and no doubt many readers are familiar with the soft velvety glaze and the ivories and pearl-greys of more recent productions, made since the recent revival of ceramic art in Denmark.

CHAPTER XXIX

CONTINENTAL—HOLLAND

Early Delft ware—The Guild of Saint Luke—English Delft.

DUTCH potters early became famous for the pottery which took its name from the chief seat of the industry in Holland, for it was at Delft that so much of the beautiful pottery covered with a fine white enamel was manufactured. In the eighteenth century some porcelain in imitation of the Chinese and Japanese was produced, but not with any great degree of success. As there were greater facilities for the transport of goods from the East, and Dutch merchants began to bring into Holland the beautiful china wares from China and other Eastern countries, the popularity of Delft ware diminished. A few of the manufacturers made efforts to retain their trade by copying the Oriental designs, and improving somewhat the appearance of their wares, but they were not successful with porcelain, and most of the Dutch pottery of the eighteenth century has been rightly called poor imitations of Oriental porcelain.

EARLY DELFT WARE.

It is the earlier wares made before the making of Delft ware was introduced into England that chiefly claim the attention of collectors. It would appear that very large quantities of Dutch Delft were brought into this country during the reign of William and Mary and throughout the first half of the eighteenth century. These useful wares were scattered about the country, and are still found in old houses. They are varied, and include Delft for household purposes, and some for commercial uses, among the latter being the famous pharmacy jars and apothecaries' vessels referred to at greater length in chapter xxxviii.

As it has already been pointed out, the town of Delft was the most important seat of the potting industry in Holland, and gave its name to the kind of pottery with its peculiar white tin enamel which was not only made in Holland, but subsequently in England and other places. The Dutch potters and other practitioners of arts and crafts in Delft were banded together in a trade guild, known as the Guild of St. Luke, which was founded early in the seventeenth century, probably about 1610. There was a register of the members of the guild, the first on the list being the name of one of the founders, Herman Pietersz. The guild members included artists, painters, glass stainers, engravers and glass-makers, potters, weavers and embroiderers of tapestry, sculptors and carvers, art printers, scabbard makers, booksellers, and dealers in paintings and engravings. They exercised some beneficial influence over their respective craftsmen, and helped to maintain the standard of quality. Like all old trade guilds, the society gradually dwindled away.

The Delft ware produced in the town of that name retained its standard of quality, and its remarkably brilliant glaze was unsurpassed, and probably unequalled, by those who copied it. This is perhaps attributable to the large quantity of pure tin used in preparing the glaze, and also to some extent due to the care and supervision in baking and firing. Among the other towns which shared the reputation which had been accorded to Delft were Amsterdam, Arnheim, Haarlem, Rotterdam, and Utrecht.

There is not much to record about the pottery which

was established in Amsterdam. Its owner is thought to have had some connection with the works at Arnheim, the products of both works being marked with the emblem of a cock ; a marked piece having the name of the town on the back is one of the few representative specimens of the old pottery at Arnheim. It is evident that there was a very early pottery at Haarlem, and it was from that town that Herman Pietersz, who was then a potter, came, and was subsequently one of the founders of the Guild of St Luke, afterwards founding important works at Delft. There was a pottery known by the sign of "The Star " at Delft, owned by Cornelis de Berg, a master potter who afterwards founded works at Rotterdam. His factory was chiefly devoted to the manufacture of tiles, and several of the more important large picture-panel tiles bear his signature, and also the name of the town. It was tiles that were chiefly made at Utrecht.

Collectors specialising on Delft ware, and securing a number of examples of that very interesting pottery, will no doubt wish to arrange and classify their specimens, either according to the names of the potters, the periods when the objects were made, or the different classes of ware produced. No less than thirty different Dutch potteries are known, and the names of their owners are for the most part those of distinguished artists in clay.

The Culick family were noted potters about the middle of the seventeenth century ; the mark they used was that of the maker's initials, to which was frequently added a number. Among the best known works of Albrecht de Keizer are some fine plaques and dishes ornamented with portraits and landscapes in blue. De Keizer's work is noted for its thinness and lightness of paste, many of the designs being ornamental in character. He was one, if not the first, of the Dutch potters to produce coloured wares in imitation of Oriental. Among other noted Dutch potters gaining renown for their colours and decorations were Augustein Reygens and Lambertus Eenhoorn. Late in the eighteenth century some very curious black Delft ware was made by Lowys Fictoor and Lambertus Eenhoorn. Frytom was a painter of plaques, and Leonard van Amsterdam became a noted decorator of finer china.

The manufacture of porcelain in Holland does not appear to have been a very successful enterprise, although it was attempted at a very early date, for we read of Wytmans at the Hague in 1614 taking out patent rights, by which he gained the monopoly of the manufacture throughout Holland of all kinds of porcelain similar to the wares made in China and Japan, a monopoly secured for five years. Porcelain was made in Amsterdam, and is known by the name of "Amstel" porcelain, called after the small river from which the capital takes its name. The potteries there were moved several times. The mark during the time the works were in Amsterdam was "AMSTEL," and when under Dr Moll's management the concern was carried on at Loordrecht, the mark used was "MOL."

The Guild of Saint Luke.

The rights and privileges of the Guild of St Luke were guarded very jealously by its members, among whom were many master potters and artists associated with the industry. The membership of the guild was very exclusive, too, for several tests of ability had to be passed before admission could be granted. The members had to prove that they were skilled craftsmen as well as employers of labour. The potters had to show that they were experts in potting, decoration, and firing. The test work had to be performed under the supervision of the guild, stringent regulations being enforced in order that the candidates might in no way receive assistance from others. The three articles they were required to make and submit were a salad bowl, a syrup pot, and a salt-cellar, which had to be fashioned out of a single lump of clay. Apparently the test was a severe one, for regulations ordained that if the samples were not up to the standard, the candidate was allowed to try again after an interval of one year and six weeks. Those were the regulations in force in 1654.

These points are of importance in that the names of many of the members appear upon specimens of pottery still extant, and collectors have the satisfaction of knowing that their specimens so marked are the work of men who were regarded in their day as having mastered more than the mere rudiments of their craft ; indeed, the membership of the guild denoted that they were highly skilled in their respective crafts.

The following abbreviated list includes the names of many well-known members whose names are found upon old Dutch pottery. The dates recorded indicate the year of their election. The marks they used were mostly either their names abbreviated, or a monogram, or their initials.

Gerrit Hermansz (1614).
Isaac Junius (1640).
Albrecht de Keizer (1642).
Jan Gerrits Van der Hoeve (1649).
Meynaert Garrebrantsz (1616).
Quiring Alders Kleynoven (1655).
Frederick Van Frytom (1658).
Jan Sicktis Van den Houk (1659).
Jan Ariens Van Hammen (1661).
Augustein Reygens (1663).
Jan Jans Kulick (1662).
Jacob Cornelisz (1662).
Willem Kleftijus (1663).
Arij Jans de Milde (1658).
Piet Vizeer (1752).
Gysbert Verhaast (1760).

Arend de Haak (1780).

Dirk Van Schie (1679).

Pieter Poulisse (1690).

Lucas Van Dale (1692).

Cornelis Van de Kloot (1695).

Jan Baan (1660).

Jan Decker (1698).

Arij Cornelis Brouwer (1699).

Leonardus of Amsterdam (1721).

Paulus Van der Stroom (1725).

Jeronimus Pieters Van Kessel (1655).

Lambertus Van Eenhoorn (1691).

Gisbrecht Lambrecht Kruyk (1645).

Samuel Van Eenhoorn (1674).

Adrianus Kocks (1687).

Jan Van der Heul (1701).

Jan Theunis Dextra (1759).

Jacobus Halder (1765).

Ambrensie Van Kessel (1675).

Louis Fictoor (1689).

Hendrik de Koning (1721).

Matheus Van Boegart (1734).

Hendrick Van Middeldyk (1764).

Rochus Jacobs Hoppestein (1680).

Antoni Kruisweg (1740).

Geertruij Verstelle (1764).

Lambertus Sanderus (1764).

Dirk Van der Kest (1698).

Johannes den Appel (1759).

Reinier Hey (1696).

Petrus Van Marum (1759).

Johannes Van der Kloot (1764).

Tripartite mark of Cornelis de Keizer and Jacob and Adrian Pynacker (1680).

G. Pieters Kam (1674).

Zachariah Dextra (1720).

Hendrick Van Hoorn (1759).

Johannes Pennis (1725).

Jan Van Duijn (1760).

Dirck Van der Does (1759).

Johannes Knotter (1698).

Pieter Van Doorne (1759).

Cornelis de Berg (1690).

Jan Aalmes (1731).

Justus de Berg (1759).

Albertus Kiell (1763).

Paul Van der Briel (1740).

Matheus Van Bogaert.

Pieter Verbur.

Willem Van Beek (1713-1758).

Anthony Pennis (1759).

Johannes Verhagen (1728).

Gerrit Brouwer (1756).

Abraham Van der Keel (1780).

English Delft.

Specific references are made to English Delft ware in the several chapters in which the work of English potters is recorded. It should be clearly understood that when so much Delft ware was being brought over to this country, and the taste was assured, English potters very frequently copied very closely the Dutch designs and colouring as well as the paste and enamel, which, of course, are so important to the collector who fully appreciates the peculiar colouring and style of the pottery made in Holland.

Dutch tiles were much copied in Liverpool, and many other specialities were imitated. Many of the apothecaries' jars and drug pots which had been first made at Delft were also imitated there. Such vessels, as well as the more utilitarian household wares in Delft ware, were also made at Lambeth and other English potteries.

Drug pots and apothecaries' jars are, however, not altogether confined to this particular class of ware; such vessels were from an early date made in many Continental towns. The collector specialising upon such objects

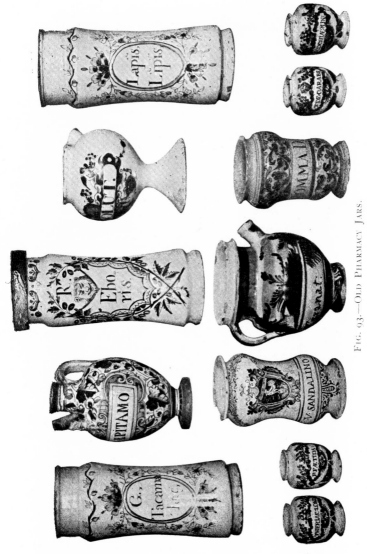

FIG. 93.—OLD PHARMACY JARS.

In the Collection of Mr. Jewell, of Piccadilly.

[To face page 308.

Fig. 94.—A Further Selection of Pharmacy Jars.

In the Collection of Mr. Jewell, of Piccadilly.

cannot very well confine himself to only Delft, and finds in similar wares fresh delights, in that every different kind of pottery or porcelain fashioned for the purpose of a drug store affords variety and adds to the collection a new charm. (Apothecaries' jars and drug pots are treated separately in chapter xxxviii. under "Specialised Collections." *See* also Figs. 93 and 94.)

Many examples of Delft are found in modest numbers in our museums, although there are few important collections of Delft on view. In the London Museum there are a few interesting pieces, chiefly English; one of these is a remarkable plate, highly decorative and richly coloured, bearing a laudatory inscription in honour of Queen Elizabeth. There are also Lambeth posset pots and caudle cups, and some drug pots, as well as a few quaintly modelled figures, one of the best being a group of a "Boy on a Dolphin."

The state rooms at Hampton Court contain some very curious pieces of old Delft ware and several massive vases. There are examples in many of our art galleries and museums, and in private collections too. In Fig. 86 there is a bowl of Delft ware, its companion bowl Fig. 87 being, of course, Oriental, decorated in the once popular English taste.

CHAPTER XXX

CONTINENTAL—ITALY, SPAIN, AND PORTUGAL

Majolica wares—Capo di Monte—Doccia—Faenza—Florence—
Venice—Spanish and Portuguese pottery.

THE connoisseur who enters the field of exploration of the mysteries of the early wares of Italy, and especially of the early majolica, is not only an advanced collector, but a specialist. The home connoisseur may, however, possess one or more examples of Italian majolica which he is anxious to locate. The brief accounts given in this chapter of the different works and the several localities where such wares and Italian majolica and porcelain were made in the past, and references to some of the best known artists who worked upon these specialistic wares, may, therefore, be useful.

It should be remembered that although old majolica is associated with the products of the earlier Italian potteries, the wares of the eighteenth century included many pieces of beautiful porcelain, such as that made at Capo di Monte, near Naples, and at Naples, under the influence and almost direct control of Charles, Duke of Naples, who afterwards became Charles III. of Spain.

MAJOLICA WARES.

The history of early Italian wares is not quite clear. At one time it was believed that the first inspirations were derived from the Moorish pottery which was among the booty taken from Majolica, or Majorca. The story is

interesting and worth repeating, even if not responsible for
the origin of later Italian wares. It was after a gallant
defence of a year or two that the Saracens gave way to the
Crusaders, who took Majorca in 1115, killed the King, and
secured much booty. As the result of that siege and
capture many pieces of Moorish pottery found their way to
Italy, and in Pisa and other places they were placed as
relics, set in the church walls. From these and other facts,
Moorish origin was at one time generally attributed to the
Italian majolica which afterwards became so famous.
Italian potters had, however, even at that early date,
acquired much skill. No doubt the beautiful lustre of the
Moorish wares which came under their notice would inspire
them to greater things than they had then accomplished,
and that may have led them to that research which resulted
in the achievement of more important results than have
been gained by either the Italian artists or Moorish
craftsmen.

The Italian majolica of which Lucca della Robia was the
fifteenth-century exponent became noted and much sought
after by ecclesiastical builders and decorators. This
famous artist held the secrets of stanniferous enamel, which
in course of time became known and adopted at Florence
and at Faenza. Mr Marryat, in his book published many
years ago, descants upon the fine majolica introduced into
Pesara in 1500. " That," he says, "was afterwards named
' porcellana,' and was very superior to the mezza majolica,
from which it differed in its composition and manufacture.
The piece," he explained, "was half fired *a bistugio*, and
then dipped into the enamel composed of oxide of tin and
lead and other combinations. The dirty colour of the paste
was thus concealed by this vitreous coating, which produced
an even white surface to serve as a ground for painting.
It required a free and firm hand to paint on the moist glaze
—there was no possibility of retouching or correction, from

the rapid absorption of the colours. This, with the accidents incidental to fusing of the glaze with the colours, accounts for any inaccuracies in the drawing or painting of the majolica. Then when the artist had finished his work the piece was returned to the furnace for its final firing."

Fortunately for the student, the materials of which the old Italian wares were composed are well known, for full particulars of the potting industry of his day were recorded by Cipriano Piccolpassoo of Castel Durante, in 1548, the original manuscript being in the Victoria and Albert Museum at South Kensington. Some of the facts recorded describe the processes which were then in vogue, and also which had been in use for many years earlier. He says that the clay, preferably that which had been deposited by a river, was to be beaten, ground in a mill, and passed through a sieve so as to bring it into a smooth state fit to be moulded on the wheel. The white enamel which he used (*bianco*) was composed of 30 parts of *marzacotto* to 12 of oxide of tin. The *marzacotto* is said to have been only powdered glass, which was a pure silicate of potash made from sand and the alkaline tartar deposited by wine. The decorations were painted on the enamelled ground sometimes before it was fired and sometimes after. The enamel before firing formed a slightly granular and very absorbent ground, like clay in the biscuit state. The earlier and more decorative pieces were painted on the unfired ground, which absorbed the colours, much of their richness being due to the colours having sunk below the ground surface. After passing through the kiln the nature and appearance of the ware was changed, a smooth, vitreous surface affording the painter who decorated such ware opportunities of showing his skill as a painter of miniatures, and alterations in detail could easily be made if necessary. Thus the difference between the early work and that chiefly decorated after firing can readily be seen.

The glaze used was made very fusible by lead, and consisted of oxide of lead 17 parts, silica 20, alkali 12, and common salt 8 parts. The colours employed were chiefly metallic oxides.

As a guide it may be pointed out that the majolica of the fifteenth century retained its purity of mediæval style and design, but a little later the work became more florid. The earlier wares were painted in blue with a yellow lustre. Many of the finest specimens are conspicuous for their figure subjects, some being scriptural, others having mottoes ; one early plate in the Louvre is inscribed, "Chi bene guida sua barcha s'entra in porto" (He who steers well his ship will enter the harbour). As a rule the shapes of majolica are plate-like in form, varying, however, in that some are dish-like and others are even like bowls and ewers in form and depth. Many fine examples may be seen at South Kensington, and also in the British Museum. Undoubtedly there are many magnificent specimens, wonderfully preserved, in the Victoria and Albert Museum, among them pieces representative of all the rarer types. One of the noted groups of Sgraffiato ware is conspicuous for its effective ornament. This curious ware was made by coating red clay foundations with white slip, afterwards cut away to the base to form designs, which were then filled in, the colouring materials being chiefly blue, yellow, and green, the whole being highly glazed.

To define the varieties of later Italian pottery and the localities where the different wares were made, it will be convenient to take the seats of the potting industry in Italy in alphabetical order.

Capo di Monte.

The works at Capo di Monte were founded in 1742 by Charles Bourbon, King of Naples, who had in earlier life

been Duke of Parma. In 1759 he became King of Spain,
and taking with him some of the best workers from Capo di
Monte, founded a porcelain factory near Madrid. That, of
course, accounts for the similar characteristics of the
designs of the Madrid wares, which are sometimes mistaken
for Italian. The products of the potteries at Capo di
Monte had little resemblance to the earlier Italian wares ;
they were, indeed, fine quality porcelain, which has, by
some, been likened to the porcelain of Plymouth and
Bow, for the porcelain of Capo di Monte was embellished
with fruit and flowers cleverly fashioned and beautifully
coloured.

After the removal of the patronage of the King the
works fell into disrepute and commercially lacked support.
The pottery was, however, re-established in 1771 at
Portici, and was carried on there for some time.

Some of the finest pieces made during the later period
of these works are found in the services made in 1787 for
George III. of England, and still preserved at Windsor
among the royal porcelain, of which there are many fine
sets at the Castle.

The mark during the period when the works were at
Naples was a crowned " N " (Fig. xlviii.).

Fig. xlviii.

DOCCIA.

A china factory was established in Doccia by the
Marquis Carlo Ginori in 1737, and carried on by the
founder's son after the death of the Marquis in 1757 ;
it flourished for many years. The earlier objects were

of hard porcelain, some after the Chinese models, others were in imitation of the Capo di Monte porcelain ; the ornaments used were chiefly in low relief, and were classical in design.

FAENZA.

It was at Faenza that so much beautiful ware was made. The style became popular, and under the name of faience it was much copied.

A marked advance was made at Faenza when Baldassare Manara, one of the master potters of the sixteenth century, introduced decorations copied from engravings. One of his finest examples is said to be a dish, the subject of the ornament of which is the " Triumph of Father Time " ; there are several examples of his work in the British Museum.

Many small factories where majolica was made are known to have existed in Faenza, and the wares made by this group of potters were so similar that identification is difficult ; many of the earlier designs were much copied at a later period, and they are almost identical in colouring and finish.

FLORENCE.

Porcelain was made in Italy in Venice as early as 1470, by one Maestro Antoni Antuonia, but no examples of this early attempt to produce porcelain like the Chinese has survived. Other attempts were made to produce similar wares, but it was not until 1735 that the first pottery was established with any degree of success. That was the factory founded at Doccia, near Florence, by the Marquis Carlo Ginori. There are, however, examples in the Victoria and Albert Museum at South Kensington, and in other museums and collections of porcelain and pottery made during the sixteenth and seventeenth centuries at the Medici factory at Florence.

The marks on the Medici china consisted of the Cathedral dome, in blue, under it the capital letter "F," which mark was added, so it is said, because it was the initial letter of Francisco I., the Grand Duke of Tuscany; but it is more probable that it was used in that it denoted the place name, Florence. The mark is represented (Fig. xlix.).

Fig. xlix.

VENICE.

The porcelain of hard paste made at the factory established by Francesco Vezzi in 1719 was continued until 1740, the mark used being "VENEZIA." After that there was a break until 1753, when another factory was started in Venice by Nathaniel Friedric Hewelke and his wife, who were refugees from Dresden. Their factory was closed in 1763. The mark they used was " V " (Fig. l.).

Fig. l.

FIG. 95.
SPANISH
16TH CENTURY JUG.

FIG. 96.
SPANISH
17TH CENTURY BOTIGO.

*Reproduced by the permission of the Proprietors of The Spanish
Art Gallery, Conduit Street, W.*

[To face page 316.

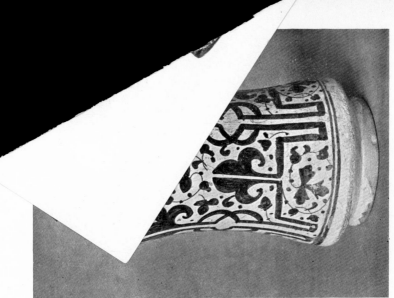

Fig. 98.—Old Spanish Pottery.
16th century blue and white jar.

Fig. 97.—Old Spanish Pottery.
15th century gold lustre dish.

In the Spanish Art Gallery, Conduit Street, W.

To face page 317.]

Another porcelain factory was founded in Venice by Giminiano Cozzi, who made beautiful vases and statuettes as well as commoner wares, marking them with an anchor in red.

SPANISH AND PORTUGUESE POTTERY.

The Moorish influence upon Spanish and Portuguese pottery is abundantly evident. There have, however, been several distinct kinds of pottery produced in these countries, apart from the Hispano-Moresque and other wares showing Arab and Persian influence. Some of these are to be seen in the Victoria and Albert Museum and in private collections. The Hispano-Moresque, undoubtedly the most beautiful of early Spanish pottery, is described in chapter xxxviii. ("Specialised Collections"), and the special characteristics of the ware given. The majolica wares of Spain and Portugal were mostly cruder in design and colouring than the Italian majolica. The coarser wares were made at Seville, Tolevera, and Valencia in large quantities in the seventeenth century; in its decoration blues, greens, and yellows were the principal colours employed. Figures and flowers were the subjects chosen, but they were seldom well done, and few pieces are attractive from an artistic point of view.

Enamelled wares of much better types were made in the eighteenth century, both in Spain and Portugal; in the latter country Rato was one of the places where enamelled pottery was made.

Some very effective pottery of red ware has been made in Spain and Portugal, not unlike the Roman Samian ware. Water jars and wine jars were often highly decorative, the colours are rich, and in some of the earlier examples the patterns are impressed. The manufacture of jars of distinctly Oriental types is peculiar to several localities; in some villages members of the same families have worked at this one branch of ceramics for centuries.

Spanish tiles (*azulijo*) coated with white enamelled surfaces decorated in colours, but chiefly lustrous in finish, are among the treasures of old Spanish pottery. (*See* chapter xxxiv.).

The illustrations given here are from examples in the Spanish Art Gallery, to the owners of which we are indebted for the photographs reproduced. Fig. 95 is a very unusual sixteenth-century ewer, standing about 7 in. high. The larger vessel, represented in Fig. 96, is, probably, of seventeenth-century workmanship. In Fig. 97 a much older piece is shown ; it is a fifteenth-century plate or dish, with raised rim on which is a knob-like ornament. The decoration is in blue, richly covered with gold lustre. Fig. 98 is a blue and white jar, standing about 12 in. high—a sixteenth-century specimen.

CHAPTER XXXI

ORIENTAL POTTERY—HISTORICAL

Dynastic classification—Chinese mythology—Deities and sacred places.

THE ceramics of the East have always held a prominent place in collections of pottery and porcelain. They have often been the chief attractions in museum galleries and exhibitions. Their quaint shapes and often graceful forms, supplemented by their highly decorative ornamentation, have added to the interest taken in them ; it is, therefore, no matter of surprise that so many have specialised upon the collection and preservation of these relics. These wares cover a period unequalled in extent ; and the productions of the potter have been continuous in China from the earliest times. The so-called prehistoric pottery of that country dates from very remote ages. It has received attention lately in consequence of large discoveries of the older wares, and as the result of extensive researches made on the site of the burial grounds from which some of the pieces have been recovered. Throughout the ages which have intervened from that early period up to the present time, pottery and porcelain have been made and handed down, so that an almost unbroken series can be secured. It is worthy of note, too, that the quaint forms and the modern conceptions of ancient designs which are among the curios imported into this country from the East make them acceptable to the collector of old china, so that many quite modern pieces are admitted into the curio cabinet, although contemporary pieces from Continental and English potteries would be cast out. This peculiarity has its advantages in that it enables the collector to compare the productions of the past and present, and helps him to see the differences in paste, glaze, and colouring of the old and the new.

The countries which have provided collectors with specimens of Oriental pottery and porcelain are principally China and Japan, although, of course, in a lesser degree, Persia, India, and other places have contributed their stores; the ceramics of the latter countries, and those of the Near East are, however, distinctive in style, and form another class quite apart from the wares fashioned and decorated in China and Japan.

The specialist has found enough to interest him in the pottery or porcelain of a single period of Chinese art, and many remarkable collections of old Chinese have been got together. The "home connoisseur" is not usually a specialist. His object is to obtain a little information about pieces he may acquire, and as far as possible to add to those pieces so as to make them more interesting by comparison with other wares from the same localities. By providing at least a single specimen of each period, so that proper sequence can be secured and the variations of the products of the same pottery observed, as its art was advanced, the collection grows more educative and its value is enhanced.

DYNASTIC CLASSIFICATION.

The long periods during which Chinese pottery and porcelain of even the cruder types were made enables collectors to arrange their specimens in well-defined series, in which the progress of art can be traced. China has had a long history, and the changes which have been made in that country have been notoriously slow. They have altered

little in pottery and porcelain, and although some advance
has been made of late years owing to the greater scientific
knowledge of the potters, there is great similarity between
the old and the new. It is also noteworthy that the
ceramics of two hundred years ago have never been
excelled ; indeed, some of the results then achieved belong
to a lost art. Great care was taken to secure good results,
and the pigments used in the decoration of the old wares
were of the very best. There was a lavish expenditure of
gold and rich colouring, and many of the finer pieces which
realise such high prices now were the result of many patient
trials and attempts ; indeed, some of the marvellous results
were the outcome of accident.

In all the well-defined periods of Chinese art some dominating influence can be traced, and the different dynastic
changes mark many of these periods, indicating the dynastic
influence on thought and inspiration. This system of classification is convenient, and in all kinds of art it is used as
pointing out changes ; the dynasties form easy landmarks
in history. Those throughout which old Chinese pottery
and porcelain were made are tabulated as follows :

The HAN	dynasty	B.C. 206	to A.D.	220
The WEI	,,	221	,,	264
The TSIN	,,	265	,,	419
The SUI	,,	581	,,	617
The T'ANG	,,	618	,,	908
The HEON TEHEON dynasty	954	,,	960
The SUNG dynasty	960	,,	1279
The YUAN	,,	1280	,,	1367
The MING	,,	1368	,,	1643
The CHING	,,	1644	,,	

(Later subdivisions to modern times.)

It will be observed that some of these periods were of
short duration, and specimens known to have been made
then are, of course, few, and for the most part rare.

X

The pottery of the Han dynasty may be termed prehistoric, even in a country like China, with its early records and history bordering upon mythology. The specimens secured during recent years have contributed to the objects which testify to the somewhat advanced arts of those early days in China.

The collector of porcelain looks with pride upon pieces of the Ming dynasty which he possesses, and it requires a long purse to collect such wares in quantity. It is the later period which comes under the ken of the householder, and many are content to own porcelain of the days when Georgian tea china was being imported into this country from the East, and when so many richly decorated punch bowls and tea-sets were being made, both in Oriental and English taste.

CHINESE MYTHOLOGY.

Before describing the decorations upon Chinese pottery and porcelain it will be convenient to refer briefly to the legends and mythology which influenced both modellers and designers. It is difficult for the Western mind to grasp the depths of such beliefs, or to understand how it was possible for them to influence design.

The pottery of very early times was *shaped*, rather than decorated, after the manner in which the hand of the craftsman was directed. It was not until the later periods that the artist had the ability to paint, gild, and ornament according to the myths with which he was familiar. His belief in those fables was still strong, and he cut and carved, moulded and shaped, and painted and pencilled to the best of his ability. Some of the works of art which have been preserved in the palaces of the Emperors must have taken much time and skill to complete.

Those were the days of great artists, and although there

are skilled artists to-day who could design anew, it is remarkable how the mythology of the ancients still forms the basis of decoration in modern factories where Chinese porcelain is made for the Western world.

It may be pointed out that the Oriental craftsman is enveloped with awe for the mysteries of his old deities, and they dominate his handicraft in a remarkable degree. The mythology of China is, of course, a subject which has attracted the attention of many learned men, who have devoted years to research into the mysteries so difficult to penetrate.

A short description of some of the myths which are pictured again and again upon Chinese porcelain should be helpful.   It must be remembered, however, that the stories or beliefs recorded are not always pictured in their entirety, and different artists throughout the long periods of ceramic art in China have varied their interpretation of the stories, and have, as time went on, shaped the symbols somewhat differently.

The Eight Taoist Immortals.

The Eight Immortals have entered largely into Chinese decoration, and most of the common objects of household use brought over to this country from China have upon them one or more of the symbols of these personages around which have been written fabled stories. The characteristics of the Immortals are as follows :

(1) HAN-CHUNG-LI, who lived in the Chow dynasty and is reputed to have discovered the Elixir of Life. He carries the *shan* with which to revive the souls of the dead.

(2) LEU-TUNG-PIN, whose emblem is a *sword*, which was given him after having overcome ten temptations, and with this he traversed the earth, slaying dragons and evil spirits.

(3)   LE-TEE-KWAE, a lame beggar, whose emblem is a *pilgrim's gourd*.   He had assumed the guise after having returned from the celestial regions, whither he had been summoned.

(4)   TSAO-KWO-KIU, who is shown carrying the *castanets*, was the son of a warrior who died A.D. 999.

(5)   LAN-TSAE-HO, a female, who carries a basket of flowers.

(6)   CHANG-KO-LAON, who is said to have ridden upon a white mule a thousand miles a day.   His emblem is a small *drum* and rods to beat it.

(7)   HAN-SEANG-TSZE, a pupil of the second immortal.   He plays a *flute*, which is his emblem.

(8)   HO-SEEN-KOO, a maiden, the daughter of Ho-tai, who is represented carrying the *lotus* flower.

DEITIES AND SACRED PLACES.

The religions, so-called, of China—some of which sprang out of the earlier mythology—have provided the artist as well as the decorator with models, although these were the creation of an earlier artist's brain.   The temples and shrines of Old China are full of objects of pottery and porcelain modelled after the forms of the "gods," copies of earlier stone and wooden figures, and objects for the use of priests and attendants.

It is from these sacred places where the rarer treasures —often labours of love in their modelling and decoration— have been stored, that collectors in this country and in America have drawn their supplies.   It is unnecessary to comment upon the way in which the rare objects have been "removed " from their original homes ; sufficient to know that temple vases and ornaments have been brought to this country in large quantities.   These are to-day being copied, and replicas are provided for the unwary and for the better informed but less wealthy collector.

The "home connoisseur" should at once learn the characteristics of the deities of Ancient China. Two of these are worthy of special note—the God of War and the God of Porcelain.

The God of War is said to have exerted his influence for centuries, and it would seem as if the myths of his splendour were not yet forgotten ! He is usually represented sitting upon a throne or chair of state. He wears a coat of mail, and is surrounded by peach-blossoms.

The God of Porcelain—Tung—is a reputed deity, for, according to legend, he was a potter when on earth, successful in making those wonderful large dragon bowls, so many of which have been produced for the imperial palaces. For his clever craftmanship he appears to have been deified, a distinction conferred upon him by the Emperor—a mere mortal. " War " and " Porcelain " often figure in pottery and the finer wares.

Among the lesser known deities are two queens : the Queen of Heaven, sometimes seated on a lotus flower, a child on her knee and a peach in her hand ; and the Queen of the Genii, whose messengers were birds with azure wings. This Queen of the Genii, who eventually became the Consort of Tung-wang-kung, is often accompanied by a maiden holding a basket of peaches, another maiden carrying a fan for her use. The God of Longevity, an old man with flowing beard, is often depicted carrying the sceptre of longevity, and frequently standing near a peach-tree.

The Buddhist priest, who has had the preservation of so many temple relics, has come in for his share of representation ; indeed, it is recorded that a Buddhist priest, in contemplation, lately added to the treasures of the British Museum through the instrumentality of the Art Collections Fund, a splendid pottery figure, is the most remarkable ceramic object which has ever come from China.

The dragon so often seen in Chinese decoration and

ornament is the emblem of the Emperor; in form and colouring the mythological creature varies, for there are four dragons, according to Chinese mythology. One of these is the "Celestial" dragon, which guards the gods, and on occasion the temple of the gods upon earth. There is the "Spiritual" dragon, which causes the rain to fall and the wind to blow—he may be called a storm dragon. The "Earth" dragon shapes rivers, and performs other mysteries of creation and transformation. Then, lastly, there is the mythical "Treasure" dragon, which is supposed to guard the metallic treasures in the mountains— the hidden wealth of the people.

The Kylin is an emblem of good and wise government, and is a favourite object. Then there are other myths, which are explained in various ways by writers upon the subject. Mrs Hodgson, in her delightful book on these wares, tells of the eight horses of the Emperor Muh-Wang, driven by his charioteer Tsao-fu. She also mentions the deer, as indicating honour and success in study; a goose, symbolical of domestic felicity; a mandarin duck as an emblem of wedded bliss; a cock and hen on an artificial rock as signifying country life; the bat as an emblem of happiness; and the hare as the emblem of the moon.

As it has been stated, the mystic beliefs have had a marked influence upon the production of Chinese pottery and porcelain, and they have also had much to do with its preservation.

The manufacture of early mortuary pottery, some of which is referred to in the description of pottery of the Han dynasty in chapter xxxii., was entirely due to ancestral worship and belief in the need of providing material things for a future state. It has been the same right through the ages. The "Old Willow" pattern made in England was drawn from Chinese designs, and typifies one of the pretty fables of Oriental conception.

CHAPTER XXXII

ORIENTAL POTTERY—ANCIENT CHINESE

The Han dynasty—Imitative pottery—The Sung dynasty.

ALTHOUGH there are examples extant of an earlier period, the pottery of the Han dynasty, to which much attention has been given of late years, is the oldest likely to come into the hands of ordinary collectors.

The earlier pottery dating back to about 1100 B.C., in the days of the Chou dynasty, has been found much incrustated, the once hard grey clay of which it was formed being now quite black. Even at that very early date incised lines were used as ornamentation, and the shapes were useful models. The pottery appears to have been modelled on the still earlier vessels of bronze with tripod feet—relics of the Bronze Age in China.

The study of Oriental pottery does indeed carry us back to times when even Chinese art was not fully developed, and the potters had but a small conception of the beautiful products of their potteries in years that were to come. It requires a somewhat cultivated taste to admire the old pottery of the cruder forms ; and yet in this very early ware there is much in which the student may revel, for in those days the inspirations which influenced the workers were those which they derived from the actualities of life by which they were surrounded, and in which they took part. Even in the very primitive forms of the vessels they used were seen reflections of the everyday life of the people, and of the things which interested them most.

327

When examining specimens of the primitive pottery there must always be taken into consideration the dual purpose of those early potters, for in addition to the vessels for use by the living, there was the mortuary pottery of contemporary dates, and often coincident in form. China had a civilisation years before the Han dynasty, and the graves of its prehistoric dead contained crude pottery upon which the objects fashioned during the Han dynasty were a marked advance. In the pottery of that dynasty, which flourished before the Christian era, there are indications of a civilisation far advanced, although it was crude when compared with the finer wares which were made later on.

THE HAN DYNASTY.

The collector naturally classes all the wares of this early period as crude, although an advance upon the very early forms. It must, however, be admitted that it is very probable that porcelain was not altogether unknown in China at that time, for there are traces of finer wares in texture and glaze, made undoubtedly at that period. As at the present time, there were varied qualities being made by different "artists," some doubtless being produced under more favourable conditions than others.

A few years ago some very remarkable discoveries were made of this old Han pottery in Hsi-an-fu, and pieces were bought for quite trifling sums by dealers, who, having first spread abroad accounts of their rarity, soon found buyers at good prices. Many of the pieces were covered with hardened incrustations, and the glazes had suffered from decomposition and oxidation owing to long burial, imparting a wonderful gold and silver iridescence. These objects give a clear insight into some of the older beliefs and customs of the people by whom this pottery was made and used.

As with the prehistoric pottery of Britain, the discovery of the ancient pottery of the Han dynasty throws some light upon other surroundings, for it tells us of the architecture, the domestic life, and even the animal kingdom represented in China at that time. It needed the experience of someone who had travelled the country to enlighten students and help them to understand the curios in which they were interested. We are indebted to Mr Berthold Laufer for the exhaustive account of his researches given in his book on *Chinese Pottery of the Han Dynasty*, written as the result of the numerous pieces he was able to collect during his travels in the Hsi-an-fu district of the Shensi Province, while on a mission to China for the American Museum of Natural History. His book is a valuable addition to the literature upon very early pottery Mr Laufer translates passages from an ancient Chinese book bearing upon the subject, and helpful to those who seek to trace the relationship of the wares so beautifully coloured by oxidation, to the old bronzes which supplied the models. One of the passages he gives reads thus : " Old bronze vessels placed in the earth for a long series of years receive the vapours of the earth, which colour them by producing flowers. The colour of the flowers is pure and clear, like blossoms which open speedily and die slowly. Some die off, and then the jar forms fruit like rust arising from water (*i.e.*, the process of oxidation). Thus they come down to posterity in an antiquated condition. The same is the case also with vessels of pottery placed in the earth for a thousand years."

When examining the early examples of the pottery of the Han dynasty one of the first things which strike us is that the potter's wheel must have been in use then, for most of the vessels give evidence of having been "thrown." That in itself is not very remarkable, for we know that at a very early date, according to Bible records, the potter's

wheel was used in Eastern countries. The pottery of the
Han dynasty, however, was not only thrown and worked
by some mechanical instrument, but it was ornamented by
hand. The modelling of the pieces which were shaped
from larger objects was very cleverly done. The workers
in clay copied very accurately the buildings around them,
and perpetuated the memory of common objects, and of
occupations like agriculture and domestic engagements.
This insight is valuable and very interesting. It has often
been deplored that the pottery of prehistoric man in Britain
does not help us to form any very clear idea of the more
advanced civilisation which some think existed in Britain
years before the great Roman invasion.

IMITATIVE POTTERY.

This so-called imitative pottery is very interesting, and
from it can be learned much of the habits of the people by
whom it was used. Mr Laufer describes some of these
objects very graphically, pointing out that the habits of
the people of the Han dynasty must have been very
domesticated. The grain mill which was in evidence
was cleverly planned. The receiver was shaped like a dish
to catch the falling grain, and in the side was a hole through
which it fell into some other vessel or basket below. These
minute details were known to the potter and copied by him
in the models he made. From their accuracy this ancient
worker must have tried hard to give reality to his work, for
in the model mill there is an imitation of the spindle in
which grooves are distinctly traceable. The upper and
the nether mill-stones are distinguishable, and, making the
action of the mill more real, the turning motion of the
stone is shown by a network of thirty-five lines radiating
from the periphery. This pottery, so beautifully glazed
with an olive green tint, obviously modelled from

contemporary mills then in use, is said to picture exactly mills still to be seen in China, so little have they changed. That in itself is an interesting feature, for although the country is fast altering and Western ideas are permeating the Celestial Empire, until quite recent days there had been little change in domestic practice in China for a thousand years or more.

Farm sheds which are represented in the pottery of the Han dynasty include models showing their interior equipment ; thus through the open side may be seen grain-crushers or rice-pounders in position, just as in the actual sheds from which the artist took his model. Mr Laufer describes one of these pottery sheds thus : " The roof consists of two sloping sides separated by a thick ridge-pole that merges at either end into a mound-like knob. Each slope of the roof is divided into five sections by four ribs of *imbrices*, the sections being covered with flat tiles (*tegulae*). Each rib shows distinctly by means of grooves. Along the ridge of the gable-ends of the roof are two massive rafters which project over the walls, and merge at either end, like the central ridge-pole, into a mound-like knob or thickened elevation. These beams should be conceived as woodwork. The framework on which the roof rests is not indicated."

In a well-known collection there are several models of grain towers. Such towers are usually placed in a bowl-like vessel, not in the centre, but on one side of it; a stairway is usually contrived in the substance of the bowl. In the bowl, near the tower, is often to be seen a well-modelled pig, feeding and fattening on the grain falling from the tower. These so-called granary urns are roofed like the pattern of Chinese roof which continued unaltered for centuries. The idea of these vessels to provide the dead with food in a similar manner to the way in which grain was stored in towers by the living in time of scarcity and famine, was not unlike that of the practice of placing food in the graves of the dead in many Western countries in prehistoric days.

Domestic objects are represented in this ancient pottery from the remote Han dynasty by such outside things as draw-wells, and by inside utensils like the kitchen stove. In the *Annals of the Later Han Dynasty* mention is made of the burial of clay stoves, some of which were of horseshoe form, others were complete with an outfit including kettle and other apparatus. The use of such stoves, from which the clay pottery models were fashioned, goes back to very early times, for the *Tsao-ming* of Li yu says " Sui jen " created the fire, but the first to continue his work (by making cooking-ranges) was Huang (2698-2593 B.C.). Small cooking-stoves and vessels in pottery are very numerous, and they mostly seem to be copies of the bronze vessels which were used at the time they were made, or possibly earlier. In addition to these larger things there are among them many curious little ladles, bowls, and dishes.

The jars and vases are fine pieces, and some are large ; they, too, have undoubtedly been modelled from vases of bronze ; the pottery shows that not only were they modelled, but many of them were moulded from the actual objects from which they were copied. The very hammer-marks of the coppersmith of those primitive times are re-produced in the object moulded from them in clay. Such marks, which show the skill of the metal worker, look rather grotesque in pottery. These moulded vessels, however, were followed at no distant period by beautifully shaped vessels modelled and worked by hand, in which the finger-marks of the potter are to be seen. Some works of the Han dynasty were ornamented with reliefs and very realistic scenes, which had probably actually occurred and been witnessed by the potters who made them. Many of the scenes were designed from natural surroundings, and were true portraiture of familiar objects, and especially of hunting scenes. It may be conjectured that the modeller, even in those early days, sometimes derived his inspirations from more ancient models—ancient even then. This is evidenced by what may correctly be termed the reproductions of fabulous creatures with which the artist was not familiar, and his ideas of them were embodied in his models as he interpreted the stories he had heard about prehistoric animals and other creatures of a mythical nature, hence the absurd grotesqueness of some of the pieces of this ancient pottery.

Among the curiosities of the pottery of the Han period are the "hill-jars," to which no definite use has been ascribed. These very remarkable pottery jars are furnished with covers which are obviously modelled in imitation of a conical hill with its ridges and slopes—another bold example of the way in which "artists in clay " (and also contemporary artists in bronze) copied the natural surroundings which impressed them most. Many of the jars, probably mortuary jars, are ornamented round the sides with reliefs in which there are animals and demons. Some of the creatures depicted are like tigers, others are more like stags, and yet others are evidently modelled from domestic animals which possibly stood calmly by while the artist modelled and shaped his clay in imitation. There are varieties of the jars, but all have well-formed feet ; the tops in some cases are much flatter than others, and conventional ornament is used in the perfection of the detail of design, contrasting with others which are simply ornamented with plain bands.

Some writers have pointed out the influence of Siberian art upon the culture of Ancient China. They trace also the spread of the knowledge of ceramics and of decoration, modelling, and ornament to Japan by way of the Korea. Students of this pottery state that the root idea of much of the decoration is found in the "flying gallop" of Scytho-Siberian art, and they note the introduction of the lion in ornament, which they rightly say could not have originated in China. It is thought that the type of the Scythian and Siberian lion came from drawings and sculptures produced by Mycenian and Greek art.

The dog has always been a favourite subject for modellers and workers in plastic materials in China. This animal is traced back to the Tibetan wolf. The ancient Turkish tribes are said to have tamed the wolf, from which it is thought came the Assyrian hound, the St Bernard, the bull-dog, and the pug. The pottery dogs, however, are mostly of the type of the Tibetan mastiff kept in China during the Mongol period, a breed contrasting so markedly with the tiny Pekin toy pugs which were so fashionable in China during the Tang dynasty.

POTTERY OF THE SUNG DYNASTY.

There is the pottery of a more advanced period which comes under the notice of the collector of old wares as intervening before the period of the beautiful and more easily collected pottery. It is the mortuary pottery of the Sung dynasty, which covers a period of upwards of three hundred years, between A.D. 960 and 1278. This pottery, so much of which found its way to the American Museum of Natural History through the instrumentality of Mr Frank Chalfont, of the American Presbyterian Mission, was discovered in 1903 in the Shantung district. It was found chiefly in tombs. Of the graves examined it is said there were some of the Ming dynasty (of a later period than the Sung), none of which contained mortuary pottery, and others of the earlier Sung dynasty. In the latter group there were many fine pieces. In one grave these were what may be termed a typical and representative

FIGS. 100 AND 101.—A PAIR OF KYLINS of the Sung Dynasty.
By the courtesy of the Trustees of the late Edgar Gorer.

[To face page 334.

FIG. 102.　　　　FIG. 103.　　　　FIG. 104.

TEAPOTS AND WINE EWER.

set, all the pieces being, doubtless, regarded as essential to the well-being of the dead, as then believed by the residents in that part of China during the Sung dynasty. These pieces were a water-jug of reddish clay with dark-brown well-glazed interior, a bowl of coarse grey clay lined with a crackled glaze, a smaller bowl, and a saucer, all of which vessels held food. These were accompanied by a sacrificial vessel lined with yellow glaze, and a water-bottle ornamented with bamboo-leaf decoration. There were lamps, too, in the Sung graves, and in one a bronze mirror. As definite proof of the approximate age of the grave there were found, along with the pottery, coins of several of the emperors of the Sung dynasty, showing from their specific dates that the pottery was of the eleventh century of the Christian era—yet the Chinese were then burying pottery vessels for the use of their dead in the spirit world, just as our Ancient Britons had done thousands of years before. The copper coins appear to have been found between the finger-bones of the skeletons ; apparently the honoured dead were given money as well as food to carry them to an unknown land, or possibly for them to use in time to come on their return.

There are splendid collections of these early objects in the British Museum, and in America a specially fine collection of Sung wares, presented to the American Museum of Natural History by Mr Chalfont of the Presbyterian Mission in Wei hsien, Shantung Province.

The illustrations of Oriental pottery shown here are taken from examples in the Gorer Gallery in New Bond Street, W., being reproduced from photographs specially taken by the courtesy of the trustees of the late Edgar Gorer. Fig. 99 represents a large and extremely beautiful pottery shrine of the Sung dynasty. The colouring of this piece is very exceptional, the creamy ground deepening to dark green, the peculiar shading having a curious effect.

Much might be said about the modelling, some of the minuter details being fashioned with great skill. It evidently represents a very noted shrine.

Figs. 100 and 101 are a pair of kylins, one male and the other female, supported on oblong bases. The colouring is excellent : the prevailing tints are green and yellow, the aubergine enamel being very rich. These are truly pieces of the finer art of the Ming dynasty.

There is something very interesting about a collection of teapots of which there are many varieties collectable. Fig. 102 is a teapot with coloured ground, having two white kakemono panels on which are landscapes, the cover being decorated with chrysanthemums in blue and yellow : it is of the Kien-Lung period. The hexagonal teapot shown in . Fig. 104 is of the Ming period ; round the base is a pointed design in red and green, the neck having six panels with diaper pattern relieved with a " Joey " head in green, yellow, and red. The wine ewer illustrated in Fig. 103 is a rare piece of the Kang-He period, having a background of powdered blue with gold tracery design relieved with panels of birds and flowers, the colours being *famille verte*.

The teapots of the Kien-Lung period shown in Figs. 106, 107, and 108 are remarkable examples. Fig. 106 has a pink sharkskin ground on which are flowers in high relief ; on either side is a shaped panel decorated with birds and flowers in colours on white ; the base has a harlequin band in blue, yellow, and red alternately. Fig. 108 is a *famille rose* teapot and cover decorated with sprays of flowers on a white ground ; on the shoulder are alternate pink and black panels relieved with flowers. Another variety, Fig. 107, has a pink sharkskin ground relieved by perforated bosses on either side ; the handle is in the form of a kylin, and round the neck is a light green band with diaper design and flowers, all the decorations being in *famille rose* enamels.

The pair of cocks in white porcelain shown in Fig. 105

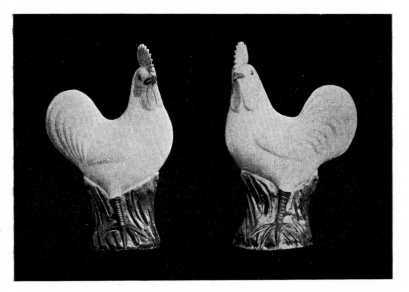

Fig. 105.—A Pair of Cocks in white porcelain, supported on
brown rocky bases, of the Kien-Lung period.

In the Gorer Gallery.

Fig. 106.   Fig. 107.   Fig. 108.

Three Remarkable Teapots.

In the Gorer Gallery.

By permission of the Trustees of the late Edgar Gorer.

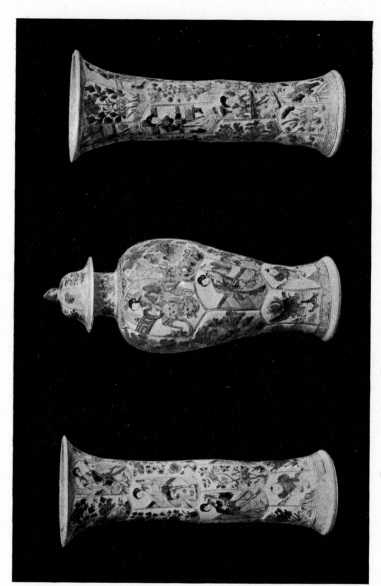

Fig. 109.—A Set of Three.—Two Beakers and One Vase and Cover.
They are in fine Famille-verte, and are of the late Ming period.

By the courtesy of the Trustees of the late Edgar Cover.

are reminiscent of many Staffordshire birds, which may well have been copied from such pieces as these, which are fine examples of Chinese pottery of the Kien-Lung period.

There are many wonderful vases in the Gorer Gallery. In Fig. 109 are shown three pieces—two beakers and a centre vase and cover—of the late Ming period. The decoration consists of female figures playing musical instruments, and dancing boys, the spaces between being filled with flowers; the colouring is *famille verte*. Fig. 110 is an oviform jar and cover decorated with various shaped panels on which are fabulous animals and flowers; between these are dragons and butterflies. The bands round the neck and base are in greens, yellow, and red. The cover is similarly treated, and has a green band round the rim ornamented with key-pattern design in black—*famille noire*. It is of the Kang-He period. Fig. 111 is a vase with black ground on which is a scroll design in green and floral panels; the spaces between are filled with chrysanthemums in white, blue, and pink, the whole in *famille rose* enamels.

The last illustration of Oriental porcelain, Fig. 112, is a large bowl with background of *rouge-de-fer*, decorated with a green scroll design and relieved with panels containing altar utensils, flowers, insects, and landscapes in *famille verte* on a white ground. Above is a broad band of green having a scroll design in white and black with small panels on which are fishes and animals. The interior is decorated in a similar manner. It is of the Kang-He period.

CHAPTER XXXIII

Porcelain enamels—Well-known varieties—Colours and glazes—
Georgian tea china—Japanese art.

AN examination of the magnificent collections of Oriental porcelain in the British Museum, the Victoria and Albert Museum at South Kensington, and some of the best known private collections, reveals the wondrous skill of the early potters in those countries where the art was practised.

The needs of imperial majesty and of the temples of the gods and their priests supplied a motif, and potters early vied with one another in supplying their royal and priestly patrons with pieces of exceptional quality and beauty.

Artistic treatment was aimed at even in the most trivial objects ; and whether it was in painting those mysterious symbols or in fashioning the cells of those beautiful *cloisonné* enamels, the artists did their best. As they had fashioned their pottery in earlier days according to their beliefs of the interests of the dead, so in later times they decorated the porcelain for the delight of the living, perpetuating, however, the traditions of their ancestors in its decoration.

PORCELAIN ENAMELS.

The porcelain of the East cannot be distinguished by the simple method of differentiating between the

338

semi-transparent and the opaque, as in more modern wares and in porcelain made in this country during the eighteenth century. The use of enamels plays an important part in the production and in the finish ; many vases of comparatively coarse pottery, when enamelled, were equal in appearance to the finer true porcelain. The term " porcelain " as applied to Chinese wares has often been defined as that ware made when the artist had learned the art of preparing and firing those wondrous glazes with which he coated his wares. It is not out of place to call the later productions of the Chinese potters "porcelain," although not technically correct when compared with the characteristics of true porcelain as described in another chapter.

It is difficult for the amateur to master the technicalities of production, neither is it necessary for him to do so in the more narrow sense as understood by the craftsman. The study of processes of manufacture is often dry, but there are some points which should be carefully noted, otherwise it is difficult to distinguish between pieces of pottery and porcelain of different potteries, for the differences are often trifling, yet even the least alteration in colour and style may make all the difference in age and in value.

In modern art China has suffered by comparison with her more go-ahead neighbour, Japan. China, however, has had a wonderful past ; but even during the periods when some of the best art was produced, craftsmen made many mistakes, due to their lack of appreciation of some of the details to which the Western world had been trained ; and they failed to understand the essentials of good workmanship which were grasped by their near neighbour. Many of the clever colour effects, rich tints, and the free use of gold lost their charm when it was noticed that the Chinese artist had evidently been sadly deficient in his appreciation of the beauty of the human form.   Another defect has been pointed out, in that the artists of Old China, although lovers of flowers and skilled painters of them, could not draw animals and birds.   Most of their attempts were crude, and even their best creations were grotesque rather than true to Nature ; this, perhaps, may be due, to some extent, to their continuation of the reproduction of mythical scenes and so often painting fabulous animals, whereas the flowers they painted were growing about them.

Porcelain was made at an early date, contemporary with coarse pottery, just as it is to-day.   During the Tsin dynasty (265-419 A.D.) blue porcelain was made. Writing in reference to this jewel-like porcelain of such a delightful blue shade, Mrs Hodgson in *The Book of Old China* tells of fragments of blue porcelain worked up as jewels and handsomely mounted, attributing " the use of blue in the colouring of that early porcelain to a fancy of the Emperor, who ordered that the porcelain of the Imperial household should be made like the colour of the heavens seen between the clouds after rain."

Some remarkable green porcelain was made by the potters of the sixth century; it was, however, during the Sung dynasty (960-1279) that such a great impetus was given to the potter's art.

WELL-KNOWN VARIETIES.

It was then that the beautiful celadon vases were first made.   The tints of this ware are so varied that when it was first brought over to this country the property of changing colour when brought into contact with poison was imputed to it.   Those were the days when witchcraft and superstition were rife.   History records that it was a celadon vase which was presented to Queen Elizabeth by Cecil, the gift being then described as " a cup of grene pursselyne."

It was also during the Sung dynasty that the famous crackle glaze was discovered ; the discovery is said to have been due to an accident, resulting in its very general adoption then and at a later date. The process of its manufacture was simple when explained. It was produced by plunging the unbaked ware when hot (by exposure to the sun) in cold water ; then when the firing was effected the vase or other object was found to be covered with small cracks, into which Indian ink was sometimes rubbed ; in this condition the ware was glazed with the curious effect so well known to collectors. The glaze was somewhat peculiar, steatite being introduced with felspar, this mixture making the ware crackle. Some pieces show a double crackle, the result of double firing and exposure.

In describing the varied works of art it is necessary to follow the dynasties in their respective order, for the story is, as it were, punctuated by these landmarks in the history of China and its productions. Great advance was made in the wares produced, in their quantity, and perhaps in their quality, when export business commenced. This was when Chinese potters made the discovery of a great European market waiting for the beautiful ceramics of China, and from that time onward there was a steady flow of porcelain into Europe from the Far East. It was during the Ming dynasty that special progress was made and a great commercial boom set in. At that time the colouring of the porcelain was chiefly blue, of that shade described by some as "Mohammedan blue." Other varieties were, however, made, among them black. Then later, in the first quarter of the fifteenth century, a great advance was made in decoration, and birds and fishes came into vogue, as well as a free admixture of flowers. A few years later the dragon was introduced, and brighter colours, especially red, were adopted.

In the sixteenth century the famous *famille verte* appeared, and wondrous indeed were the pieces thus decorated.

The pottery and porcelain of the Ching dynasty, beginning in the year 1644, is that which is best known to collectors. It may, however, be pointed out that many of the older designs have been reproduced or copied ; thus it is that really expert knowledge is needed to distinguish between them and to accurately decide between the original and the copy ; yet, notwithstanding the clever way in which Chinese potters of the past and present have tried to follow the old masters, there is a difference when old and new are compared.

COLOURS AND GLAZES.

The body of Oriental wares, especially Chinese, may be pottery or it may be semi-transparent, and therefore, judged from the European standpoint, porcelain ; the after-coating of the glaze, however, gives it an appearance, in many cases, from which it is hard to define the ground-work ; therefore, as it has been pointed out already, it is not desirable to differentiate between pottery and porcelain when describing the finer Chinese ceramics. Kaolin, or china clay, and felspar are the chief constituents in the material from which the potter formed the base on which to lay, after drying, his glaze and colouring.

The various methods of treatment, some of which have been referred to already, followed in the order in which they were discovered or introduced from other countries into China. The blue, which was afterwards used so successfully in England and elsewhere, was easy to apply, and it adhered to or became absorbed by the paste and was therefore a simple and effective colour under glaze. In connection with blue the glaze employed was usually

FIG. 110.—An Oviform Jar
and Cover of the Kang-He
period. Famille-verte colours
on a white ground.

In the Gorer Gallery.

FIG. 111.—Vase and Cover,
with scroll design decoration.
In fine Famille-rose enamels.
The Kien-Lung period.

By permission of the Trustees of the late Edgar Gorer.

FIG. 112.—A LARGE ORIENTAL BOWL, with background of rouge-de-fer, decorated with a green scroll design and relieved with various shaped panels, containing altar utensils, flowers, insects and landscapes, in Famille-verte tints on a white ground. The interior of this fine bowl, which is of the Kang-He period, is decorated in a similar manner.

In the Gorer Gallery in New Bond Street, London.

By permission of the Trustees of the late Edgar Gorer.

white, but not always, for some of it was of a light bluish tint. Red and blue were not infrequently used in conjunction, some of the richest and softest colourings being composed of these tints.

The black foundation—the rare *famille noire*—was decorated with gold ornament, a form of enrichment which was early adopted to make effective and more brilliant the green enamels known as *famille verte*. In the use of these various enamels it is well to note that reds and greens were added after glazing, whereas blue was almost invariably applied before glazing. The Chinese potters made, doubtless, many experiments before they were successful with what became favourite, if rare, shades. The yellows and purples are among the scarce and choicest examples. The yellow, mostly confined to imperial purposes, goes by the family name *la jaune*, and is derived from cadmium and iron, the beautiful tints being produced from manganese. The rare rose tint derived from the lavish use of gold was the basis of the splendid decoration on the Chinese wares which comes under the designation of the *famille rose*.

An important and almost distinct variety is the group distinguished as enamelled in colour—the decoration consisting of rare tints produced by the use of unusual pigments. Of these self-coloured enamels it may be explained that the blue of the very early times—that lovely sky-blue —was quite distinctive from the deeper blues of later years ; indeed, many of the tints of the same colourings made at different times, and in some instances made at contemporary dates, are distinctive. Take, for instance, the "mazarine " blue, so much used afterwards by English potters and conspicuous in the blue of Worcester and the blue of the blue-and-white of the Kang-hsi, or Kang-he, period, which is greatly admired.

There are self-coloured reds, but red has always been used in decoration, and many of the best results have been produced by shading. In the reds come, of course, the *famille rose*, obtained from gold, the most costly and the most beautiful of the pigments.

The black of the *famille noire* is among the rarities, and genuine specimens of this ground colour, often richly ornamented by contrasting tints, are costly to buy. The yellow of the imperial palaces is varied in tint and is designated by such fanciful names as "mustard," "canary," and "lemon."

A few other shades should be mentioned, like the " sea-green " made in the sixteenth century, developing later into what are known as " apple-green," " emerald-green," and " pea-green." Brown glazes are not very interesting, although some of the self-coloured lustrous browns are enriched by floral sprays in colour on panels of white.

Next in order to the self-colours are those which consist of more than one coloured enamel or glaze ; some of these first moulded and then picked out in colours, like the gaudy Chinese pilgrim bottles, owe their origin to Persian influence.

The style of design which runs through so many of the periods of Chinese art was influenced by the prevailing thought, which led to the almost constant employment in decoration of those deities or their attributes. There are, however, a few well-known patterns which are for the most part made up of floral sprays of the prunus blossom, which is such a feature in the Chinese landscape. The famous hawthorn pattern is but the prunus blossom transformed in colour. Among other flowers may be mentioned the chrysanthemum, the poppy, the lotus, and the aster, all of which flowers figured on the older porcelain, and were used again and again in after years for the decoration of more modern works of art.

The marks seen upon the different wares are much too

varied to deal with *in extenso*. It is interesting to know that marks on china are "no new thing." The custom of marking wares is said to have originated about the year A.D. 1005, by order of the Emperor, who ordered that a special symbol or mark should be placed on all porcelain used in the imperial palaces, much of it then being made at the pottery at King-tê-chên.

GEORGIAN TEA CHINA.

The English market was valuable to the Chinese potter during the last half of the eighteenth century. It was then that the wealthy in this country were anxious to obtain Oriental porcelain not then produced in England after the same manner. The industry, specially directed towards the supply of porcelain suitable for the English market, flourished under the patronage of the Chinese Emperor Ch'ieng-lung, who did all he could to foster foreign trade. With his death—after a reign of sixty years—the manufacture of antique porcelain valued so such by the collector came to an end ; for although much beautiful pottery and porcelain have been produced during the last hundred years or so, it is largely made up of replicas, or modern adaptations of old styles and designs, and not so distinctive or interesting in the eyes of connoisseurs.

The collector will learn more about the colouring and the charming decorations of old Chinese porcelain by inspecting a good representative collection than from either descriptions or illustrations. The Salting Bequest placed the nation in possession of an unrivalled collection of Oriental ceramics, as well as other treasures. These beautiful and truly representative wares are to be seen in the Victoria and Albert Museum, at South Kensington. Arranged in cases, classified and representative of well-known potteries, ancient and modern, they include examples of all the important varieties. From these examples the early products of the potters of the Han dynasty may be inspected. These are in close proximity to the finer ceramics of the Tang and Sung periods, followed by Ming porcelain and the greater varieties of the Kang Hsi, very conspicuous being examples of the very rare *famille rose* and *famille noire*. Besides these works of art of the older dynasties, there are examples of modern porcelain, from which the taste of modern artists and connoisseurs may be judged.

JAPANESE ART.

During the last quarter of a century Japanese art has advanced. It is, however, questionable whether in the eyes of the collector of pottery it has improved. The art of Japan has moved along with the commercial growth of the nation, and its artists have learned that while many of the articles made for the European markets are valued because of their curious and sometimes startling decorations, others are purchased on account of their suitability to European needs. The pottery of Old Japan is sought after because of its beauty and rich ornament, but the arts of modern Japan are appreciated in proportion to their assimilation to Western ideas.

Mr James Bowes, the Japanese consul in Liverpool, in his excellent book, *Japanese Pottery*, says, in reference to the thoughts and subjects which actuate the workers in clay : " The decoration of Japanese pottery has, perhaps more than that of any other art works of the country, afforded an opportunity for the illustration of the senti- ments of the people, the subjects employed embracing not only the flowers, shrubs, and trees, for the beauty and dignity of which Japan is so justly celebrated, but there is also found upon these wares a record of many of the thoughts which have influenced their lives : the fabulous creatures associated with the Imperial House, the crests of the *daimio* and the *samurai*, the historic battles and the portraits of the noble men and gentle women of ancient times, whose deeds and virtues still thrill the hearts of their descendants, poetic associations of flowers and birds ; their festivals, traditions, and superstitions ; views of the sacred mountain, and of the beautiful spots renowned for groves of the almost worshipped *oumai, sakura,* and *matsu ;* the gods of fortune ; the *takara mono* and other ornamental forms instinct with meaning."

It is thus that the collector must approach the study of Japanese porcelain, which, while similar in many respects, differs from that of its neighbour China.

It is said that the potter's wheel was introduced into Japan in the eighth century, but it was not until long after that that any marked progress was made, for Kato Shirozayemon, who has been named the " father of pottery " in Japan, did not live until the thirteenth century. He visited China and there learned the mysteries of the craft.

The potting industry in Japan at the present time is well illustrated in the numerous vases and ornamental works —copies of older models or more recent adaptations of ancient designs.

Hozen was early noted for its wares, the chief kiln being at Karatzu. Pottery was made for the imperial household in Yamashiro more than a thousand years ago. It was, however, not until the sixteenth century that the art progressed much. Towards the close of that century an important industry sprang up in the Satsuma province, where it received the encouragement of Prince Shimadzu Yoshihiri soon after he had visited the Korean potteries. He had brought back with him several skilled workmen, who were entrusted with the founding of kilns in Japan. They discovered suitable clay in Satsuma and there began to make pottery covered with the peculiar style of ornament for which the district became noted. The colouring of this ware consisted chiefly of red, green, and gold, the best examples coming from Tokio.

In the seventeenth century several other districts became noted for their potting, each distinguishing itself by the introduction of ornament and design different from any other, and quite different from the characteristics of the older Satsuma. One of these potteries was founded in Kago, and another at Owari, where much beautiful porcelain was made, notably the celadon ware of Setsu.

It may be useful to note a few well-known characteristics in the ornament adopted pretty generally throughout Japan. The *Ho-ho* bird of rich plumage, with its tail of long, waving feathers, and the *kiri* tree are frequently seen; both are specially favoured decorations of the imperial palace. According to the legend the *Ho-ho* bird dwells in the regions above, only descending to earth upon the birth of an emperor.

The following symbols (arranged alphabetically) are often seen in Japanese ornament :

FUNDO, a commercial weight.

HOJIU-NO-TAMA, a sacred jewel, signifying everlasting.

IKARA, or an anchor, indicating safety.

KAI, a shell. The shell represents wealth; in olden times shells were used as money.

MAKIMOND, an unrolled scroll representative of wisdom.

SANGOJU, rarity.

TSUCHI, a hammer, a symbol of the god of riches.

There is a peculiar beauty about the older wares, and many of the vases and other objects, although not always graceful in form, have a special attraction about them. Signs of age and even rough usage rob many of the early pieces of the full beauty of the delicate pencilling of gold and colour, but their owners would not exchange them for any modern work of art, however handsomely decorated. It is the same with almost every other class of curio !

CHAPTER XXXIV

TILES

Ancient Roman tiles—Mediæval tile-making—Dutch and later
English tiles.

THE modern use of clay as a material from which to produce
tiles and architectural pottery and garden ornaments is to a
large extent but following plans and methods of ancient
peoples. The Romans, whose long occupation of this
country enabled them to understand the advantages of
clay and to make use of it as a material from which to
produce useful building tiles, erected kilns wherever
suitable clay was to be found near the sites of their camps
and cities.

ANCIENT ROMAN TILES.

The lasting quality of the Roman tiles was well known
to those builders and architects who in the Middle Ages
made use of so much of the old material which they found
scattered about the sites of camps and towns, which were
deserted after the Romans left these shores.

One of the most striking examples of the re-use of such
tiles in even important buildings is seen in Saint Alban's
Abbey, which was in mediæval days built of bricks, locally
made, relieved by patterned work, in some cases very
decorative, formed by the extensive introduction of layers
of old Roman tiles, which were then very plentiful among
the ruins of Verulam, near by the Abbey grounds. Although Verulam has for centuries been ploughed over and
almost every vestige of that once-important city has

349

disappeared, broken tiles are not infrequently turned up in the fields.

The Roman tiles were thin and of a standard size quite different from that adopted in England in the Middle Ages, and therefore easily distinguished from more modern products. They are, however, often found almost side by side with those of much later times, for mediæval builders not only used up old tiles, but supplemented them by the use of new tiles of different sizes, made locally, often from the same old clay beds which had served the Romans. In mediæval days the purely builders' tiles for roofing and for flooring purposes were supplemented by many quaintly handsome decorated tiles, which were used in finishing the walls and floors of ecclesiastical buildings in the days when many sought to save their souls by building religious houses, and contributing to the erection of great abbeys and ecclesiastical establishments. It was thus that an impetus was given in those days to decorative tile-making and like industries.

It is extremely interesting to trace the connecting links between the past and the present in all industrial enterprises, especially in districts where natural supplies of raw material have fostered a continuation of the industry without break. This is not difficult in the tile industry, for in several localities tile-making has been carried on, although perhaps at intervals, for nearly two thousand years. In many instances kilns for the manufacture of tiles have been erected on the sites of old tile-making yards ; and years after the making of tiles has ceased there, when it has been almost forgotten, some adventurous worker in clay has discovered, or rather rediscovered, the excellent qualities of the local material, resulting in a new tile kiln being erected.

The county of Worcester is so well known to collectors of ceramics that it may appropriately be mentioned as a

FIG. 113.—15TH CENTURY INLAID TILE,
from Monmouth Priory.

In the British Museum.

[To face page 350.

Fig. 114.—Panel of Four Inlaid Tiles,
15th century.

In the British Museum.

locality where the tile-making industry can be traced to quite early times and followed up. In the fifteenth century many tiles were made there. In the year 1833 ancient kilns were found at Malvern; it was thought that they had been connected with Malvern Priory. In the neighbourhood the tiles discovered have often been found to be decorated with sacred symbols; others have upon them armorial bearings and some floral ornament. Many of these are of red clay, some having patterns which have been filled in with white liquid slip, the whole being afterwards coated with yellow glaze.

Broseley was an important seat of the tile industry in the seventeenth century, a record being extant of an order being placed there, in 1650, for one thousand tiles for the purpose of repairing the Bridge chapel at Bewdley. In recent days tile-making has become a feature of the county. At Worcester, Chamberlain made encaustic tiles much after the style of those afterwards made by Mintons at Stoke. The tile works at Worcester in 1850 were transferred to Mr Maw of Broseley, by whom an important modern tile trade was founded.

MEDIÆVAL TILE-MAKING.

The illustrations in this chapter are all of early tiles selected from the numerous examples in the British Museum. Fig. 113 is a fifteenth-century tile from Monmouth Priory, an exceptionally fine piece of inlaid work. Fig. 114 is a panel of four tiles of similar date, also in the British Museum. Those tiles shown in Figs. 115 and 116 are particularly interesting and very large, measuring 16 in. square. The upper panel represents Iseult (disguised) with others in a ship, and the lower panel King Richard in combat with Saladin.

The mediæval tiles which have been found in England,

and which were used in the building of great abbeys and ecclesiastical and public buildings, are something quite different to the earlier types of Roman and Romano-British tiles which have been found so extensively in this country. The commoner tiles which were made locally in England between the twelfth and the seventeenth centuries were not unlike Roman, in that they were made of red earth, but they were different in substance and also unlike them in decoration. Such tiles were usually square, and did not measure more than $\frac{3}{4}$ in. in thickness, the sizes varying from about $4\frac{1}{2}$ in. to 5 in. square. These tiles were used not only for ecclesiastical buildings, but for floors in Tudor mansions, and in some of the still earlier castles. In the Guildhall Museum, in London, there is a very fine selection of these early tiles, most of them having been found in the Metropolis itself. Some of these have been taken out of ancient buildings, and not only their age and undoubted genuineness authenticated, but the places where they were in actual use are well known. In some instances, probably, ancient records mention the builder's name, the architect who specified them, and the pottery from whence they came, if not actually the artist who fashioned them.

Some of these tiles in mediæval days were emblematic, and made specially for the buildings where they were used. There are many, of course, with ecclesiastical ornament, and some decorated with Royal arms and emblems. There are many on which may be seen the *fleur-de-lis*, and on others a five-petalled rose. There are designs of interlaced triangles, and there are some of lozenge form divided into squares by a cross with foliated ends. One very remarkable tile, which is said to have come from Chinnor, in Oxfordshire, is ornamented with a full-faced bust within a double circle crowned, and is said to resemble the head of Edward III. as seen on his groats and other silver currency.

There are some tiles, evidently parts of sets, which, when complete, formed a larger and more elaborate pattern. One set when complete, by correctly arranging four tiles in a block, represents an interlaced triangular design with a *fleur-de-lis* in the centre, and a lion's head within a small circle in each outer angle of the square formed by the four tiles. Another set of four which were found some years ago in Brook's Wharf, London, when joined together form a *fleur-de-lis* within an octofid, with five-petalled roses, between a double circle. There is another similar set on which are represented the heads of animals; and one consisting entirely of *fleur-de-lis* decoration. There are three tiles belonging to a set of four, which, when complete, make up an eight-petalled rose within two circles with a border of oak leaves between segments of circles and flowers in the outer angles.

The Royal arms are seen on many tiles, especially on some found under St Matthew's Church, in Friday Street, London. In the same place were discovered some tiles ornamented with shields of arms, and others with a cross formed of four *fleurs-de-lis*. No doubt some of these tiles of different patterns have been used conjointly, forming a more elaborate scheme of decoration. Most of the tiles are in coloured relief, the patterns formed of raised designs in one colour being less frequent; some of them were evidently used as paving tiles of floors.

There are Tudor wall-tiles extant, some of them very decorative. In the collection in the Guildhall there are Tudor wall-tiles covered with a yellow-brown glaze, the ornament being composed of masque, sword, Tudor rose, *fleur-de-lis*, and other decorative ornament. There are others with a crowned mailed figure in relief in the centre, the tiles coated with a green glaze having a very effective appearance. A very curious tile discovered some years ago in Gun Wharf, Wapping, was evidently used for wall tiling.

Its decoration consisted of a man supporting a capitol with his uplifted hand.   Another tile found at the same time during excavations was ornamented with a man's head and body terminating with a fish-tail.   One of the handsomest in the Guildhall collection is a yellow-glazed tile, the design in relief consisting of a crown surmounting the Royal arms, supported by a lion and a dragon, beneath which is another crown, and the Royal monogram, "E R " (Elizabetha Regina).

Another type of mediæval tile was introduced in the sixteenth century, and seems to have been made until towards the close of the eighteenth century.   It was a tile with a white-glazed surface, decorated in blue ; and sometimes in blue, yellow, and green.   Such tiles, generally designated "polycromic tiles," have frequently been found in London.   One discovered in Coleman Street, a rare tile exhibited before the British Archæological Association some years ago, is described in the Guildhall catalogue in the terms suggested by the late W. Syer Cuming, F.S.A., Scot., who defined it as follows : " An effigy of a male personage, the face slightly turned to the right.   The head covered with a huge cap, the front probably made up of three broad fan-shaped flaps of a rich brownish-orange colour. The white shirt has a broad collar encircling the throat embellished with a yellow trellis, doubtless meant to represent gold embroidery.   An ermine-lined mantle of ample proportions hangs upon the shoulders, and falls on either side of the effigy."   Mr Cuming thought that the figure represented Prince Arthur, brother of Henry VIII., who died at Ludlow Castle on April 11, 1502.

Other tiles of this period are covered with interesting figures and ornamentation.   One represents a cock with a foreground of grass and rushes ; another a figure carrying a spear and blowing a horn, with a foreground of trees within concentric circles.   Other tiles show respectively a hare, a dog jumping, the flight of wild duck, bunches of grapes, and designs of tulips, as well as Moorish designs, evidently copies of Oriental tiling.

DUTCH AND LATER ENGLISH TILES.

Again, a change in fancy came when Dutch pottery was imported into this country, and while some of the more elaborate tiles of the eighteenth century just referred to were being made for special purposes, a vast quantity of Dutch tiles was brought over to England. It is, of course, well known that such tiles were made along with Delft wares in some of the English potteries, such as Lambeth and other places, but there is a distinctive difference in genuine Dutch tiles. It is probable that the tiles which had been used so extensively in Holland at even an earlier period were made by the Dutch potters, even before they began to make wares ornamented in blue and white, which were sent over to this country during the reigns of William and Mary and subsequent sovereigns; but the seventeenth century was an important period during which these tiles were brought over to England in considerable numbers.

The uses of such tiles were varied ; it is said, however, that they were used to a much larger extent in Holland as wainscoting than they were ever employed in this country. The Dutch builders found them decorative and less expensive than wood. But in the seventeenth century they began to be used in England in making up the interiors of fireplaces, and for similar purposes, but they did not take the place of wood wainscoting to the same extent they had done in Holland.

Many remarkable designs were produced, but scriptural subjects seem to have been the most popular. It is quite true, while the collector associates Dutch tiles with the blue and white types, there are others of different texture and decoration.   In the British Museum there is a series of upwards of twenty reddish-brown tiles, decorated and moulded in relief.   Some are covered with scriptural subjects, others are historical.   Many tiles may be seen in the Victoria and Albert Museum fitted up round suitable contemporary grates ; and, again, some very excellent examples of Dutch tiles taken from old houses in London may be examined in the London Museum.   Some of them have been set up so as to show their original use.   In the Guildhall Museum there are many specimens which have been dug up, and found in old houses, and taken out of buildings which have been demolished.   The collector, by examining this series, forms a good idea of the varieties there are, and of what he may hope to collect.   Briefly described, such tiles may be classified as scriptural, architectural, landscape, and domestic.   The scriptural tiles are very quaint in drawing, and in the evident ideas of the artist.   Heading the list there is, of course, Adam and Eve and the Serpent at the Tree of Knowledge.   This once very favourite story of our first parents is supplemented by such subjects as the Israelites worshipping the golden calf ; David playing before Saul ; Jonah cast ashore by the whale ; the baptism of Christ in Jordan ; the Crucifixion ; and the angel at the open sepulchre.

The architectural tiles include a water gate and towers, a bridge, a walled town, and a group of buildings.

There are landscapes in which houses and rivers and mountains are introduced ; and winter landscapes and summer scenes ; there are men fishing, and shepherds with their flocks.   Cottages and bridges over rivers are popular, and there are agricultural scenes.

The domestic series shows common household occupations, and some traders' work.   There are many such tiles in the Guildhall Museum, and many in private collections, too, while the collection in the British Museum (from which the examples shown in this chapter are taken) is unrivalled for early mediæval tiles of historic interest.

In late years the Dutch tile-makers, finding that their small tiles for wall panelling were successful, attempted the manufacture of the larger pieces. Some of the slabs covered over with floral and natural history subjects were very decorative, and would, to a certain extent, serve as panel tiles in the upper portions of walls, taking the place of tapestry. Some of these panels were fully 3 ft. square, and must have been somewhat difficult to fire. Their painters drew their subjects from pictures of well-known Dutch artists ; others in their landscapes and floral designs introduced the arms of their patrons. Again, other tiles were obviously made to fit certain spaces, the sets including elaborate border tiles. Perfect examples of these old Dutch plaques or large tiles are now very difficult to obtain.

In the chapters relating to the English Delft works mention is made of the important tile industry carried on at some of the works in this country, where Delft ware was made in imitation of the Dutch. At several factories tiles formed an important part of the output. For instance, immense quantities of tiles were made in Liverpool, notably at the works at Shaw's Brow, founded by Alderman Shaw, a peculiarity of the tiles being that although they were very similar in style and design to the Dutch tiles of earlier date, they were made with bevelled edges holding them in position, an improvement of considerable architectural value. Some of the Liverpool tiles were decorated with local views, excellent examples being shown in the Liverpool Museum ; indeed, most of the Liverpool tiles were artistic as well as useful.

There was a tile factory at Warrington where Zachariah Barnes made very hard tiles for dados and wall linings.

His tiles were thin and mostly followed Dutch styles of ornament. Tiles have, of course, been made in more recent years for other purposes, not only at the well-known ceramic works, but at places where the whole industry has consisted of tile-making and the manufacture of ornamental panels. Tile-making is still carried on in England at Broseley, at Poole in Dorset, in the Staffordshire Potteries, and other places, for architectural tiling has in modern years been very much in vogue.

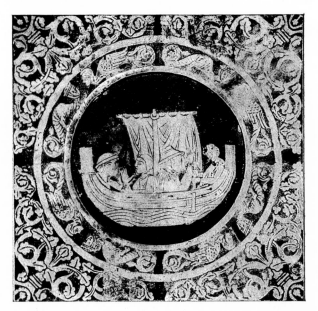

Fig. 115.—The Chertsey Panels—
Iseult with others in a Ship.

Fig. 116.—The Chertsey Panels—
King Richard in combat with Saladin.
In the British Museum.

[To face page 358.

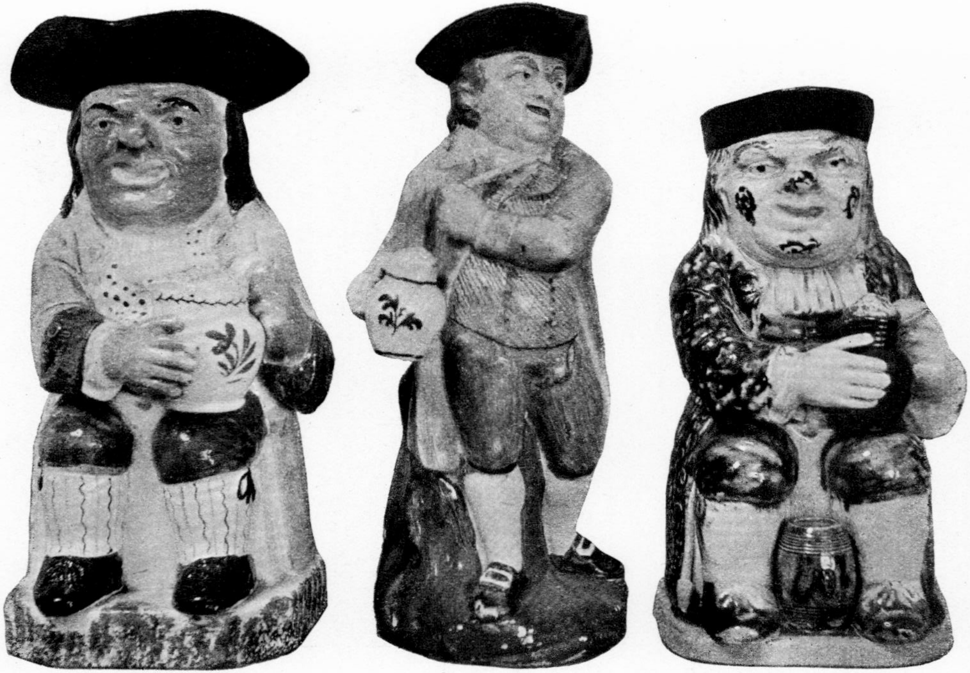

FIGS. 117, 118 AND 119.—THREE TOBY JUGS, various types.

At the Manor House, Hitchin, by favour of Mr. Phillips.

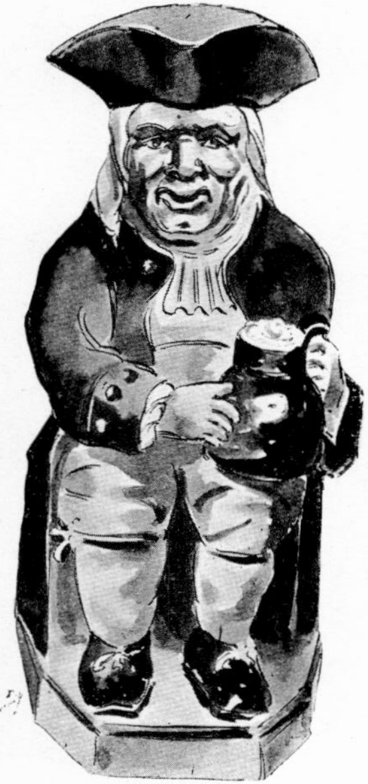

FIG. 120.

A TOBY JUG.

In the Author's Collection.

CHAPTER XXXV

TERRA-COTTA

Museum collections—Tangara figures—Antique lamps.

TERRA-COTTA cannot be overlooked altogether by the collector of pottery and porcelain, although there are many who do not regard the different substances and effects produced as having much in common. Those, however, who admire the beauty of ancient classic art, its sculptures and architectural reliefs, see in terra-cotta an early adaptation of the commoner and easily worked materials to the purposes of decoration and ornament. The material employed in the manufacture of old terra-cottas was of course the common clay of which bricks were made ; but much of the true terra-cotta of classic times was distinguished from the common clay figures and building materials in that the clay body was coated over with a thin layer—a species of white enamel—which was very suitable for painting upon.

The terra-cotta objects, specimens of which are to be found in our museums and in more important collections, cover a wide field, and represent the efforts of clay-workers in several distinct districts, and throughout the various periods during which the art flourished. From these museum examples it is evident that the ancients made use of terra-cotta for ornamentation of the more important buildings, designed and erected under the direction of noted architects and builders, and for many smaller and less important purposes. It is the lesser pieces that collectors chiefly obtain, and very many of the figures, most of which have been used as votive offerings, are well executed.

The use of terra-cotta for builders' purposes has not been confined to olden times, for some of the finest comparatively modern buildings, like the Natural Museum at South Kensington, are almost entirely enriched with terracotta reliefs and medallions.

The collector of miscellaneous pottery scarcely discovers from the oddments he gets together the full beauty of terracotta ornament, and rarely realises how in the past, and in the present, it has contributed to decorative architecture. Yet the clay-workers who modelled the objects they fashioned were not far removed from the great artists! The treatment of clay figures for pediments and panels for exterior use was necessarily different from that accorded to the smaller objects, which were enamelled and sometimes painted.

The collector desirous of specialising upon terra-cotta finds a variety of objects among the fragments of architectural pottery which come under his notice, and he has an ample opportunity of getting together a representative collection of such well-defined objects as lamps and figures. There are many relics of ancient peoples, for Lower Italy and Sicily, as well as the islands of the Mediterranean, have yielded up great treasures.

Roman art in terra-cotta was chiefly confined to architectural purposes, but many of these pieces still extant are very suitable for even a private museum or a cabinet of the cruder pottery, such as early English and pieces of Romano-British, and even mediæval pottery. The Greek terra-cottas are mostly figure subjects, and form a separate group of themselves.

The renaissance of art on the Continent gave great impetus to arts of all kinds, not least to workers in clay;

for at that time a new demand sprang up for terra-cotta
statuary for both indoor and exterior adornment.

MUSEUM COLLECTIONS.

As in so many other branches of art, the student of
terra-cotta is indebted to the zeal and enthusiasm of the
advanced collector, who has so frequently spent much time
and money in the pursuit of his hobby, the result of his
labour in course of time finding its way into one or other of
the public museums. Again, museum authorities have
exceptional opportunities of acquiring such treasures in
bulk, and also of obtaining isolated specimens which may
be required to fill up vacancies in the proper sequence of a
display which aims at being educative as well as interesting
in its completeness. Thus it is that in the Victoria and
Albert Museum at South Kensington there are many
splendid pieces of terra-cotta, representing all the known
periods of its manufacture. The British Museum, too,
contains many specialised collections and groups, especially
of the early Greek terra-cottas. The specimens there are
arranged in order according to the different periods of
Greek art, leading up from the earliest archaic times to the
later period of Romano-Greek art. The vase rooms are
remarkably rich in enamelled objects; many have been
found on the sites of ancient towns, other pieces, like the
votive offerings, have been discovered in the islands of the
Grecian Archipelago, and some have been brought from
Egypt. It is truly remarkable how fresh some of them
look, their long burial or entombment having in no way
impaired their beauty of form or of colouring. Terra-
cottas break easily, and therefore many of the figures are
mutilated and in some instances are mere fragments of
groups which, when complete, may have been among the
choice works of the best artists of that day.

During recent years there have been some remarkable finds in Cyprus, Crete, and in other islands which in ancient times were under similar influences to those which prevailed in Athens and other leading cities of the Greek Empire when at its best. The beliefs and legends of Greek mythology are seen in the paintings upon the vases, and the figure grouping shows the inspirations from which the principal subjects were taken. In the Victoria and Albert Museum there is a fine group representing Aphrodite and Cupid. Another group is intended to typify "A soul about to enter Charon's bark."

Quite a distinct group of terra-cottas comes from Northern Africa, the subjects being undraped figures, wearing head-dresses representing, perhaps, the latest fashion in head-gear of those times!

TANGARA FIGURES.

Figure subjects are always pleasing, for they represent life, and many of them are true to nature in that they represent the people of the age in which they were made, and the customs and habits of their owners, and in many instances their clothing and the household goods with which they were associated. There is a peculiar attraction about those Greek figures which were modelled from the athletes who had attained such perfection through rigorous training; many athletes must have posed to the workers in clay as well as to the sculptors in stone and marble.

Greek art was very general, but there were certain places where the potter chiefly flourished. It is only during recent years that research has produced evidence of specialised work. The late nineteenth-century discoveries which led to the finds of so many figures in the tombs of Tangara, once an important Bœotian town on the high road from Athens, leading northward, threw much light upon the subject.

Describing the formation of Tangara figures and other objects of contemporary dates, an expert says that they were made of soft clay pressed into a mould, the objects showing marks of having been formed in two parts and then joined together. This method of manufacture left a hollow figure, and an examination of the curios shows that there is a small hole at the back which was evidently placed there to allow the moisture to escape when firing. The heads were solid, and the fact that the other part of the figures was hollow has resulted in the preservation of many of the heads, whereas the remainder of the bodies has perished. It appears that it was customary to colour the figures, and in many instances there are distinct traces of the colours, some of which have been wonderfully preserved. From some of the best specimens the idea of the general scheme of colour can be ascertained. Rose and blue were the favourite colours of the drapery of the female figures, and the gold ornaments they were often represented wearing were shown in gilding which has retained its brilliance in a very remarkable way. It is a noticeable characteristic that the hair is generally red or auburn. The representations of human figures show two types of women, and their perfect forms are the admiration of all who examine them: some represent nymphs, others cupids, and some were evidently deities which are recognised by their own peculiar attributes. The value of these figures to those who seek to ascertain what the people of that far-away time were like is great, for it is generally admitted that there is abundant evidence of the accuracy of the modeller, the painter, and the artist, all of whom must have been familiar with the women and maidens of their day.

The variety of the figures is also of much value to the

connoisseur, as he is naturally desirous of making his collection as varied as possible.   There are both standing and seated figures.   Girls and matrons are shown in many poses ; some are holding fans, others have wreaths in their hands.   Women are playing musical instruments, girls are dancing, and some are amusing themselves with playing at the game of "knuckle-bones."   Among the deities Eros seems to be the most popular, for he is represented in many forms, sometimes being shown riding, at others flying, and often standing in repose.

Some claim that there is a special interest in the figures without a fan, in that the fan was not introduced into the East until the fourth century, thus marking a dividing line between the older figures and those made after the introduction and adoption of the fan.

The ease with which modern artists are able to copy the old terra-cotta, and even to give quite recent pieces a close resemblance to the antique, has caused the forger to give much attention to Tangara figures.   The more popular subjects have been much copied ; the collector must therefore beware.

Antique Lamps.

The terra-cotta lamps which have been found in so many parts of the world known to the ancients, show how in very early times ornament and decoration were applied to quite common objects, even those the main purpose of which was strictly utilitarian.   The lamp was then essential, and charged with oil was used on all occasions, for otherwise houses and streets were unlighted.   The torch was the primitive lamp or lighting medium, and the curious have speculated upon who it was who gave to the world the first lamp, and thus ushered in a new era ; for the lamp, however crude it was, marked a new departure and indicated a step forward in civilisation. The honour of the invention has been accorded to the Egyptians, for the earliest known examples come from the tombs of Egypt. Some of these early lamps are of silver, bronze, and even of gold, but the plastic clay in which the Egyptians were clever workers was undoubtedly, at a very early period, modelled in the form of lamps taking the shapes of bulls, dogs, and other animals, many of which have been found at Memphis. Red terra-cotta lamps in the form of birds have been discovered in many parts of Africa. At Carthage the Phœnicians used lamps shaped like shells, and similar lamps have been found in Sardinia, Sicily, and in Malta. Greek and Roman tombs have yielded up many specimens. The earlier examples were strong and without much ornament, but most of those which have come into collectors' hands show signs of decoration. At first they were covered with pagan emblems, but as times altered the Christian symbols were substituted, and not a few have been found in the Roman catacombs, where many of the early Christians were forced to live.

CHAPTER XXXVI

HISTORIC POTTERY

The famous Willett collection—Souvenirs of royalty and statesmen—
Scriptural subjects, music, and art.

THE specialistic collector is often one who makes his hobby
a sequel to study or some previous experience and occupation. The man who has studied history, and who may,
if only in a lesser degree, have taken part in the making of
history, naturally likes to associate historical reminiscences
with his hobby. If a connoisseur of old china, he has
ample opportunities of combining historic reminders with
his love of rare specimens, or of pieces representing different
pastes, glazes, and schemes of ornament. History is
traceable in the vast quantity of souvenirs in pottery and
porcelain which have been made in the past, and which
potters still make whenever any great historic event occurs.
There have been royal souvenirs on pottery representing
almost every reign in English history since the time of
Elizabeth, including "jubilee " mugs of the reign of Queen
Victoria, and cups and jugs commemorating the coronations
of the late King Edward VII. and his present Majesty King
George V.

Some pieces are historic in that they commemorate
events which mark progress and show the tastes and habits
of the people in the day in which they were made. They
hand on to posterity vivid pictures of amusements and
public functions. There is the group of pottery which tells
of the early days of our national game—cricket. One of

these is a mug which was made by Fletcher & Co., of Shelton, on the front of which is a view of a cricket match, fully described by the inscription upon it, which reads, " Grand Cricket Match, played at Lord's Ground, Mary-le-bone, June 20 (1790) and following day, between the Earls of Winchester and Darnley for 1000 guineas." It is printed in red, a choice little specimen, which changed hands at Christie's some time ago for about forty guineas.

Then again there are mementos of naval battles, one little mug of salt glaze ware being covered over with pictures of the old "wooden walls" of England, the inscription upon it reading, " The British glory revived by Admiral Vernon. He took Portobello with six ships only, November 22, 1739." This little mug, which measures only 5¼ in. high, was sold a short time ago for twenty guineas.

The commemorative pieces reminding us of battles and sieges are truly numerous, but it is only when viewing a complete and really comprehensive collection that the real value and merit of historic pottery can be fully appreciated.

THE FAMOUS WILLETT COLLECTION.

Some well-known collectors have found great interest in surrounding themselves with a collection of grotesque figures, finding amusement in what may have been caricatures even when modelled, but still conveying to the intelligent observer a basis of truth, and conveying by the clothing and colouring of the figures or characters some very useful knowledge of the times when either the figures were being made or those historic characters they portrayed lived. There are others who have collected groups or figures of historical characters, such pictures and forms of ornament as those referred to in the foregoing

paragraphs.   But it is the inscriptions as well as the dates
and mottoes upon such pieces that give such unqualified
delight to the historical collector.

One of the most important collections, carefully made
with a view of illustrating popular British history, that has
ever been got together, was that collected by the late Mr
Henry Willett of Brighton.   Some years ago the collection
was the central feature of attraction at the Bethnal Green
branch of the Victoria and Albert Museum.   Since the
death of Mr Willett that unique collection has passed into
the hands of the Public Library Museums and Fine Art
Galleries at Brighton.   By the courtesy of the Director of
the Museum we are enabled to refer to some of the chief
characteristics of that interesting collection, which has
been so much admired.   It is interesting because of its
completeness, and the examples illustrating most of the
characters which have been pictured upon pottery.   It is no
new thing to commemorate public men by giving to the
world statues and busts by which their personality can be
handed down to posterity.   But pottery brings such
portraiture to the masses.

Mr Willett's collection included British historical
characters, the list being headed by Royalty.   Then came
military and naval heroes, statesmen, philanthropists, men
associated with architecture, and architectural subjects.
These were followed by groups illustrative of music, drama,
poetry, science, literature, sports, pastimes, and amusements, and other pieces relating to domestic incidents.
The object of the collector was to show how the history of
the country may be traced on homely pottery ; and in
grouping the catalogue of that collection the author tells
us that the classification is not so much in reference to the
maker, the time, and place of manufacture, but rather in
regard to the human interest presented by the different
objects.   That suggests quite a different motive from that

usually pursued by the collector of china, and yet it is a very laudable one, and in itself should be a sufficient motive to induce some home connoisseurs to take greater note of their so-called commoner wares, perchance now on a kitchen mantelpiece, and to inspire them to add to such collections.

In the Willett Collection there are pieces dating from the sixteenth century side by side with those of the middle of the nineteenth century. The connection with Royalty in some of the earlier pieces of Delft ware and old English stoneware is merely that of the Royal monogram like the Tudor rose, and the initials " E. R." on a yellow-glazed earthenware sconce for candles of Elizabethan days. There is a dish with a portrait of Charles I. and a statuette of Oliver Cromwell. There is a group, truly historical, representing Charles II. in an oak tree. Then on some old Dutch Delft dishes may be seen portraits (?) of William III. and Mary. On an old Fulham stoneware mug there is a portrait of Queen Anne. It was a commemorative piece, for the inscription upon it reads, " To the Memory of Queen Anne, made 1721." There is a plate of blue decoration, of Delft ware, on which is a loyal inscription, " God save King George, 1716."

The portrait pieces, consisting of mugs, jugs, teapots, and plates, include a series of Royal portraits, among them George II., George III., George IV., William IV., and Queen Victoria. Commemorative of a domestic incident, yet one of much interest to the nation, is a cream-ware jug on which is a portrait of George III. inscribed with the legend,

> "Britons rejoice, cheer up and sing
> And drink this health, Long Live the King."

The jug was made to celebrate the King's recovery from illness in 1789. There is also a bowl commemorative of the jubilee of George III., on which there are several verses. To some the military heroes have peculiar interest, like the black basalte medallion bust of the Duke of Marlborough, a statuette of General Wolfe, and another of General the Marquis of Granby.

Early in the nineteenth century much pottery was made commemorative of the Duke of Wellington, and of his successes which culminated on the field of Waterloo; naval heroes, including Lord Rodney, Earl Howe, Admiral Sir Sydney Smith, and Lord Nelson, were frequently pictured, and represented by pottery busts or statuettes. Inscriptions, too, of a military character are frequently met with.

In the Willett collection there is a Staffordshire mug of earthenware, printed in blue, made, probably, about 1800, inscribed,

> " The Volunteers Success attend,
> And all that are Old England's friend."

The old volunteer movement has been superseded, but Britain's territorial army is still doing its duty.

SOUVENIRS OF ROYALTY AND STATESMEN.

There are many historical pieces commemorative of English and French wars, some showing the connection between Great Britain and the United States of America. There are portrait busts and portraits on plaques of George Washington. There is an English mug made about 1790, inscribed, " Civil and Religious Liberty to all Mankind."

A punch bowl, on which is printed the arms of the United States, has on it a portrait of Benjamin Franklin; a plate printed in blue, with a view of Massachusetts State House at Boston, was made in Burslem about 1820; and there is a cream-ware printed jug on which is an American eagle in colours, inscribed, " Peace Commerce and honest Friendship with all Nations. Entangling Alliances with none. Jefferson. Anno Domini 1804."

The British statesmen who have received honour at the hands of potters include the Earl of Chatham, William Pitt, Charles James Fox, Earl Grey, Lord John Russell, Lord Brougham, George Canning, Daniel O'Çonnell, Sir Robert Peel, and Lord Palmerston. In this group is a famous flask of brown stoneware, representing Lord Brougham, and inscribed, " Lord Brougham's Reform Cordial."

There is an interesting series of statuettes and figures, specially classified to show costumes and characters. In this category are figures of an old town-crier, a crossing sweeper, Josiah Wedgwood, a wheelwright's shop, and a jug printed with a barber's shop, inscribed,

> " Shave for a penny Hair drest for twopence
> And a Glass of Gin into the bargain."

To these may be added a sweep, the Jewish seller of old clothes, the pedlar, the "buy-a-besom " girl, and a shoe-maker fitting a lady with a pair of shoes, for all these subjects came in for attention at the hands of the modeller. Architecture is represented by well-modelled quaint little cottages and other buildings referred to in another chapter, and also by pieces on which are printed pictures and representations of architectural buildings.

Scriptural Subjects, Music, and Art.

In a group labelled " Scripture History " in the Willett Collection there are some very quaint representations of old Biblical stories interpreted according to the fancy of the artist. There are religious groups and paintings of a controversial and denominational character. One of the best-known groups picturing church procedure in olden time is

that known as the " Vicar and Moses " (*see* Fig. 37).   There
are verses, too, upon jugs and mugs relating to the same
subject.   The doings of the vicar and parish dignitaries
seem to have come in for a large share of attention.   One
remarkable group, painted on a porcelain jug made at Bow
in 1760, now in the Brighton Museum, represents several
clergymen and their parishioners carousing at the sign of
The Horns.   There is also a cup there on which are the
heads of the Pope and the Devil, the inscription reading,
" While the Pope absolves, the Devil smiles."   There is
another interesting figure of coloured earthenware, representing John Wesley preaching from a pulpit.   To some,
doubtless, the brown-ware Rockingham bust of the Rev.
John Wesley in the form of a pepper pot was somewhat
derogatory to the founder of Wesleyanism, but there was
not always much connection between vessel and ornament.
An earthenware group is inscribed, " The New Marriage
Act," and represents " a marriage in church," a companion
group representing " a marriage under a tree," both groups
being in colours.

Music has always been a favourite subject for the artist
to represent in picture form and sculptured groups.   It is
seen on some of those marvellous groups made in Chelsea,
now among the most valuable ceramic treasures.   Mr
Willett was able to gather together a very delightful case of
figures, busts, and groups, chiefly of old Staffordshire.   He
secured figures representing a girl playing on a guitar, a
boy playing on a pipe, a one-legged negro figure, a negress
dancing, a boy with a hurdy-gurdy, and many other equally
interesting pieces.

Old English amusements and occupations are represented in this collection by printed decorations, illustrating
bull and bear baiting, prize fighting, cock fighting, racing,
coaching, shooting, stag and fox hunting, coursing, archery,
cricket, ballooning, fishing, dancing, farming, marketing,

gardening, and harvesting—a truly remarkable collection well worth a journey to Brighton to inspect. In these days when we have fast-speed motor-cars, and aeroplanes overhead, the earthenware plate printed in blue, showing a man riding on a velocipede in 1810, is worth noting, as well as its inscription,

> " I scud along on this machine,
>   While many a crowd is gaping seen ;
>   Accelerating power,
>   Gaining ten miles an hour."

CHAPTER XXXVII

GROTESQUE POTTERY AND FIGURES

The grotesque in ancient pottery—Mediæval figures—Old puzzle
jugs—Curious cups—"Toby" jugs—Quaint figures.

HUMAN nature is very varied ; some see the humorous side
very quickly, others need more than usual novelty and
grotesqueness to stir up their feelings. What is amusing
and even upsets the gravity of most stolid men scarcely
calls forth a smile from others. Then again, there are some
who fail to see in the coarse jokes or in the crude representations seen on some pottery anything to interest ;
indeed, such pictures and sentiments repel ; whereas
others, although equally refined in their own feelings and
actions, simply revel in what they term grotesque pottery,
in that to them it has a charm all its own, and they are able
to disassociate it from the circumstances under which it
was made and used.

It would appear that potters of all ages have realised
the varied tastes of those for whom they were catering, and
have endeavoured to please in all directions. To-day
collectors try to obtain antiques according to their fancies,
and what to some would have no interest are to them full
of delight. When we remember that much of the old
pottery now carefully stored in drawing-rooms and museums
was at one time in constant use in ale-houses and taverns,
in the days when tipplers and roisterous mirth were the
common associations of such places, it is not to be wondered
at that the subjects chosen by potters for the decoration of

374

such vessels were of types which were in accord with the surroundings of the places where they would be used, and with the times in which they were made.

THE GROTESQUE IN ANCIENT POTTERY.

The grotesque appeals to many ; they see in it a peculiar value, in that such pottery so well represents the doings of the times in which it was used ; and, consequently, such pieces are in many respects of historic value, just as the more delicate pottery and porcelain objects which were printed over with portraits of famous generals and political leaders, and which by their devices commemorate great events on land and sea.

Among the earlier mediæval pottery of this country many pieces are grotesque, and their forms and colourings are suggestive of scenes far removed from those of to-day.

In the pottery of Ancient Egypt, China, and other Oriental countries, there are many early specimens which a collector of grotesque pottery would include in his specialistic collection.

In the pottery of the Han dynasty in China there are many quite utilitarian pieces which are grotesque enough to please the most fastidious in his selection, and yet they were based upon the common objects with which the potters were then familiar, such as the farm-sheds of the agricultural population by which the village potters would be surrounded. In *Chinese Pottery of the Han Dynasty*, by Berthold Lanfer, there is an illustration of a sheepfold, in pottery, containing five quaintly modelled sheep in front of a mill. It is a delightful specimen of ancient grotesque design. That piece is representative of the grotesque in form and modelling. Other contemporary ceramics are grotesque and quaint in design rather than in form, such,

for instance, demon-like figures on Han bas-reliefs. The
pottery representing the forms of animals, mythological and
actual, is quaint enough, and vessels taking such forms
are spread over the greater field of ceramic art; from the
pottery mastiffs of the Han dynasty to the present-day
races of dogs—fierce and wild, and tame and domesticated
—have been modelled. Legends, myths, and fables have
been perpetuated by such creations. There are the great
hunting dogs of Mongolia upon ancient pottery, and to-day
English makers model lap dogs and grinning Cheshire cats
in pottery as ornaments (?).

MEDIÆVAL FIGURES.

Collectors of old copper and brass are familiar with the
quaint metal ewers and jugs, in the forms of animals, which
were hammered into shape so laboriously in mediæval
England. The coppersmith formed vessels in the shapes
of horses, and knights mounted on prancing chargers.
They imitated the animals with which they were familiar,
in more or less grotesque form, caricaturing, in their
inability to fashion them aright, sheep, cattle, and dogs.
When the clever modellers among the potters of that
period began to fashion figures and to shape them so that
they could be used as jugs and drinking cups, from the
grotesqueness of the figures they shaped they appear to
have copied the work of the coppersmith rather than to
have modelled their vessels from the animals which one
would have thought were easy of access, and would have
been more realistic models. Among the remnants of old
mediæval pottery of this grotesque type, however, the
vessels were curious in that they differed as far as possible
from actualities. Those met with in this country were
doubtless at first brought over from foreign lands, for
they are very much like the grotesque pottery from Eastern

countries which has already been referred to in this chapter. There is, however, abundant evidence that the curious old glazed pitchers, now so rare, were not infrequently copied by English potters who then sought fresh inspirations. They were grotesque indeed, although here and there not at all a bad illustration of a mounted knight or a venerable pilgrim on horseback is met with. These old drinking cups, for that was the form such vessels took, are valuable when in anything like good preservation. In very few instances are they more than fragments, but often sufficient to indicate their original form when complete.

OLD PUZZLE JUGS.

The employment of puzzle jugs to amuse, to create laughter at the expense of the uninitiated, to while away the time, and perhaps with an eye to the increased sale of liquor, was a common practice in olden time. Such jugs, which were much in evidence at the village inn in years gone by, were perforated at the neck or under the handle. To drink without spilling was not easy, for the feat to be performed lay in closing with the fingers all the holes or spouts except the one used. Others again, especially some made in the seventeenth century, had wide-open necks, only a narrow passage being reserved for their contents, the true outlet of which was ingeniously concealed. The larger jugs so common in the tavern were supplemented by more graceful, although equally troublesome, puzzle cups, which were found on the tables of the refined, who had them for the amusement of their guests. They were much in request at hunting parties, the ornaments and decorations being in keeping with the pleasures of the chase.

Puzzle cups and jugs were made in Delft ware and in stoneware, and other serviceable materials, and their

embellishment suggests the source of the ornaments afterwards adopted by the Staffordshire potters, who used
hunting scenes in their modelled designs so successfully in
the eighteenth century.

To collectors the charm of such vessels is often found in
their inscriptions as much as in the moulded ornament.
Suggestive of the difficulties of imbibing liquor from them
there were such invitations as, " COME TAKE ME IF
YOU CAN."

Among the curious inscriptions upon old puzzle jugs
may be mentioned one which reads,

> " Here, Gentlemen, come to try your skill !
> I'll hold a wager if you will,
> That you don't drink this liquor all
> Without you spill or let some fall."

Another inscription is perhaps more original than the last.
It is,

> " From Mother Earth I took my birth,
> Then formed a jug by man,
> And now stand here filled with good cheer,
> Taste of me if you can."

CURIOUS CUPS.

Grotesque cups, quaint jugs, and tankards used under
special conditions have been made by potters from quite
early times. The Norman potters made some curious
figures in earthenware representing knights on horseback,
their pottery being coated with a green glaze. Those
curious figures, which were hollow, served as drinking cups.
Later we have the old puzzle jugs and puzzle cups so
common in the Tudor period. Then there is the Astbury
bear-shaped jug from which liquor was drunk. Another
interesting feature in quaint drinking cups is found in those
made in Chesterfield, Leeds, and in Staffordshire in the form
of animals' heads, such as the heads of bears, foxes, dogs,
and deer.

Delft ware was much favoured for curious cups, just as the jugs of an earlier date had often been made of that material.   Many of these cups were inscribed.   One of the oldest dates known on Lambeth Delft is a mug inscribed on a band round the rim, " WILLIAM AND ELIZABETH BURGES, 24th AUGUST 1631-1632."

The quaint drinking or hunting cups, formerly made in Staffordshire, and so much reproduced, were chiefly of Whieldon or Elers ware, and of Rockingham or Derby china.   The Astbury bear-shaped jug or cup has already been referred to in the description of the Astbury pottery. It was rough, however, and quite different to the well-finished drinking cups modelled in the form of foxes' heads, dogs' heads, and other animals associated with hunting. Some few of these cups were also made in Liverpool. The large cider mugs with two or three handles, at one time common in Devonshire, were supplemented by the huge heads of stoneware which were hung out by tavern keepers indicating that cider was sold.   Some of these cider mugs were of curious forms and decorations, such, for instance, several of those made at Worcester in Dr Wall's time.

Another curious freak was the frog-jug of Sunderland ware, in which was a frog at the bottom of the cup concealed from the drinker until a considerable portion of the liquor had been consumed.   Some of the inscriptions on the Sunderland jugs were naval, but naval views and representations of ships were by no means confined to the potteries in Liverpool, Sunderland, and other seaport towns, for they were made in considerable numbers in Staffordshire.   The drinking vessels in the form of cows were all noted in a variety of ways, one of the scarcer types being that with the " Willow " pattern ornament. Those copied in modern times are chiefly the painted cows—and very poor imitations most of them are, too !

" Toby " Jugs.

There have been many varieties of so-called " Toby " jugs, although some of them have been far removed from the original model. Different potters and their workmen have variously interpreted the idea, which in its original form was to represent an old man dressed in the costume of the period, such as then might have been seen seated in many a village ale-house, or on a bench outside, holding a jug in one hand and a pipe in the other. The "Toby fill-pot " was the name given to that jug, and graphically it portrayed the character of many frequenters of taverns in the eighteenth century. The little jug the old man was shown holding in his hand was often filled to overflowing, and the figure represented a man who was addicted to hard drinking. Other varieties represent a somewhat more aristocratic-looking individual, indicating from the knee-breeches and the ornamentation of his coat a superior station in life.

The colouring of the " Toby " jugs varies, too, some being very realistic and not at all extravagant, whereas other jugs were cruder in colouring, although their forms were modelled with a certain degree of accuracy. Then, besides the richly-coloured jugs, in which blues and greens and yellows are conspicuous, there are " Toby " jugs in brown ware, sombrely dressed individuals enjoying their jug or pint of ale, some varieties representing the more polite service of a beaker with a jug in reserve. The quaintly-shaped clay pipe, although generally in evidence, is sometimes absent, and even the well-filled jug or pot of ale is omitted at times when a somewhat stout-looking individual, standing in rather a cramped position, has both hands occupied in the act of taking a pinch of snuff. Such jugs are sometimes represented with adjuncts such as

FIG. 121.—A PUZZLE JUG.
In the British Museum.

FIG. 122.—A STAFFORDSHIRE FIGURE OF FALSTAFF, after the
Chelsea style, marked "WOOD AND CALDWELL."
By favour of Mr. Phillips.

[To face page 380.

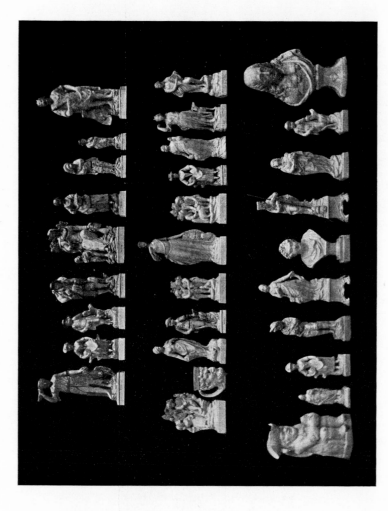

Fig. 123.—Figures made by Ralph Wood, of Burslem, and other Staffordshire makers.

In the Collection of Mr. C. B. Morgan, of Hale, Cheshire.

a barrel, and occasionally the old man is accompanied by his dog.

There are "Toby" fill-pots of Staffordshire make of almost every conceivable form and variety, and such jugs were made also at the Rockingham Works, near Swinton, and in some of the minor potteries. There are many modern replicas of the old "Toby" jug, which has been so well copied that it is difficult at times to distinguish between the old and the new, although the glaze and signs of use and age are helpful indications, as well as the softer tones and colouring, although bright, of the older examples. The Rockingham jug was of a rich chocolate brown, a streaky lead glaze being one of its characteristics. There are also "Toby" bottles, which are a sort of development of the "Toby" jug.

The "Fair Hebe" jug by J. Voyez, a Frenchman who modelled for Wedgwood, is one of the curious, if not actually grotesque, pieces of pottery. The base of the jug is a group of figures modelled in high relief.

Several varieties of "Toby" jugs are illustrated in Figs. 117, 118, 119, and 120. Fig. 121 is a rare puzzle jug in the British Museum.

QUAINT FIGURES.

The subjects which were chosen for figures were of many types; some were, of course, of exquisite forms, like the Greek models; others were copied from real life, and were faithful representations of then well-known personages. The historical series of portrait figures forms a distinct class, and is valued for the remembrances of the people long dead which they carry with them. (*See* chapter xxxvi., " Historic Pottery.")

Many of the figures, although to a certain extent historical, are, however, quaint and almost grotesque in the way in which persons and objects are represented. No doubt many of the groups are far from faithfully picturing real life, even as it was when times and conditions were very different from what they are now. To many the chief charm lies in the quaint forms of the figures and groups, notwithstanding their obvious incorrectness ; others, again, delight in the rich colouring of the figure subjects. The choice lies in great variety between the beautiful figures of Bow, Chelsea, and Derby, and the cruder forms and colouring of the less costly Staffordshire figures. All these have been referred to under the notices of the respective works where they were made.

It may be a moot point whether the choicer groups of Chelsea are rightly described as quaint, yet few will deny that the gorgeous raiment of most of the subjects is quaint enough. Even the magnificent groups already referred to, like that in the London Museum (*see* Fig. 29), are quaint, but they are beyond the pocket of the average " home connoisseur," who will rarely find hidden away in an old cupboard or in a disused attic anything so choice.

The products of the Derby Old Works included some choice rarities, the pair of " Dwarfs " being the best known. Another curious Derby pair represents " Peace " and " War."

Pottery busts of old divines were very popular in the Staffordshire Potteries at the close of the eighteenth century. They stood upon brackets and tables in the best parlours of middle-class homes, and were favourite chimney ornaments. Some of the less expensive figures served the working classes, who also bought freely such wares. John Wesley was the subject of many such figures, and his bust and a companion piece, that of Whitfield, were to be seen in many places. There were, too, followers of the arts, especially of music. Handel was modelled by several of the Staffordshire potters. Discoverers and scientists were subjects chosen by some potters ; especially by Ralph Wood, who about 1780 made some exceptionally large figures of Sir Isaac Newton and Benjamin Franklin. John Wilks, the philanthropist, probably modelled in 1765, had already become popular. Some preferred earlier historical characters for ornamental busts and statuettes, choosing Chaucer, Shakespeare, and a few of the best-known reformers.

The " Wood " figures were fired at a high temperature, coloured when in a biscuit state with metallic oxide glazes applied with a brush, and then fired for a second time at a lower temperature.

These figures have been the subject of special study by Mr. Cecil B. Morgan, of Hale, who has been successful in securing an exceptionally representative collection, which has for some time past been on view at the Whitworth Institute at Manchester. Mr. Morgan kindly sends photographs of many of these pieces, a few of which are reproduced. Fig. 123 shows quite a number of the figures, which should, however, be seen to be fully appreciated. Other specimens are illustrated in Figs. 124 to 130.

Among the Staffordshire figures some are obviously grotesque, although interesting mementos of olden time. Such, for instance, the coloured earthenware " town crier " standing upon a base, holding in one hand a bell and in the other a scroll, from which he is making some announcement. Many such figures were made during the closing years of the eighteenth century.

It may be pointed out that the " home connoisseur " possessing but a few or even an isolated example of figure subjects need not despair, for one or two such objects add interest to a collection of " old pottery," and, as antiques, apart from their interest to the connoisseur of ceramics, have a quaint beauty all their own.

Another branch of grotesque ware is that which is

formed by the decoration rather than the form of the pottery. The ornament used by various artists is referred to under the separate notices of the respective potters and mention of their products. One instance, as illustrating the type of grotesque ornament, will be found in the old Delft ware plates and dishes, especially in those curious portraits (?) of William III. and Queen Mary II. On such painted plates William stands, crowned, holding a sceptre in one hand, often in conjunction with his Consort, who carries the orb, thus indicating their joint sovereignty. In some instances William III. is given as an equestrian figure, which certainly does not do much credit to the artist by whom it was drawn; such patterns are grotesque enough in their conception.

Potters found new designs in the hunting scenes, which were more varied in the subject matter they provided than the humbler domestic and rural scenes and episodes which for so long served the artist. The production of hunting cups, puzzle jugs, and " Toby fill-pots " were in succession smart, business-like ventures, for they suited the tastes of the hunters, they found pleasure and amusement for the drinker, perchance giving him fresh incentive to imbibing liquor, and provided the inn-keeper and the consumer of ale with a decorative tankard suggestive of a typical frequenter of ale-house and a seat on the village green outside the tavern. To-day collectors are charmed with such relics of a past age, and often forget the incidents connected with their use.

Some have specialised collections of china and pottery models of cottages. These seem to have been made at quite a number of places in the Staffordshire Potteries ; also at Worcester and Coalport or Coalbrookdale. The Rockingham cottages have won some repute, for at one time they were very popular as chimney and fireplace ornaments. Not only were the cottages of the district

FIG. 124.

In the Collection of Mr.
C. B. Morgan.

FIG. 125.

[To face page 384.

FIG. 126.   FIG. 127.   FIG. 128

STAFFORDSHIRE GROUPS.

In the Collection of Mr. C. B. Morgan.

FIG. 129.   FIG. 130.

FIGURES BY RALPH WOOD, of Burslem.

In the Collection of Mr. C. B. Morgan.

To face page 385.]

drawn upon as models, but old buildings were represented on these quaint little pieces. There are examples representing Norwich Castle, and old town towers and gateways. Many of the " cottages " form boxes, the roof of the house serving as the lid. Such groups are often highly ornamental, although somewhat crude in colouring. They are frequently embellished with rustic work outside, sometimes very good representations of roses and climbing plants almost covering portions of the exterior. There have been modern replicas of these old ornaments, and it requires some little experience to distinguish between the old and the new, for some excellent replicas have been made. Perhaps the mauve-coloured Rockingham cottages are among the best of the originals.

These pleasing objects seem to have been used for a variety of purposes, one being that of pastille burners, fragrant smoke coming into the room through the little chimneys on the cottage roofs. It should be noted that most of the examples met with in dealers' shops were made a little later than the usual types of collectable pottery and porcelain, being objects much favoured during early Victorian days.

CHAPTER XXXVIII

SPECIALISED COLLECTIONS

Salt glaze ware—Lustre ware—Apothecaries' drug pots—Teapots.

THE "home connoisseur" is naturally inclined to gather together a representative collection of the different periods during which pottery and porcelain have been made, or to collect specimens of the products of potteries which exist or have existed in times gone by in that particular district in which he is living. It often happens that private collections are an assemblage of specimens either handed down as remains of sets or portions of sets which have been family possessions, supplemented by specimens which had been bought from time to time either as souvenirs of places visited, or because of their apparent good value ; when attending a sale, or visiting some town where there is an old curio shop, an obvious bargain is seen and taken advantage of. The average householder likes to secure specimens of the antique, and old china is one of the favourite subjects, especially domestic china, things which have been used in other households, or in the same dwelling in years gone by. Such general and mixed collections are, of course, the rule, but to every rule there is an exception, and even the "home connoisseur" without any intention to become an expert collector is at times induced to become a specialist.

To many there is a peculiar interest in a specialised collection, and this branch of collecting presents a field of intense interest to the student, and to those who like to dip deeply into whatever hobby they take up. The specialist in his selection is sometimes guided by his inclination, which may be towards the artistic and the beautiful in form and colouring; or his interests may lie in those objects which have to him a peculiar delight in that they were made in some place with which he was once familiar, although it may be far removed from his present dwelling.

There are some who have specialised on old china made in their native land and possessing peculiar characteristics; such, for instance, those printed wares commemorative of historical events, and of persons who have lived and won for themselves fame. There are others who by their specialisation seem to render a silent tribute to those who in early days made the best possible use of local clays and their environment, which gave them special opportunities of manufacture of which they were not slow to avail themselves. There are some who like to specialise on peculiarities of finish, such as a miscellaneous collection of pottery made in different places, but according to a generally accepted system or recipe, like the salt glaze ware, the outcome of an accidental discovery, which gradually became the method of glazing adopted in many different potteries.

Among the most noted specialists are those who, while seeing beauty of form and colour in the more ordinary wares, prefer to gather around them the ornamental rather than the useful. Thus we have specialists in figures, so many delightful examples of which are found in the now valuable pieces made at Chelsea, Bow, Derby, and other places. The different wares have come in for specialisation, especially those distinctive substances and methods of glazing, like the Delft ware, covered with an enamel giving it such a characteristic distinction from the pottery which was made at the time that Delft ware was introduced into England. The specialist, too, can take up a branch like Dutch or English Delft wares; and there are others who find sufficient variety in Delft ware made for similar purposes, such, for instance, the old apothecaries' jars, drug pots, and vessels used by chemists, who secured their shop fittings from Holland, and afterwards obtained replicas in this country. Another important sub-division is found in the very extensive variety of old Staffordshire figures, of which such splendid specialised collections have been gathered together.

Ancient customs have provided the specialist with other varieties ; thus, reminiscent of the days of hard drinking, a collection of punch bowls may be formed. Others may see more variety and take greater delight in a collection of "Toby" jugs, which are so realistically fashioned and perpetuate the memory of the customs and habits of the people who frequented ale-house and tavern, and who drank great jugs and mugs of ale, finding potters a ready market for such striking pieces as those found in specialised collections.

Articles of a like nature and purpose have often served the specialist, such as a diversified collection of old teapots. In such collections, of course, there have been many Oriental varieties. It is perhaps fortunate for the specialist that the manufacture of fine wares and delicate porcelain was long deferred in this country, otherwise it would have been difficult to have obtained so many beautiful specimens of Oriental tea china, such as are seen in our museums and private galleries. The Oriental nations were famous for their beautiful wares centuries ago, when the only pottery made in this country was produced from local clays, fashioned in crude and somewhat un-interesting forms.

It is probable that more specialised collections of old Chinese porcelain have been made than any other variety, and very remarkable indeed are some of the old Chinese works of ceramic art. The Chinese go back to an early period, and even their cruder forms, contemporary with our prehistoric pottery, are things of beauty and of remarkably artistic designs.   In most of the old Oriental countries the varieties of pottery and porcelain are sufficient to provide the specialist with an ample selection, and to give him a wide field to explore.   Very costly indeed are the rare pieces of early Chinese porcelain, especially of those periods when certain rare colours were produced, the mixing of the pigments being now a lost art.   Such specialised collections naturally gain value and interest, for the number of collectors increases, and it is not at all likely that any finds of rare porcelain will to any appreciable extent increase the supply.

English collectors have hitherto paid little attention to European pottery, and comparatively few amateur collectors have thought well to specialise on Continental wares.   Yet there are many opportunities, especially in the pottery of those countries which in early days were influenced by the art of Eastern nations, and those countries where great artists lived and left their mark on the world. Such men are few, it is true, and the remaining examples of their efforts and successful work too costly to specialise upon—such objects, for instance, as Palissy ware, made by Bernard Palissy, who stood out so conspicuously in France in the reign of Henry III. (of France).

Again, the specialist has many opportunities of research when taking up old lustre, especially if he includes in his collection Hispano-Moresque ware, very beautiful, although, it must be admitted, difficult to secure.   That, of course, shows marked traces of its Moorish origin.

Thus it will be seen that the collector with ample means can surround himself with a specialised collection of rare antiques of accruing value and increasing rarity, while those with less abundant means can specialise in many ways.   For a trifle they can secure specimens of prehistoric pottery from many parts of the world. They can specialise on Roman ware at a small outlay; they may also gather around them representative collections of the less costly productions of the English eighteenth-century potters, and according to opportunities and space at their command can specialise upon the larger ceramic works or confine themselves to miniatures, like the delightful Wedgwood plaques, cameos, and trinkets.

In short, the collector has either a narrowed view engendered by confining his attention to the minute details of some particular branch of study, or he possesses a wider outlook, and desires to make his collection instructive and interesting to those having less specialistic knowledge than himself. As in the case of most collectable objects, the interest to an outsider, and to some extent to the collector himself, is intensified when the specialistic collection is classified and arranged. The true scheme of arrangement of such a collection is that of a museum display arranged either in chronological succession, classified according to different potteries, or arranged so as to show in different groups particular characteristic designs and colourings, or to give an idea of the relative qualities and perhaps monetary values of the rarer specimens when compared with the commoner examples.

To explain what the aim of a museum should be we cannot do better than quote what the late John Ruskin said. " A museum," he declared, " should be primarily not at all a place of entertainment, but a place of education ; but a museum is, be it secondly observed, not a place of elementary education but for that of already far advanced scholars." Pottery in its crude forms carries us back to the earliest times—times before history was written, when there were not even inscriptions upon tablets of stone and clay. The modern collector, be he a specialist upon one particular group or one who concentrates his attention on the potter's art as a science, ranks with kings, poets, statesmen, artists, and men and women of all ranks who have been devotees of ceramics and specialists in their studies of the ancient art of the potter, so differently interpreted throughout the ages.

Salt Glaze Ware.

In another chapter the story has been told of the accidental discovery of salt glaze by a servant employed by Mr Joseph Yates, at Stanley, near Bagnall, not far removed from Burslem in Staffordshire, when preparing in an earthen vessel brine for pickling pork. When the fire became too hot and the brine boiled over, a delightful glaze on the rough earthen vessel resulted in the discovery of how to make salt glaze. It is quite true that some of the greatest inventions and discoveries that have ever been made have been the result of simple domestic arrangements and everyday operations, and they have not always been made by scientists. The salt glaze once discovered, and applied by Adams at Golden Lane, and by Wedgwood at Etruria, was soon found to be a simple and satisfactory process, and its fame spread until salt glaze became an accepted method of glazing pottery.

The specialistic collector, having decided that nothing but those objects coated with salt glaze should appear in the selection, naturally examines every piece coming under his notice. He gradually acquires proficiency, and understands the minutest indication of quality in the ware and in the glaze. He knows very well that the salt thrown into the kiln, vaporising, deposits a fine glaze over the surface. The firing is not always equally successful, but unless there has been some accident or some deterring agency the glaze will be found to have settled pretty equally all over the surface. The advantages of a naturally distributed glaze, like that imparted by the vaporising of the salt over a mechanically applied glaze, or one put on by hand, are obvious, the chief characteristic being that the salt glaze does not detract from the sharpness of the design. It coats over the surface equally. Naturally, as the eighteenth-century potters applied this glaze, and as they became more efficient in the firing of their kilns, they recognised that there were some precautions necessary in order to secure satisfactory glazing. As it has been pointed out, the salt was cast into the ovens by firemen through holes, and distributed pretty equally over the interior of the kiln. Then, having been distributed, the glazing became automatic—a natural process. The ovens chosen for salt glaze ware were usually large. Some precaution had to be taken in arranging the ware in the perforated saggers so that there should be nothing to impede the proper circulation of the vapour.

It is said that in olden time, when salt glaze was general in Burslem, the firing-up took place once a week, and at a stated time. Burslem to the uninitiated was like a miniature Mount Etna, for the fumes were dense and the white smoke very disagreeable. The glaze evenly distributed spread over the pattern, and most of the old salt glaze wares were moulded, the pattern sometimes being sharpened by moulding tools, all superfluous clay being scraped away. The colouring was, of course, another process, but salt glaze was effectively used on many blue wares. Then came the Oriental style, and the beautiful cream-ware which Wedgwood perfected. In a collection there are useful table services, ornamental salt glaze butter-bowls and butter-boats, some curiously moulded teapots, some of the Staffordshire teapots having striking resemblance to Oriental ware in form, and sometimes in decoration. It is, however, on salt glaze ware the collector is specialising, and all specimens offered to him are critically examined, for it is from that view-point that he admires them or rejects them.

Although much of the salt glaze ware was utilitarian in character, a specialised collection contains many artistic and ornamental pieces. Some very beautiful salt glaze vases are obtainable; they are, of course, ornamental. Then again, there are plaques and reliefs, and Staffordshire figures coated with salt glaze. Pottery figures in salt glaze, which are usually small, are rare; sometimes they are modelled by hand, but generally moulded. The commoner objects of this type are animals and birds in pairs and occasionally grouped. Some of the table appointments would doubtless then be regarded in many households as superfluous, for they were exceedingly decorative, especially salt glaze sweetmeat dishes, some of which were used for pickles and other delicacies.

As it has been stated, much of the salt glaze ware is self-coloured; other pieces are coloured with blue decoration, scratched blue being a common form, the cobalt being dusted into the scratched incisions. Occasionally black or brown slip was used, and some of the salt glaze ware, like that made by Littler, at Brownhill's, and afterwards at Longton Hall, was of a deep cobalt blue, the ware being ornamented with white tin enamel.

Specialists on salt glaze find much to admire in the fine coffee-pots, now getting scarce, which are much handsomer than many of the teapots, and are frequently covered with floral ornament, many excellent sprays being painted in blue. Some of these very fine pieces may be seen in the Victoria and Albert Museum. From the decoration of the larger specimens the difference in the characteristics of the chief periods or stages of salt glaze is clearly shown. The first period was, of course, that in which stamped ornament was used, and was mostly earlier than 1720. Then came the moulded period, in which animals, shells, and natural history objects were fashioned ; at that time in mixing the paste ground flint was used instead of sand. Then about 1750 coloured ornament was very generally employed, both Oriental and English styles of decoration being adopted. Collectors may also discover among coffee-pots later specimens on which the deep cobalt blue was employed.

Lustre Ware.

In a specialised collection the connoisseur who takes an interest in the peculiarities of the ware, its finish or its decoration, searches the products of many different potteries in order to make his cabinet representative. If, however, the objects of his pursuit are limited to the output of some one works or group of works, his aim is simplified, and perhaps somewhat narrowed.

In such a group as lustre ware the scope is widened, for not only has the collector a wide field to cover, but the manufacture of lustre ware is spread over many centuries, for when it was revived in this country in the eighteenth century it was by no means new. Moreover, there is ample choice in rarity and in comparatively inexpensive pieces. This gives collectors who cannot afford to indulge in costly specimens an opportunity of pursuing their hobby and gathering together many interesting pieces, which, although inexpensive, are pleasing in that they represent a very widespread industry.

In the direction indicated the collection of lustre ware has recently presented an attractive outlook, for such a specialistic group, including, it is true, the rare pieces of Hispano-Moresque ware, also includes many "bits" of old English pottery and china, which can still be picked up for quite trifling sums.

In this chapter, through the courtesy of the proprietors

of the Spanish Art Gallery, some very good examples of old Hispano-Moresque ware are shown in Figs. 95, 96, 97 and 98. Such pottery, brilliant with its lustrous finish, has indeed many peculiar characteristics about it. It was obviously a foreign art introduced and followed very closely by the Spanish artists and potters, for it is distinctly Moorish in design, and can without difficulty be traced back in its affinity to the Persian pottery of much earlier times. It is said that the potters of Bagdad in the ninth century were in possession of the old secret of making metallic reflex and imparting that peculiar lustre which is, of course, the chief characteristic of Hispano-Moresque ware. From Bagdad through Northern Asia the Moors carried the secret to Spain, and there it flourished as early as the twelfth century. There are no specimens of the earliest period extant, for it is quite clear that the earliest examples known are of a somewhat advanced art, and were probably made after many earlier attempts to perfect the ware, and to introduce at any rate some of the European features of ornament in the Oriental-looking pottery.

In course of time Valencia became the most notable centre of the manufacture of Hispano-Moresque ware, and many of the beautiful pieces collectors so gladly secure came from those well-known potteries.

The illustrations of this beautiful ware, taken from examples in the Spanish Art Gallery, where many choice pieces of this old pottery are on view, are described on p. 318. There is a wondrous sheen about the lustre which it is impossible to describe. It differs much from the commoner imitations and also from the more modern wares in which English potters have tried to copy the peculiar lustre of this Spanish pottery. The blue and white jar illustrated in Fig. 98 is, of course, very different in appearance, but the design of its decoration is, like the contemporary lustre ware, distinctly Moorish in character.

Collections of these wares are far from common, and it is only in the larger museums that there are sufficient examples to enable connoisseurs to form any adequate idea of the variety of types and the different effects produced by the metallic lustrous decoration.

Collectors of this European type of lustre ware will, doubtless, bear in mind the lustre made in Persia and Egypt, and also the Italian lustre wares, the manufacture of which spread over a period extending from the twelfth to the early part of the seventeenth centuries. In the British Museum is a marvellous collection of these lustres, representative of the art of Oriental countries and of Spain.

The English potters of the eighteenth and the early part of the nineteenth centuries introduced this form of ornamentation. They produced some excellent effects, different lustres being achieved after many experiments. The metals they experimented with were chiefly gold, copper, and platinum, but they produced many varied effects and different shades of colour by combinations of metals and by varied treatment in firing. The large quantity of English lustre still to be met with—many of quite common or inexpensive kinds—shows that the lustrous finish was popular. The Staffordshire wares include what are defined by collectors as " pink," " rose," " purple," " ruby," and " spotted " lustres. The commoner wares ornamented with " copper " lustre decorations are of red-brown, that colour of body paste having been found to be the best on which to produce the rich orange or golden-copper metallic hue. The richness of the golden lustre was often enhanced by an under-band of yellow glaze. The Sunderland lustre was chiefly gold.

The purple and pink lustre effects were produced on a white body of hard paste ; those, too, were made at Sunderland, although many ascribed to the potteries on the banks of the river Wear were doubtless made in Stafford-shire. A specialistic colouring peculiar to Staffordshire was the ruby-coloured lustre made chiefly by the firm of Allerton at Longton.

The less expensive examples which may readily be procured include tea-services, and especially bowls, basins, and mugs. Curious plaques on which are views of Sunderland, and sometimes mottoes and rhymes, are bordered with copper and golden lustre. The silver lustre is far from decorative, although it has been much copied in modern wares. To the specialist who wishes to collect quaint domestic and decorative pieces, distinctive in their characteristics, and not very expensive, lustre ware as made in the eighteenth century is to be recommended.

APOTHECARIES' DRUG POTS.

At first sight it seems a strange thing to specialise upon " shop fittings " and those vessels which have been used as receptacles of drugs—the older jars and canisters of the trader. When, however, we realise that about such things there is a halo of romance, and an association with the mystic and uncanny, more than usual interest is found to surround such things.

The alchemist of old in secret compounded his mysterious ingredients in ancient bronze mortars—now curios of considerable value. The "witches' cauldron," if we are to believe William Shakespeare, was the receptacle for many strange things.

The old pharmacy jars held drugs, herbal compounds, and preparations from the vegetable and animal kingdoms which would cause the most ardent believer in the medical skill of past generations to scoff, were their efficacy recommended by modern practitioners.

The vessels in which these preparations were

compounded, mixed, and stored were of suitable forms and sizes, and the monks and men of medicine, and the apothecaries of olden time who doled them out, had their jars lettered and often decorated accordingly.

In the sixteenth century, before the dissolution of the monasteries, most of the drugs were obtainable from the monks, and from the religious houses whose apothecaries compounded them.   Indeed, many of the early jars and drug pots secured on the Continent by their emblems and lettering show signs of having been used in the drug store of the monastery or convent.

In the *Encyclopedia of Antiquities*, published in 1825, at a time when most of the Delft and other jars hereinafter described were in actual use, some interesting facts about apothecaries are recorded.   It is said chemists and druggists were the *pigmentarii*, *pharmacopolae*, and *medicamentarii* among the Romans who sold herbs and drugs, but the physicians mixed their own medicines.   In Italy in later times the apothecaries obtained a legal status by an edict of Frederick II. in the thirteenth century.   In England the grocers and apothecaries were formerly in association, but they afterwards separated.   As the result of much dispute King James took the matter in hand, and appears to have administered a scathing rebuke to the grocers, for in answer to the complaints of the grocers, who objected to the apothecaries separating from them, he replied : " Another grievance is that you have condemned the patents of the apothecaries.   The grocers are but merchants.   The mystery of these apothecaries were belonging to the apothecaries wherein the grocers were unskilful, and therefore I think it fitting they should be a corporation of themselves."   A charter was granted in 1617, and when members had satisfied the master and wardens they were allowed to keep a shop and to " prepare, dispense, commix, or compound medicines."   The

Apothecaries Company, whose Hall is in Blackfriars, formerly held, under a grant by Sir Hans Sloane, Bart., dated February 20th, 1722, "a Botanic and Phisic Garden at Chelsea, for the purpose of growing medical plants and the promotion of the knowledge of medical botany." These interesting facts may with advantage be kept in mind when studying the inscriptions on old Delft pharmacy jars and drug pots.

The collectable drug pots are varied in shapes, colouring, and in the styles of their decorations. Although most of them are of Delft ware, some of the more decorative pieces are of finer materials, and the paintings upon them are well executed and look well upon the smooth surface of the finer glaze. Such decorations are frequently symbolic, and generally in accord with the purposes for which the jars were to be used.

It is probable that even now some of the rarer types are in use in out-of-the-way places in England. In Flanders and Holland many vauable jars are still in use in the shops of old-established apothecaries. Good specimens bring large sums when offered in the sale-rooms, but the less important types may sometimes be bought quite cheaply in dealers' shops, especially in country towns, where there is not so much demand for this particular variety of ceramics.

The source of drug pots is of some importance, although not always easy to trace. The earlier wares were Italian, many were made in Holland, and in the seventeenth and eighteenth centuries such vessels were made in England.

One of the finest collections of pharmacy jars ever got together is that of Mr J. E. Jewell, the present proprietor of Heppell & Co., the well-known chemists of Piccadilly, by whose courtesy the illustrations Figs. 93 and 94 are given. They are thoroughly representative of the different styles he has collected from all parts of the world, and of all periods, for among them is an early vessel dated 1562 (*see* top row, right hand, Fig. 94). It is a beautiful syrup jar on which are depicted roses, and the label, painted in yellow, reads "ROS. SOL" (Solution of Roses). It is a particularly valuable piece, the paste of which is of a soft brown colour, coated with a very hard enamel. In the same group will be noticed a spouted jar which is lettered "A. Melonis"; the decoration, appropriately of melons, is richly coloured and covers the vessel. The open jar, lettered "SEM. SINAP," once contained mustard seed; other vessels in the group show by their labels a wide difference in age, origin, and use. The early Spanish jar in the bottom row with its indications of Eastern ornament, contrasts with the dainty paintings of fruit, flowers, and peacocks upon the larger jar with a metal cover in the upper row.

Fig. 93 represents another group of pharmacy jars. In the centre, in the bottom row, is an exceptionally early Italian piece. Most of the examples are of European origin. The four small jars, however, are doubtless English Delft, one reading "THERIAC: LOND.," the others showing by their inscriptions that their contents were likewise prepared in accordance with the London pharmacopœia.

This remarkable collection contains upwards of 300 specimens, chiefly purchased on account of their rarity, or in order that Mr Jewell might make his collection fully representative. Taking at random a few specimens other than those pictured, mention may be made of two beautiful little Italian jars dated "17ii," lettered, in burnt sienna colouring, "ALLIA MONTAGNA"; these, with many others of similar shapes, once belonged to a monastic institution.

In such an extensive collection as that at Heppell's the different processes of finishing Delft ware can be seen, examined, and understood by comparison better than in most collections of specialists, in that the specimens have been gathered from so many places and represent the paste, glaze, and enamels of so many different potteries. Some have thick enamelled surfaces, others show a fine gloss, on which are painted fruits, flowers, and other objects—a truly interesting collection.

The apothecaries' jars and drug pots seen in lesser numbers in other private collections and in public museums are not without interest. In the London Museum there are some very early pieces ; one very fine jar found in Lothbury is coated with a green glaze which has a bluish tinge, and from the Latin inscription upon it was evidently intended for the storage of "preserved quince." There are also exceptionally good specimens in the Bethnal Green Museum and in the Guildhall collection of pottery. Liverpool Delft ware jars are well represented in the Liverpool Museum.

At the Nuremburg Museum there is a fine collection of drug pots made in that town and at Frankfort. There is a room fitted up as an old drug store, and very realistically are shown the various vessels as they were intended to be used. The " shop " is in the style of an old pharmacy, and has old-time fittings, which, of course, suit the jars and drug pots and other vessels shown therein.

TEAPOTS.

Since the introduction of tea into this country, and its gradual use as a household beverage, teapots, subsequently supplemented by tea-services, gradually gaining in completeness, have been made in this country. There is scarcely a maker of porcelain who has not at one time or other produced some of these delightfully varied useful

2 c

objects. A specialised collection of teapots includes rare and quaint specimens from China such as came over to this country with the early shipments of tea, the remarkable teapots and kettles from China and Japan, some none the less acceptable although made during recent years, and the teapots, large and small, produced in Staffordshire, Derby, Worcester, Lowestoft, Bristol, Leeds, and many other places. Teapots were rarely made exclusively for ornament, although the best tea china might only have been exposed on special occasions. Consequently the teapot has often come to grief ; spouts have been injured, lids cracked, and the appearance of much use stamps many teapots as being old, although that is no guarantee that they are genuinely antique. There are, of course, salt glaze teapots of many forms, beautiful red teapots of Elers ware, Broseley teapots covered with "Willow " pattern enriched with gold, as well as lustre teapots in gold, copper, and silver, charming Leeds ware teapots, and rare panelled Worcester. Then, again, there are those choice jasper ware pots made by Wedgwood and by Adams, with their different coloured grounds and their exquisitely modelled cameo reliefs. There are the Chinese designs and the painted floral designs. The Billingsley rose may be seen on some of them, and among the gems of the collection may be a Swansea or Nantgarw teapot contrasting with the richly decorative Crown Derby in blues, reds, and greens. They may vary in age from the red Elers and Astbury wares to the Rockingham teapots, not altogether artistically designed, although welcome parts of very beautifully decorated tea-sets. Many of the early teapots are only complete when accompanied by their stands, which add so much to the attractiveness of cabinet specimens. The collector who specialises is often a close observer of minute details in decoration, and will reject a specimen on account of flaws in decoration and glaze. He becomes critical ; for a specialised collection, to be interesting and valuable, must as far as possible consist of perfect specimens. Then again the question of marks of identification is an important factor, and the collector who can point to marked specimens as authentically placing his varied specimens adds to their value, although there may be some few characteristic designs, like the cauliflower ware, which point definitely to a well-known period, but not always to any particular maker.

CHAPTER XXXIX

REPRODUCTIONS AND RESTORATION

Avoiding the fabricator—Some forgeries—The restorer at work.

THE path of the collector of pottery and porcelain is strewn with difficulties, and it is soon realised that there is much to be learned before an amateur can distinguish between the products of different potteries from their paste and fabric and general appearance. The collector, too, is beset with reproductions—some will more bluntly point them out as forgeries. Such reproductions have been made in good faith by copiers of the antique, who have placed on the market copies of genuine pieces which have won more than passing renown. They have sold them as reproductions, and many honest dealers are careful to label them clearly, so that there can be no mistake as to their origin or purport. Unfortunately there is another class of maker, chiefly found on the Continent of Europe, who produces as near as possible copies of old English and other porcelain, forging marks, and in every possible way attempting to hoodwink the unwary. It is regrettable that such makers are backed up by some dealers who seek to make an extra profit out of the sale of such wares. Of course it is only the amateur who is deceived by these imitations, but it is vexatious for those who have to discover their mistakes after having paid dearly for their experience.

The faker has been at work in all kinds of antiques; not always successfully, for it is curious how many kinds of old china are a sealed book to the imitator and forger,

404

while on the other hand there are a few branches which seem to lend themselves to reproduction, and modern makers and artists are able to produce and colour very successfully some of the well-known types of old pottery.

The "home connoisseur" who values china because it represents some household possession that he has acquired by inheritance or by gift, and perhaps knows something about its history, has not quite the same amount of trouble with the fabricator, although in some wares there are pieces made only fifty or sixty years ago from the same moulds used by the first modellers of those designs and by early potters. Some firms, who have a long history going back far into the early days of the potting trade, pay a tribute to their founders by using the old moulds and by reproducing in modern porcelain patterns and styles which won them such fame a hundred years ago. It is indeed a tribute to the designers of a former age, in that their works are acceptable in modern times, when art has reached such a high position and artistic training has become so general.

Avoiding the Fabricator.

It is obvious that one of the first things that the collector or " home connoisseur " should do is to become acquainted with the chief characteristics of paste and glaze, decoration and gilding, colouring and marks. Undoubtedly the best education is found in the study of well-known collections, such, for instance, those collections which are to be seen in our more important museums. In the Victoria and Albert Museum at South Kensington the ceramic galleries contain examples of most English potteries and of some of those most famous works on the Continent ; and they are especially rich in Oriental porcelain, the Oriental galleries containing specimens of all periods and practically all countries. In the British

Museum there is a magnificent collection of English porcelain, as well as some Oriental, and the finest collection of prehistoric and mediæval pottery to be found anywhere. The advice given to the amateur is to visit one or other of these galleries as often as possible—not once, nor twice, but many times.

It may be well at first to obtain a general idea of the characteristics of the different potteries, but even if the collector aims at securing a general collection for his cabinet, he will do well to take the potteries one at a time, and become thoroughly conversant with their peculiarities, for there are distinct characteristics noticeable in Worcester, Derby, Nantgarw, and the still scarcer products of Lowestoft. By carrying out this suggestion many pitfalls may be averted, and in a short time the amateur will gain confidence, and be able when visiting a secondhand shop to put on one side, without hesitation, obviously doubtful pieces. When looking in a shop window he will quickly recognise a preponderance of reproductions, and will wisely give that shop a wide berth. It is true some buy reproductions, and are quite satisfied with them, valuing and judging them as mere ornaments, for, probably, a modern showily-furnished house. The collector of antiques, however, will look upon such fakes with abhorrence, especially such modern imitations of old Worcester, Mason's ironstone china, " Toby " jugs, Staffordshire figures, and other wares so frequently copied.

The question has been raised sometimes whether it is desirable to ask for a written guarantee when purchasing old china. The reliable dealer selling a costly antique is always willing to guarantee the genuineness of the object he sells as " old." There are some dealers not so well informed, who may be well assured in their own minds that certain objects are antique, knowing their source, but for the want of actual knowledge of the special products of certain potteries they will hesitate to give any guarantee. Collectors must, of course, themselves assess the value of statements given to them ; but in all fairness to the would-be honest dealer they must to some extent rely on their own judgment ; and although they may at times have to pay dearly for experience, they are wise in acquiring confidence as the outcome of study and research, which will enable them to decide between a reproduction and a genuine specimen. The best judge is liable to make mistakes, and especially is this the case in values. Dealers naturally have some regard to the cost of the goods they are selling, and they themselves may have given too much—a very common mistake in the sale-rooms. It is some little consolation to the amateur to know that the errors he commits are of greater assistance to him in his knowledge of old china than any bargains he acquires.

SOME FORGERIES.

The forgeries of Crown Derby china are fairly common, especially copies of old Derby figures.   Usually the modern replicas are more perfect and have clearer features than those given to the early pieces by the original modellers. The painting is harsh, the soft effect of the colouring of the old Derby figures being absent.   Then, again, the gilding is inferior. Apparently forgers of Derby have aimed high, for they have attempted to copy some of the more valuable pieces, and have used the coloured mark which is only found on perfect and more beautiful specimens.   It has been pointed out that a peculiarity of genuine old Chelsea figures is that the under eyelid is almost invariably absent, whereas on modern replicas this feature has been supplied. The glaze of the forgeries is glassy looking, and apparently thinner than the glaze of the genuine antique.   Replicas are usually of hard paste,

It is not always easy to locate the origin of imitations. It is well known, however, that some of the finest imitations and replicas come from France, where every kind of rare porcelain seems to have been copied. There is the square-marked Worcester, Old Nankin, and rare Sèvres to be bought for an " old song." English pottery has been much copied ; not only the finer wares and the more decorative brilliantly coloured " Toby " jugs, but even the brown posset pots of the seventeenth century have been imitated. The commoner types of copper lustre have been imitated, and there is much that is stamped with the appearance of copies, if not actually posing as "antiques."

The Restorer at Work.

The art of restoring broken pottery has been acquired by the riveter and by the more skilled artist, who, with paste and composition, the ingredients of which he carefully conceals, makes good defects, and afterwards paints and glazes in imitation of that which was missing. If those who gaze in wonder at the "perfect" examples of Etruscan art in museums only knew how many are "restored," it would come with a shock ; yet, notwithstanding defects known to curators, and cleverly covered up, these otherwise damaged wares serve every purpose of the collector and the student, *for they have been restored by experts.* It is said that the best restorers to be found in Rome and Naples have been engaged in nearly all the museums of Europe upon the restoration of Etruscan ware. The employment of experts makes all the difference, and their work contrasts with the clumsy work of amateurs, who so often disfigure much that might otherwise have been made very beautiful.

It is not always easy to secure the services of a true artist-craftsman, but the collector adds to the pleasure of his hobby when he is able to repair pieces he acquires in a damaged condition, or which may be accidentally broken while in his possession.

The rivet and the drill should be avoided as relics of a barbarian age in repairing china; there are many excellent cements which serve better to restore or repair cabinet pieces, and the workers in such materials can produce exact counterparts of missing pieces by practising modelling and fitting, afterwards colouring or painting the restored portions. Sometimes in the case of ancient pottery it is desirable to scrape down to the rough clay paste or body. Under the hands of the man who understands the materials —old and new—upon which he has to work, it is possible to fit in, and even dovetail, by filing grooves, pieces of other vases of a similar nature, and then with cement and plaster to make good defects.

In some cases plaster of Paris is the best medium; then afterwards it is enamelled, painted, and varnished, until the restored vase looks "perfect."

Porcelain is not so satisfactorily handled as the rougher wares; it can, however, be restored; and handles, knobs, and entire lids can be made to fit broken treasures. Wire, and even bent hairpins, serve as foundations on which to build, and stiff cardboard is often the base of a missing piece of a jug or vase which it is necessary to repair or to restore by adding " a lost piece."

The " home connoisseur " finds much pleasure, and profit, too, in restoration. The wealthy collector may scorn the broken " crock," but all are not in such a fortunate position, and many broken family pieces which have been restored are valued more by their owners than perfect specimens of unknown origin.

CHAPTER XL

PRICES

Some sale considerations—Advice to collectors.

THE market value of curios, and especially of collectable pottery and porcelain of well-known characteristics, is the first consideration of the would-be purchaser of a new specimen. It is a matter of great importance to the owner of an old collection or of a few rarities, bequeathed or acquired. The actual cost to their owners can never be regarded as a true estimate of the worth of old pottery and porcelain, because the market prices of these things are constantly changing, and with few exceptions—such, for instance, adverse conditions of sale, like the war period, which has depleted the resources of many curio collectors—there is an upward tendency. The increasing scarcity of genuine antiques, brought about by the growing interest in such things, makes the market firmer, and prices rise.

Then again there is always some shrinkage of supplies owing to breakages sustained, and the increasing number of public museums and galleries in which curios are "locked up"; for the collections belonging to such bodies are rarely dispersed. The tendency is, therefore, to attach an accruing value to collected pieces, the ratio of which value is higher in perfect specimens and rarities, for which there is always keen competition, than in the commoner types.

The numerous sales of fine china at the London auction rooms, and in the country when old houses are sold and their contents dispersed, and old homes broken up, afford

410

some little guide to prices. That is to say, a marked sale catalogue tells what figures have been paid for certain articles which are more or less accurately described. In the more costly antiques, sold separately, the prices realised can be allocated to the actual article under consideration. In less valuable ceramics where several pieces, with a somewhat vague description, are included in one lot, it is difficult, if not impossible, to fix definitely the money given for any one article, as so many considerations weigh with the buyer at sales.

Some Sale Considerations.

The public auctions are attended by dealers and by collectors. The former buy on commission, when they have a definite order on their books from a collector, or they buy whatever they think exceptionally good value and saleable stock. They are out to buy, to sell, and to make gain, and the dealer's estimate of price is based not so much upon the market value of the article, judged from previous standards, as from his knowledge of demand and prospects of sale at a profit which necessarily fluctuates, although usually rising. The silence of the well-known dealers in the same line of business in the face of keen competition for the goods offered for sale between two or more competitors should prove to the amateur buyer that the price—probably a high one—actually realised on behalf of the lucky vendor was in consequence of some special demand, and not because the actual market had suddenly risen.

The prices paid by the speculative dealer who knows his business and is buying for the replenishment of his stock, having no commission or special reason for buying, are the best guide to present-day value.

Skilled knowledge is of great value when buying. It

embraces first knowledge of the curio, certainty that it is actually the product of the pottery it purports to come from, and some assurance that the curio—ceramic or other product of olden time—is in the best possible condition, or in what degree its market value has been affected. The second consideration is knowledge of market value as gauged by prices paid for similar goods, under similar conditions, recently.

The main differences in conditions of sale are those of the auction room, where the connoisseur is competing with the trader, and the conditions under which a dealer having a legitimate eye to profit is offering it to the collector. There is yet another condition often encountered in these days, when so many opportunities are offered in the Press for the disposal of curios to strangers by amateurs : it is that when two amateurs are trading together the one usually over-estimates the worth of his possession, the other tries to run down the price and buy as cheap as he can.

The collector is a hunter—perhaps not of big game, but certainly one who finds keen delight in searching for treasures in out-of-the-way places, and sometimes far afield. The treasures which may be seen, examined, and purchased almost every day in London during the season are brought together from dealers in other towns and other countries, and they are sent to the auction mart to be sold by dwellers in remote places.

The auction mart is not always the best place for bargains, for it is frequented by the most experienced dealers and experts ; but minor bargains which do not appeal to the dealer are snapped up by amateur collectors.

To attend auction sales is no doubt the easiest way to acquire curios, and it is one which gives collectors much insight into market values. To attend a few sales of old china is in itself an education in prices. The real pleasure of the hunter is, however, when the collector is "thrown on his own," and without guidance from the bids of dealers or experienced collectors has to fall back upon his own knowledge and experience when making a bid for a coveted treasure.

Americans are keen hunters, and have carried away treasure in the past from all European countries. There was a time when in the region of the Old Plantations ceramic treasures could be procured from the houses which had not changed family ownership since the days of George III., when the States had not declared Independence.

New York and many parts of the United States were in years gone by happy hunting-grounds for the manufacturers of this country, who shipped large quantities of fine pottery and porcelain to the American continent. Although some of the American factories are of a respectable age, few date back to the times when old china, as judged from an English standpoint, was being made. Nevertheless, there are collectors in the States who like to discover specimens of Queen's ware which was made at the Queen's Ware Works in Pittsburg in 1854, chiefly from clay found in the State of Missouri. At that time common earthenware was being manufactured near Pittsburg on the Ohio River, and Fenton's patent flint enamelled ware was made near Charleston, in South Carolina.

Things and conditions have changed, and collectors have to be very wide awake to secure bargains ; indeed, the keen collector's spirit found so strongly in Americans is to some extent responsible for the inflated prices which have been paid of late years for very fine pieces.

Collectors in this country and in America are always on the look-out for more treasures. In this they differ from the "home connoisseur," strictly so-called, in that his chief interest lies in identifying family pottery and porcelain, and in adding to them in order to enhance their value and interest rather than in the accumulation of an extensive collection.

ADVICE TO COLLECTORS.

In conclusion, the collector of old pottery and porcelain should visit the London museums, so rich in representative collections, and the provincial museums, in which there are so many rare pieces of local interest, as often as possible. By so doing he will become familiar with the chief peculiarities of form, style of decoration, and colour ; he may not be allowed to handle the objects on view, and therefore cannot note all the differences in paste and glaze which the expert learns to understand by touch ; but some of the differences in paste and glaze are obvious at sight. In first-class dealers' shops the collector can critically examine the characteristics of the ceramics on sale, and can also obtain useful information from men who have had exceptional opportunities of judging of the genuineness of pieces, and know, too, their relative values. The collector —even the " home connoisseur "—gradually becomes conversant with the points of interest and the signs of identity, relying in time more upon these than on marks, which are sometimes uncertain and not always genuine. As in antique furniture, so in pottery and porcelain, the different styles and ornament used at certain periods become familiar to the connoisseur, and as these characteristics stand out clearer and he treads with more certain steps, the pleasures of collecting and the delights of possession become greater. " Knowledge is power," and it undoubtedly gives strength and confidence to the searcher after more treasures, making the path clearer and the beauty of ceramics more fully appreciated.

GLOSSARY

Agate Ware.—The paste produced to resemble veinings of agate and natural stones, the clays being twisted together forming layers of different colours, is known as "agate ware." "Surface agate" was simply an ordinary cream body grained and splashed.

Basalt or Basalte.—Wedgwood describes basalt as a fine black porcelain bisque, of nearly the same properties as natural stone. It takes a high polish, and even serves as touchstone for metals, and will strike fire with steel ; further, basalt will resist acids.

Biscuit.—The condition of the clay figure or vessel before glazing. Biscuit was often fired once, then decorated, and after glazing fired again.

Blue-Printing.—Blue was at one time almost the only colour used in printing china. It was found suitable for the under-glaze printing which came in vogue about 1780. The process thus became known as "blue-printing," and was often used afterwards as a general term for under-glaze printing.

Calcareous Clay.—The clay containing lime, used chiefly in the body of Delft ware.

China Clay.—The china clay discovered in Cornwall, consisting of disintegrated granite, was procured in the days when old china was being made, secured by the disturbing or breaking up the so-called clay, then turning on streams of water, producing a milk-white liquid afterwards conducted by "launders" into a cistern or tank, in which the pure creamy substance was deposited. After passing through several minor processes and washings the deposit when dried became of the consistency of cheese, and was cut up into blocks or cubes, placed in drying sheds ready to be packed in casks or carted loosely to the coast, from whence it was shipped ; in early days transport was effected by small coasting vessels and thence taken from the coast by canal barges inland to the Staffordshire potteries. The kaolin was practically the same substance as the material used by the Chinese, taking its name from a Chinese word signifying a lofty ridge, Chinese kaolin being obtained from a hill near King-te-chin.

The Dorset clay from the neighbourhood of Poole which is of great value was discovered by the Romans. Several varieties of this clay are shipped to the different potteries. Freight charges have varied : the cost of clay to makers was immense before transport was made easier. In 1728 clay cost 50/- per ton, delivered in London; by the close of the eighteenth century the price had fallen to 14/-. The clays of Poole have of late years been used chiefly for tiles, many of which were made in the district as early as 1770.

Cream-Ware.—Cream-ware is a generic term applied to all light-coloured earthenware from about 1750 onwards. Wedgwood's cream-ware was a variety. Much of the so-called cream-ware paste when broken presents a white appearance.

Delft Ware.—Early Delft ware was made in Holland from 1600, and was afterwards copied in Liverpool, Lambeth, and elsewhere. The chief difference in its composition from that of ordinary wares is that the paste of the Delft ware is earthenware covered with a tin enamelled surface of much thicker substance than glaze. The surface coat is quite opaque and entirely covers and obscures the ground body; the enamelled surface is usually decorated in colours, in the earlier wares blue predominating.

Enamels.—The term "enamel" indicates the colours used either in painting or printed decoration over glaze, although the term more correctly applied indicates the coating covering such pastes as Delft ware.

Glaze.—The liquid with which the body of the pottery or porcelain is covered before firing. This coating is distinguished by different terms. Thus, there is lead or galena glaze, the glaze formed by sulphide of lead in powder, dusted on the ware as in the earlier forms of pottery. Afterwards a liquid lead glaze in which vessels were dipped was used. Salt glaze was the glaze produced by throwing common salt into the kiln, the vapour which resulted depositing a fine layer or glaze over the ware.

Ironstone China.—The body known as ironstone consists of ironstone slag and flint added in large proportions to the clay. The first patent in reference to ironstone china was taken out by Miles Mason in 1813.

Jasper Ware.—The fine, hard, unglazed stoneware, so richly decorated in cameo relief, first employed by Wedgwood, afterwards imitated by other potters. This body contains a large proportion of barum sulphate (barytes).

Kaolin.—This, the purest form of clay, was found the most suitable for porcelain in China, where it was first used. It is a hydrated silica of alumina. The kaolin found is England—chiefly in Cornwall—is frequently spoken of as "Cornish clay."

Lustre Ware.—The remarkable lustre decoration of earthenware, producing varied metallic hues, is formed by thin layers of gold, platinum, copper, or silver.

Marks.—The marks of makers of pottery and porcelain were sometimes impressed with a metal stamp when the paste was in a soft state, at others painted under the glaze, and a few instances over glaze. They were indications of owners of the works, of the artist who modelled or decorated the piece, of the pattern, of ornament, or form of the object. They were also in some instances indications of quality, different coloured marks being used to distinguish between some of the finer pieces and ordinary models. Then, again, many marks were changed, indicating transfer of ownership, the incorporation of other works, Royal patronage, and change in the composition of the paste or body of the ware. (For further reference to marks, see mention of specific potteries.)

Opaque China.—A term sometimes applied to earthenware having a white or chalk body, finished to give it the external appearance of porcelain.

Oven.—The oven or kiln is the furnace in which the saggers containing the pottery are placed for firing. There are varieties of ovens or kilns, including the muffle-kiln used for glazing after decoration.

Over-Glaze.—This denotes the condition of manufacture appertaining to decoration or painting applied on the glazed body, the decoration being afterwards fixed by a second firing.

Paste.—Paste is the term denoting the body of the pottery or porcelain. Soft paste was usually obtained by the use of a large proportion of bone ash in the composition, hard paste denoting the porcelain body consisting chiefly of felspar and kaolin.

Pearl Ware.—A kind of white earthenware containing a larger proportion of flint and china clay than the cream-ware. It was blued somewhat with cobalt. It is said to have been first used by Josiah Wedgwood.

Sagger.—A fire-clay box or receptacle in which the pottery or porcelain is baked in the oven. The sagger is used to protect the ware in the oven during firing.

Scale Decoration.—The particular decoration having the appearance of scales of a fish, usually forming a background, generally blue in colour. Scale decoration was used in England at Worcester, and at an earlier date on old Chinese porcelain.

Slip.—The semi-fluid material of clay and water applied in making pottery, sometimes in decoration.

Slip Decoration.—A form of decoration produced by running slip in pattern over the pottery before firing. Slip decoration is usually effected by using different coloured slips, producing colour effects without painting.

Spurs.—Spurs are largely used as supports of pottery during glazing operations. They are made of fire-clay and prevent the objects from touching the sagger or kiln, allowing the heat to circulate.

Transfer Printing.—Transfer printing from designs engraved on copper plates, transferred on tissues, is a method of ornamenting pottery frequently resorted to. The transfers on paper, after being applied to the surface of the ware, are fixed by heat.

Tortoise-shell Ware.—This beautiful effect was produced by coating cream-coloured wares with mingled glazes, cleverly imitating tortoise-shell markings and shades.

Under-Glaze.—This term is used in reference to the form of decoration or painting applied on the biscuit before glazing or firing. It is a process of transferring the print from the tissue to the biscuit, which is afterwards glazed and fired. The process was used at Caughley about 1780, and soon afterwards adopted at Worcester, the Staffordshire Potteries, and elsewhere.

INDEX

PRINTED BY THE ANCHOR PRESS, LTD., TIPTREE, ESSEX.